ServiceNow Cookbook

Over 50 practical and immediately applicable recipes to help you manage services in your enterprise environment efficiently

Ashish Rudra Srivastava

Pack<t>

BIRMINGHAM - MUMBAI

ServiceNow Cookbook

Copyright © 2017 Packt Publishing

All rights reserved. No part of this book may be reproduced, stored in a retrieval system, or transmitted in any form or by any means, without the prior written permission of the publisher, except in the case of brief quotations embedded in critical articles or reviews.

Every effort has been made in the preparation of this book to ensure the accuracy of the information presented. However, the information contained in this book is sold without warranty, either express or implied. Neither the author, nor Packt Publishing, and its dealers and distributors will be held liable for any damages caused or alleged to be caused directly or indirectly by this book.

Packt Publishing has endeavored to provide trademark information about all of the companies and products mentioned in this book by the appropriate use of capitals. However, Packt Publishing cannot guarantee the accuracy of this information.

First published: February 2017

Production reference: 1240217

Published by Packt Publishing Ltd.
Livery Place
35 Livery Street
Birmingham
B3 2PB, UK.
ISBN 978-1-78588-052-0

www.packtpub.com

Credits

Author
Ashish Rudra Srivastava

Reviewer
Sukhwinder Wadhwa

Commissioning Editor
Kartikey Pandey

Acquisition Editor
Rahul Nair

Content Development Editor
Mehvash Fatima

Technical Editor
Varsha Shivhare

Copy Editor
Safis Editing

Project Coordinator
Kinjal Bari

Proofreader
Safis Editing

Indexer
Pratik Shirodkar

Graphics
Kirk D'Penha

Production Coordinator
Nilesh Mohite

About the Author

Ashish Rudra Srivastava is an ITIL and Service-Now Certified Professional who has assisted multiple global organizations in ITSM, CRM, BPM and Infrastructure Management implementations and solutions delivery. He holds a bachelor degree in Computer Science & Engineering and a dabbler at Artificial Intelligence, Big Data, Cloud & mobile application development, Enterprise architecture frameworks and ITSM applications. He works as a Service-Now consultant, developer and trainer and has trained numerous industry professionals in ITSM tools like Service Now, BMC Remedy and JIRA in administration, development and implementation areas. He is a strategic partner to clients in Insurance, Banking and Manufacturing domains.

His research interest lies in Artificial Intelligence based network security systems. He has propounded an innovative concept of *PMA-Hardware* utilising an indigenous framework called NFCL model. His research paper on this titled **Hardware Based Total Secured Networks** was published in IJFCC journal in 2012. `http://www.ijfcc.org/papers/93-F0040.pdf`.

You can find him on LinkedIn `https://www.linkedin.com/in/ashishsrivastava03`

I would like to express my gratitude to Lord Ganesha for giving me strength, my Father Rudra Pratap Srivastava and my mother Reeta Srivastava who have nurtured me into the person who I am today. My special thanks to Mehvash Fatima for editing and composing the book. Last but not least, my thanks to all those people I have been associated with whose names don't find mention here but have contributed in shaping this.

About the Reviewer

Sukhwinder Wadhwa is currently working as a Senior Consultant - ServiceNow at Infosys Ltd. He has 8.5+ years of experience in IT Service Management Consulting, ITSM Tools Functional Consulting and Pre-sales. He has rich experience in Business Analysis, Solution Design, IT Service Delivery and Operations.

For his qualification, Sukhwinder has done B.Tech (IT) and MBA(IT) and is a ServiceNow Certified Administrator and ServiceNow Certified Implementation Specialist. In addition, he has certifications in, ITIL v3 foundation, CoBIT 4.1 and IBM Certified Solution Advisor - Cloud Computing Architecture V2.

www.PacktPub.com

For support files and downloads related to your book, please visit `www.PacktPub.com`.

Did you know that Packt offers eBook versions of every book published, with PDF and ePub files available? You can upgrade to the eBook version at `www.PacktPub.com` and as a print book customer, you are entitled to a discount on the eBook copy. Get in touch with us at `service@packtpub.com` for more details.

At `www.PacktPub.com`, you can also read a collection of free technical articles, sign up for a range of free newsletters and receive exclusive discounts and offers on Packt books and eBooks.

Mapt

`https://www.packtpub.com/mapt`

Get the most in-demand software skills with Mapt. Mapt gives you full access to all Packt books and video courses, as well as industry-leading tools to help you plan your personal development and advance your career.

Why subscribe?

- Fully searchable across every book published by Packt
- Copy and paste, print, and bookmark content
- On demand and accessible via a web browser

Customer Feedback

Thanks for purchasing this Packt book. At Packt, quality is at the heart of our editorial process. To help us improve, please leave us an honest review on this book's Amazon page at "Amazon Book URL".

If you'd like to join our team of regular reviewers, you can e-mail us at `customerreviews@packtpub.com`. We award our regular reviewers with free eBooks and videos in exchange for their valuable feedback. Help us be relentless in improving our products!

Table of Contents

Preface — 1

Chapter 1: Getting Started with Service-Now — 7
- **Introduction** — 8
- **Service-Now prerequisites** — 9
- **Service-Now and the ITIL framework** — 9
  - How it works… — 9
  - See also — 11
- **Understanding Service-Now procurement** — 12
- **Understanding Service-Now roles and licensing** — 12
  - There's more… — 13
- **Understanding the Service-Now setup** — 14
- **Accessing the Service-Now application** — 14
  - Getting ready — 14
  - How to do it… — 14
  - How it works… — 17
  - There's more… — 17
  - See also — 17
- **Microsoft Active Directory authentication** — 17
  - Getting ready — 18
  - How to do it… — 18
  - How it works… — 19
  - There's more… — 20
- **Logging in to the Service-Now application portal or end user view** — 20
  - Getting ready — 20
  - How to do it… — 21
  - There's more… — 23
  - See also — 23
- **Creating service requests from the Service-Now portal** — 23
  - Getting ready — 23
  - How to do it… — 24
  - There's more… — 26
- **Understanding the Service-Now IT view** — 27
  - Getting ready — 27
  - How to do it… — 27

How it works…	28
There's more…	32
See also	32
Understanding Service-Now's self-service application	32
Getting ready	32
How to do it…	33
See also	34
Understanding Service-Now's service desk application	34
Getting ready	34
How to do it…	35
Understand unique record identifier	37
Getting ready	37
How to do it…	37
There's more…	38
See also	38
Using the incident management application	38
Getting ready	38
How to do it…	38
How it works…	40
There's more…	40
See also	41
Using the related lists of applications	41
Getting ready	41
How to do it…	41
See also	46
Using the problem management application	47
Getting ready	47
How to do it…	47
How it works…	48
There's more…	48
Using the change management application	49
Getting ready	49
How to do it…	49
There's more…	51
See also	51
Creating the change/problem task from the incident task	51
Getting ready	51
How to do it…	52
Chapter 2: Performing Core Configuration and Management Tasks	**55**

Introduction	56
Setting up basic configuration	56
Getting ready	56
How to do it...	56
Understanding LDAP servers	61
Getting ready	62
How to do it...	62
Understanding user administration	67
Getting ready	67
How to do it...	67
Understanding group administration	71
Getting ready	72
How to do it...	72
Using service-now plugins	76
Getting ready	76
How to do it...	77
Configuring the Service-Now form	80
Getting ready	80
How to do it...	80
There's more...	87
See also	87
Configuring UI policies on Service-Now forms	87
Getting ready	87
How to do it...	87
Configuring UI actions on forms	91
Getting ready	91
How to do it...	92
Understanding deployments or update sets	95
Getting ready	95
How to do it...	95
There's more...	103
See also	103
Getting into CMDB	103
Getting ready	103
How to do it...	103
There's more...	107
See also	107
Setting up an SLA/OLA/underpinning contract	107
Getting ready	107

How to do it…	107
See also	111
Setting up system rules	111
Getting ready	111
How to do it…	111
There's more…	114
Understanding the system dictionary	114
Getting ready	114
How to do it…	115
Understanding the Service-Now tables schema	117
Getting ready	117
How to do it…	118
Getting into system security	120
Getting ready	120
How to do it…	121
There's more…	125

Chapter 3: Building Data-Driven Application — 127

Introduction	127
Starting a new application	127
Getting ready	128
How to do it…	128
Getting into new modules	134
Getting ready	134
How to do it…	134
Getting into the client script	143
Getting ready	144
How to do it…	144
Getting into the server-side script	148
Getting ready	149
How to do it…	149
Understanding the team development plugin	158
Getting ready	158
How to do it…	158
Understand web services	161
Getting ready	162
How to do it…	162
See also	168
Understanding development best practice	168
Getting ready	168

How to do it…	168

Chapter 4: Configuring Alerts and Notifications — 171

Introduction	172
Understanding the Service-Now system mailbox	172
Getting ready	172
How to do it…	173
Creating a new e-mail notification	179
Getting ready	179
How to do it…	180
Creating an e-mail template	186
Getting ready	186
How to do it…	186
Creating an e-mail notification script	190
Getting ready	190
How to do it…	190
Setting up an inbound e-mail action	193
Getting ready	193
How to do it…	193
Inbound e-mail action – new	197
Getting ready	197
How to do it…	197
Inbound e-mail action – forward	202
Getting ready	203
How to do it…	203
Inbound e-mail action – reply	207
Getting ready	207
How to do it…	207
There's more…	211
E-mail Notification by event registry	211
Getting ready	212
How to do it…	212
E-mail notification troubleshooting	218
Getting ready	219
How to do it…	219

Chapter 5: Building and Configuring Reports — 223

Introduction	224
Viewing and running reports	224
Getting ready	224

How to do it…	224
Creating new reports	**227**
Getting ready	227
How to do it…	227
Scheduling reports	**230**
Getting ready	230
How to do it…	230
There's more…	234
Sending multiple reports in one e-mail	**234**
Getting ready	234
How to do it…	234
Creating a table-specific report module	**238**
Getting ready	238
How to do it…	238
Creating a dashboard	**243**
Getting ready	243
How to do it…	243
Including the date in a report's e-mail notification	**247**
Getting ready	248
How to do it…	248
Working with the report's header and footer template	**250**
Getting ready	250
How to do it…	250
Working with the report sources	**255**
Getting ready	256
How to do it…	256
Working with the report range	**260**
Getting ready	260
How to do it…	260
Creating a database view	**263**
Getting ready	263
How to do it…	263
Chapter 6: Creating and Configuring Workflow Activities	**269**
Introduction	270
Understanding the Service-Now workflow	**270**
Getting ready	270
How to do it…	270
Attaching a workflow with the service catalog	**280**
Getting ready	280

How to do it…	280
Attaching workflows with current/new modules	**282**
Getting ready	282
How to do it…	283
There's more…	285
Workflow troubleshooting	**286**
Getting ready	286
How to do it…	286
Setting up an approval activity	**289**
Getting ready	289
How to do it…	289
Working with condition activities	**294**
Getting ready	294
How to do it…	295
Working with task activities	**301**
Getting ready	301
How to do it…	301
Working with workflow utilities	**307**
Getting ready	307
How to do it…	307
Setting up e-mail notifications from workflows	**317**
Getting ready	317
How to do it…	317
How to configure a timer in workflows	**322**
Getting ready	322
How to do it…	322
Understanding the approval engine	**325**
Getting ready	325
How to do it…	325
Chapter 7: Auditing and Diagnosing Service-Now	**327**
Understanding auditing in Service-Now	**327**
Getting ready	327
How to do it…	328
Working with auditing tables	**330**
Getting ready	330
How to do it…	330
There's more…	332
See also	332
Understanding Service-Now upgrades	**332**

Getting ready	332
How to do it…	332
Working with system logs	**338**
Getting ready	338
How to do it…	338
There's more…	341
See also	341
System diagnostics	**342**
Getting ready	342
How to do it…	342
Working with background scripts	**348**
Getting ready	348
How to do it…	349
Working with Field Watcher	**350**
Getting ready	350
How to do it…	350
Working with JavaScript logs	**353**
Getting ready	353
How to do it…	353
Index	**357**

Preface

The genesis of this book owes to the fact that several students who attended my training programs in the last few years have been struggling with ITSM implementations or application support upon their initial assignments. They keep on texting and calling me to seek guidance and often solutions to roadblock which though unforeseen yet are very natural to any project. This paved way for the thinking that a concise yet comprehensive literature dealing with the practical and real life problems during implantation is needed. This book is my humble attempt to the goal. It provides step by step approach to ITSM implementation or resolving development or support using Service-Now, common pitfalls, impediments and errors and their possible solutions. Apart from the general framework for a Service-Now implementation to facilitate a robust design, it also provides general guidelines for planning implementation in such a way as to avoid most of the situations which may result in a not-so-clean design later on.

This book provides insights into the various stages from planning through implementation and maintenance with specific focus on what to expect at individual stages and how to be prepared or counter the common as well as rarely occurring pitfalls that arise from time to time by following best practices recommended by Service-Now.

What this book covers

Chapter 1, *Getting Started with Service-Now*, covers Service-Now basic modules and is focused on individuals who have never been associated with any ITSM applications and want to shift their career path in ITSM/Service-Now application.

Chapter 2, *Performing Core Configuration and Management Tasks*, deals with common issues, administration, database, contract configuration and other topics useful for deployments. It is focused on professionals who are working on ITSM applications or Service-Now already and want to enhance knowledge of Service-Now platform administration.

Chapter 3, *Building Data-Driven Application*, deals with development, enhancement and maintenance of new and existing custom applications. This includes server side, client side and web service side scripting with specific focus on best practices. On many occasions professionals struggle deciding the structure of the application. This chapter provides a general guideline for that.

Chapter 4, *Configuring Alerts and Notification*, deals with development and configuration of inbound and outbound alerts and notifications, dynamic and static content and watermarking.

Chapter 5, *Building and Configuring Reports*, explains how to develop and deploy reports for specific support group or team and developing relevant dashboards.

Chapter 6, *Creating and Configuring Workflow Activities*, this chapter covers development and configuration of application workflow activities, triggers, approval groups and usage of components like timer, switch and so on. This chapter is important for the entire audience of this book as this part is the heart and soul of Service-Now.

Chapter 7, *Auditing and Diagnosing Service-Now*, focus of this chapter hovers upon the troubleshooting capability in Service-Now. It deals with auditing, debugging and version control.

What you need for this book

Service-Now is cloud hosted enterprise level application so you require standard browser (Internet Explorer/Firefox/Safari/Google Chrome) only to access it. Apart of your organization Service-Now instance, you can claim your personal Service-Now instance by registering on at this link `https://developer.servicenow.com`.

Who this book is for

This book targets IT professionals and administrators who have some experience of working with ITSM or Service-Now already and are looking to solve regular or unique problems that surface when using Service-Now. It's advisable to have a basic level of administration experience with Service-Now. Familiarity with JavaScript is assumed.

Sections

In this book, you will find several headings that appear frequently (Getting ready, How to do it, How it works, There's more, and See also).

To give clear instructions on how to complete a recipe, we use these sections as follows:

Getting ready

This section tells you what to expect in the recipe, and describes how to set up any software or any preliminary settings required for the recipe.

How to do it…

This section contains the steps required to follow the recipe.

How it works…

This section usually consists of a detailed explanation of what happened in the previous section.

There's more…

This section consists of additional information about the recipe in order to make the reader more knowledgeable about the recipe.

See also

This section provides helpful links to other useful information for the recipe.

Conventions

In this book, you will find a number of text styles that distinguish between different kinds of information. Here are some examples of these styles and an explanation of their meaning.

Code words in text, database table names, folder names, filenames, file extensions, pathnames, dummy URLs, user input, and Twitter handles are shown as follows: If you want to open a new record of the table, then you can type `table name.do` in the search box, and if you want to open see all available records in the table, then you can type `tablename.list`.

A block of code is set as follows:

```
action.setRedirectURL(current);
current.assigned_to = gs.getUserID();
current.setForceUpdate(true);
current.update();
```

New terms and **important words** are shown in bold. Words that you see on the screen, for example, in menus or dialog boxes, appear in the text like this: "If there are any errors then resolve the errors, and click on **Commit Update Set** to deploy your code in the target instance such as the testing or production instance."

> Warnings or important notes appear in a box like this.

> Tips and tricks appear like this.

Reader feedback

Feedback from our readers is always welcome. Let us know what you think about this book-what you liked or disliked. Reader feedback is important for us as it helps us develop titles that you will really get the most out of. To send us general feedback, simply e-mail feedback@packtpub.com, and mention the book's title in the subject of your message. If there is a topic that you have expertise in and you are interested in either writing or contributing to a book, see our author guide at www.packtpub.com/authors.

Customer support

Now that you are the proud owner of a Packt book, we have a number of things to help you to get the most from your purchase.

Downloading the example code

You can download the example code files for this book from your account at http://www.packtpub.com. If you purchased this book elsewhere, you can visit http://www.packtpub.com/support and register to have the files e-mailed directly to you.

You can download the code files by following these steps:

1. Log in or register to our website using your e-mail address and password.
2. Hover the mouse pointer on the **SUPPORT** tab at the top.
3. Click on **Code Downloads & Errata**.
4. Enter the name of the book in the **Search** box.
5. Select the book for which you're looking to download the code files.
6. Choose from the drop-down menu where you purchased this book from.
7. Click on **Code Download**.

Once the file is downloaded, please make sure that you unzip or extract the folder using the latest version of:

- WinRAR / 7-Zip for Windows
- Zipeg / iZip / UnRarX for Mac
- 7-Zip / PeaZip for Linux

The code bundle for the book is also hosted on GitHub at https://github.com/PacktPublishing/ServiceNowCookbook. We also have other code bundles from our rich catalog of books and videos available at https://github.com/PacktPublishing/. Check them out!

Downloading the color images of this book

We also provide you with a PDF file that has color images of the screenshots/diagrams used in this book. The color images will help you better understand the changes in the output. You can download this file from https://www.packtpub.com/sites/default/files/downloads/ServiceNowCookbook_ColorImages.pdf.

Errata

Although we have taken every care to ensure the accuracy of our content, mistakes do happen. If you find a mistake in one of our books-maybe a mistake in the text or the code- we would be grateful if you could report this to us. By doing so, you can save other readers from frustration and help us improve subsequent versions of this book. If you find any errata, please report them by visiting http://www.packtpub.com/submit-errata, selecting your book, clicking on the **Errata Submission Form** link, and entering the details of your errata. Once your errata are verified, your submission will be accepted and the errata will be uploaded to our website or added to any list of existing errata under the Errata section of that title.

To view the previously submitted errata, go to https://www.packtpub.com/books/content/support and enter the name of the book in the search field. The required information will appear under the **Errata** section.

Piracy

Piracy of copyrighted material on the Internet is an ongoing problem across all media. At Packt, we take the protection of our copyright and licenses very seriously. If you come across any illegal copies of our works in any form on the Internet, please provide us with the location address or website name immediately so that we can pursue a remedy.

Please contact us at copyright@packtpub.com with a link to the suspected pirated material.

We appreciate your help in protecting our authors and our ability to bring you valuable content.

Questions

If you have a problem with any aspect of this book, you can contact us at questions@packtpub.com, and we will do our best to address the problem.

Getting Started with Service-Now

Service-Now, probably is the most spoken IT Operation / IT Service Management application/tool these days. So what exactly is Service-Now and what does it does? Service-Now is the cloud-based enterprise application which offers everything-as-a-service, Service-Now has large portfolio of services including platform as service, finance, marketing, field operation and so on. Service-Now holds vital position in the market of IT service management, IT operations management and IT business management applications. If anyone asks me what it is, then I always say that it may be an application/tool which might address most of your IT operational issues. If we go the little further on application level then we can say that Service-Now application is the collection of many small applications which are committed to different processes. Service-Now does provide the capability to application developers to develop a desired application in less time as well, which makes it more powerful and preferred to the customers. Many IT and non IT companies are moving from their legacy service management suites / help desk tools to the cloud-based Service-Now. So, the question that arises is, why is Service-Now attracting many IT and non IT customers? To answer this question, we should go to the ground zero of Service-Now, which will help to understand Service-Now from delivering business values. I will start with the ground zero of Service-Now and will gradually move toward the top with some very interesting recipes.

In this chapter, we will cover the following recipes:

- Service-Now prerequisite
- Service-Now and ITIL framework
- Understanding Service-Now procurement
- Understanding Service-Now roles and licensing
- Understanding Service-Now setup

- Accessing Service-Now application
- Microsoft Active Directory authentication
- Logging in to the Service-Now application portal or end user view
- Creating service requests from the Service-Now portal
- Understanding the Service-Now IT view
- Understanding Service-Now self-service application
- Understanding Service-Now service desk application
- Understand Unique record identifier
- Using the incident management application
- How to use create related lists of applications
- Using the problem management application
- Using the change management application
- Creating the change / problem task from incident task

Introduction

Many customers from different industries such as banking, insurance, manufacturing, oil, and gas are using Service-Now software, but please keep in mind that every practice or customer may have its own unique operational environment. So now let's begin the Service-Now journey! You know by now that Service-Now is a service management suite but if you are thinking that it is the only one in the service management applications market then you are not correct. Names that come to my mind when I think about the other service management tools include: BMC Remedy, HP Service Manager, and VMWARE Service Manager.

Service-Now is based on the **Information Technology Infrastructure Library (ITIL)** framework, which is an integrated, process based, best practice framework for managing IT services. The recipes in this chapter will give you a detailed overview of the Service-Now modules and the ITIL v3.0 framework, and we will also see how Service-Now is leveraging the ITIL framework.

Service-Now prerequisites

To start with Service-Now, you should have a basic understanding of Java scripting and SQL. Please keep in mind that as an admin or developer you are not allowed to access the database layer or application code layer but Service-Now provides its own classes, functions, and methods for development and other work. In addition, if we talk about the supporting technology behind this application, then Service-Now is Java-based and uses Oracle, MySQL, and SQL server databases and as a web server, Tomcat is being used.

Service-Now and the ITIL framework

Service-Now is an IT service management tool and it follows the ITIL v3.0 framework but, now Service-Now is currently expanding its footprint into many other portfolios as well, such as legal management, marketing management, and cost management and so on.

How it works...

The ITIL v3.0 framework has five phases, but Service-Now has supporting modules or applications for the following ITIL phases only:

- Service design
- Service transition
- Service operation

The following phases are not supported by Service-Now:

- Service strategy
- Continual service improvement

Service Strategy	Service Design	Service Transition	Service Operation	Continual Service Improvement
Portfolio strategy	Capacity management	Transition planning and support	Service desk	The 7- Step process improvement process
Financial management	Availability management	Service assets and configuration management	Incident management	Quality management system
Service portfolio management	Service management	Change management	Event management	Business question for CSI
Release management	Continuity management	Service validation and testing	Request fulfillment	ROI for CSI
	Demand management	Knowledge management	Access management	Service management
	Service catalogue management	Deployment management	Application management	Service reporting
		Evaluation	IT Operation management	
			Application management	
			Technical Management	

ITIL v3.0 Framework – Reference: https://en.wikipedia.org/wiki/ITIL

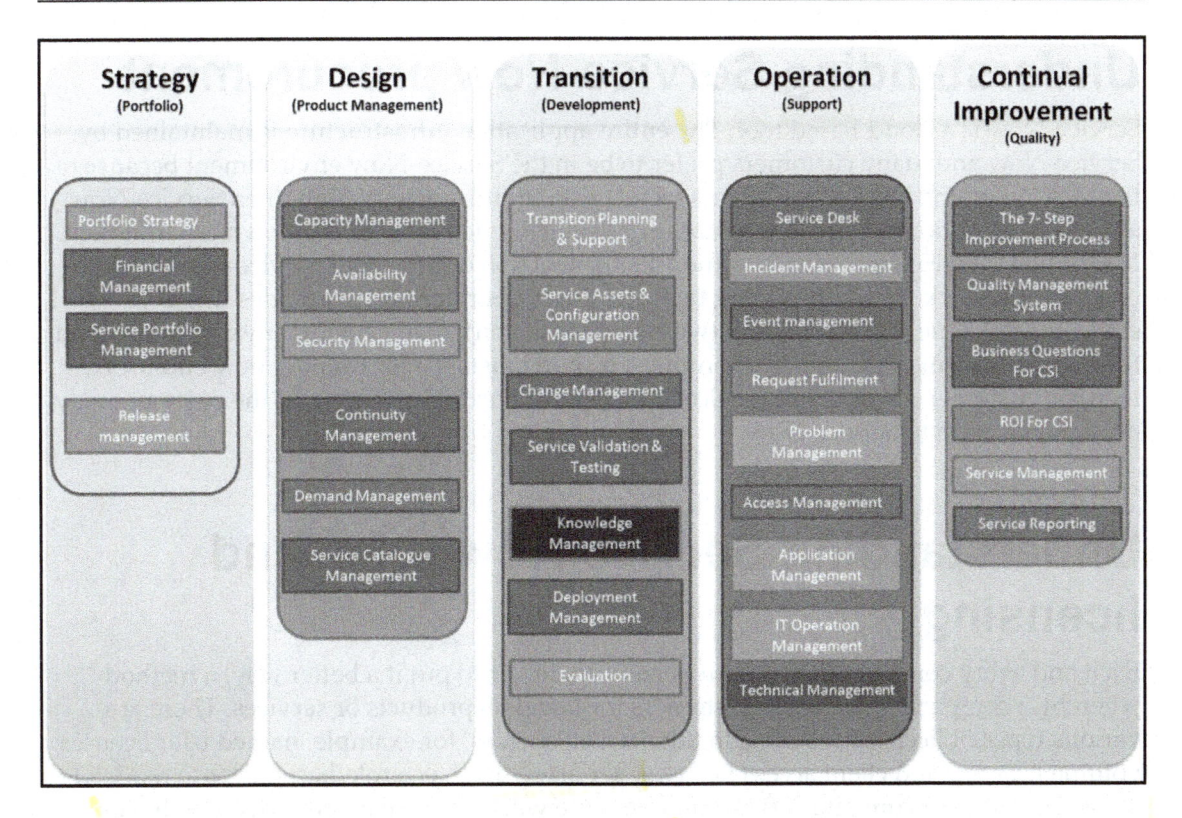

ITIL v3.0 Framework

See also

To read more about the ITIL framework please follow:

- https://en.wikipedia.org/wiki/ITIL,http://wiki.servicenow.com/index.php?title=ITIL#gsc.tab=0
- http://www.upenn.edu/computing/isc/training/archived/lunchtime/Overview%20to%20ITIL.pdf

Understanding Service-Now procurement

Service-Now is a cloud-based tool. The entire application infrastructure is maintained by Service-Now and many customers prefer to be in the Service-Now environment because of the cost constraint, but if a customer's security standards are very high, then Service-Now also gives an option to the client to opt for hosting Service-Now in their own environment. In addition, Service-Now provides the VPN connection option from Service-Now to the customer network. After processing the sales orders, Service-Now provides three environments (one production and two non-production). If any customer wants more than three environments, such as, for example, a training instance for training new end users, then the customer can ask Service-Now to provide an extra instance, but the customer may need to pay extra to Service-Now.

Understanding Service-Now roles and licensing

Each and every company has its own license model, or to put it a better way, a method whereby a company will charge customers for using its products or services. There are various types of licenses available in the market, such as, for example, named user licenses, volume licenses, and client access licenses. Service-Now, has a role-based license model. For instance, if in your company 1,000 employees are working, then all employees will have access to Service-Now as an end user, which means they are allowed to raise requests or incidents on Service-Now, but for handling all those service tickets there are one 100 IT employees and all have Service-Now ITIL role access: According to for the Service-Now licensing model, your company would need to pay for 100 licenses only.

In an IT operational environment, a requester may be referred to as an end user who can do any of these tasks:

- Create, view, or modify their own request
- Search service catalog
- Access knowledge base
- Access public pages
- Undertake surveys
- Set own notification preferences
- View assets assigned to a user
- Initiate a chat session, or access and post to live feed.

In an IT operational environment, a fulfiller may be referred to as a support group member who can perform all the tasks of a **requester,** as well as the following tasks:

- Create, delete, and modify any record
- View, create, delete, and modify any report
- Perform development and administrative activities, and approve requests routed to a user

In an IT operational environment, an **approver** is a manager, a lead, or a high-level management person who can perform all the tasks of **requesters** and can also approve or deny a routed record.

In my experience, many customers don't want to purchase an approver license for various reasons.

Approval by e-mail is counted as a license. In such special cases, you can deactivate the my approval module from the self-service application so that the module won't be visible to users and can create approval e-mails for all kinds of requests with the help of e-mail templates.

There's more...

As a Service-Now application administrator, you should be always careful before giving role to any user as there may be some approvals are required from higher management. This is why it's very important to know the roles in Service-Now.

> In my experience, many customers don't want to purchase an approver licenses due to for various reasons. Usually **Approval** by e-mail is not counted as license but clients contracts varies as well. In such special cases, you can deactivate the **My Approval** module from **Self-Service Application** so that the module won't be visible for users and can create approval e-mails for all kinds of requests with the help of **Email Templates** module.

Understanding the Service-Now setup

Service-Now is a cloud-based application; that's why your client is not required to set up any infrastructure to support Service-Now in their environment. By reading the *Understanding Service-Now procurement* recipe, you should know that Service-Now provides three environments (one production and two non-production). As a setup, these environments are called instances and may be classified as development, testing, and production. Consider the following examples of Service-Now instances or web addresses:

- `packtprod.service-now.com`
- `packtdev.service-now.com`
- `packtest.service-now.com`

If the customer is Amazon and has requested more than three instances from Service-Now, then the web addresses may look similar to the following:

- `amazon.service-now.com`
- `amazondev.service-now.com`
- `amazonqa.service-now.com`
- `amazondev2.service-now.com`

Each Service-Now instance has a unique, secured web address, but administrators are allowed to create a custom URL which can redirect to the original URL.

Accessing the Service-Now application

You don't need to install any client-side application on your local machine to access Service-Now in your environment. It is easily accessible by a standard web browser, which makes it appear as a web browser application for a customer. Here it is important to note that instance addresses or links (`http://{instancename}.service-now.com`) will always be company specific.

Getting ready

To access Service-Now, you need a standard web browser (you may use Google Chrome, Internet Explorer, or Mozilla Firefox) to access the URL with an active Service-Now instance, and valid credentials.

How to do it…

1. Open any standard web browser.
2. Type the Service-Now instance web address provided for your company in the address bar (`http://{instance_name}.service-now.com`).
3. If customer has given external authentication, then are you are automatically logged in. To read more about external authentication follow: `http://wiki.servicenow.com/index.php?title=External_Authentication_(Single_Sign-On_-_SSO)` link.
4. If customer has not been given external authentication, then you will see a login page as follows, where you need to enter the **User name** and **Password** in the respective fields:

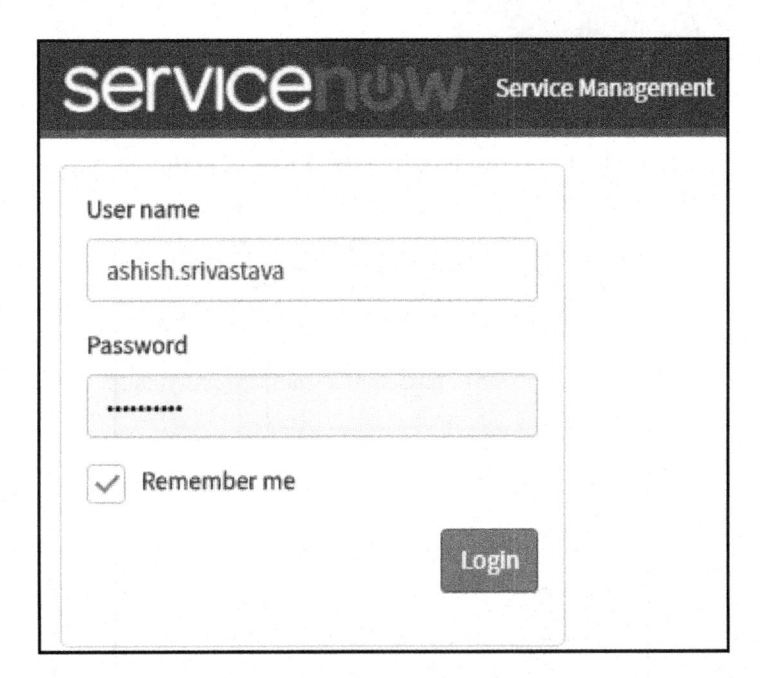

Service-Now login screen

Getting Started with Service-Now

5. Now click on the **Login** button. If your credentials match, then Service-Now will allow you to move further and show the following application screen:

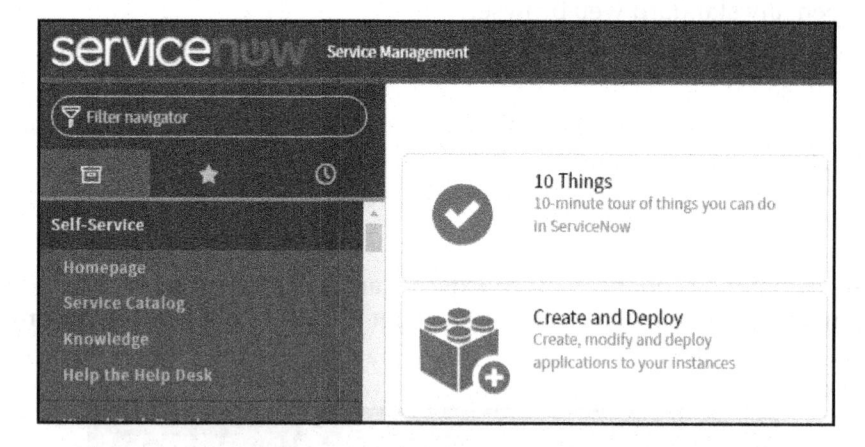

Service-Now application screen

6. If your credentials do not match, then Service-Now denies access and shows you the following error message as follows:

Service-Now error screen

How it works...

If an external authentication is not being used, then the **User name** and **Password** authentication is done by the Service-Now user table (`sys_user`), which will serve only as the master source of the user's data. So, when you enter the username and password, Service-Now verifies the user's account against the user table and after successful verification, Service-Now allows you to move further. However, if Service-Now is not able to match the credentials you entered, then it does not allow you to login and show error message.

There's more...

Each Service-Now instance has unique, secured web address but administrators are allowed to create a custom URL which can redirect to original URL. Here it is important to note that instances address (`http ://{ instance_name}.service-now.com`) will be always company specific.

See also

To read more about external authentication follow:

- `http://wiki.servicenow.com/index.php?title=External_Authentication_(Single_Sign-On_-_SSO)`

Microsoft Active Directory authentication

It's not feasible to manually maintain a large set of users in any enterprise level application. This is why every organization maintains a master source of all users on a server. So, Service-Now should be integrated with the master source to import users for user's access.

Getting ready

In many organizations, the Microsoft Active Directory server is used as the master source of employee or user records. Users are allowed to log into the assigned laptop or desktop using active directory's or Windows username and password. Service-Now provides an inbuilt **Lightweight Dictionary Access Protocol (LDAP)** server to integrate with Microsoft Active Directory to import all users' records. To step through this recipe, all you need is an active Service-Now instance and valid credentials and an admin role.

How to do it...

1. Open a standard web browser and type the web address (http://{instance_address}.service-now.com) of the **ServiceNow** instance which is provided by the organization.
2. Now, for instance, if Service-Now is integrated with **Microsoft Azure**, then you will see the following login page:

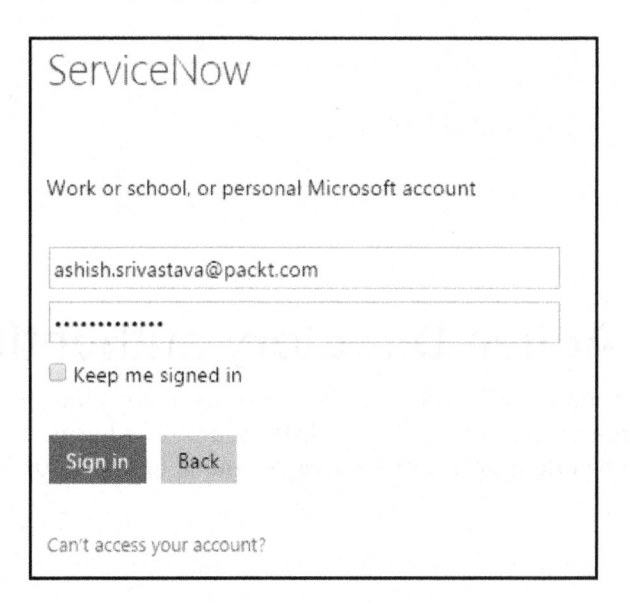

![ServiceNow login page with Microsoft Azure - Work or school, or personal Microsoft account, showing email ashish.srivastava@packt.com, password field, Keep me signed in checkbox, Sign in and Back buttons, Can't access your account link]

Microsoft Azure page for Service-Now login

3. Now, on the login page, enter active directory's username and password to log in. Please note, active directory's username and password are commonly referred to as windows credentials, as by this, you are allowed to log in on your organization's machine.

4. On successful authentication, Service-Now, will allow you to log in to move further but if the username and password are not matched, then Service-Now will show an error message.

5. Sometimes, you may observe that some fields in a user's records are not being imported in the Service-Now user table (sys_user) properly so, in such cases, you may ask for access to Microsoft active directory where you can validate whether data is available in active directory or not. Refer to the following screenshot to see what the user record looks like in active directory:

User details in active directory server

How it works...

When the user enters the network domain credentials (username and password) on the login page, the Service-Now instance passes it to the LDAP server and the LDAP server responds with an authorized or unauthorized message which Service-Now determines whether to grant access or not. It is important to note that Service-Now can allow new users to login to an instance even if the user does not have an account. When the new user tries to login in to Service-Now, it automatically issues a query to the LDAP server and if the user record is found, the integration tries to authenticate it with the password. If the password is valid, Service-Now creates an account for the user.

There's more...

There are mainly two types of accounts – the network domain level account (authorized by the LDAP server – active directory integration) and the manual account (which is directly created in the Service-Now user table). So, for instance, if your customer's active directory server is not available or is down, then Service-Now will not allow any user to login on the instance because the LDAP query authentication fails. However, if as an admin, you want to access Service-Now, then you can access it via the manual account which is not authenticated by LDAP server. It is important to note that as an admin, you should have a non-AD or manual account for critical situations.

Logging in to the Service-Now application portal or end user view

Out of the box, Service-Now provides a **Content Management System** (**CMS**) application, which is the soul of the Service-Now front-end (portal). By using the CMS application, you can create web pages and enhance the look and feel of the Service-Now platform for the end users. It is a single place from where all users can raise incidents or requests. If you are a beginner and you not aware of incidents or service requests, then read the following standard definitions:

- An incident is an unplanned interruption to an IT Service or reduction in the quality of an IT service (source: `https://en.wikipedia.org/wiki/Incident management_ (ITSM)`).
- A service request is a user request for information or advice, or for a standard change (a pre-approved change that is low risk, relatively common, and follows a procedure), or for access to an IT service. An example of a standard request is a password reset (source: `https://www.sunviewsoftware.com`).

In this recipe, you will learn about the Service-Now CMS site basics and navigation as an end user.

Getting ready

To step through this recipe, you should have an active Service-Now instance and valid credentials only.

How to do it…

1. Open any standard web browser.
2. Type the `service-now` instance web address (`http://{instance_name}.service-now.com`) provided by your company in the address bar.
3. By default, upon login, you will see the home page but, depending on the login rule, you may be redirected to the Service-Now portal or end user view. To read more about the login landing page click `http://wiki.servicenow.com/index.php?title=Specifying_a_Login_Landing_Page#gsc.tab=0` link.
4. On the Service-Now platform, you are allowed to create more than one site but the URL suffix must be different for each and every site. By default, Service-Now provides the site by web address (`http://{instance_name}.service-now.com/ess`). You can also create a new site by web address (`http://{instance_name}.Service-Now.com/IT`). It is important to note that the instance name must be same.
5. The following screen shows the default portal of Service-Now, which the end user will see after login based on the landing page configuration:

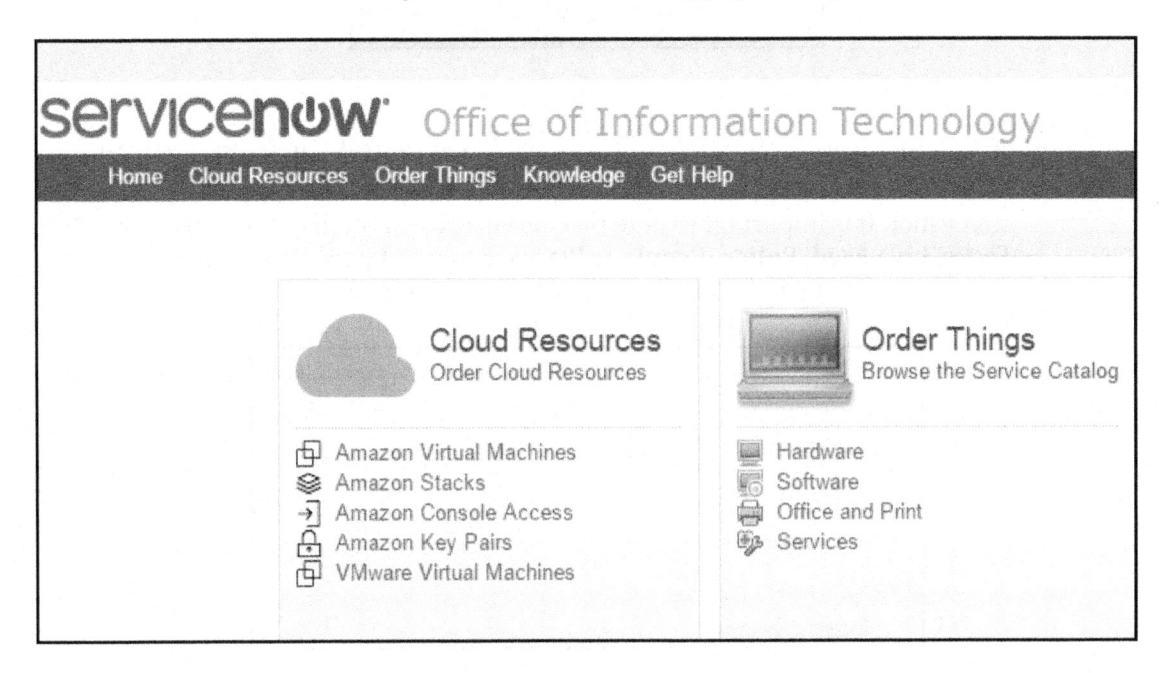

Service-Now frontend (portal)/end user view

6. Now after login, you are allowed to create a service ticket (incident, task or service request). It is important to note that every organization configures Service-Now as per their business requirements so sometimes only middle-level managers, such as team leader or manager, are allowed to create service requests on your behalf. . Let's understand this by an example so if you are joining a new organization on contractor position then to start work from day one you need certain things access like laptop, printer access, VoIP access, application access and so on, then in such scenarios the only manager or lead raise service request so don't be surprised by such kind of Service-Now configuration.

7. Often, a user wants to follow up on a service ticket so for fulfilling such a requirement, Service-Now provides a search facility by Zing, which is a text indexing and search engine. As an admin or end user, you can enter the ticket number in the search box as given following but it is important to note that end user has access level is less as compared to admin's access level. For an example as an admin if you enter incident number INC0010108 in search box:

Search incident on CMS

8. Service-Now allows for a text search on the CMS site as well. You can type the desired text in the search box and you will see a page similar to the following screenshot. It is important to note that Service-Now search criteria are limited to **Tasks, Live Feed, Policy, People & Places, Knowledge & catalog**, and you can filter out any of them by unchecking the respective box:

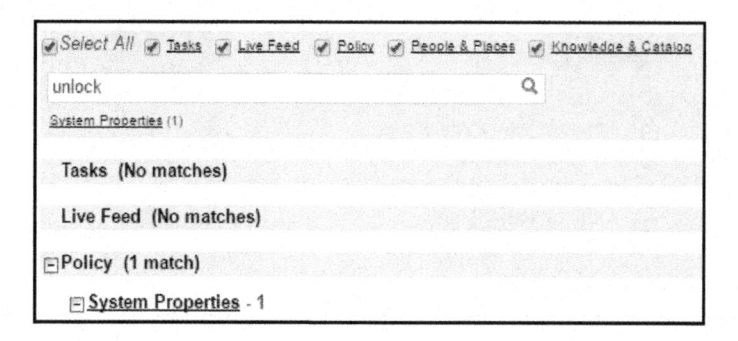

There's more...

Out of the box, Service-Now provides **Content Management Application** (**CMS**) which supports application portal or end user view. Under CMS application, **Login Rules** module supports landing page of portal after successful login. For better understanding let's take an example, users without any roles should be redirected to Service-Now portal and with user ITIL, should be redirected to IT View

See also

- To read more about the login landing page click on `http://wiki.servicenow.com/index.php?title=Specifying_a_Login_Landing_Page#gsc.tab=0`
- To read more about searching `http://wiki.servicenow.com/index.php?title=Introduction_to_Searching#gsc.tab=0`

Creating service requests from the Service-Now portal

As a beginner, you can co-relate the service requests with a web-based form like a movie booking, an exam form and so on, in which you need to enter your details only but depends on required information Service-Now form may be simple or complex. In this recipe, you will learn about the service requests of Service-Now. For better understanding let's take a better example so if you want a laptop from your organization then on the service request form you might have to choose screen size, ram, hard drive and so on or many organization categories then laptop in the executive laptop, standard laptop, high configuration laptop.

Getting ready

To step through this recipe, you need an active Service-Now instance and valid credentials.

Getting Started with Service-Now

How to do it...

1. Open any standard web browser.
2. Type the Service-Now instance web address (`https://{instance_name}.service-now.com`) provided by your organization in the address bar, now enter your credentials in respective fields.
3. After login, you will be redirected to the Service-Now frontend/portal. Once you are on the main portal then in the **Order Things** section, click on the **Hardware** button:

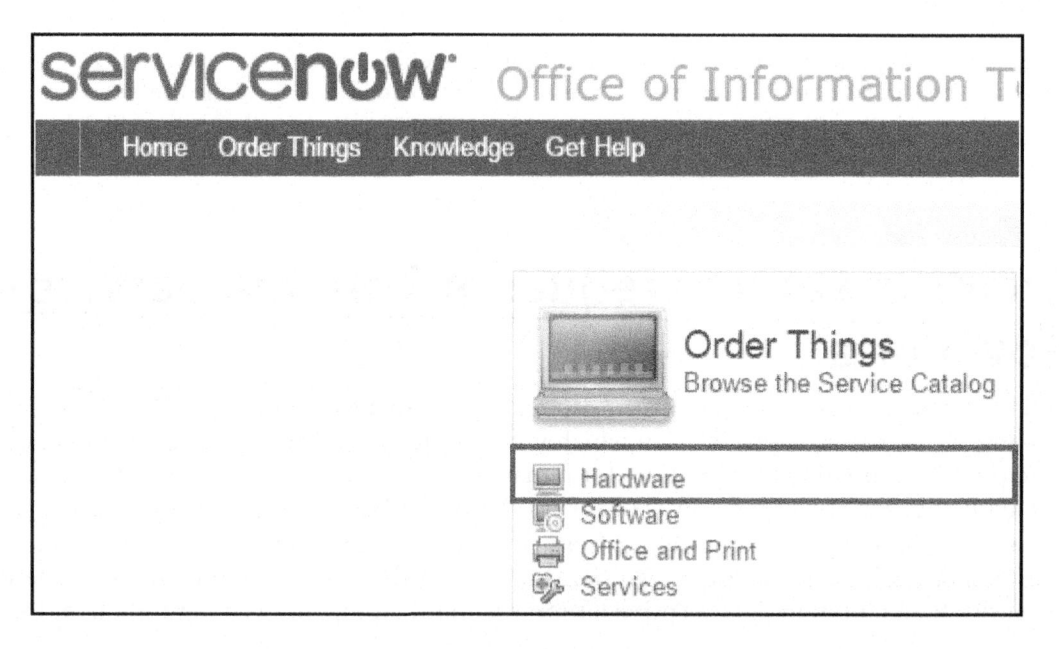

Service-Now Portal Menu Block

Chapter 1

4. After clicking on the **Hardware** button, you will be redirected to the catalog page where you can see all available catalogs. Now select **Sales Laptop Access** form the options, after that you will be redirected to the following screen:

Name
Ashish Srivastava

Optional Laptops
- ☐ Executive Laptop
- ☐ Standard Laptop
- ☑ High Configuration Laptop
- ☐ Desktop

Software Requirements

MS Office, Citrix

Catalog item request form

5. In the catalog item **Sales Laptop Access** request form, enter your name, describe your request, and click on Order Now. You will now be redirected to the following screen where you can view your request number, delivery date, stage, and price:

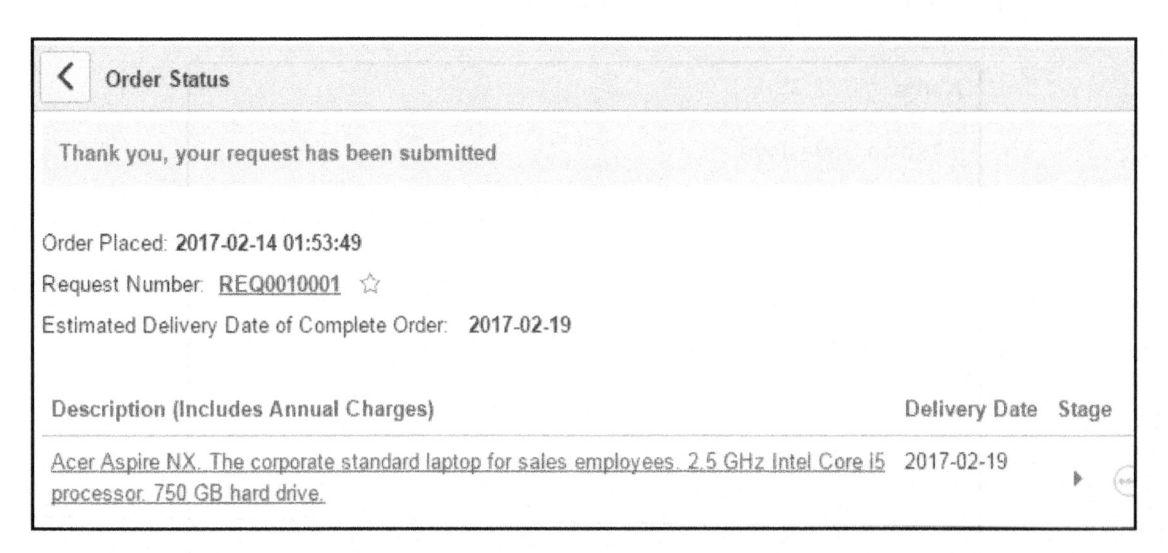

```
< Order Status

Thank you, your request has been submitted

Order Placed: 2017-02-14 01:53:49
Request Number: REQ0010001
Estimated Delivery Date of Complete Order: 2017-02-19

Description (Includes Annual Charges)                                              Delivery Date   Stage

Acer Aspire NX. The corporate standard laptop for sales employees. 2.5 GHz Intel Core i5    2017-02-19
processor. 750 GB hard drive.
```

Catalog item request order status

There's more...

Out of the box, Service-Now provides **Service Catalog Application** to support catalog item and under the application, **Maintain Item** module is available for viewing existing catalog item (Sales Laptop) or creating new catalog item.

Service-Now portal/end user view may be classified in many ways according to organization's business and it is important to note that here may be many catalog items for serving different purpose like for facilities, legal, IT, procurement, marketing and so on.

Understanding the Service-Now IT view

Similar to other enterprise applications, Service-Now also maintains two views. The first is for the end user and another is for admins or ITIL or fulfillers. In this recipe, you will learn about the IT view of the Service-Now application.

Getting ready

To step through this recipe, you should have an active Service-Now instance and valid login credentials.

How to do it...

1. Open any browser (Internet Explorer, Google Chrome, Safari, or Mozilla Firefox).
2. Type the Service-Now instance web address (`http://{instance_name}.service-now.com`) provided by your organization in the address bar, now enter your credentials in respective fields and press enter button.
3. The following screen is the IT view of Service-Now, where all the applications and modules are available:

Service-Now IT view

How it works...

- **Section 1** in the preceding screenshot is a search box where you type the name of the desired module. If you know the table name, then you can simply type the table name, which works in two ways: If you want to open a new record of the table, then you can type table name.do in the search box, and if you want to open it to see all the available records in the table, then you can type tablename.list:

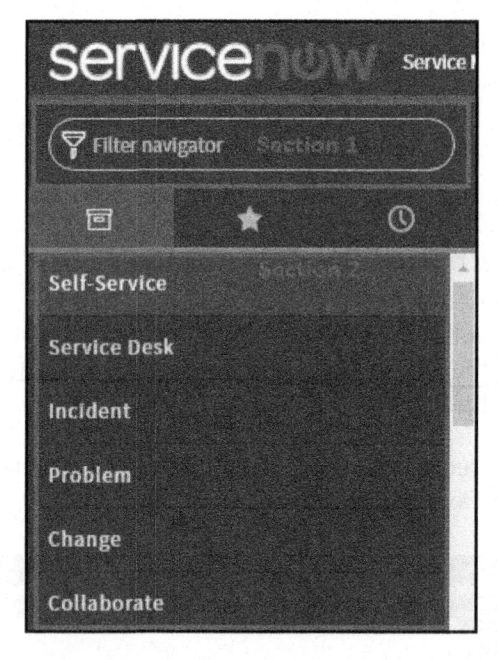

Section 1 and Section 2

- **Section 2** is dedicated to applications; you can view all the applications, whether they are system or custom applications.
- **Section 3** is dedicated to login user details; you can do the following tasks:
- You can view your Service-Now profile
- You can impersonate other users to view their views
- If you have the security_admin role, then you can elevate privileges

- If you want to log out from Service-Now, then you can click on **Logout**:

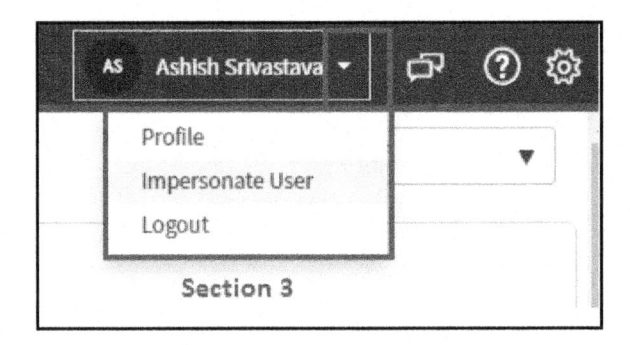

Section 3

- **Section 4** is a global search box, which is dedicated to finding records from multiple tables:

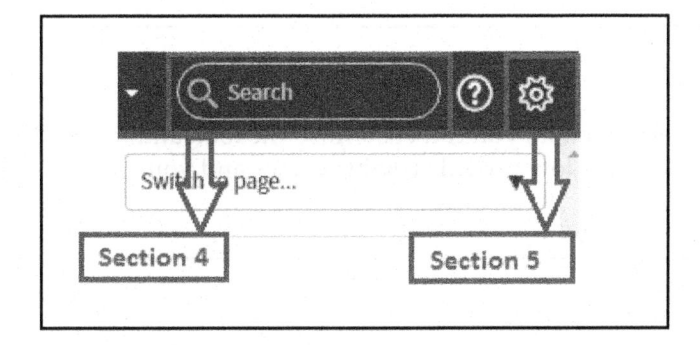

Section 4 and Section 5

- **Section 5** is a **settings** button from where you can customize your Service-Now view. The settings section is a combination of the following four items:

- In the **General** section, you can customize the time zone, user interface, and so on:

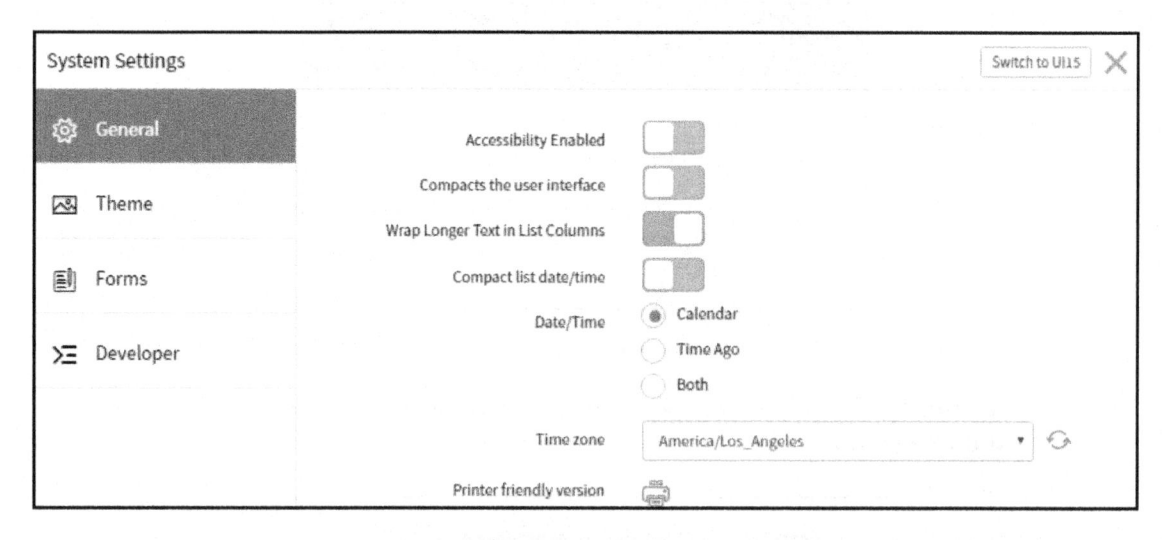

Service-Now System Settings – General

- In the **Theme** section, you can customize the look and feel of the backend. Out of the box, Service-Now provides eight themes and you are allowed to choose any one of them:

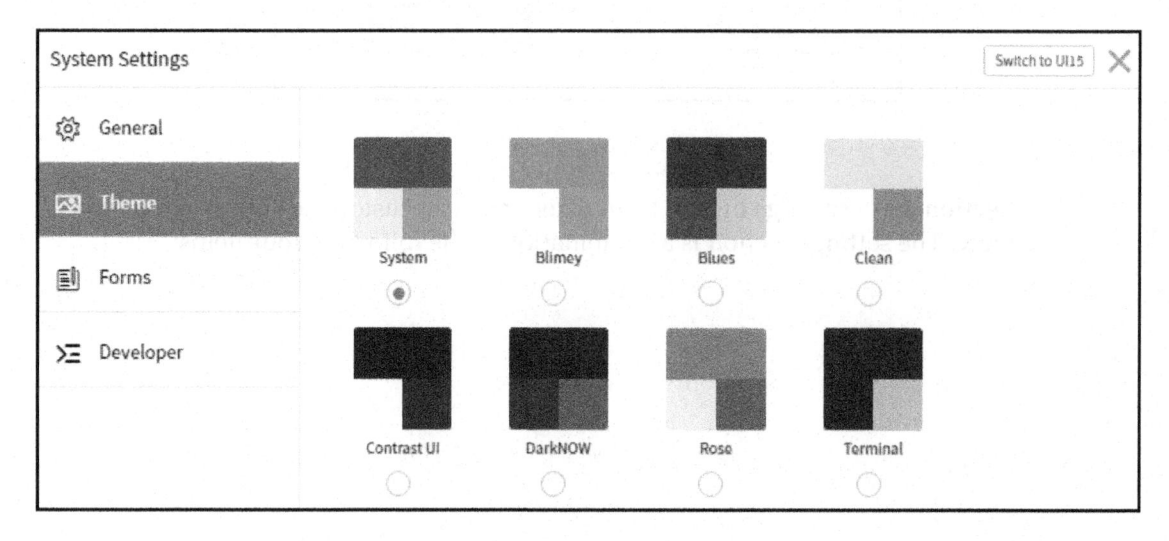

Service-Now System Settings – Theme

- In the **Forms** section, you can customize forms layout at the IT view and the related list loading time as well. Out of the box, Service-Now provides three options. If you want to load the related list with the form, it consumes more time to load as compared to the **After Form Load and On-demand** options:

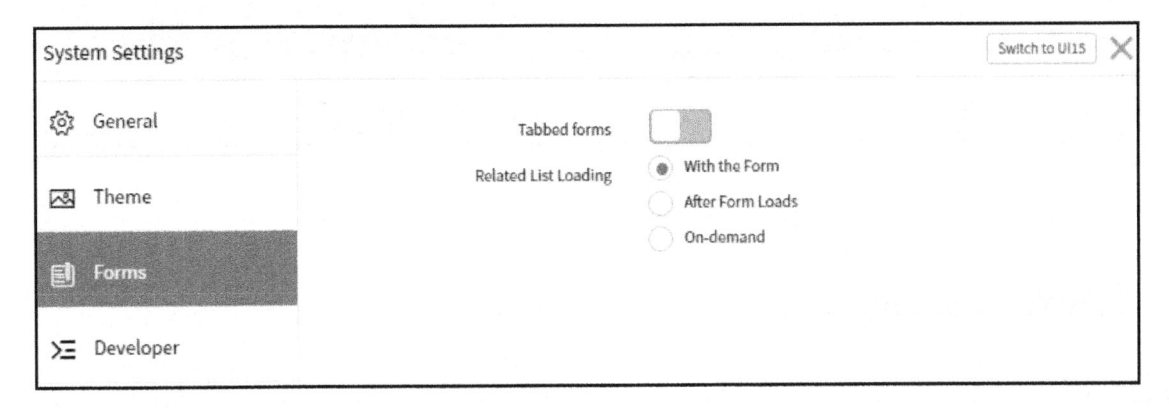

Service-Now System Setting – Forms

- In the **Developer** section, Service-Now provides features to add current update sets and the current application in the backend:

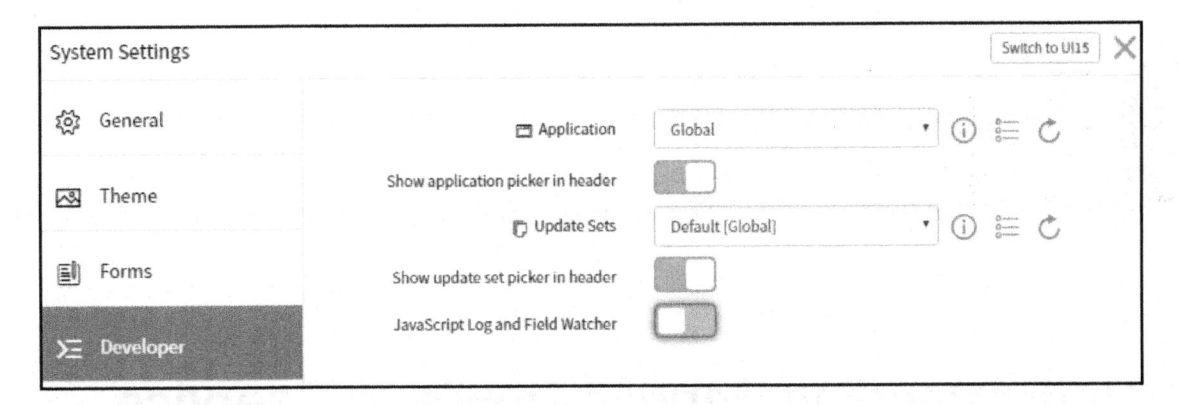

Service-Now System Settings – Developer

- Once you turn it on, you will able to view the current update set and application in the top banner:

Service-Now development feature

There's more...

As an admin, Service-Now provides you a way to directly open the new record or view record. It is important to note that you must know the table name for applying it. If you want to open a new record of the table, then you can type table name.do in the search box like incident.do, and if you want to see all available records in the table, then you can type `tablename.list` like `incident.list`.

See also

- To read more about the navigation and user interface click on https://docs.servicenow.com/bundle/geneva-servicenow-platform/page/administer/navigation_and_ui/concept/c_NavigationAndTheUserInterface.html
- To read more about the filter and breadcrumbs click https://docs.servicenow.com/bundle/geneva-servicenow-platform/page/use/using_lists/concept/c_UsingFiltersAndBreadcrumbs.html

Understanding Service-Now's self-service application

Service-Now's Self-Service module is available for all users, whether it's an end user or any ITIL role holder. The self-service application is the best place from to manage major tasks.

Getting ready

To step through this recipe, all you need is a Service-Now instance address and valid credentials.

How to do it…

The Self-Service application module is available in the IT view for all users. To view this application module, the user doesn't need role. This self-service application has many modules but let's take a look at some key ones:

- **Watched Incidents**: As a support group member, usually you want to denote your reporting manager or lead or any other user regards to the incident so in such a case you can add their name in **watched list** field. Once users are added on the incident form, they will start getting all email notification for each and every update regards to the task like incident, problem, and change and so on:

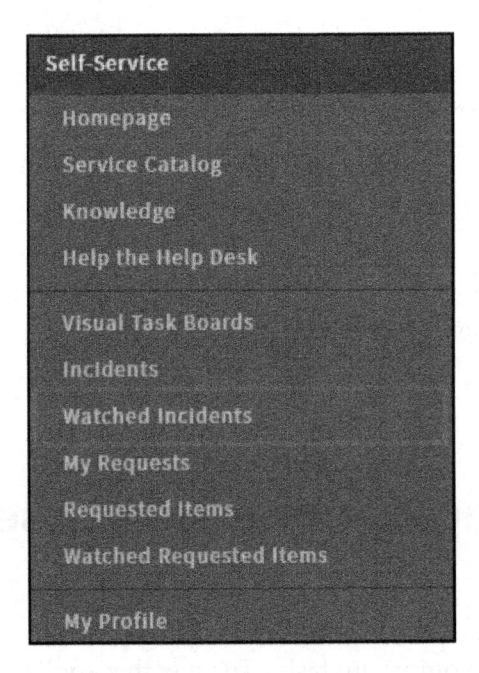

Service-Now self-service module

- **Homepage**: Mostly, the resolver manager wants to see the overview of all calls; so, in such a case, Service-Now provides out of the box modules where any manager, lead, or team member can view the overall status of all calls, which can be customized based on the requirement:

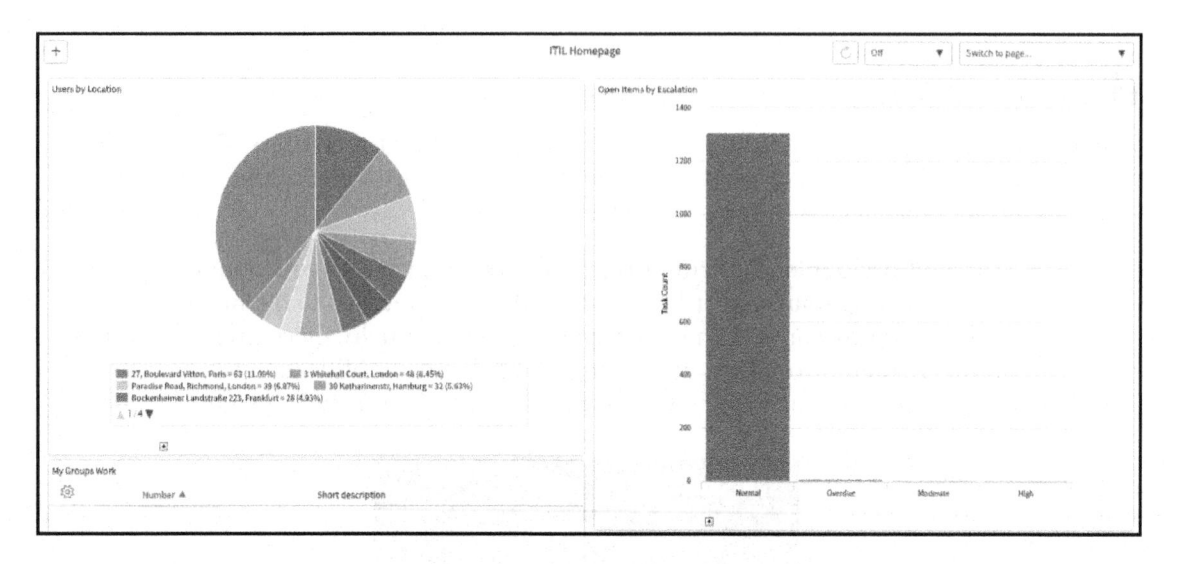

The ITIL Homepage

See also

- To read more about the Self-Service application click on https://docs.servicenow.com/bundle/geneva-servicenow-latform/page/use/employee_self_service/reference/r_EmployeeSelfService.html

Understanding Service-Now's service desk application

Out of the box, Service-Now provides a service desk application from which you can manage all your tasks and your group tasks. To view this application, you should have an ITIL/Fulfiller role that is licensed.

Chapter 1

Getting ready

To step through this recipe, you should have an active Service-Now instance and valid login credentials and an ITIL or admin role.

How to do it...

1. Open any browser standard browser.
2. Type the Service-Now instance web address (http://{instance_name}.service-now.com) provided by your organization in the address bar, now enter your credentials in respective fields and press enter button
3. On the left-hand side in the search box type **Service Desk** and Service-Now will search out application for you or navigate to Service Desk application. In the **Service Desk** application, many modules are available, but let's take a look at key ones only:

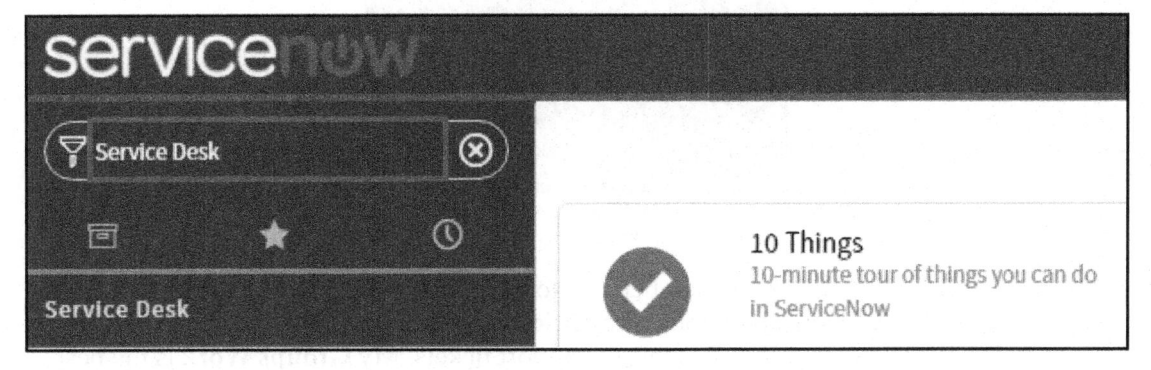

Searching the Service Desk application

Getting Started with Service-Now

4. As a support team member, you will receive your all your task in **My work**. If you want to see all the calls that are assigned to you, then you can simply click on **My Work**. The **My Work** module records all calls that are assigned to you regardless of the type of task. So, for example, if you have a problem, incident, or catalog task in your queue, then by clicking on **My Work** you can view all the calls that are in your bucket:

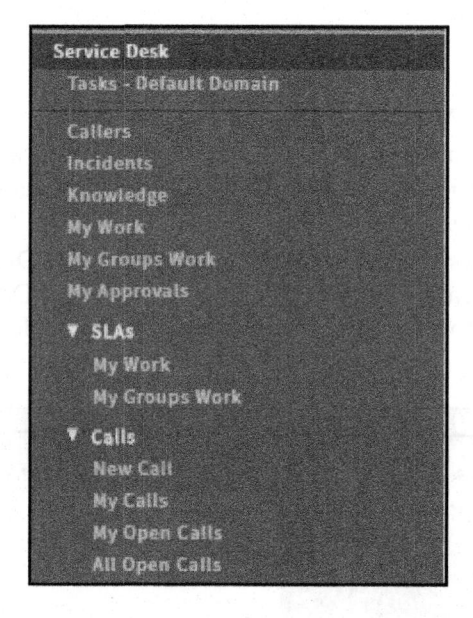

Service-Now Service Desk

5. Every support person belongs to some support group, but in many cases, a support group member may belong to more than one support group as well; so, to view all group's support tickets, **My Groups Work** is the best place to manage all calls that are assigned to your groups.
6. **Service Level Agreements (SLAs)**, contracts between service providers and end users that define the level of service expected from the service provider, are critical for any resolver group or any service company, where the service company has an agreement with the clients that if any issues come to them they will resolve the issues in the agreed timeframe. So, by clicking on **SLAs (My Work)** you can monitor your own SLA, and by clicking on **SLAs (My Groups Work)** you can view your group's SLA.

7. Approval is one of the key functions of any service management tool. On a daily basis, we raise many requests and most of them require a manager's approval, so managers can directly go to the Service-Now instance; but if your client wants to avoid the approval license cost, then you can configure the e-mail approval functionality.

Understand unique record identifier

For maintaining the uniqueness of each record Service-Now generates a 32 character global unique ID which is called `sys_id`. You can view **SysID** in any standard browser address bar.

Getting ready

To step through this recipe, you should have an active Service-Now instance, a role, and valid login credentials.

How to do it…

1. Open any browser standard browser.
2. Type the Service-Now instance web address (`https://{instance_name}.service-now.com`) provided by your organization in the address bar, now enter your credentials in respective fields and press **enter** button.
3. In the browser you can view SysID. Let's understand this by an example. In following screen shot you can view `sys_id=3D4301f1084f053200abb3b3728110c70e`:

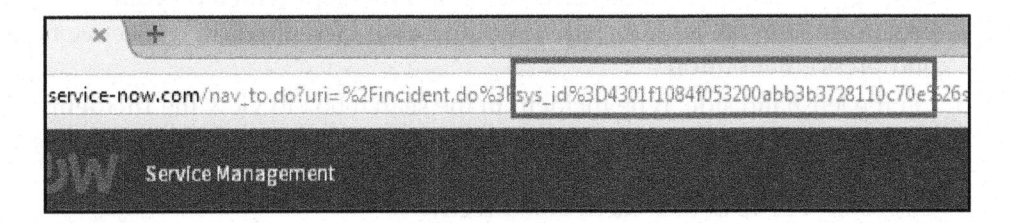

Record `sys_id`

There's more...

It is important to note that same sys_id value is never generated more than one time. If two record share same sys_id value then one was copied to other at database level outside of Service-Now application.

See also

To read more about the `sys_id` click at: http://wiki.servicenow.com/index.php?title=Unique_Record_Identifier#gsc.tab=0

Using the incident management application

Incident management is one of the key applications of Service-Now. As per the ITIL definition, an unplanned interruption to an IT service or reduction in the quality of an IT service is referred to as an incident. Application login error, antivirus error, server room fan and so on can be considered as incidents examples.

Getting ready

To step through this recipe, all you need is an active Service-Now instance, valid credentials, and an admin/ITIL role.

How to do it...

1. Open any browser standard browser.
2. Type the Service-Now instance web address (`http://{instance_name}.service-now.com`) provided by your organization in the address bar, now enter your credentials in respective fields and press enter button.
3. On the left-hand side, type Incident in the search box to view the **Incident application.** To create a new incident record, you can directly type `incident.do` in the search box. If you want to see all incident records, then you can type `incident.list` in the search box directly:

Chapter 1

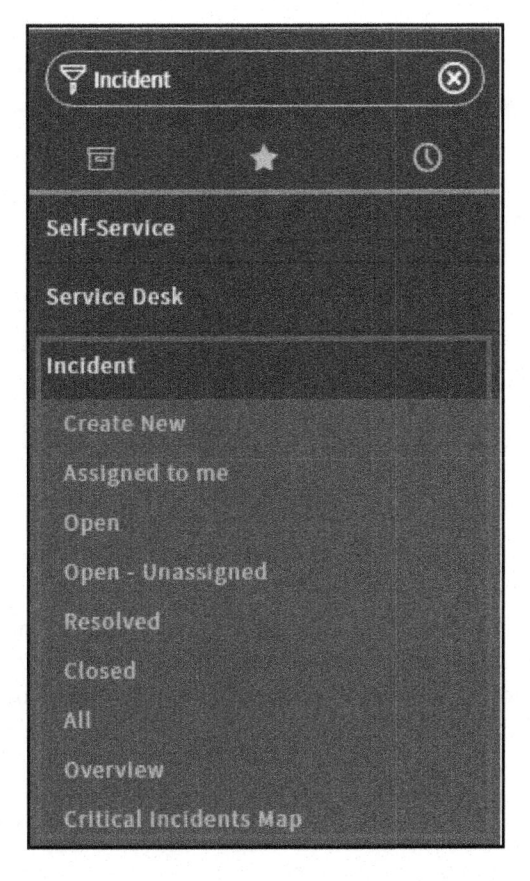

Service-Now Incident Management module

4. If you want to create a new record by the incident application then you can click on **Create New** module. After clicking on **Create New** module the incident form is opened on screen, now enter the relevant fields on incident form and click on **submit** button:

Getting Started with Service-Now

Incident Form

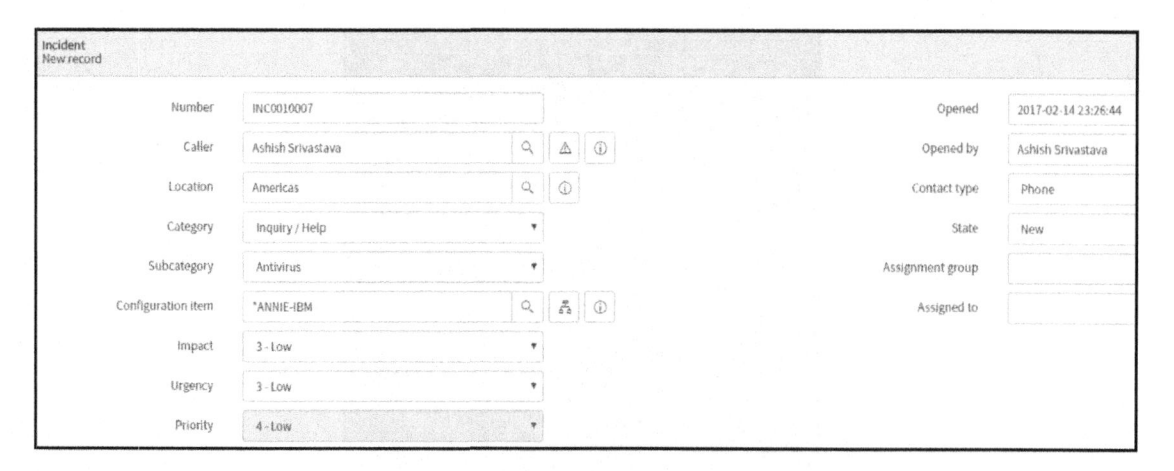

5. After submission of the form, an incident number will be generated for an example INC0000055, which will serve as a reference number for the users
6. Once the form is submitted, an incident is assigned to the respective support group to resolve it. Any group member can check a new incident under **My Group Work** and assign it to them. After resolving the incident they can click on the `Resolve Incident` button.

How it works...

The incident table extends the task table by which it gets all the properties of the task table. When you click on **Create New** module, an incident form appears and you fill in the details. After clicking on the **Submit** button, Service-Now generates an incident number with the unique number called SysID. For the assignment of the support group, a relationship is defined under **System Policy Application** in **Assignment Lookup Rules**, **Assignment** and **Data lookup Definitions** modules which store the relation of category and subcategory and when a condition is met, it assigns an incident to the support group.

There's more...

End users or users without any role are not allowed to create the incident from IT view as they don't have access to view this application but ITIL users can create the incident from the IT view. It is important to note that there is no workflow for incident application.

See also

- To read more about the incident management click at https://docs.servicenow.com/bundle/geneva-it-service-management/page/product/incident_management/concept/c_IncidentManagement.html

Using the related lists of applications

Related lists are highly useful when we need to build a relationship between the two tables and for reporting as well, there is always a relationship of parent and child, which can be established by a system definition application (relationship module).

Getting ready

To step through this recipe, you need an active Service-Now instance and a valid credential or role (admin).

How to do it...

1. Open any browser standard browser.
2. Type the Service-Now instance web address (http://{instance_name}.service-now.com) provided by your organization in the address bar, now enter your credentials in respective fields and press enter button.
3. On the left-hand side in the search box, type incident, and under the **Incident Application** click on **Open Module:**

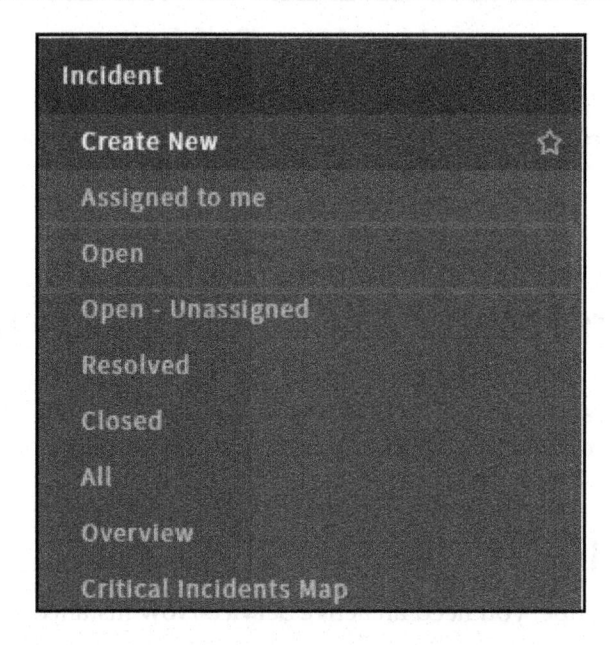

Incident Application – Open Module

4. After clicking on **Open Module,** you will able to view all active incident in the list format as follows:

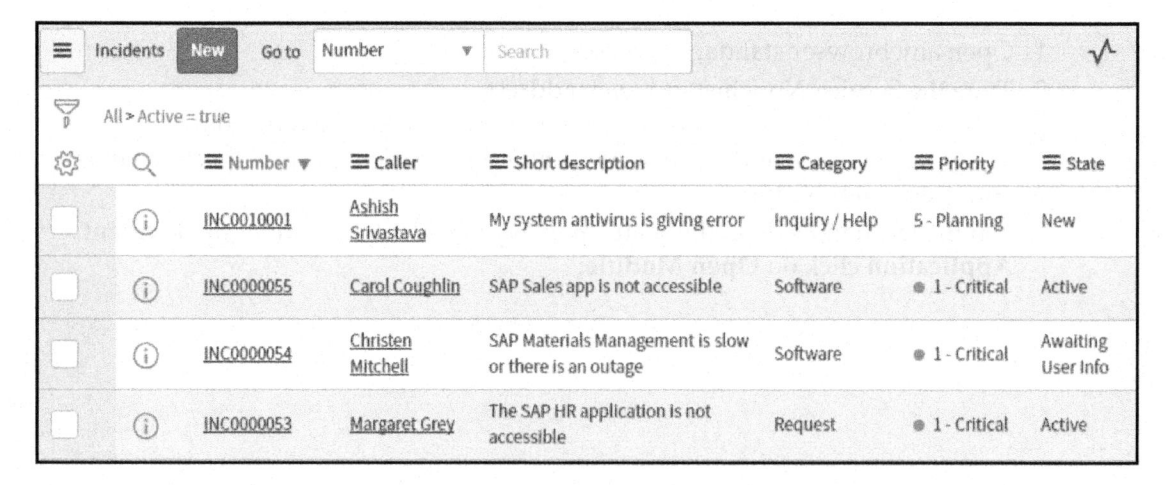

		Number	Caller	Short description	Category	Priority	State
		INC0010001	Ashish Srivastava	My system antivirus is giving error	Inquiry / Help	5 - Planning	New
		INC0000055	Carol Coughlin	SAP Sales app is not accessible	Software	1 - Critical	Active
		INC0000054	Christen Mitchell	SAP Materials Management is slow or there is an outage	Software	1 - Critical	Awaiting User Info
		INC0000053	Margaret Grey	The SAP HR application is not accessible	Request	1 - Critical	Active

Incident Records – List View

Chapter 1

5. Now, you can click on any incident record but for now, so let's suppose you have clicked on **INC0010001** record. After opening the incident record, you need Right-click on the header of the incident form. After that, select **Configure** and in the configure options, select **Related Lists** as follows:

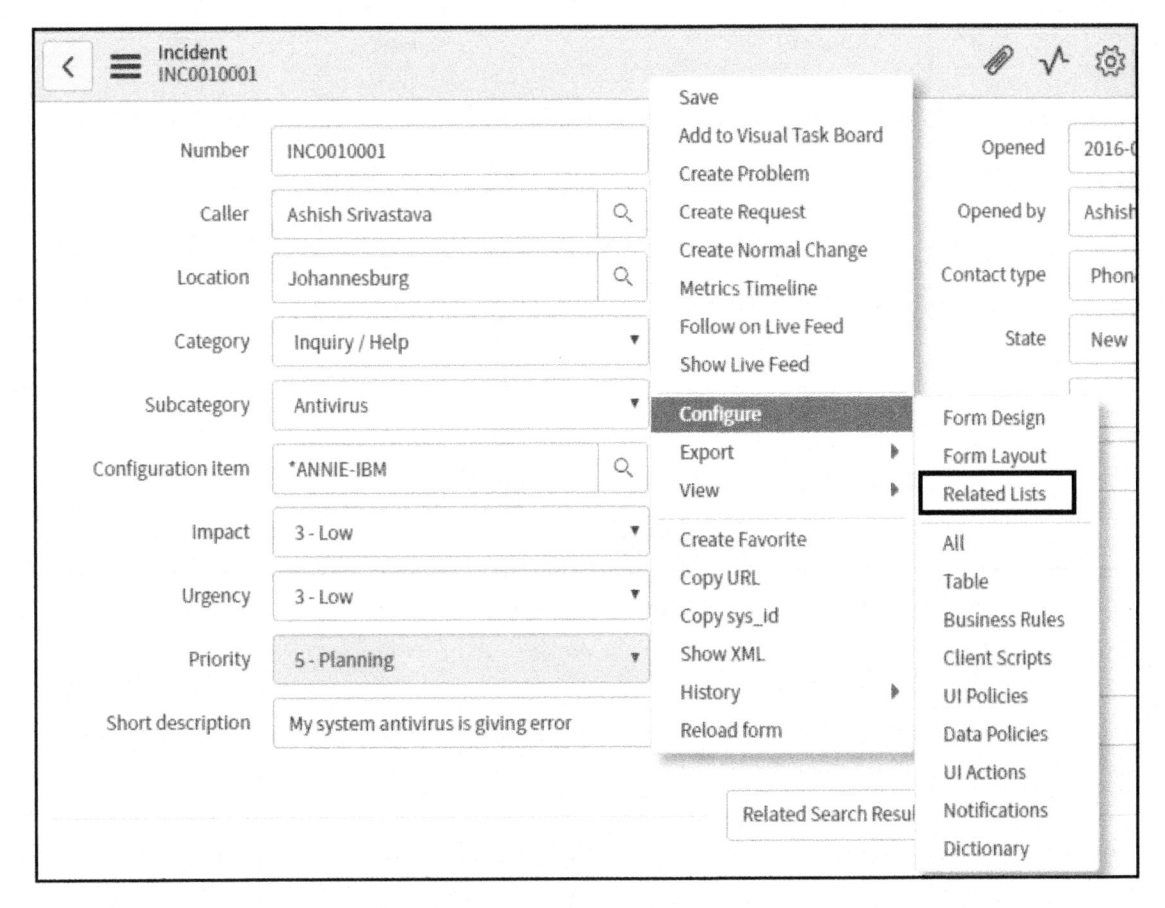

Configuring related lists from the incident form

6. Out of the box, all related lists are available and you can move any related list to the **Selected** box from **Available box** as shown following:

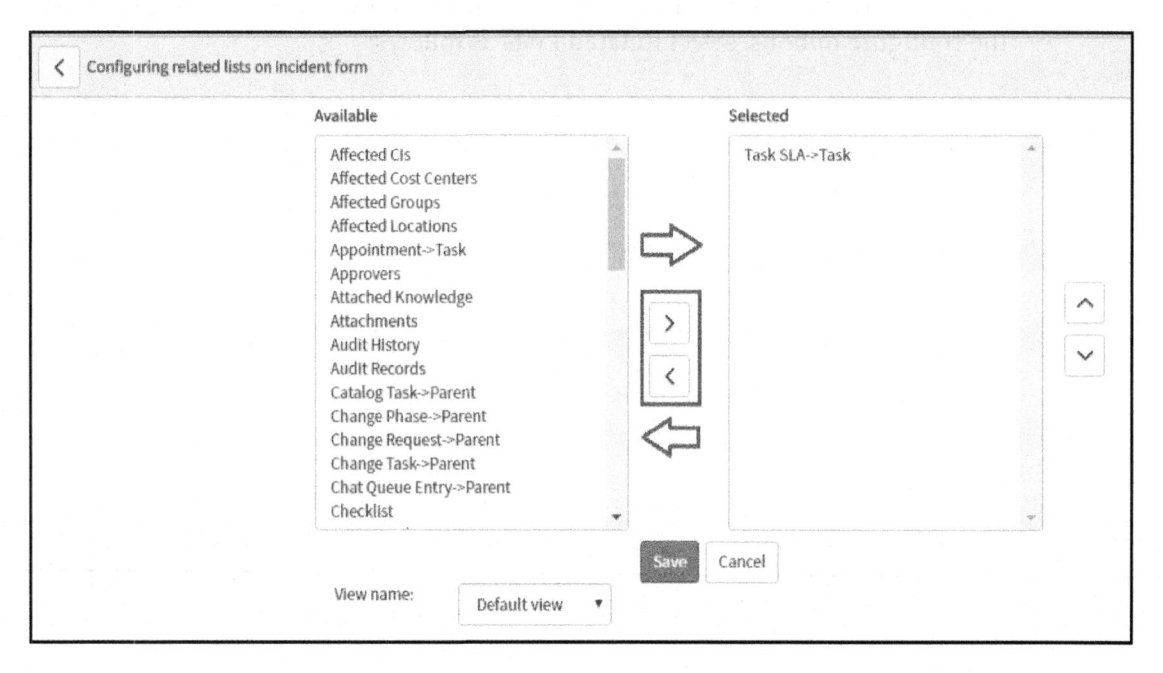

Adding related lists to the form

7. The available box holds out of the box relationships and you can move as many as you want from available box to selected box but for now, let's support you have moved *Affected CIs* related list from **Available** box to **Selected** box as shown following and click **Save** button:

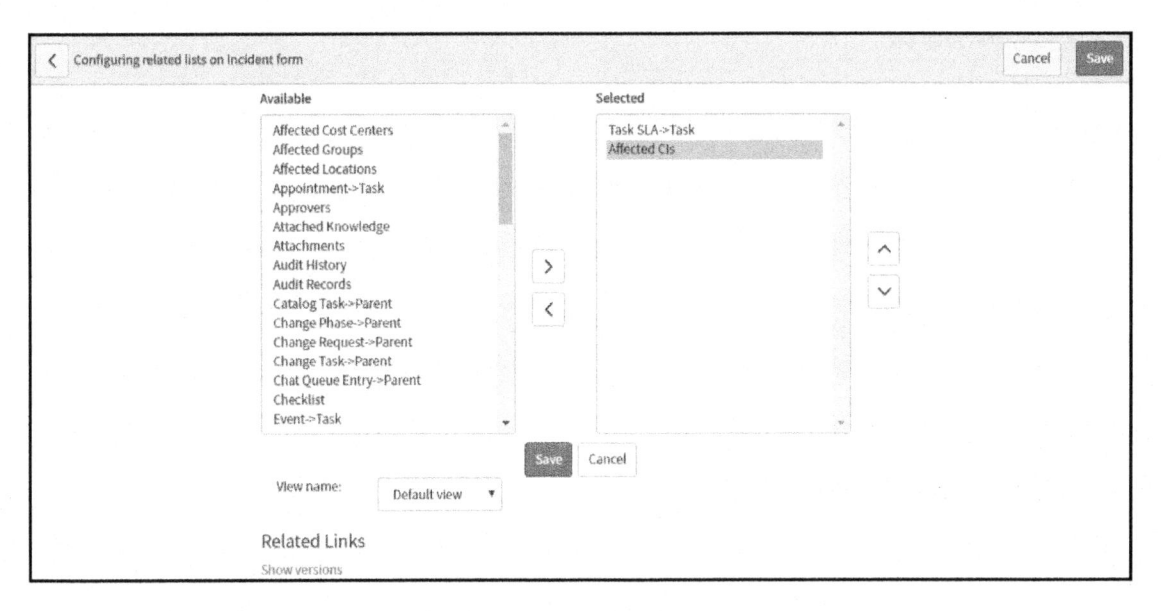

Adding Affected CIs related on the incident form

8. After clicking on **Save** button, you will able to view **Affected CIs** related list bottom on incident form. It will show all Cis which are affected by the incident as follows:

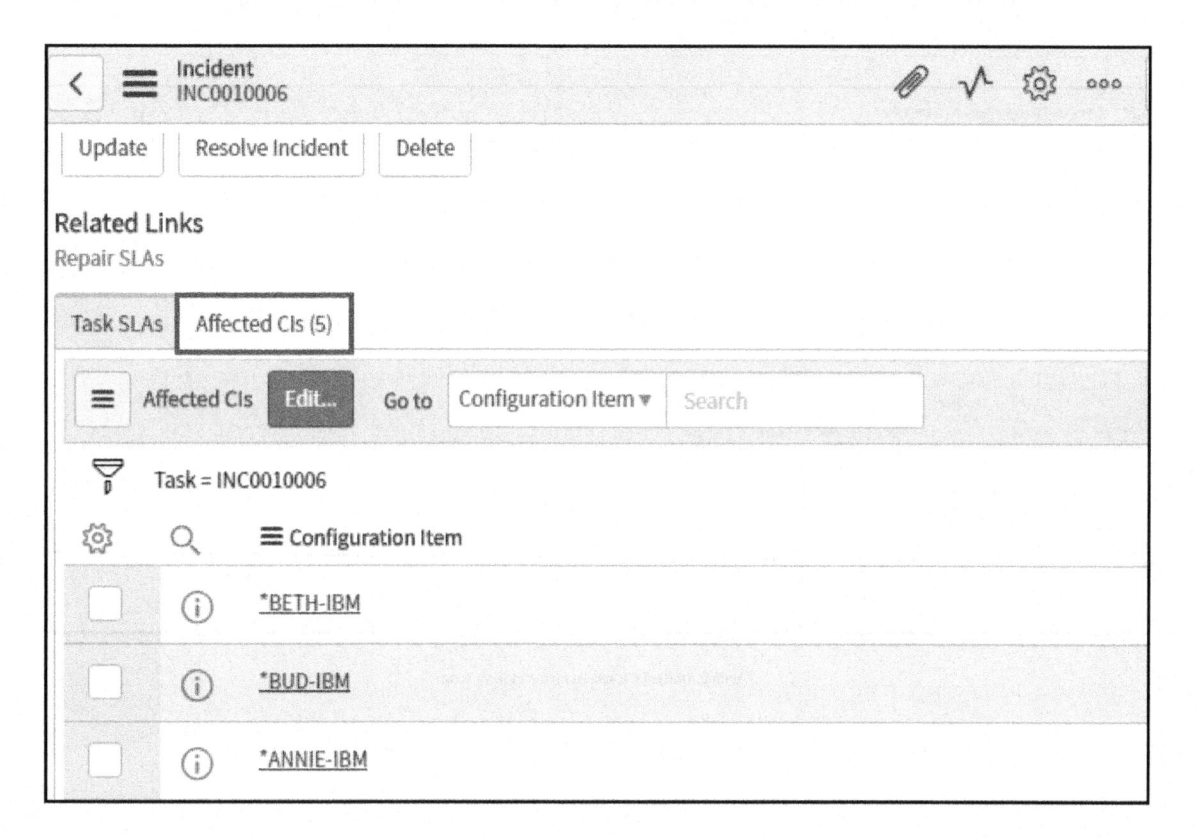

See also

- To read more about the configuration item click on http://wiki.servicenow.com/index.php?title=ITIL_Configuration_Management#gsc.tab=0 **and** http://wiki.servicenow.com/index.php?title=Attaching_Configuration_Items_to_an_Incident#gsc.tab=0

Using the problem management application

Out of the box, Service-Now provides problem management application for facilitating the problem management process. If we talk about the problem as per ITIL then 'Problem' is the unknown cause of one or more incidents, often identified as a result of multiple similar incidents, In general words if your support team is receiving many incidents related to one CI (Configuration Item) then it is considered as a problem and a problem ticket must be created for permanent fix.

Getting ready

To step through this recipe, all you need is an active Service-Now instance, valid credential and Admin/ITIL role.

How to do it...

1. Open any browser standard browser.
2. Type the Service-Now instance web address (http://{instance_name}.service-now.com) provided by your organization in the address bar, now enter your credentials in respective fields and press enter button.
3. To search the problem application you need to type Problem and Service-Now will search out *Problem Application* for you. As an option, you can directly type problem.do to create a new record or to view all the records in the problem management module type problem.list in the search box.
4. Now, under the problem management application, click on the Create **New** module to create a new problem record:

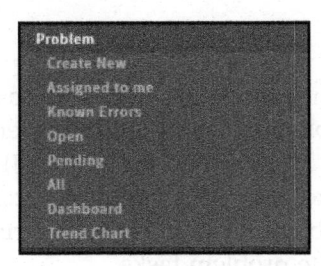

Problem management application

5. After click on the `Create New` module, you will able to view blank problem form so now enter necessary details in the form and click on **Submit** as follows:

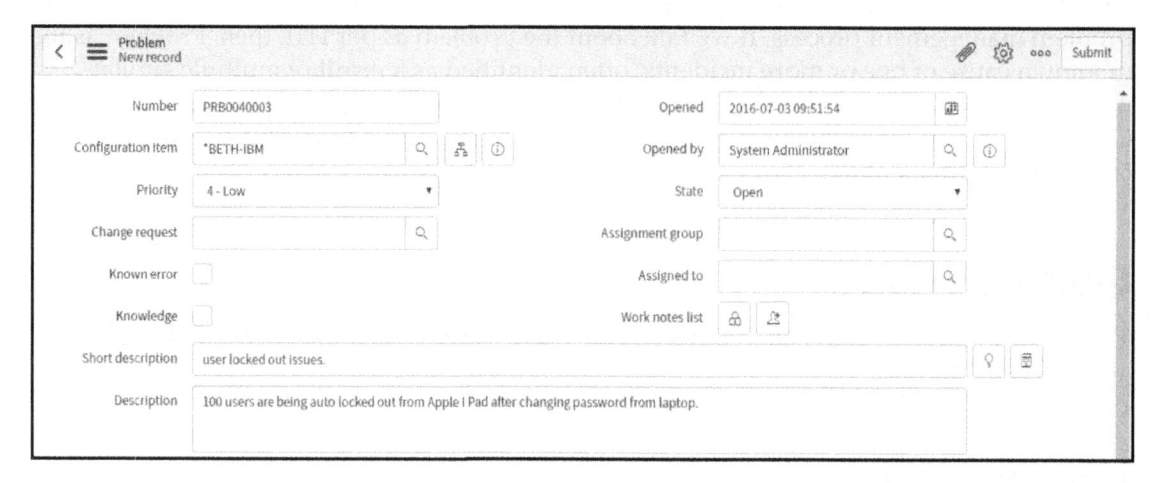

Problem management form

6. Now, a new problem ticket generated `PRB0040003` for reference purpose of the user.

How it works...

A dedicated problem table is available in Service-Now. When you click on **Create new** in the problem management module, a default problem management form appears, and after submission of the problem task, a unique `sysId` and number is assigned to the problem task, which serves as a parent.

There's more...

To manage, problem management process Service-Now has **problem table** and all problem-related records are stored in problem table only which extends to the **task** table. In addition, a part Service-Now admins, only IT users or users with ITIL roles are allowed to create problem records. It is important to note that many organizations have dedicated **problem manager** positions to handle problem related task so in term of process only problem manager may have access to create problem tasks.

Using the change management application

Disraeli, a British prime minister, said that:

> "Change is inevitable. Change is constant."

So, let's see how Service-Now uses the ITIL framework in its application. Every organization goes through a transition phase to achieve new goals to improve their services, user experiences, stability, or increase their product line for internal or external customers. In the ITIL framework, change management is a process used for managing the planned deployment of alterations to all configuration items in the configuration management database that are a part of production and test UAT environments along with any other environment that a business wants to have under change management. To manage the change management process, Service-Now provides the change management application.

Getting ready

To step through this recipe, all you need is an active Service-Now instance, valid credentials, and a role.

How to do it...

1. Open any browser standard browser.
2. Type the Service-Now instance web address (http://{instance_name}.service-now.com) provided by your organization in the address bar, now enter your credentials in respective fields and press enter button.
3. On the left-hand side in the search box, type Change and Service-Now will search out Change management application for you. For creating new change record click on **Create New** module under **Change application** as follows:

Getting Started with Service-Now

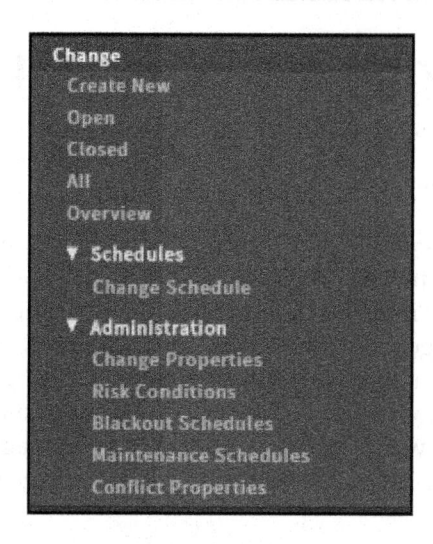

Change
Create New
Open
Closed
All
Overview
▼ Schedules
    Change Schedule
▼ Administration
    Change Properties
    Risk Conditions
    Blackout Schedules
    Maintenance Schedules
    Conflict Properties

Change management application.

4. As an option, you can type change_request.do in search box to directly open change management form. If you want to see all change records, then you can type change_request.list in the search box.
5. After clicking on the **Create New**, you will able to view the change request form as follows:

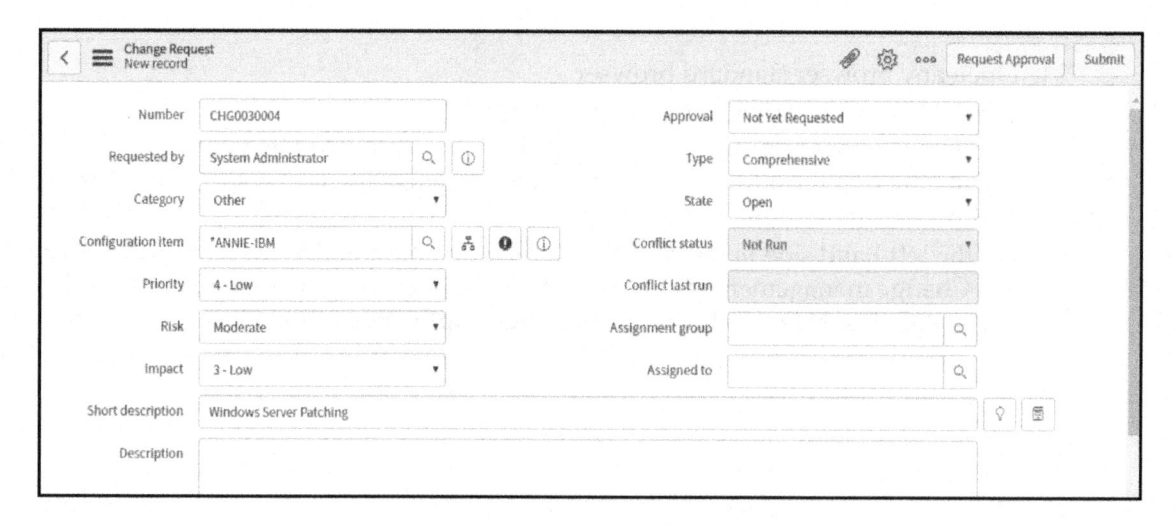

Creating a new **Change Request** form

[50]

6. Change management is a very critical process and many organizations use their own customized version of change model, now in change request form, you need to enter necessary details in change management form fields with be modified through change request.

There's more...

To support change management process, Service-Now provides a change_request table which extends to **task** table. Please note in numerous organizations, there a dedicated **change manager** to handle change requests. It is important to note that change management process guided by 3 workflows comprehensive change, emergency change and routine change and you can modify as per your organization requirement.

See also

To read more about the change management: https://docs.servicenow.com/bundle/geneva-it-service-management/page/product/change_management/concept/c_ITILChangeManagement.html

Creating the change/problem task from the incident task

Incident/problem/change may be inter-dependent. Let's understand this by an example so if your support group has received many incidents INC0000075/ INC0000091/ INC0000059 and so on related to user account which may lead a problem ticket or an emergency change ticket to deploy the permanent fix of issue. Out of the box, Service-Now provides functions to create a change or problem task from an incident task.

Getting ready

To step through this recipe, all you need is an active Service-Now instance, an ITIL or Admin role, and valid credentials.

How to do it...

1. Open any browser standard browser.
2. Type the Service-Now instance web address (http://{instance_name}.service-now.com) provided by your organization in the address bar, now enter your credentials in respective fields and press enter button.
3. Go to the Incident application.
4. Now, under incident application, click on **Open** module which will show all active incident records.
5. You can select any incident task to create a problem/change task but for now let's suppose you have opened INC0000044, now right click on incident form header through computer mouse as follows:

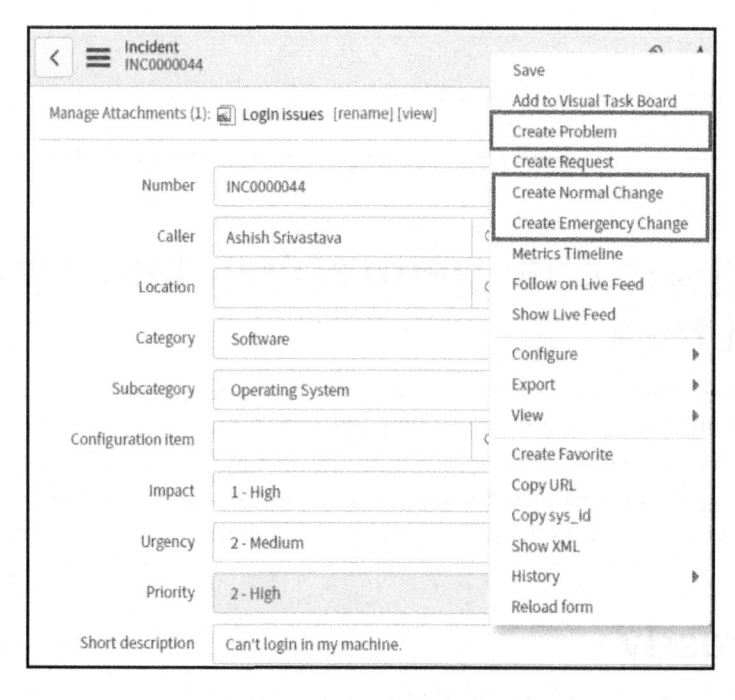

Creating a change/problem ticket from an incident

Chapter 1

6. If you want to create a change task from an incident, then click on **Create Change**. Once you click on the **Create Change** button, Service-Now will redirect you to the change form with some of the basic fields auto-filled.
7. If you want to create a problem task form incident, then click on **Create Problem**. Once you click on **Create Problem**, Service-Now will redirect you to the change form with some of the basic fields auto-filled:

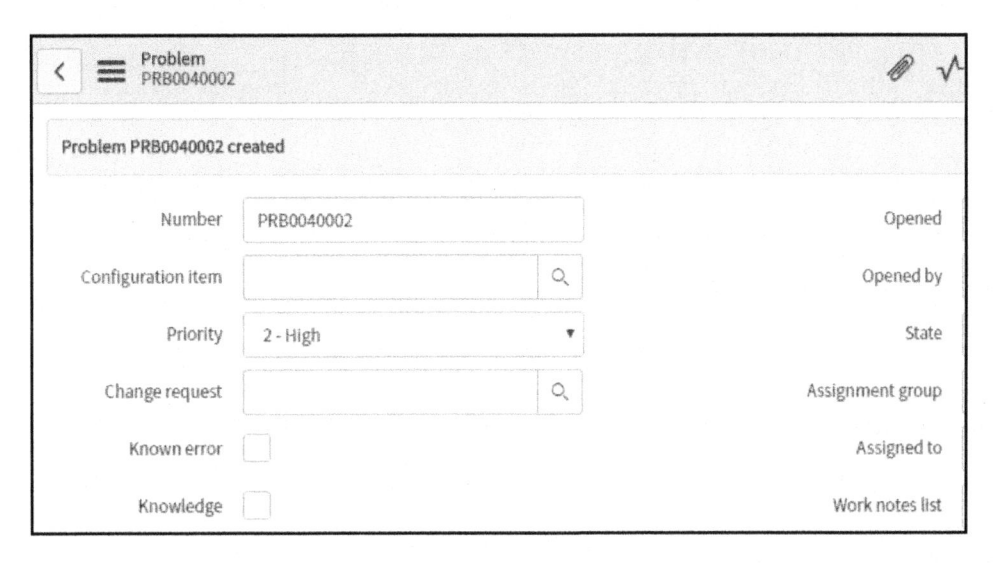

Problem task created Incident Form

8. Now problem task `PRB0040002` is created from `INC0000044` with other information as well like Priority, Opened by and so on but `INC0000044` will serve as a parent of problem task as follows:

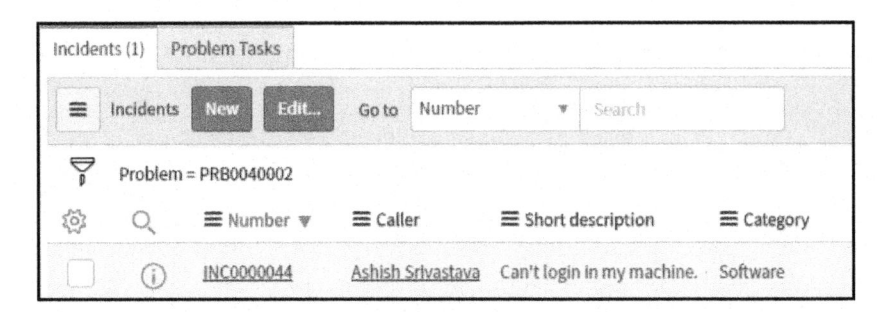

Problem-related Incident

[53]

2
Performing Core Configuration and Management Tasks

In this chapter, we will cover the following recipes:

- Setting up basic configuration
- Understanding LDAP servers
- Understanding user administration
- Understanding group administration
- Using Service-Now plugins
- Configuring the Service-Now form
- Configuring UI policies on Service-Now forms
- Configuring UI actions on forms
- Understanding deployments or update sets
- Getting into CMDB
- Setting up an SLA/OLA/underpinning contract
- Setting up system rules
- Understanding the system dictionary
- Understanding the Service-Now tables schema
- Getting into system security

Introduction

After purchasing Service-Now, the customer receives one production instance and two non-production instances, which are out-of-the-box and need to be configured as per your organization's requirements. In this chapter, you will learn to perform core configuration and management activities.

Setting up basic configuration

From Service-Now, a customer receives an out-of-the-box instance. Note that each and every organization has its own marketing and branding policies for IT applications. Basic configuration is an essential part of a Service-Now instance, in which you need to configure the entire Service-Now website (portal or frontend) for end users. From the IT point of view (where you can see incident, problem, change, self-service, and other such modules), you are allowed to change the theme of Service-Now and split the application pane at your convenience.

Getting ready

To step through this recipe, you should have an active Service-Now instance, valid credentials, and admin role.

How to do it...

1. Open any standard web browser.
2. Type the Service-Now instance web address provided by your company in the address bar (`http://{instance_name}.service-now.com`).
3. If you want to change the logo of service-now instance then on left hand side in the search box, type `system properties` and select **My company** module under system properties application:

Chapter 2

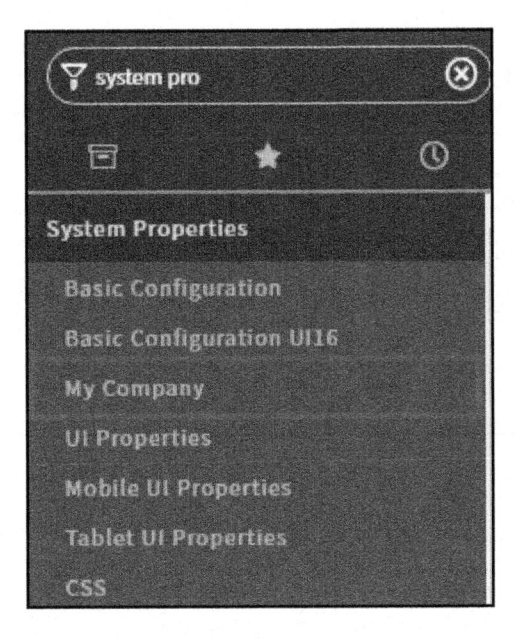

Change logo

4. After clicking on **My Company**, you need to click on **Banner image [update]**:

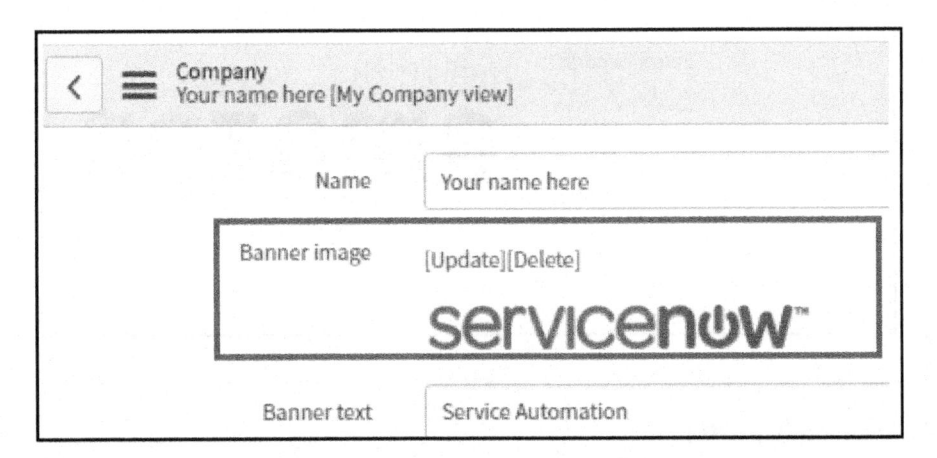

Update logo

[57]

5. After clicking on the **[Update]** button, click on **Choose File**, upload your logo, and click on **Ok**:

Upload your company

6. After clicking on **OK**, the new logo will be uploaded:

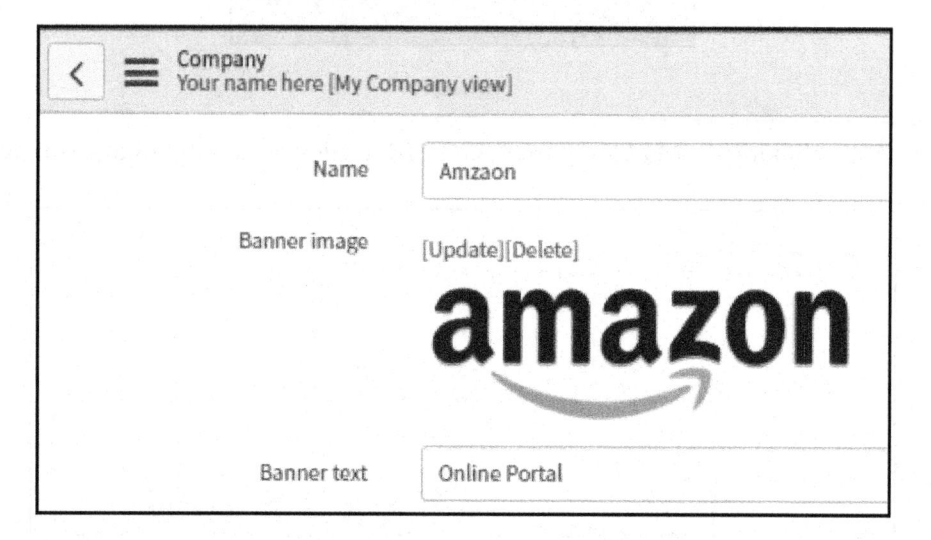

New logo

7. Click on **[Update]**.
8. If you want to modify Service-Now as per your company's branding, then on the left-hand side in the search box, type `system UI` and select **Themes**:

Chapter 2

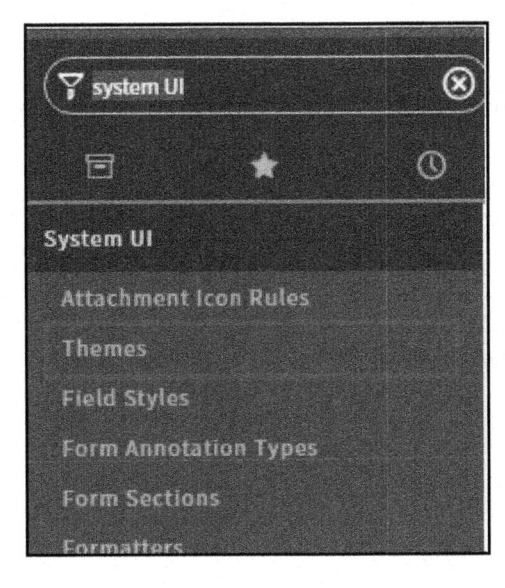

System Themes

9. After selecting **Themes**, you need to click on the **New** button:

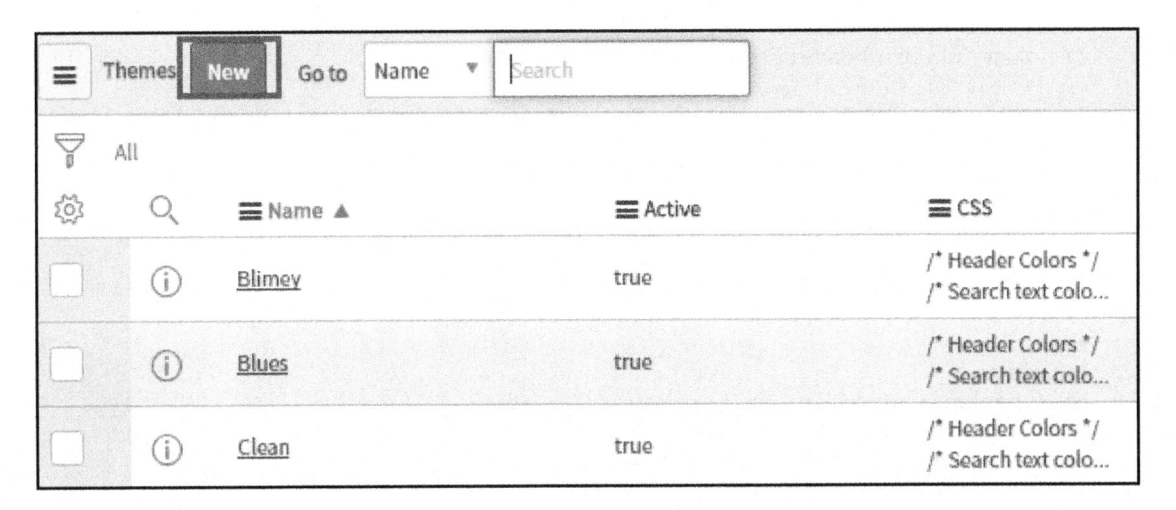

Themes records

[59]

Performing Core Configuration and Management Tasks

10. Now you need to configure the theme to your company branding:

    - **Name**: Amazon
    - **Active**: True
    - **CSS**:

```
 /* Texts in forms, Lists, Bookmarks, cards border_mouseover, Live-feed,
Context Menu & Form right side Icons */
$text-color: #3e1431
/* Input boxes, Buttons tabs top color, pagination_vcr & Form Icons */
$highlight-color: #6ab90d
/*  Hover color for TR, Form Icons    */
$accent-color: #6ab90d
/*  Favorites, Bookmark Mouse over , Icon-Hover-Focus-Color*/
$accent-color-dark: #6ab90d
/* Border-colors */
$lightest-color: #027864

/* Navigation-border-bottom-colors */
$color-light: #6ab90d
/*  White background for Nav Items, Buttons, Pagination VCR & Form labels
*/
$color-lightest: white
/*  Edge_flyout_header section_title & anchor text */
$color-dark: #000000
/* Bookmark column & Navigator, Table Header, Form Header, Form right side
Icons   */
/*$color-lighter: #14846c*/

#/* Additionally We can change the color for Banner */
base.color: #6ab90d
banner.description.color: #222222

###
# Legacy
body.background.color: white;
table.background.color: white;
list.row.even.background.color: white;
list.row.odd.background.color: #027864;
```

    - **Device**: doctype

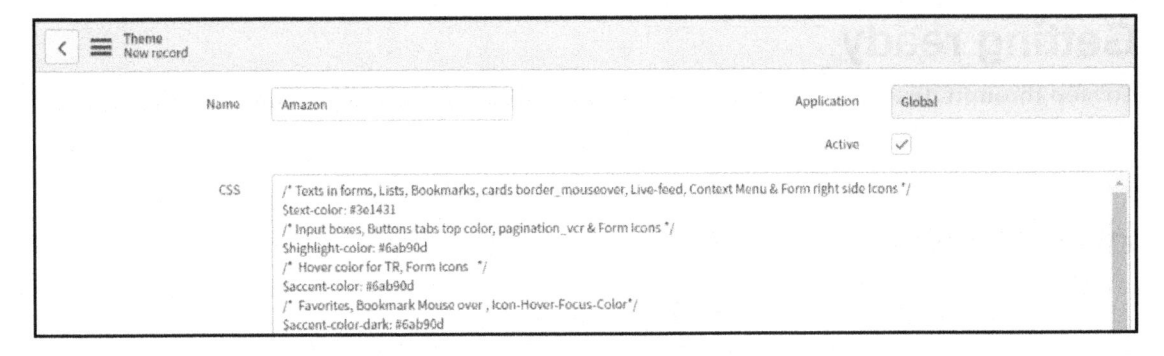

Create new theme

11. Click on **Submit**.
12. Now your new theme is added under **Theme**:

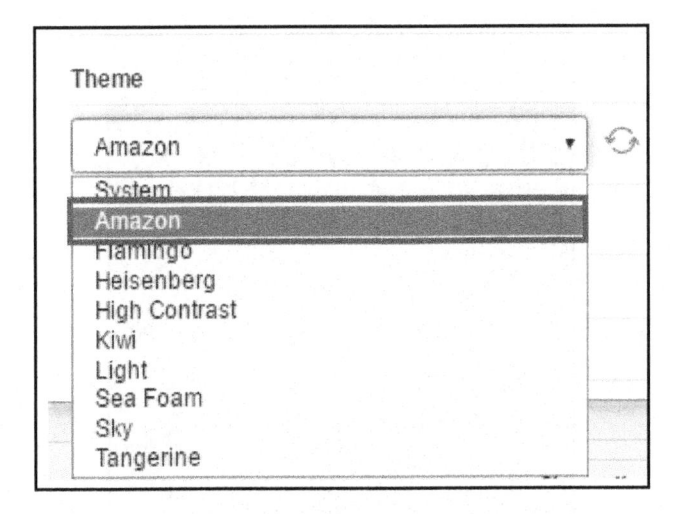

New theme added

Understanding LDAP servers

If the LDAP server is the master source of user date, then it won't be wrong. Out of the box, Service-Now provides a built-in LDAP server, so for streamlined user access, you can integrate your company's Active Directory with Service-Now, so whoever is in the company's Active Directory is allowed to log in with their company Windows or system credentials.

Getting ready

To step through this recipe, you should have an active Service-Now instance, valid credentials, and an admin role.

How to do it...

1. Open any standard web browser.
2. Type the Service-Now instance web address provided by your company in the address bar (http://{instance_name}.service-now.com).
3. Type `system ldap` on the left-hand side, and service now will search out the module. Now you need to click on **Create New Server**:

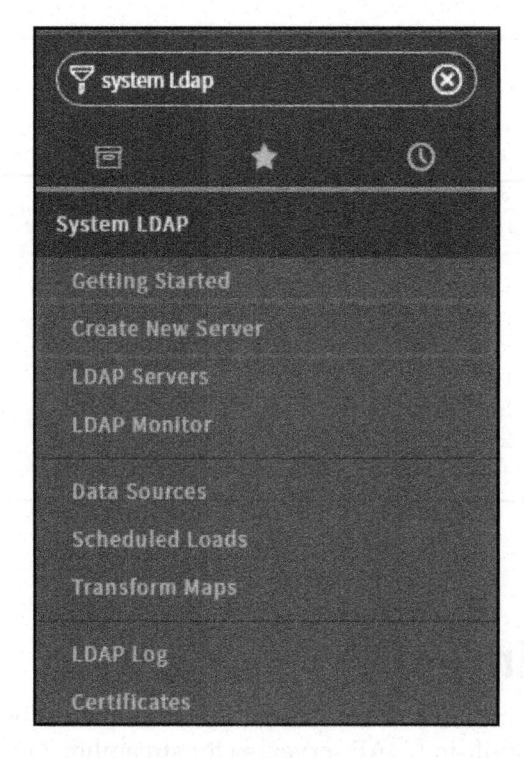

System LDAP

4. You have to configure it to streamline user access, as follows:

- **Type of LDAP Server**: **Active Directory** (You can give your own name)
- **Server name**: AD Server
- **Server URL**: ldap://10.10.10.3:389/
- **Starting search dictionary**: DC:packt,DC=com

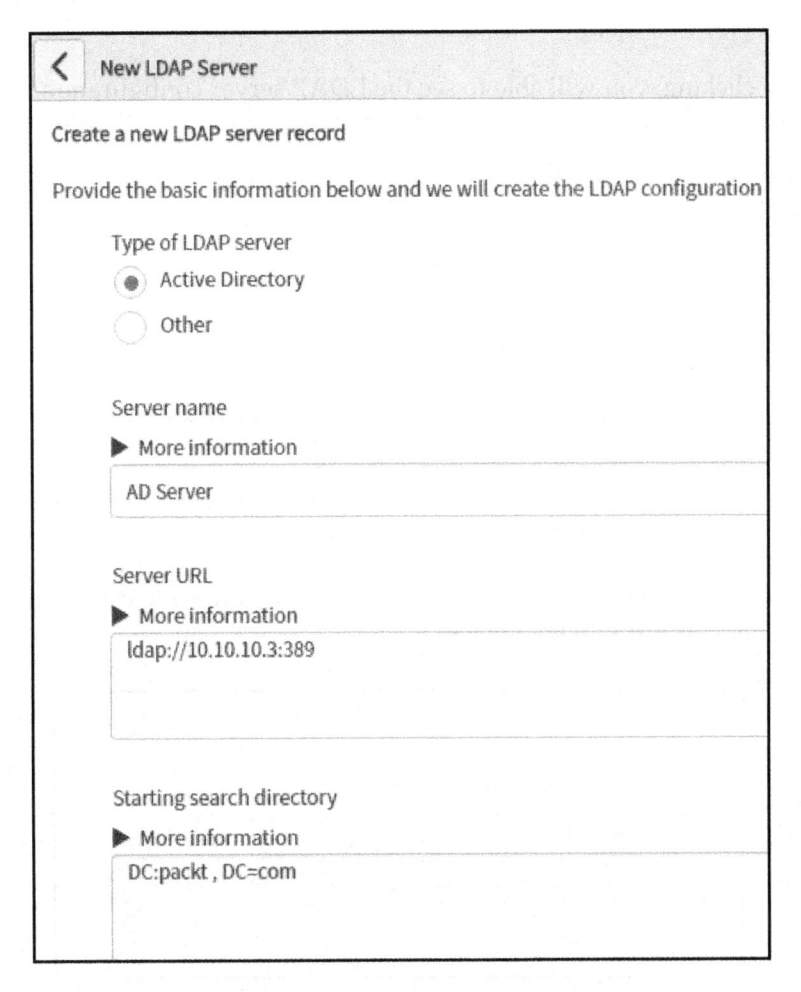

LDAP server configuration

5. Now click on **Submit** button.

Performing Core Configuration and Management Tasks

> Standard LDAP integration communicates over TCP on port 389 by default, which is not secure, so if you want to go with port 389, you can implement a **Measurement Instrumentation Discovery** (**MID**) server in your organization to communicate securely outside your company network LDAPS (an SSL-encrypted integration) to communicate over 636 by default, which requires a certificate. You can `ldap://10.10.10.3:636/` instead of `ldap://10.10.10.3:389/` in Server URL field.

6. After clicking, you will able to see the LDAP server configuration page, where you need to provide configuration attributes to import data from `AD Server`:

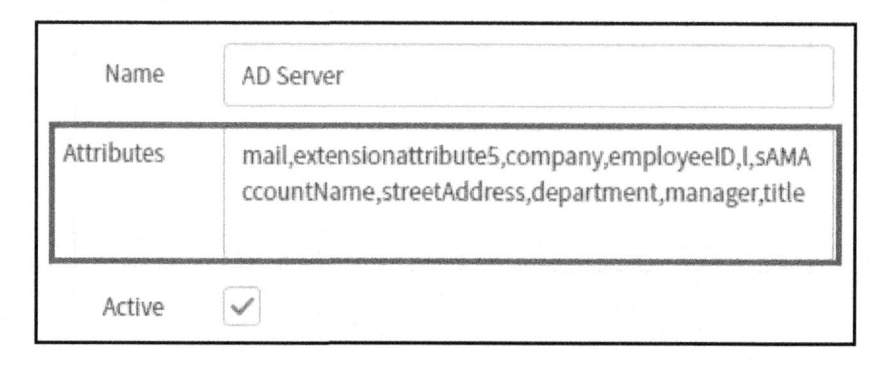

Name	AD Server
Attributes	mail,extensionattribute5,company,employeeID,l,sAMAccountName,streetAddress,department,manager,title
Active	✓

LDAP server attributes configuration

7. After configuration of `AD Server` attributes, you need to configure the account by which import will take place:

Application	Global
Login distinguished name	admin
Login password	********
Starting search directory	DC=packt,DC=com
MID Server	

LDAP server admin account configuration

Chapter 2

8. You can configure advanced options, as shown here:

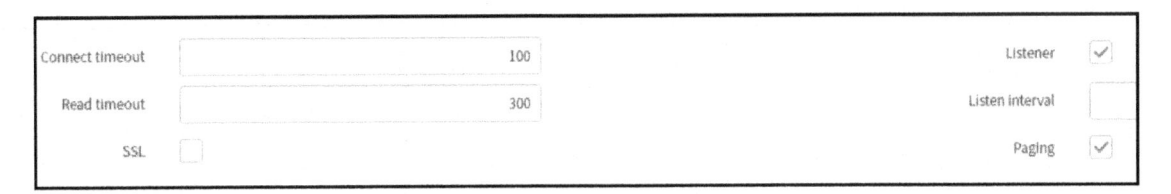

Connect timeout	100		Listener	✓
Read timeout	300		Listen interval	
SSL	☐		Paging	✓

Advanced option configuration

9. You can click on the **LDAP OU Definitions** related list, as shown in the next screenshot, to view further configuration of LDAP:

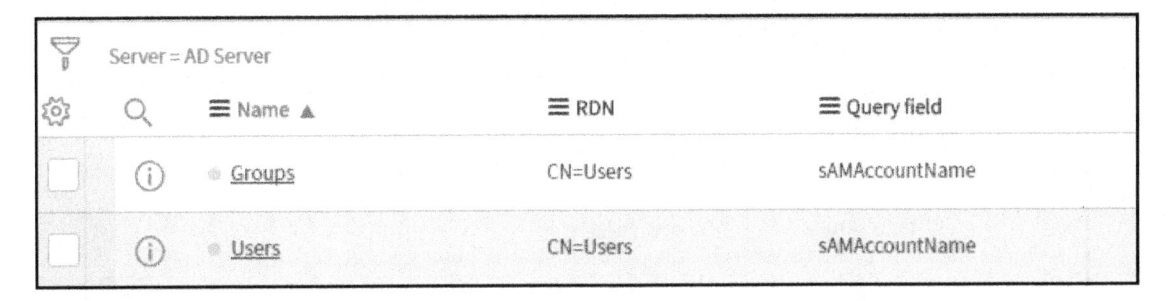

		Server = AD Server		
⚙	🔍	≡ Name ▲	≡ RDN	≡ Query field
☐	ⓘ	Groups	CN=Users	sAMAccountName
☐	ⓘ	Users	CN=Users	sAMAccountName

LDAP OU definitions

10. On many occasions, you may come across a situation where you want to change the daily import time of user records. To view that, click on **Scheduled Loads** under the system LDAP module, as shown in the following screenshot:

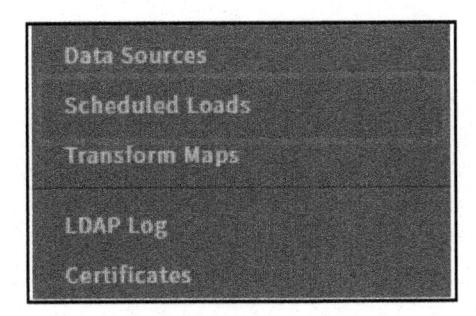

Data Sources
Scheduled Loads
Transform Maps
LDAP Log
Certificates

Scheduled loads to configure daily import

[65]

Performing Core Configuration and Management Tasks

11. After clicking, you will able to see following job created for LDAP data import. Now click on **AD Server/Users Import** to see it's configuration:

ⓘ AD Server/Groups Import	Daily	AD Server/Groups
ⓘ AD Server/Users Import	Daily	AD Server/Users

Actions on selected rows... ▼

Daily job to import data

12. After clicking, you will able to see the configuration page, as shown in the next screenshot. Mark it **Active** if it isn't. To change the time of daily import, change the value in the **Time** field:

Name	AD Server/Users Import
Data source	AD Server/Users
Run as	System Administrator
Active	✓
Execute pre-import script	☐
Execute post-import script	☐

LDAP user import configuration

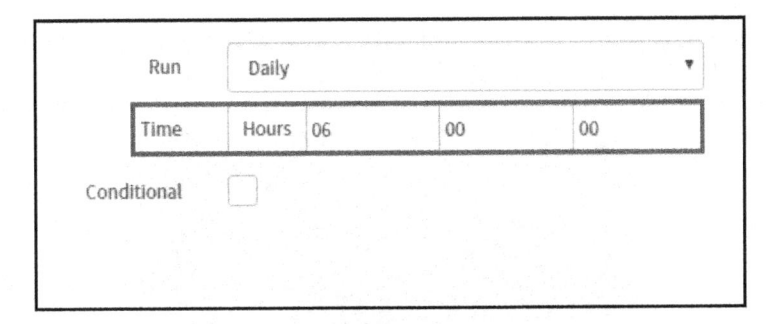

LDAP user import time configuration

13. Click on **Update**, and you will able to see the schedule in the **Scheduled Loads** module. Now, the data import will start everyday at 6.00 AM to get user records from Microsoft Active Directory.

Understanding user administration

Users are a critical part of any organization, and application access should be smooth, so for streamlined access to applications, you can integrate Service-Now with your company's LDAP server. Out of the box, Service-Now provides an LDAP server and user administration modules for configuration.

Getting ready

To step through this recipe, you should have an active Service-Now instance, valid credentials, and an admin role.

How to do it...

1. Open any standard web browser.
2. Type the Service-Now instance web address provided by your company in the address bar (http://{instance_name}.service-now.com).

3. After login, type `user admin` on left hand side in the search box and Service-Now will search out application for you as follows:

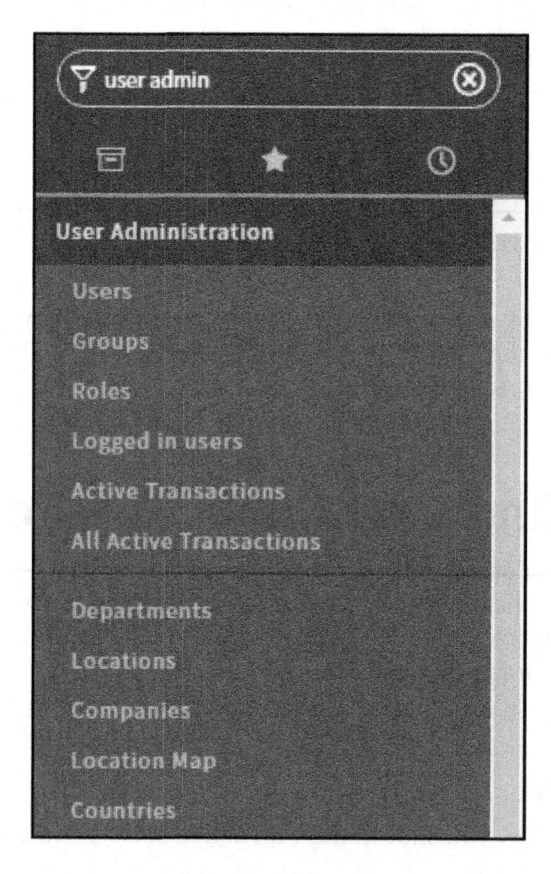

User administration module

4. Under the **User Administration** module, Service-Now provides many other modules, but I'll cover a few key modules in this recipe.
5. The **Users** module is the place where Service-Now holds all Service-Now user accounts.

6. Click on the **Users** module, and you will see user records, as shown in following screenshot:

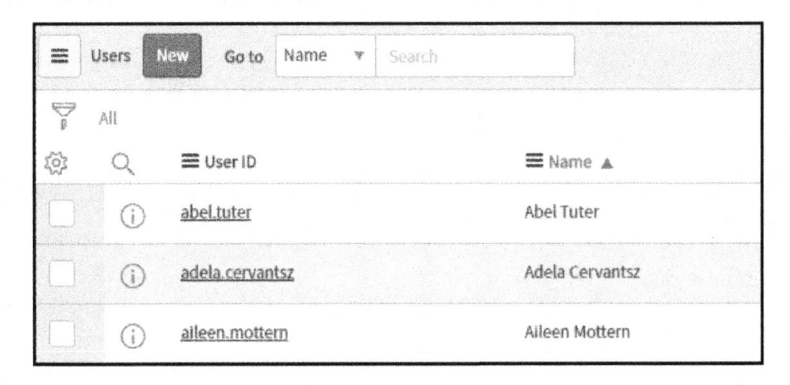

User accounts

7. In order to create a manual account or user, click on the **New** button and fill in the required information:

Create new user

Performing Core Configuration and Management Tasks

8. Now, newly created user is ready to login in Service-Now.
9. As you know, Service-Now is a role-based system, so a user without any role will act as an end user. To assign any role to a user, you need to open the user record again:

Click Edit

10. You can find all system roles and custom roles in **Section 1**, and to assign a role to a user, you can use the right arrow icon and add it to **Section 2**, as shown here:

Chapter 2

```
Add Filter    Run filter   (?)

       -- choose field --         ▼    -- oper --    ▼    -- value --

Collection        Section 1                 Roles List    Section 2
🔍                                          Ashish Srivastava

activity_admin                              admin
activity_creator
agent_admin
approval_admin
approver_user
assessment_admin
asset                              >
assignment_rule_admin
bsm_legacy                         <
bsm_legacy_admin
business_rule_admin
catalog
catalog_admin
catalog_editor
catalog_item_designer
catalog_lookup_admin
catalog_lookup_manager

                         Save   Cancel
```

Add role to a user

11. Now click **Save** button and as an output a role will be assigned to user account.

Understanding group administration

A group is a logical combination of the same skill set or common purpose. In an IT support environment, there may be many support personnel with the same skill set but different levels, such as L1, L2, and L3, where L3 are experts and L1 may have beginners.

Getting ready

To step through this recipe, you should have an active Service-Now instance, valid credentials, and admin role.

How to do it...

1. Open any standard web browser.
2. Type the Service-Now instance web address provided by your company in the address bar (http://{instance_name}.service-now.com).
3. Type your credentials in respective fields.
4. After login, type user administration on left hand side in the search box and Service-Now will search out application for you. Now click on **Groups** module as shown following:

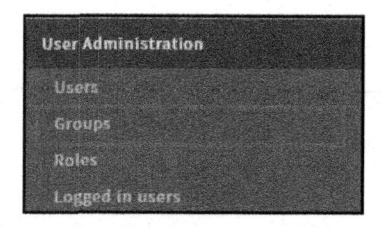

Group module

5. After clicking, you will see **Groups** records, as shown here, where you need to select the **New** button:

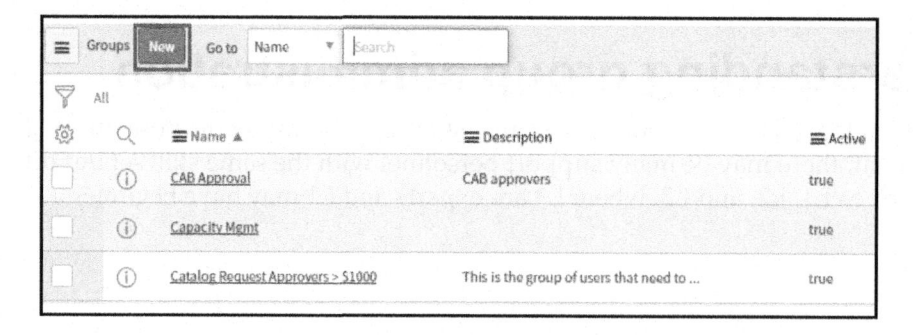

Group Records

6. After clicking, you will need to configure the group, as follows:
   - **Name**: `ServiceNow Support`
   - **Manager**: `Ashish Srivastava`
   - **Group email**: `ServiceNowSupport@example.com`
   - **Description**: `L3 Support Group`

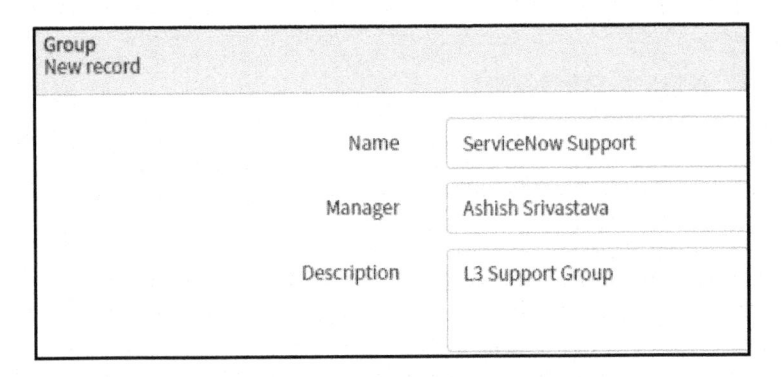

New group configuration part 1

New group configuration part 2

7. Now click **Submit** button.

8. After submitting, you will able to see three new related lists – **Roles**, **Group Member**, and **Groups** as shown in following screenshot:

Group related list

9. You can assign a role to a group, but keep in mind that by assigning a role, you are granting the role to all group members, as shown in the following screenshot. It is important to note that as best practice, Service-Now recommends adding the role to groups so that by group membership, **Group Members** also get the role:

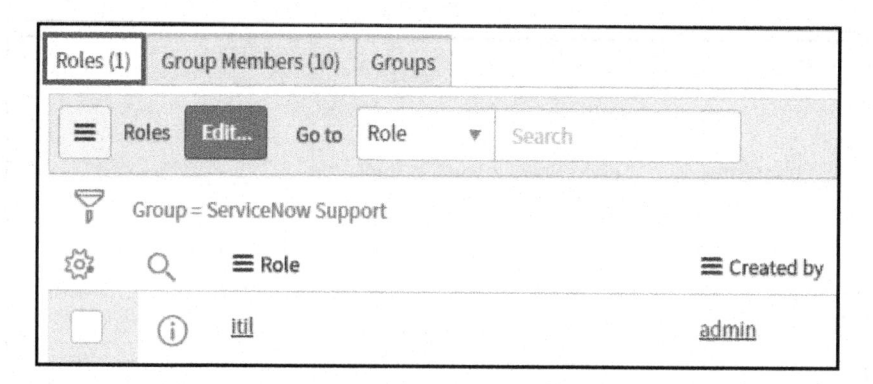

Add role to group

10. After granting the role to the group, you need to add group members to it who will work on support tickets. To add a group member, click on the **Group Member** related list and then on **Edit...**:

Chapter 2

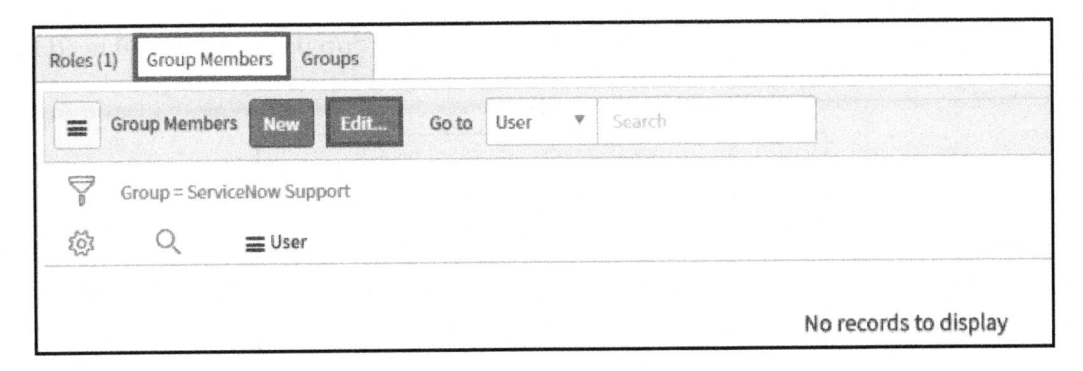

Add group member

11. **Section 1** refers to the user table; you will able to see all users in it. Now you can add a group member, as shown in the following screenshot:

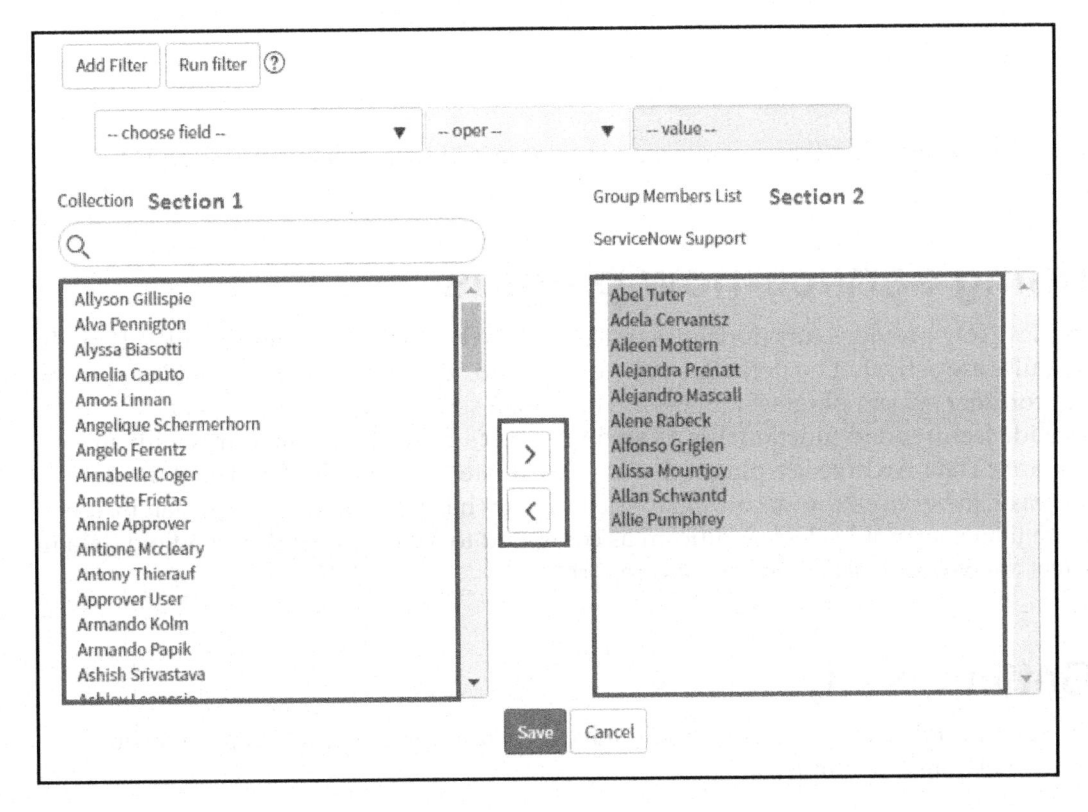

Adding users in group

[75]

12. Click on **Save**, and you will be redirected to the group page, where you need to click on the **Update** button:

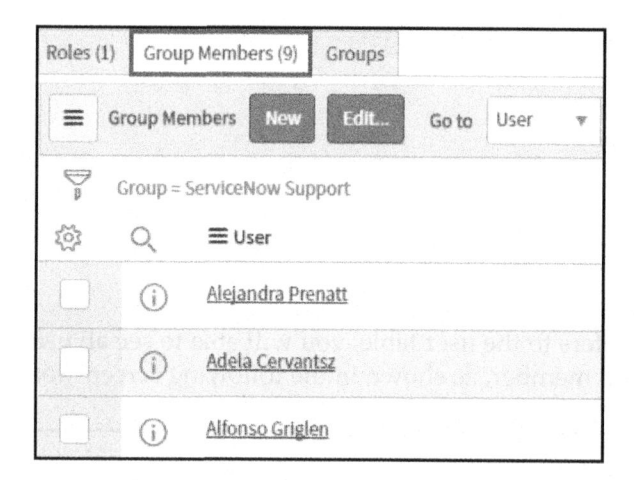

Group members

13. As an output, now you group is created and with nine member and ITIL role.

Using service-now plugins

Service-Now provides functionalities or features in the form of system modules. Usually, modules are activated by default, but if you want to add additional functionality, then you can consider system plugins. Plugins are like small software components that provide features and functionality as an option. Let's better understand this with an example: **Data Archive** is a plugin that is not activated by default. The size of the data increases in Service-Now according to the time that has passed; for example, an incident more than a year old is less significant as compared to a current incident, and old data may affect the performance of queries and reports.

Getting ready

To step through this recipe, you should have an active Service-Now instance, valid credentials, and an admin role.

How to do it...

1. Open any standard web browser.
2. Type the Service-Now instance web address (`http://{instance_name}.sservice-now.com`) provided by your company in the address bar. Now, enter your credentials in respective fields.
3. Type `plugins` on left hand side in the search box and Service-Now will search out the plugin module for you. Now Click **Plugins** module under system definition application as follows:

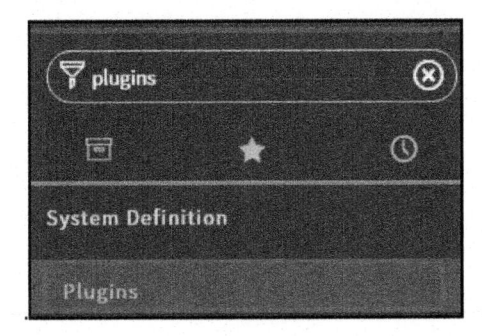

Plugin Modules

4. After clicking on the module, you will see the **System Plugins** page, shown next. It is important to note that **System Definitions** plugins are free to use, and you can activate any plugin as per your requirement:

Name	Version	Status
Activity formatter	1.0.0	Active
Aggregate Web Service	1.0.0	Inactive

System plugins

Performing Core Configuration and Management Tasks

5. If you want to activate any plugin, you can look for that plugin using the search box. For an instance, if you want to create and manage communications related to major business issues or incidents, you can activate the `Incident Alert Management` plugin. Search for and click on it. After that, you will be able to view the plugin details, as shown here:

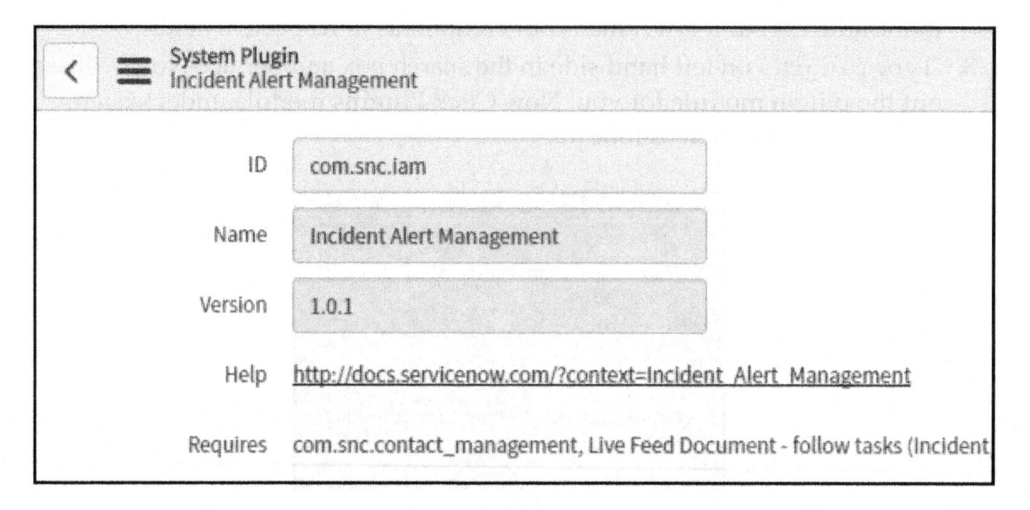

Plugin details

6. If you want to activate it, you can click on the **Related Links Activate/Upgrade** related list:

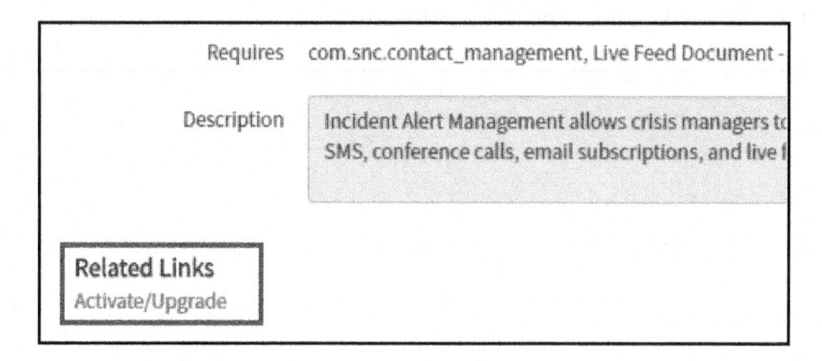

Plugin activation

[78]

7. After clicking, you will see a popup windows, where you need to click **Activate** button:

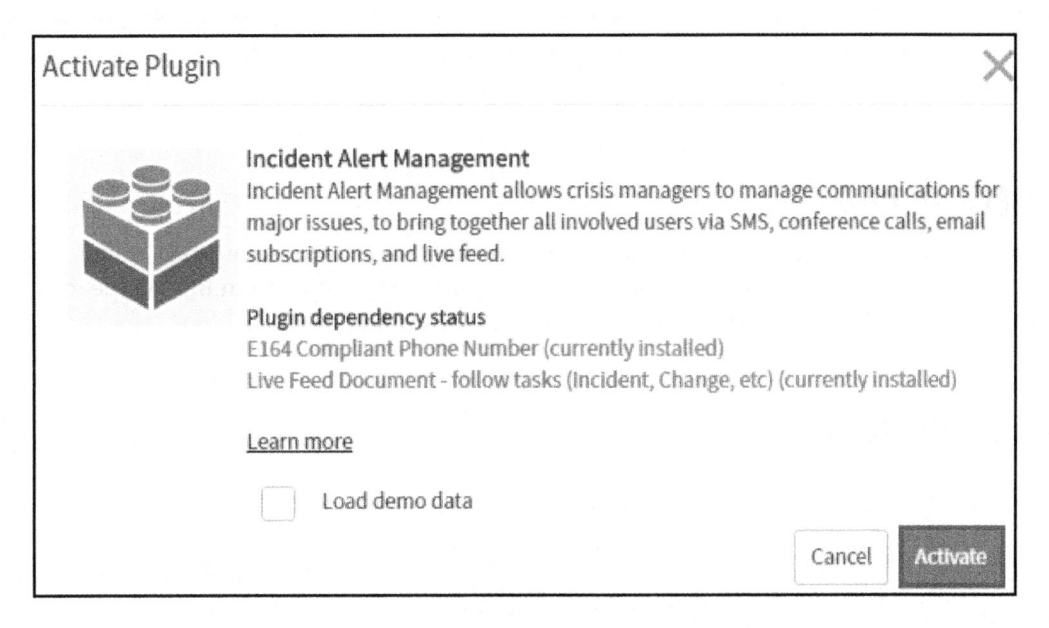

Plugin activation button

8. Now as an output, you will see plugin information popup window as shown in following screenshot:

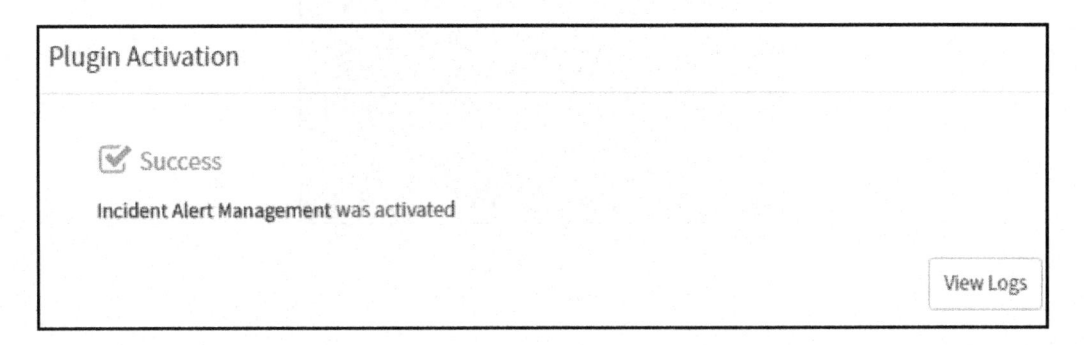

Plugin activation info

9. Now, click on **Close** button and reload form. After that refresh the page, you will see activated plugin on left hand side in application menu.

Configuring the Service-Now form

Configuration of the Service-Now form is critical as it holds a lot of information regarding the user, issues, impact, priority and assignment groups, and so on. In this recipe, you will see how you can configure the form as per your requirement.

Getting ready

To step through this recipe, you should have an active Service-Now instance, valid credentials, and an admin role. We are configuring the incident form in this recipe, but you can similarly configure any other form.

How to do it...

1. Open any standard web browser.
2. Type the Service-Now instance web address (http://{instance_name}.service-now.com) provided by your company in the address bar. Now, enter your credentials in respective fields.
3. Go to the **Incident** applications and click on the **Create New** module:

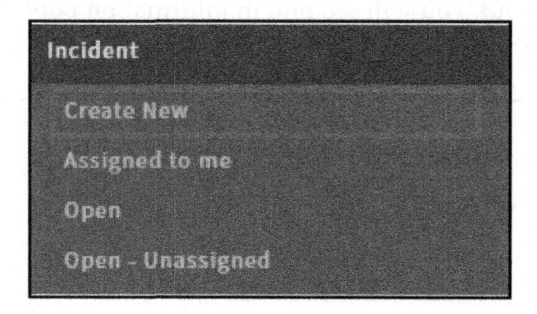

Incident module form configuration

Chapter 2

4. Now, you will able to view a new **Incident** form.
5. On the **Incident** form header, hover the mouse cursor and right-click:

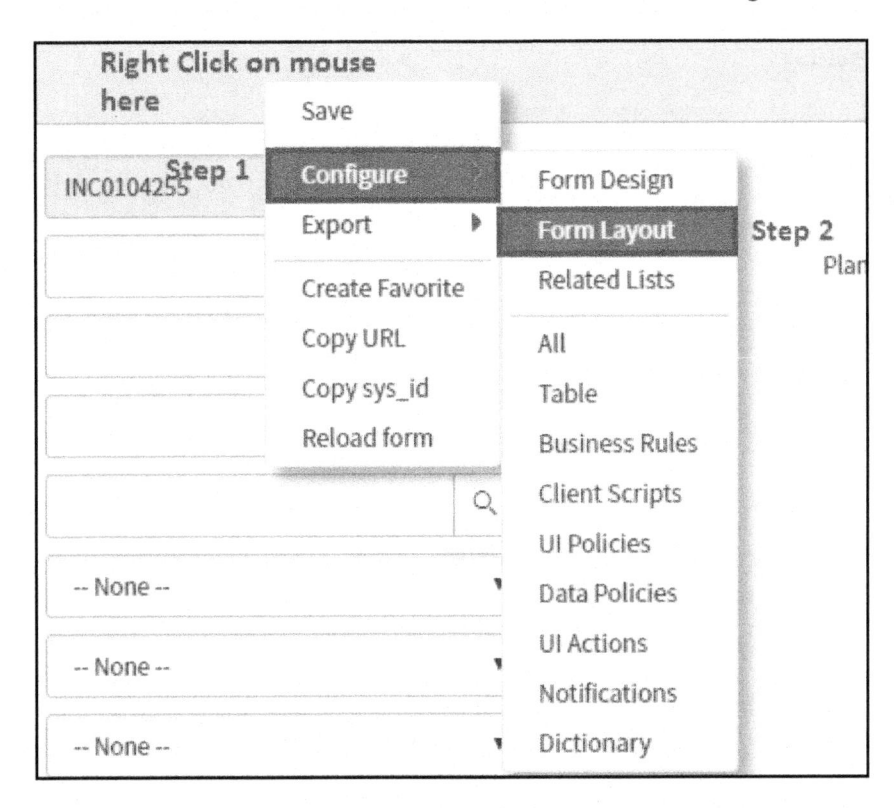

Incident form configuration

Performing Core Configuration and Management Tasks

6. After right-clicking, a header a menu appears; hover again over the **Configure** button and click on **Form Layout options**:

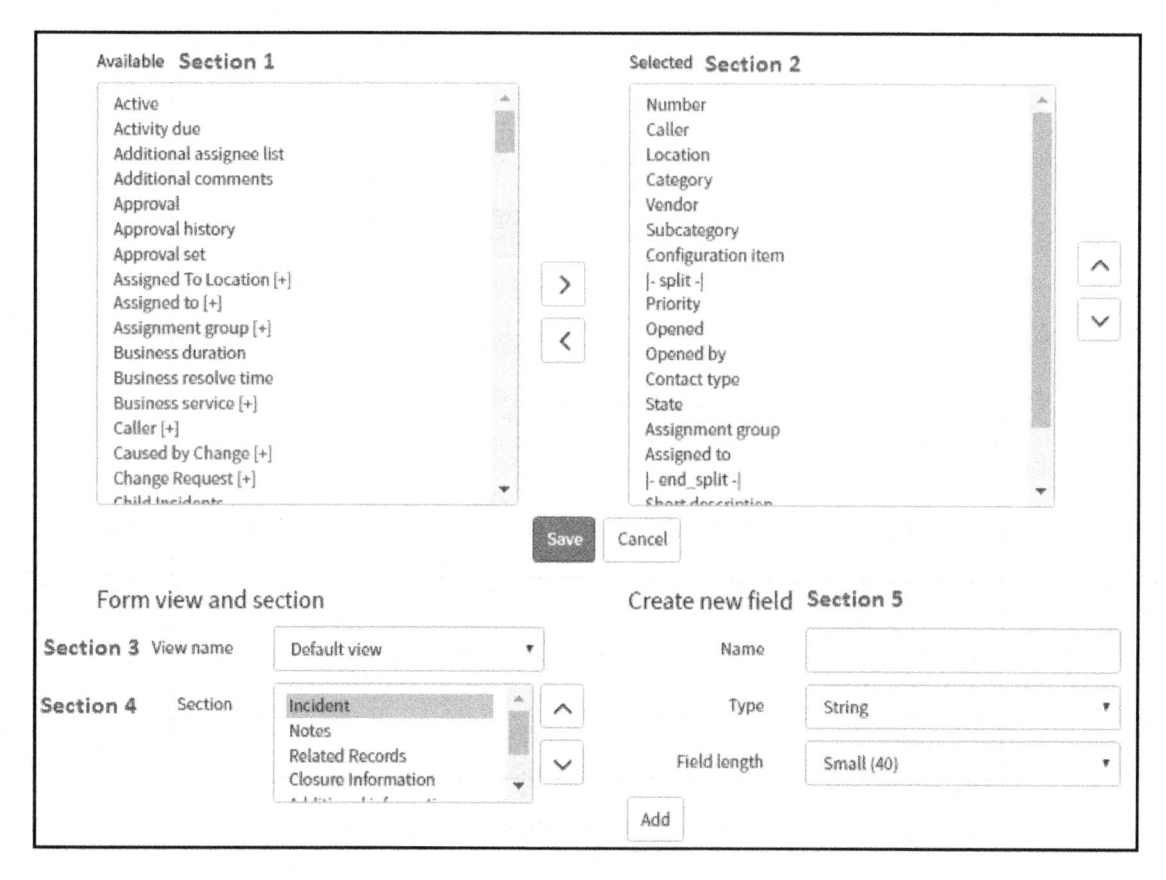

Incident form layout

7. After selecting the **Form Layout** option, you will be able to see the following page:

- **Available** (**Section 1**): This holds all the tables' variables or fields and you can move any fields on the form.
- **Selected** (**Section 2**): This holds all the fields that are visible on the form.

- **View name (Section 3)**: There may be more than one view of the form. A view controls the field on the form that appears when a user opens a form or list. Let's understand views by an example when you want to view all views of a form. To do so, you can refer to the following screenshot; as an admin, you are allowed to see all the views of the incident form.

    For instance, if you are an end user, you are allowed to view fewer fields on the form as compared to a support person, and if you compare a support person with an admin, admins are allowed to view all fields compared to a support person. To read more about this, go to http://wiki.servicenow.com/index.php?title=View_Management#gsc.tab=0:

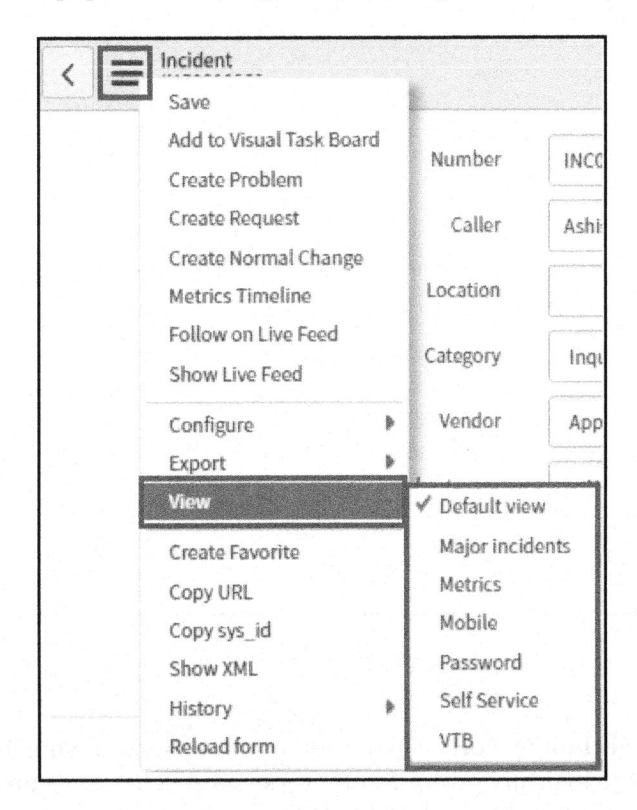

Incident form views

Performing Core Configuration and Management Tasks

8. Now, if you want to know how the incident form will look on mobile devices, go to **View** | **Mobile** . After clicking on **Mobile**, you will be able see the mobile device view of the incident form, where you easily identify that mobile device views have fewer fields as compared to the default or self-service view:

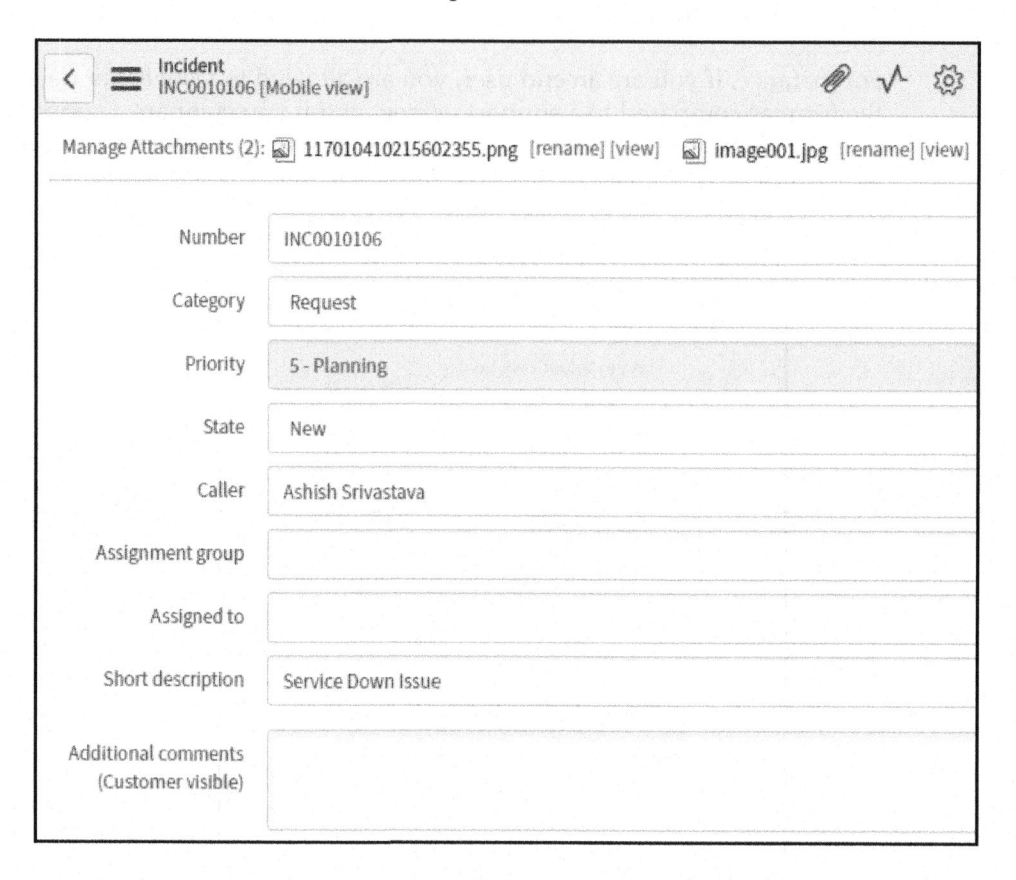

Incident form: mobile view

- **Section (Section 4)**: Forms are divided into sections, as shown here. Sections are just a way to logically group common-purpose fields. Let's understand this with an example. For instance, the **Closure Information** form section should contain closed date, closed by, and closed code data:

Chapter 2

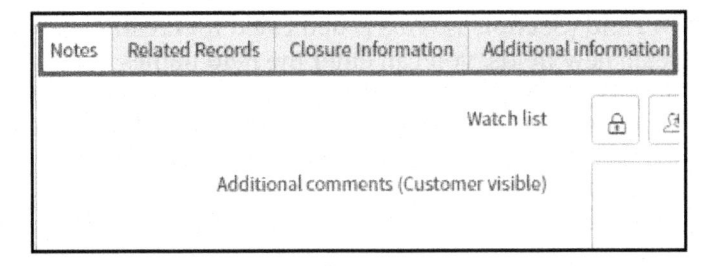

Incident form sections

9. If you want to add more fields to any section, such as a note, then you need to select `Notes` from **Section**, after which you will be able to see the fields that are available in the `Notes` section. Now you can move the desired field from **Section 1** to **Section 2**:

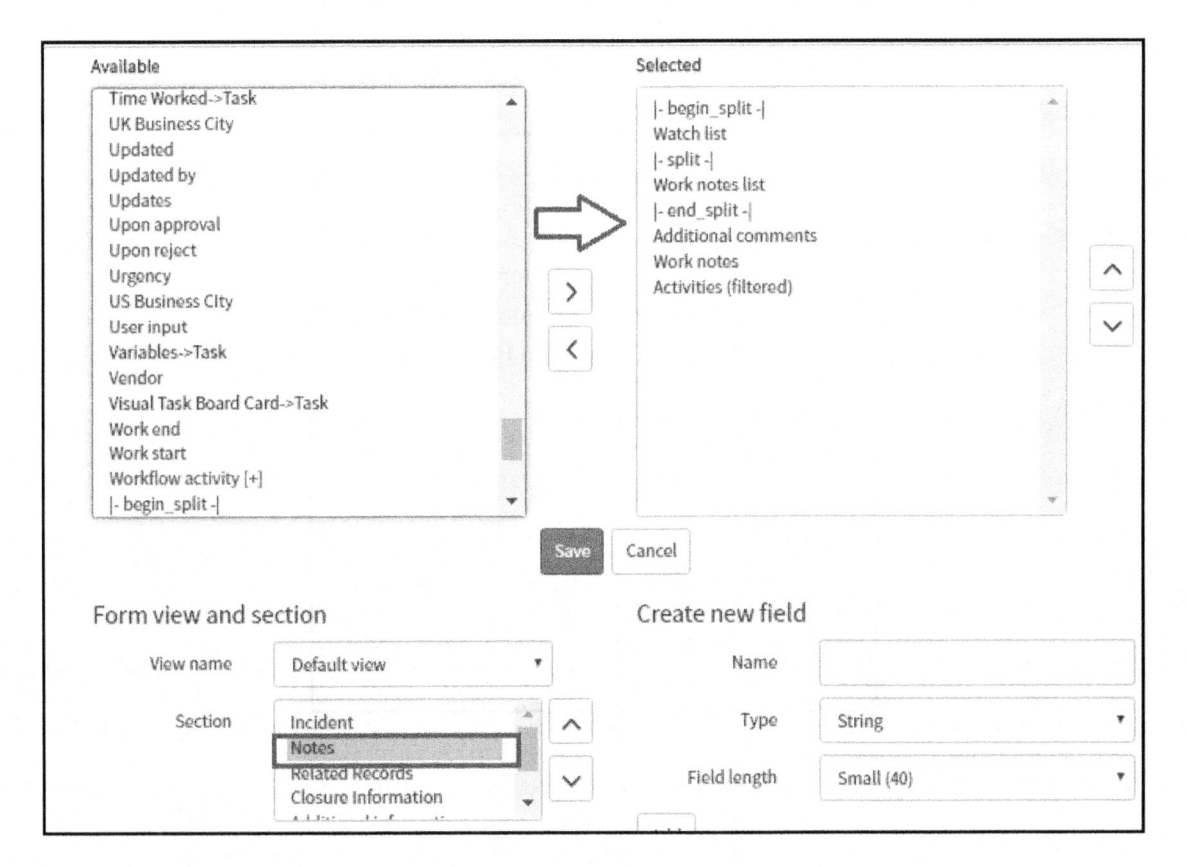

Add field in form section

[85]

Performing Core Configuration and Management Tasks

- **Create new field (Section 5)**: This is dedicated for creating new fields. If you want to create new fields, you can enter the field names here.

10. Let's suppose you want to add a new field in the **Incident** section, as shown here:

- **Name**: Age In Days
- **Type**: String
- **Field length**: Small (40)

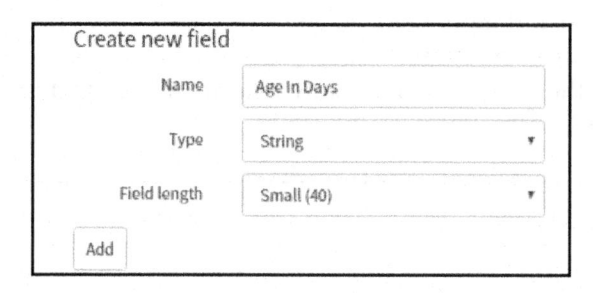

Create new field

11. Follow the given steps to create the field:
    1. Click on the **Add** button and then on Save.
    2. A new field will be added to the selected container.
    3. If you want to make a reference field, you can, as follows:

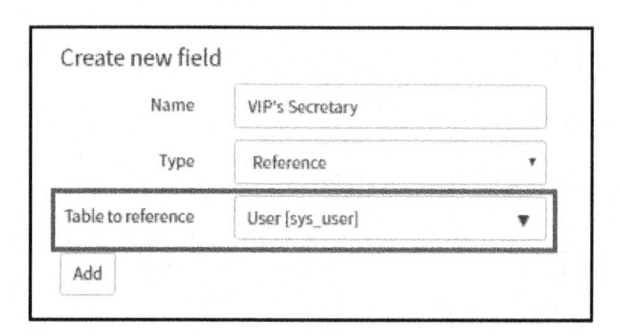

Create reference field

[86]

There's more...

It is important to note that by **Form Layout** option is available under **Configure** for all modules and you can configure by any application like change, problem, contract, cost, and so on in same way.

See also

To read more about the follow on: `http://wiki.servicenow.com/index.php?title=View_Management#gsc.tab=0` link.

Configuring UI policies on Service-Now forms

UI policies are applied to the Service-Now form to customize the behavior of the form, such as read-only access or showing or hiding a field base on a condition. Keep in mind that UI policies run after the client script does.

Getting ready

To step through this recipe, you should have an active Service-Now instance, valid credentials, and an admin role.

How to do it...

1. Open any standard web browser.
2. Type the Service-Now instance web address (`http://{instance_name}.service-now.com`) provided by your company in the address bar. Now, enter your credentials in respective fields.
3. Go to the **Incident** module and click on the **Create New** module.
4. Right-click on the header of Incident form.

Performing Core Configuration and Management Tasks

5. Click on **Configure** and then on **UI policies**:

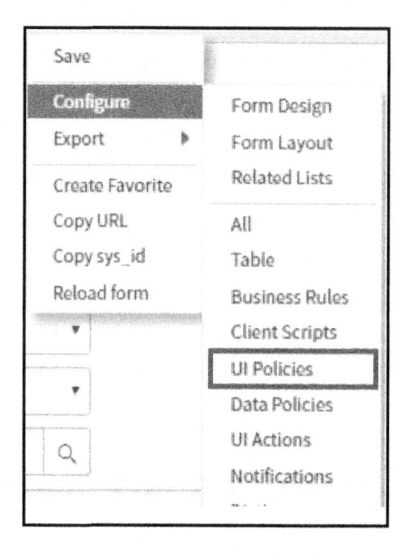

UI Policy button

6. Now you will be able to see the **UI Policies** page, as shown in the following diagram. Here, you need to click on the **New** button:

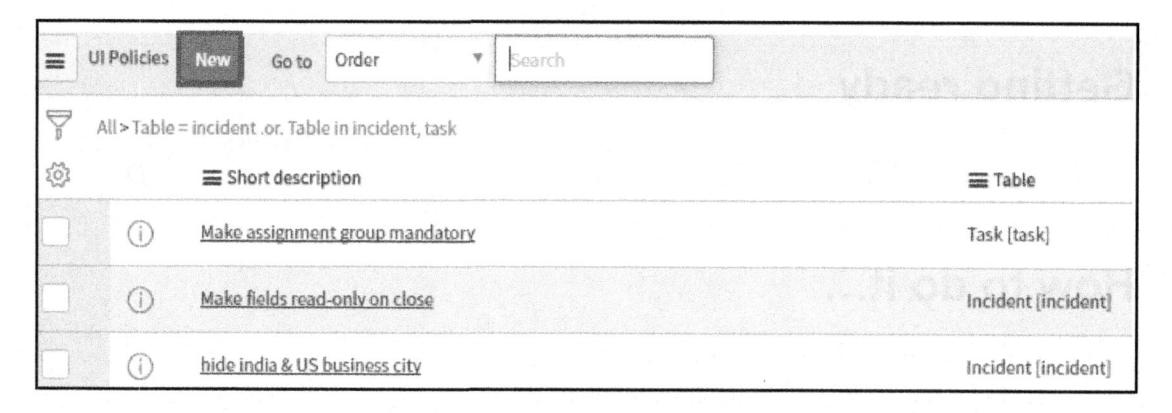

	Short description	Table
	Make assignment group mandatory	Task [task]
	Make fields read-only on close	Incident [incident]
	hide india & US business city	Incident [incident]

UI policies records

Chapter 2

7. Now you need to configure the UI policy as follows:
    - **Table**: `Incident [incident]` (table will be auto selected as you are making a policy on the Incident table)
    - **Short description**: `make fields read only / mandatory` (you can enter a different short description as per your convenience)
    - **Order**: 100

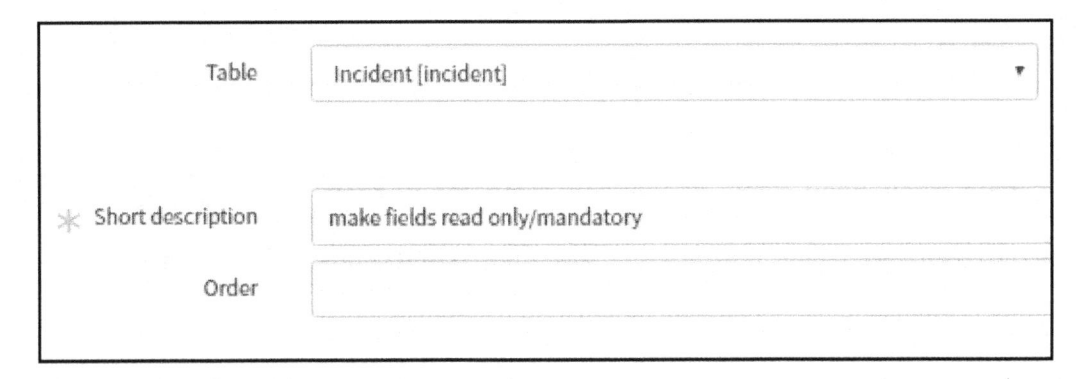

Table	Incident [incident]
* Short description	make fields read only/mandatory
Order	

Configure UI policy part 1

8. Now you need to decide when you want to apply your UI policy; set the condition as given here (When state is new) and click on **Submit** button:

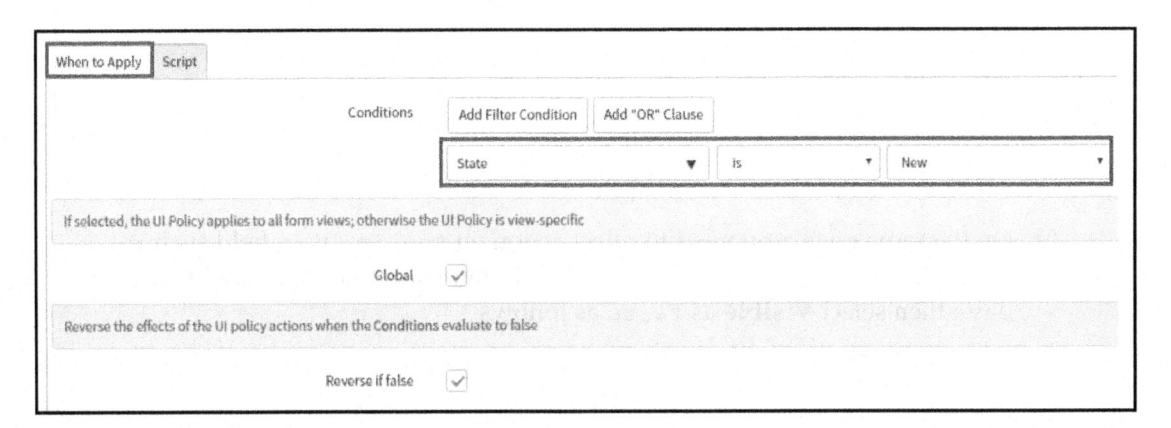

Conditions	Add Filter Condition Add "OR" Clause
	State is New
If selected, the UI Policy applies to all form views; otherwise the UI Policy is view-specific	
Global	✓
Reverse the effects of the UI policy actions when the Conditions evaluate to false	
Reverse if false	✓

Configure UI policy part 2

[89]

Performing Core Configuration and Management Tasks

9. Once UI policy is created a new related list **UI Policy Actions** will be available at the bottom of **UI policy** configured form. Now click on **New**:

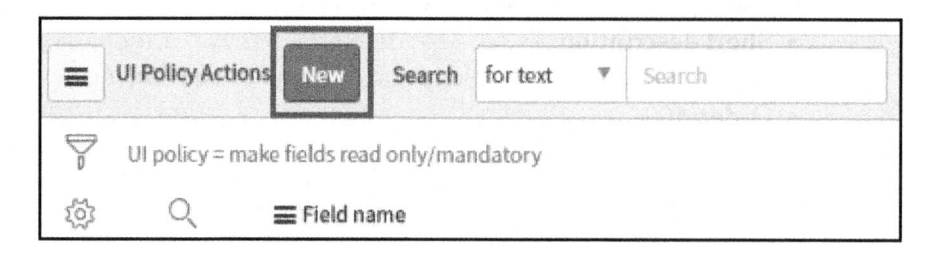

Configuration UI policy part 3

10. It is important to note that for each and every **UI policy** there will be a **UI policy action** which will be executed when **UI policy** conditions are matched.
11. Now, you will be redirected to **UI Policy Action** configuration page. Here, you need to select a field `Age in Days` on which you want to apply **UI Policy Actions** when conditions are matched as given here:

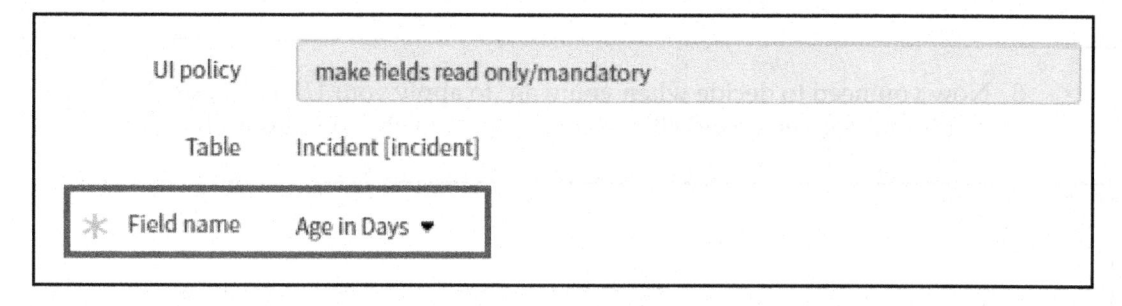

Configuration UI policy part 4

12. On the same page, you need to select action on `Age in Days` field such as `Visible`, `Read Only`, or `Mandatory`. If you want to hide the field `Age in Days` then select **Visible** as `false` as follows:

[90]

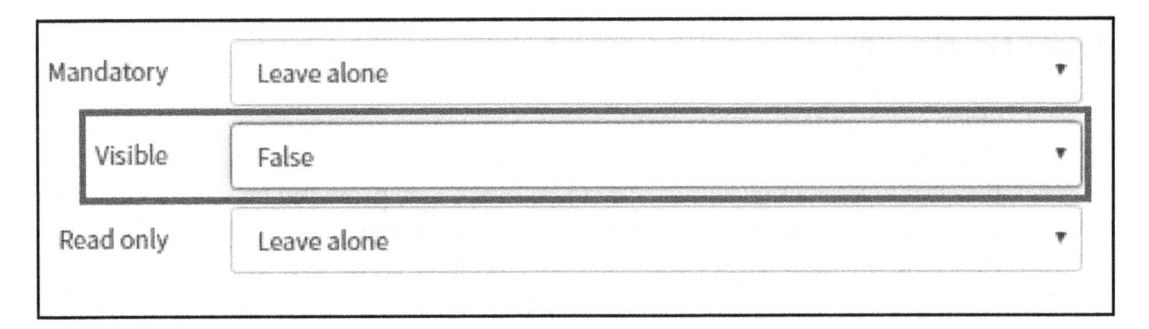

Mandatory	Leave alone ▼
Visible	**False** ▼
Read only	Leave alone ▼

Configuration UI policy part 4

13. Now click **Submit** button. After submitting, you will be redirected to UI policy page. On UI policy page click on **Update** button again in order to save entite configuration.

> It is important to note that UI policy actions fields `Mandatory`, `Visible`, or `Read only` are Booleans only and you are allowed to select either `true` or `false`.

14. As an output, If incident state is new by then UI policy `Age in Days` will be hidden but for other state (Awaiting user info, Resolved and so on)it will be visible.

Configuring UI actions on forms

A UI action is a form button used to perform actions, such as saving a record or creating a new ticket, change ticket, or problem ticket.

Getting ready

To step through this recipe, you should have an active Service-Now instance, valid credentials, and an admin role.

How to do it...

1. Open any standard web browser.
2. Type the Service-Now instance web address (http://{instance_name}.service-now.com) provided by your company in the address bar. Now, enter your credentials in respective fields.
3. Go to the **Incident Application** and click on the **Create New** module.
4. Now, you will view an empty incident form or on existing incident form right-click on the header of the incident form through mouse and click on **Configure** and then on **UI Actions** option:

UI Action button

5. You will now see all the **UI actions** of the table. You need to click on the **New** button, as shown here:

New UI actions

6. Now, you will see the UI Actions page, which needs to be configured as follows:
   - **Name:** Take this task (you will need to enter the name)
   - **Table:** Incident [incident] (auto-populated)
   - **Action name:** Take this task (helpful while calling from the client side)

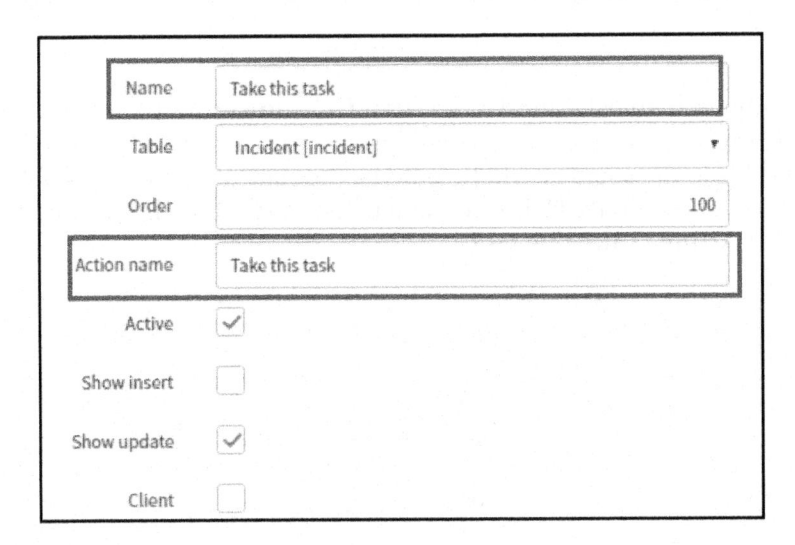

UI action configuration part 1

Performing Core Configuration and Management Tasks

7. Now, you need to decide where this UI action will be placed on the form. Out of the box, Service-Now provides eight places, where you can place a button as per your convenience:
    - **Form button**: If you check the **Form button** option, the button will be placed on the form header:

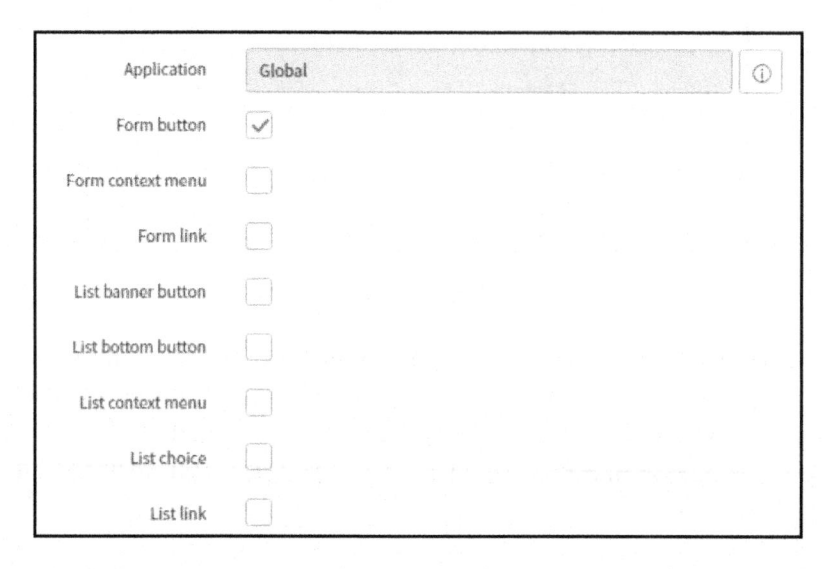

    UI action configuration part 2

8. Conditions are most critical apart from **UI action** (button) as based on conditions only Service-Now decides who will be able to see or on what state UI action will be visible to the users or what would be the state after clicking on the **UI action** (button), as here only ITIL/resolver (customized role)/admin should have access this **UI Action (Take this task)**:

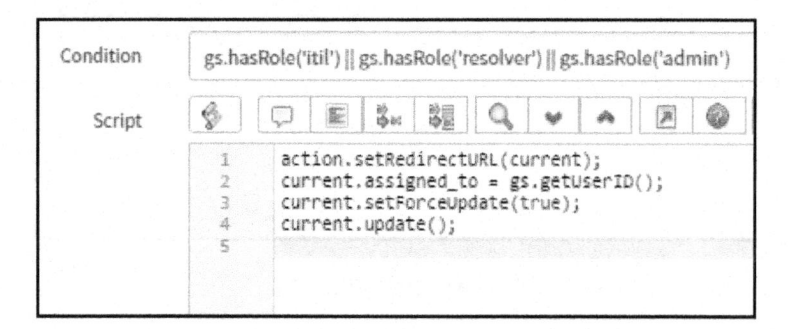

    Condition: `gs.hasRole('itil') || gs.hasRole('resolver') || gs.hasRole('admin')`

    Script:
    ```
    action.setRedirectURL(current);
    current.assigned_to = gs.getUserID();
    current.setForceUpdate(true);
    current.update();
    ```

    UI action configuration part 3

[94]

- Script:

    ```
    action.setRedirectURL(current);
    current.assigned_to = gs.getUserID();
    current.setForceUpdate(true);
    current.update();
    ```

9. After adding the script in **Script** box, click on **Submit** button.
10. As an output, the **Take this task** button is added on the incident form:

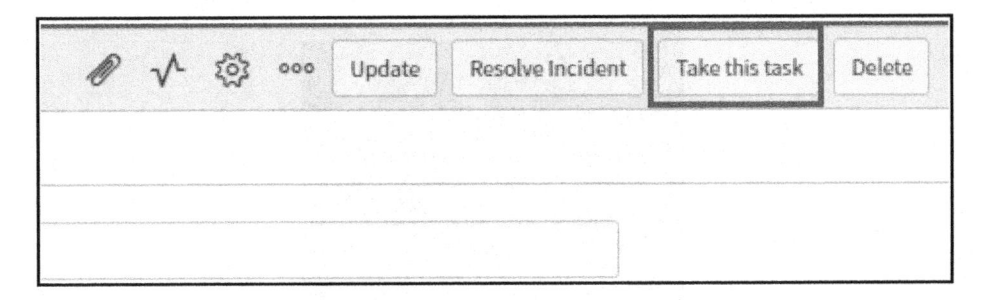

New UI action added on incident form

Understanding deployments or update sets

An update can be considered as a customized package of development items; you know by now that any Service-Now customer gets three instances or environments: One production and two non production. So, all new requirement or development work is done on the development instances, and all end-user testing is done on the testing environment. Once everyone is happy, the code is deployed in the production environment, but remember that only configuration can be captured in the update set, not data. To read more about update sets, click on `http://wiki.servicenow.com/index.php?title=Using_Update_Sets#gsc.tab=0`.

Getting ready

To step through this recipe, you should have an active Service-Now instance, valid credentials, and an admin role.

How to do it…

1. Open any standard web browser.
2. Type the Service-Now instance web address (https://{instance_name}.service-now.com) provided by your company in the address bar. Now, enter your credentials in respective fields.
3. Type update Set in the search box and Service-Now will search out the System update sets application for you as follows:

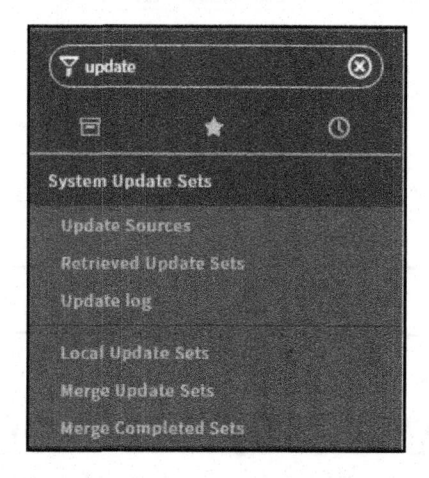

System update set module

4. To create a new update set, click on **Local Update Sets** module. You will see all update sets of instance, where you need to click on **New** Button as shown in following screenshot:

Update set records

5. Now you need to configure update set configuration page as follows:
    - **Description**: `item development includes |-new employee on board |-new asset order` (you can provide your own description)
    - **Name**: `item development` (you can give your own name as well)
    - **State**: **Update Sets** have three states:
        - **Progress**: This is to track customization
        - **Completed**: When you are done with customization, then you can mark the update as completed
        - **Ignore**: When you are no longer working on an update set, it is recommended you delete and ignore the update set, but keep in mind that to delete an update set, you will need to delete all update set items

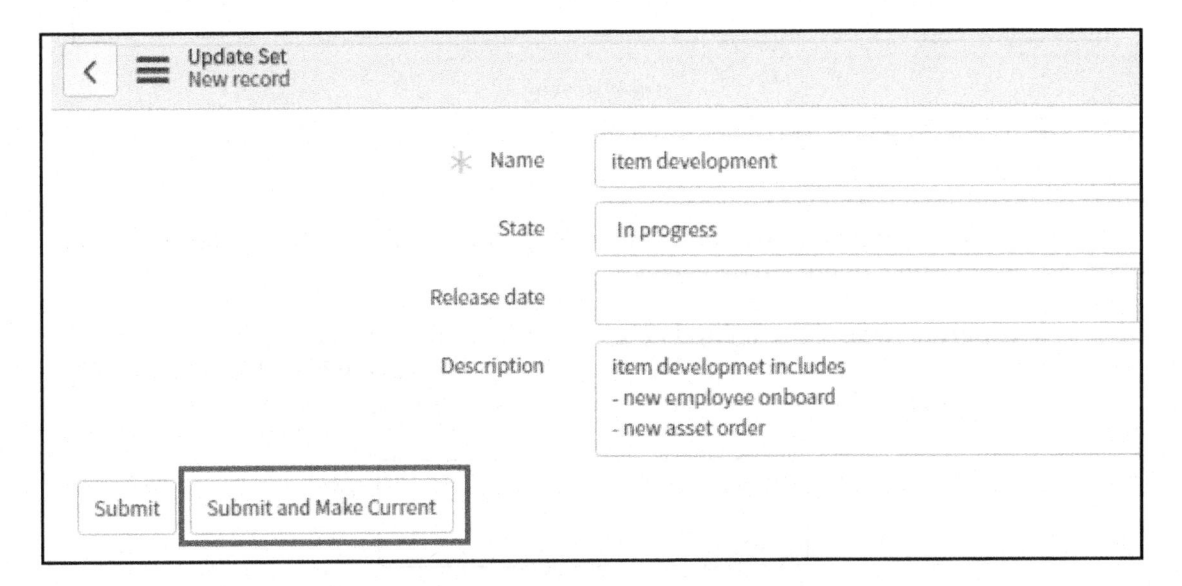

Local update set creation

Performing Core Configuration and Management Tasks

6. By clicking on **Submit and Make Current** button, all the new development items will be captured in **Item development** update set only, as shown here:

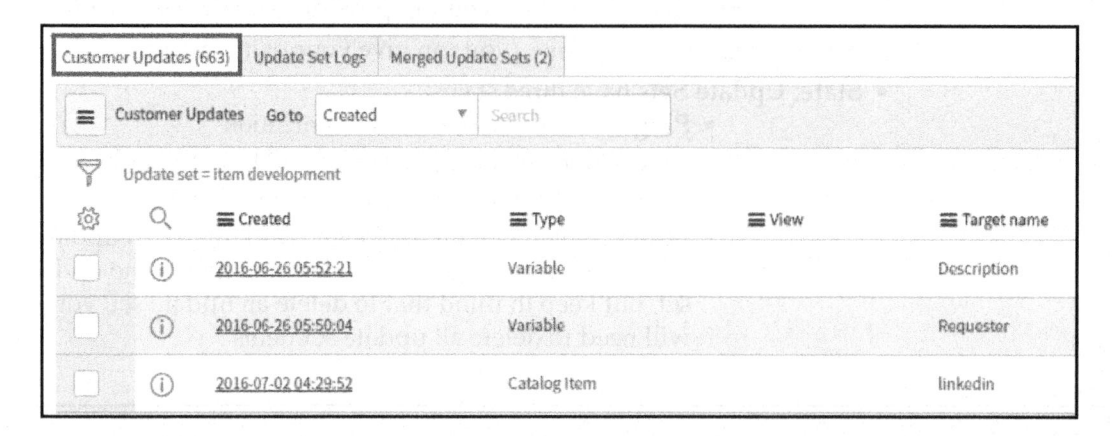

		Created	Type	View	Target name
	(i)	2016-06-26 05:52:21	Variable		Description
	(i)	2016-06-26 05:50:04	Variable		Requester
	(i)	2016-07-02 04:29:52	Catalog Item		linkedin

Captured in update set

7. If you are done with development then mark the update set **Item development state as completed.**

8. Now for deploying **Item development** update set in the testing instance for end user testing, there are two ways:

- **Export to XML**: Once an update set is marked completed, a new **Related Links** appears at the bottom of update set. If you click on **Export to XML** then update set **Item development** will be downloaded to your local machine in XML format:

Related Links
Export to XML
Merge With Another Update Set

Export Local update set in local machine

9. Once the update set XML file is downloaded to the machine, you can even rename the file as per your convenience. Now to deploy the development items in the testing instance (`https://packtest.service-now.com`) or production instance(`https://packtprod.service-now.com`), open the target instance and type **Retrieve Update Sets in** the search box and click on it as follows:

[98]

Chapter 2

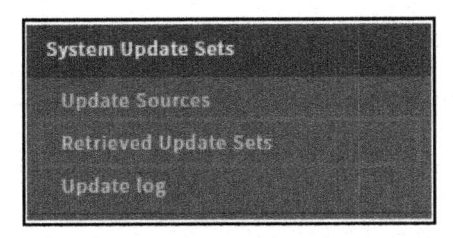

Retrieve update set to deploy update set

10. At the bottom of page, on clicking on **Retrieved Update Sets**, you will see the Retrieve Update Sets page where you need to click on **Import Update Set from XML** button as follows:

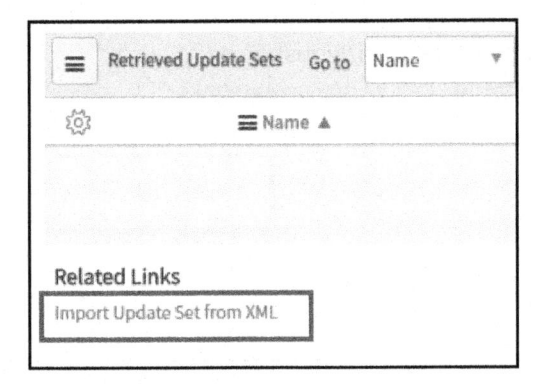

Related link to import

11. After clicking on **Import update set from XML** button, you will see the Import XML page, as shown here, where you need to upload the update set **Item development** by clicking on **Choose File** to upload the file from your local system and click on **Upload button**:

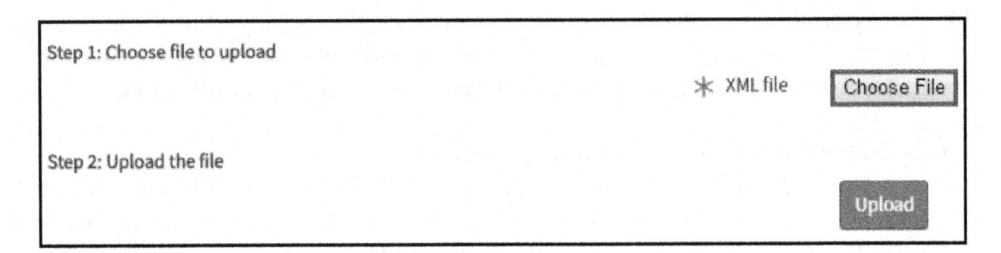

Import update set on other instances

[99]

12. Now the update set **Item development** is uploaded in the target instance let suppose `https://packtest.service-now.com`. Open the record again and click on the **Preview Update Set** button as follows:

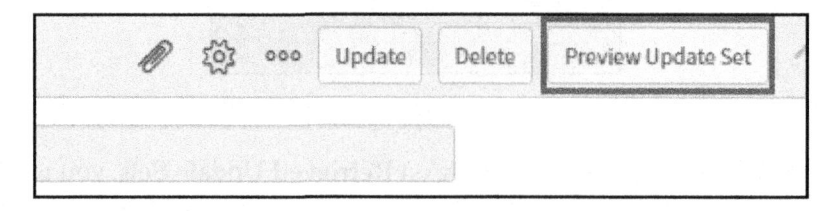

Preview loaded update set

13. If there are any errors then resolve the errors, and click on **Commit Update Set** to deploy your code in the testing instance (`https://packtest.service-now.com`):

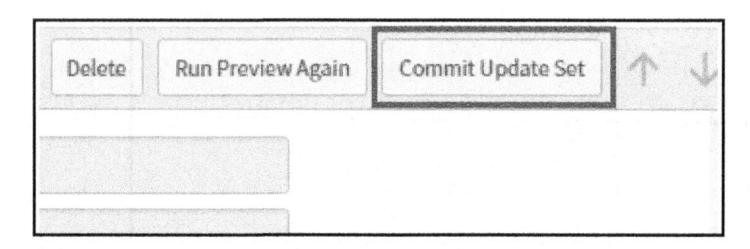

Commit update set to deploy customization

- **Retrieve Update Set**: If your target instance is connected with your source instance, then you can use this option as well. Directly, you may click on the **Retrieve Update Sets** option and follow the process described in step 1. To connect two instances, you can follow the same process.

14. Now update set **Item development** is successfully deployed in testing instance (`https://packtest.service-now.com`) and your development items are moved from development instance to testing instance for end users.

- **Retrieve Update Set**: If your target instance (`https://packtest.service-now.com`) is connected with your source instance (`https://packdev.service-now.com`) then you can use this option as well. Directly, you may click on the **Retrieve Update Sets** but if both instances (testing and development) are not connected then you can connect both as well as follows.

Chapter 2

15. Under the **System Update Sets application** click on the **Update Sources** module as follows:

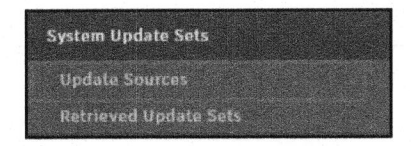

Update Source Module

16. After clicking on it, you will see the following configuration form:
    - **Name**: `PacktDev` (you can give your own name)
    - **Type**: `Development`
    - **Short description**: `PacktDev update set`

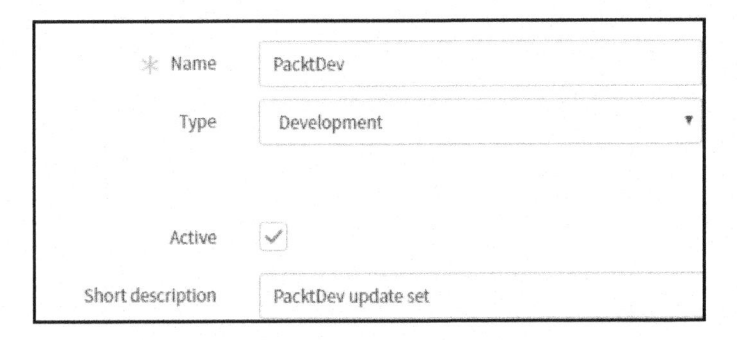

Update source configuration part 1

- **URL**: `https://packtdev.Service-Now.com`
- **Username**: `admin`
- **Password**: ....

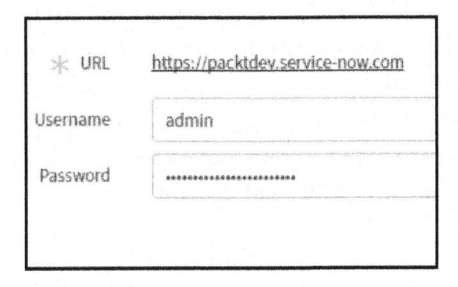

Update source configuration part 2

[101]

17. Click on **test connection** and then click on **Submit**.
18. Now a new remote instance record is added under **Remote Instance** as shown in following screenshot:

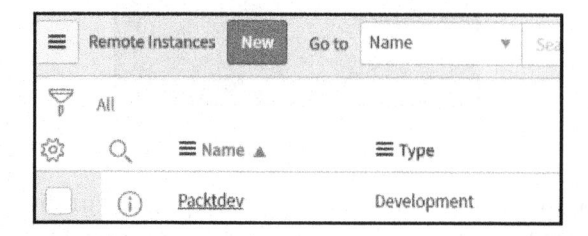

- Now whenever you want to import an update set from the development instance (https://packdev.service-now.com) to the target instance (https://packtest.service-now.com), click on open update source again and then on Packtdev. You will be redirected to the following page, where you need to select **Retrieve Completed Update Sets** in **Related Links**:

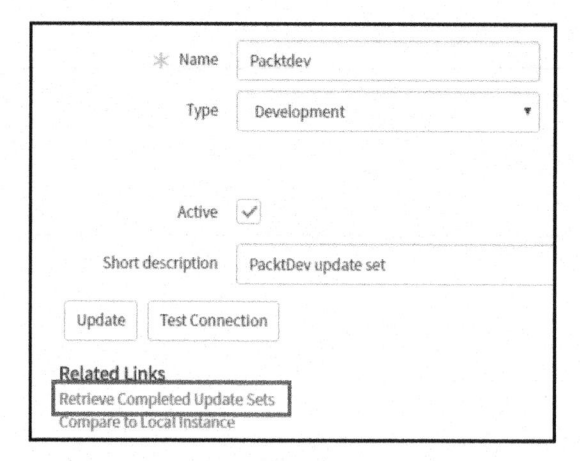

- Now by clicking the **Retrieved Completed Update Sets** button, all the update sets which are in completed state in https://packdev.service-now.com instance will be moved in https://packtest.service-now.com instance.
- Now To deploy update set in the target instance, you can select desired update set from **Retrieved update Sets** records and click **Preview Update Set button** and at last click on **Commit Update set** button.

There's more…
It is important to note that data cannot be captured in update sets; configurations can be captured in update sets and only after committing the update set development items will be visible in target instance.

See also
To read more about the update sets click on `http://wiki.servicenow.com/index.php?title=Using_Update_Sets#gsc.tab=0` link.

Getting into CMDB
CMDB stands for configuration management database. Let's understand this with an example. For instance, if you purchase a laptop, then you can easily maintain or install software, but in an enterprise environment with, say, 10,000 systems in different locations, it's not an easy task to maintain (monthly patching, installing new software security, and so on) such large numbers; that's why asset management tools are on the market; they search for devices and store them in Service-Now CMDB tables.

Getting ready
To step through this recipe, you should have an active Service-Now instance, valid credentials, and an admin role.

How to do it…

1. Open any standard web browser.
2. Type the Service-Now instance web address (`https://{instance_name}.sservice-now.com`) provided by your company in the address bar. Now, enter your credentials in respective fields.

Performing Core Configuration and Management Tasks

3. Type `configuration` in the search box, and Service-Now will search the module for you:

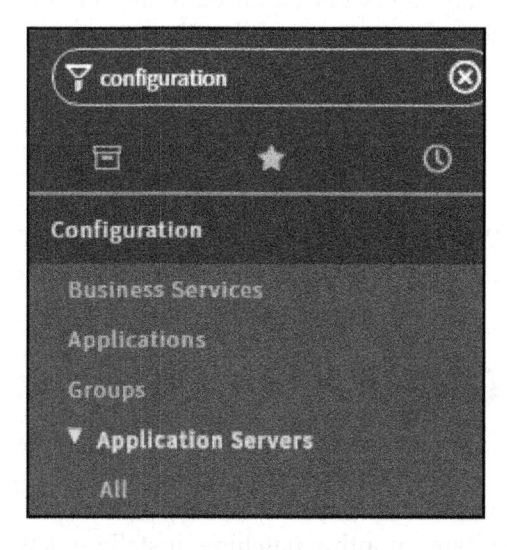

Configuration management module

> It is important to note that out of the box, Service-Now CMBD has different classes to store different types of records such as hardware, software, server, printer, policy server, and so on.

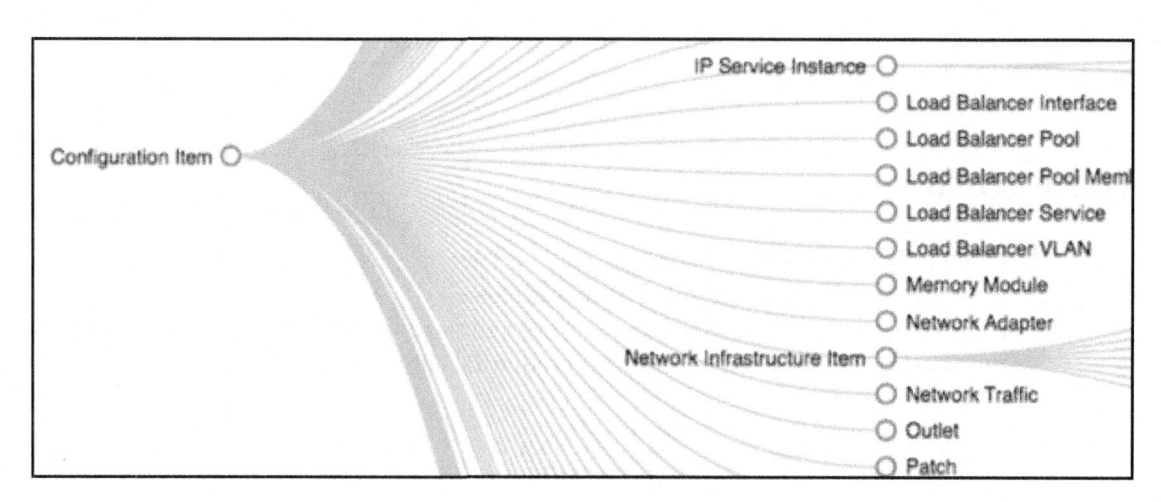

CMDB schema map

[104]

4. It's is important to note that if your requirement is not being fulfilled by out of the box tables then you can even extend CMDB. So, let's understand this better with an example. If your organization has more than 10,000 iPads and the management wants assets on Service-Now CMDB and tag them with user's profile, then you can extend CMDB to store iPad devices.
5. On the left hand side, type tables in the search box and Service-Now will search out **Tables** module for you then click **Tables** module as shown in following screenshot:

Service-Now tables

6. Now, you will now be able to see all system and custom tables here, as shown here. Now you need to click on the **New** button:

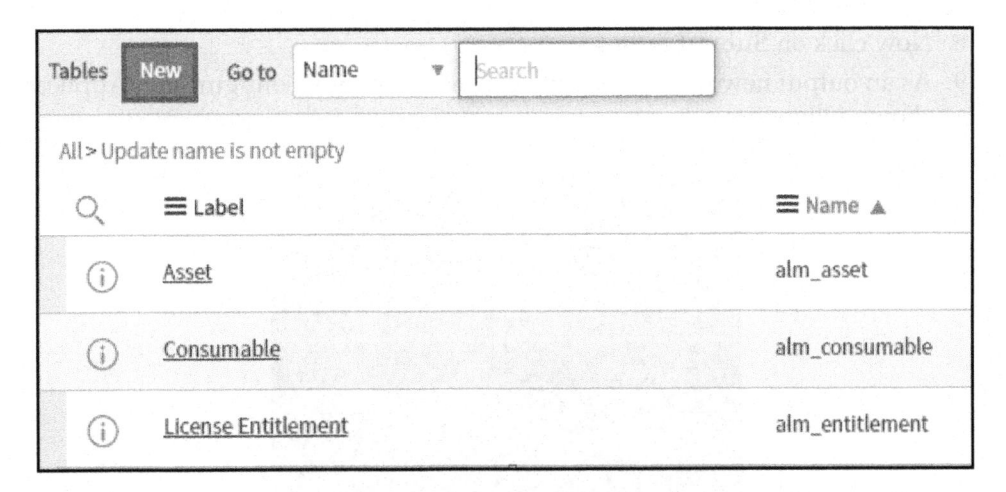

Label	Name
Asset	alm_asset
Consumable	alm_consumable
License Entitlement	alm_entitlement

Create new Service-Now table

[105]

Performing Core Configuration and Management Tasks

7. Now you can configure new table which will store Ipad devices as follows.
    - **Label** : `Ipad`
    - **Name** : `u_ipad` (Auto popup)
    - **Extends table** : `Computer`
    - **Create module** : `true`
    - **Add module to menu** : `Configuration`

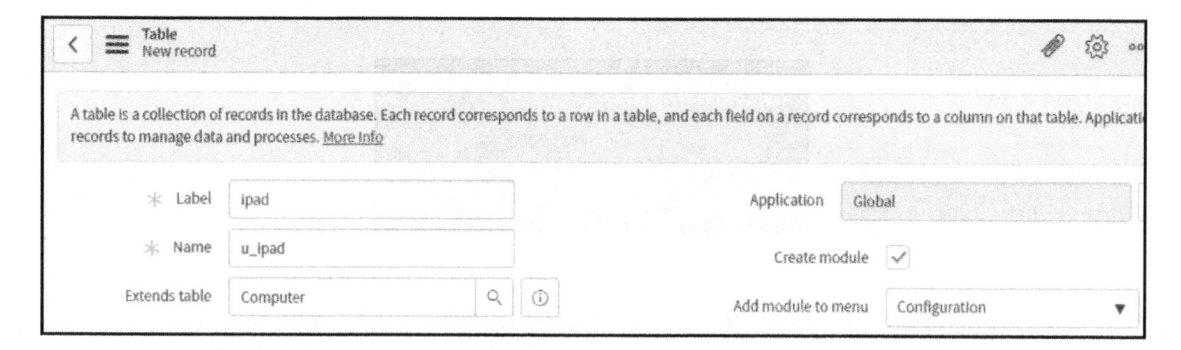

Extending CMDB

8. Now click on **Submit** button.
9. As an output new iPad class will be available under Configuration Application as shown following:

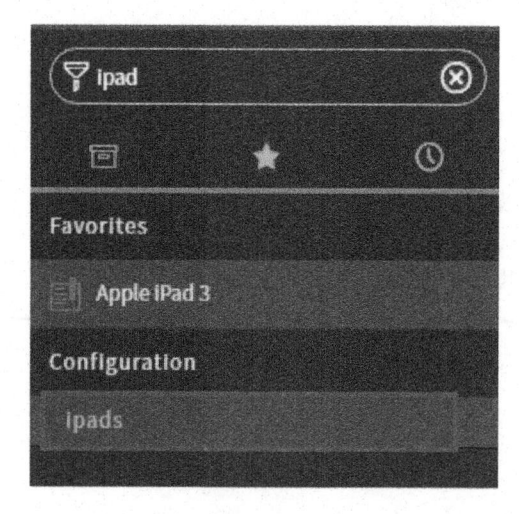

New iPads class

[106]

There's more...

It is important to note that service-now provides extended CMDB plugin which includes a collection of modules for specialized configuration items, such as radio hardware, test equipment, and voice system hardware.

See also

To read more about CMDB and extended CMDB click on following link:

`https://docs.servicenow.com/bundle/helsinki-it-service-management/page/product/configuration-management/reference/r_CMDBAndExtendedCMDB.html`.

Setting up an SLA/OLA/underpinning contract

In an IT support environment, every support group, vendor and so on work under certain time contract based on priority of task; this contract can be referred to as SLA or OLA or underpinning contracts. SLAs are used to ensure that the support team completes the task in the set amount of time.

Getting ready

To step through this recipe, you should have an active service-now instance, valid credentials and an admin role.

How to do it...

1. Open any standard web browser.
2. Type the Service-Now instance web address (`https://{instance_name}.service-now.com`) provided by your company in the address bar. Now, enter your credentials in respective fields.

3. Type `service management` in the search box and Service-Now will search the **Service Level Management application** for you. Click on the **SLA Definitions** module, as shown here:

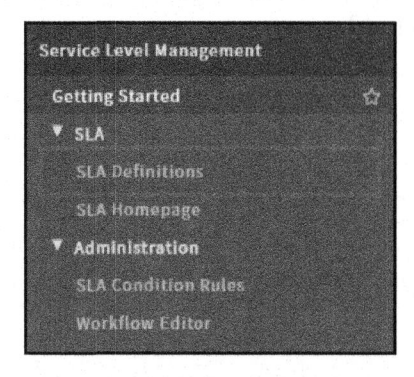

Service-Now management

4. You will now be able to see the following screen, where you can see all SLA records. Click on the **New** button to create new SLA:

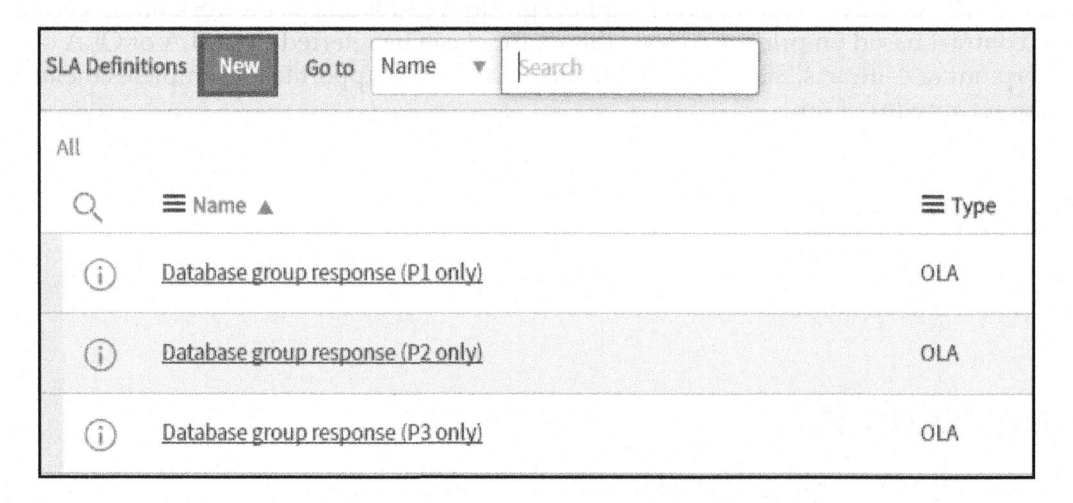

Create new SLA record

5. It is important to note that that an SLA has three conditions (state, pause and stop) and if conditions are not set properly then the SLA may be cancelled automatically. Now configure the SLA definition as follows:

- **Name:** `AD Server Issue`

- **Type** : SLA
- **Table** : Incident[incident]
- **Workflow**: Default SLA workflow (auto attached)

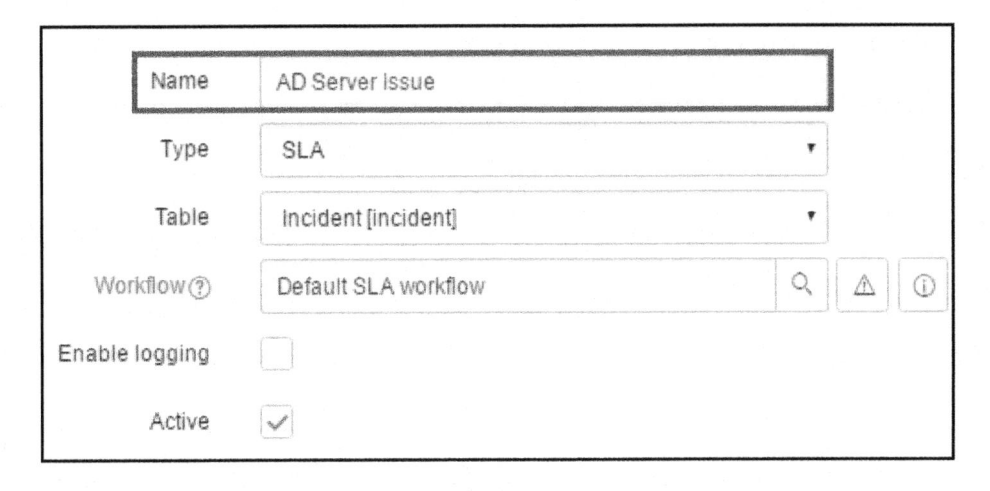

SLA configuration part 1

- **Duration type** : User specified duration
- **Duration** : 4 Hours
- **Schedule** : 8-5 weekdays

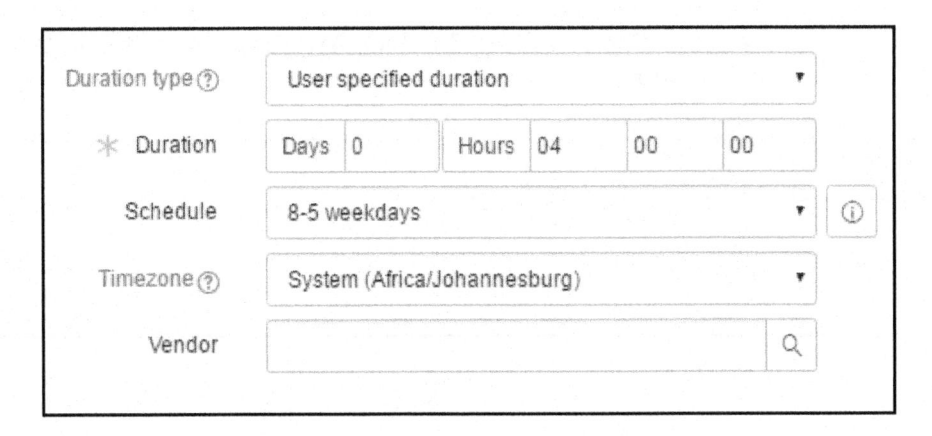

10. SLA configuration part 2

- **Start condition**: Define the start condition of the SLA, such as timer start condition, as on a new state or on a ticket description. You may choose the state, category, subcategory, or business services to kick off
- **Category**: Software
- **Subcategory**: Business Software
- **Business Services**: Active Directory

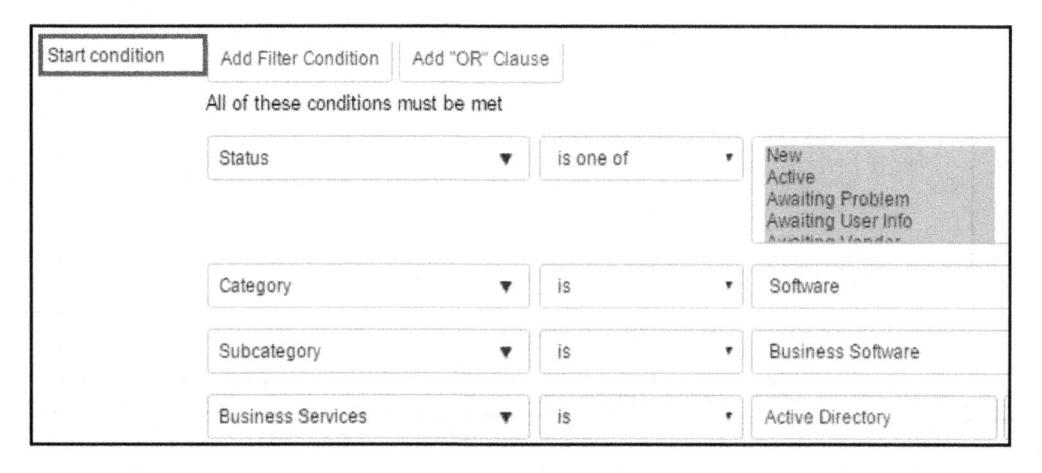

SLA start condition

- **Pause condition**: Define the pause condition of the SLA such as timer pause conditions as when you want any details from end users you can make the pause condition when the state is awaiting user info. **Awaiting Problem** and so on.
    - State : Pick **Awaiting Problem**, **Awaiting User Info**, or **Awaiting Vendor**

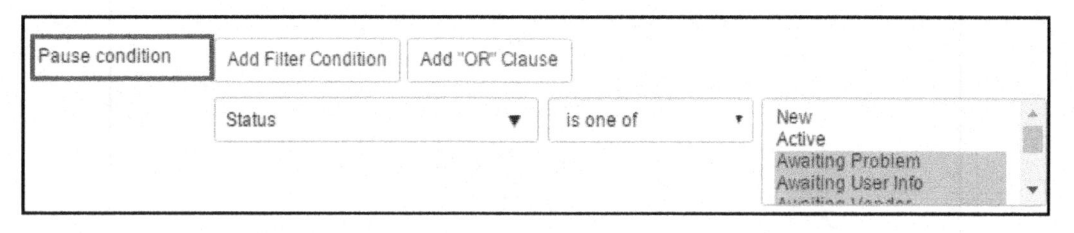

SLA pause condition

- **Stop condition**: Finally, you need to configure when the timer should end, such as when the task state is resolved or closed. Note that out of the box, Service-Now has a business rule that closes resolved incidents after 5 days

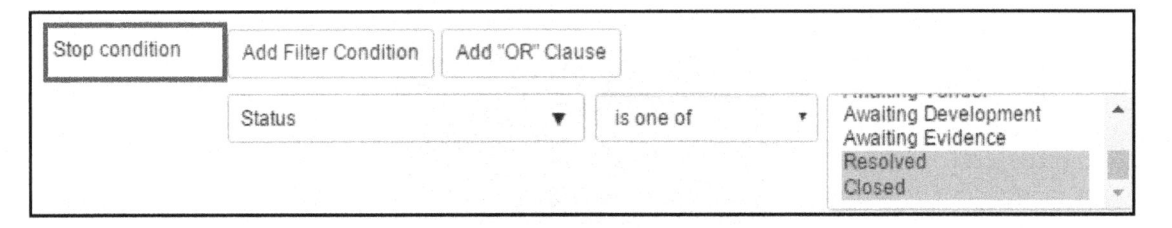

SLA stop condition

6. Click on **Submit**.
7. As an output, when these conditions are matched the SLA **AD Server Issues** will start execution.

See also

To read more about the SAL follow `http://wiki.servicenow.com/index.php?title=Service_Level_Agreements#gsc.tab=0` link.

Setting up system rules

Out of the box, Service-Now provides data lookup and assignment rules to automatically assign a task to users or groups.

Getting ready

To step through this recipe, you should have an active Service-Now instance, valid credentials, and an admin role.

How to do it...

1. Open any standard web browser.
2. Log in to the Service-Now instance with the credentials.

3. Type `system policy` in the search box and service-now will search system policy application, and under the rule section you can find all related module such as **Data lookup Definitions**, **Assignment Lookup Rules**, **Assignment**, and so on:

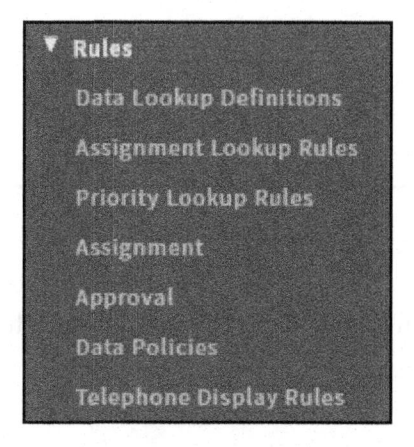

System Policy – rules

4. To assign values in the assigned to or assignment group fields, you can use assignment look up:
5. Click on the **Assignment Lookup Rules** module, as shown here:

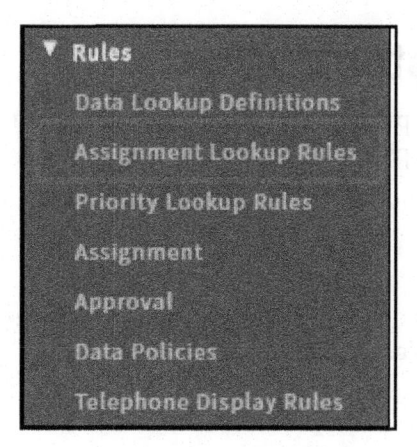

Create new assignment look up rule

Chapter 2

6. You will now be able to see the assignment rule configuration page:
    - **Name:** `Hardware Assignment`

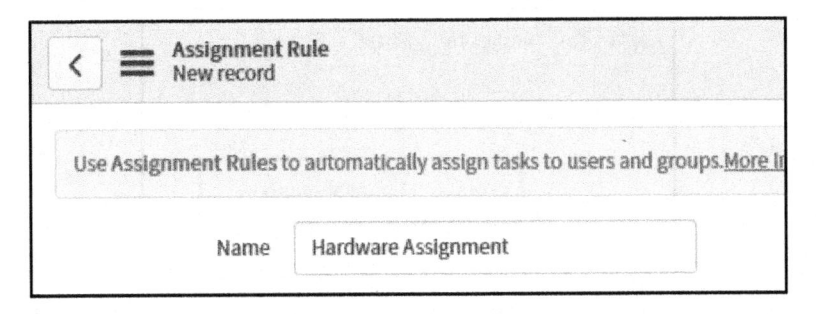

Assignment rule part 1

7. Now, you need to set conditions for the assignment, as follows:
    - **Category:** `Hardware`
    - **Subcategory:** `Wireless`

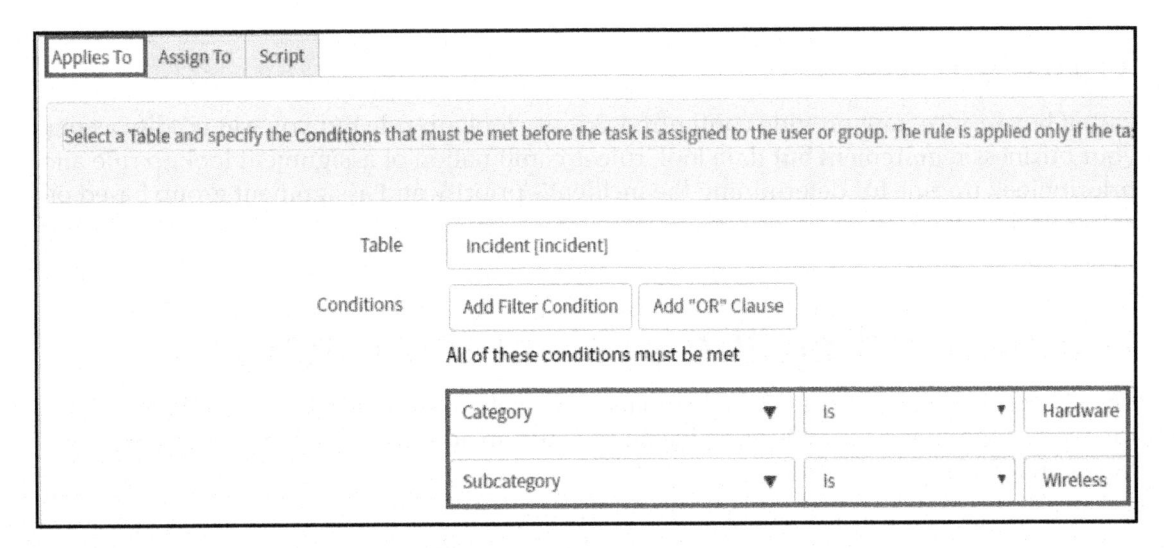

Assignment rule part 2

8. Now you need to assign based on the conditions, which means that when the earlier conditions are matched, then the following will be the assignment group:

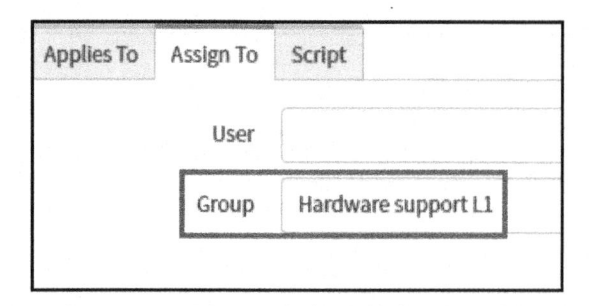

Assignment rule part 3

9. Click on the **Submit** button, and now, when the conditions (category: hardware and subcategory: wireless) match on the incident form, then the assignment will be `Hardware support L1`.

There's more...

Out of box service-now provide configured priority look up rule but you can modify as per your business requirement but data look rule is combination of assignment lookup rule and priority look up rule for determining the incident's priority and assignment group based on matcher fields.

Understanding the system dictionary

The system dictionary is a special table that contains details for each table and definitions for every column on each table in an instance. Being an admin, you are allowed to modify tables and fields.

Getting ready

To step through this recipe, you should have an active Service-Now instance, valid credentials, and admin role.

How to do it…

1. Open any standard web browser.
2. Type the Service-Now instance web address (`https://{instance_name}.service-now.com`) provided by your company in the address bar. Now, enter your credentials in respective fields.
3. On the left-hand side, in the search box, type `dictionary`. Under the **System Definition** application, you will able to see the **Dictionary** module:

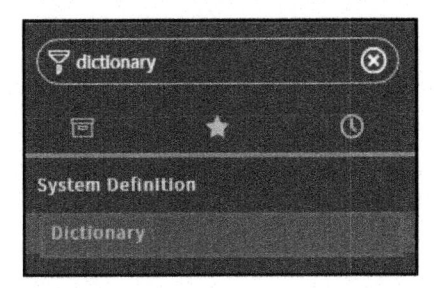

Dictionary Module

4. Click on **Dictionary** module. After click you will able to view screen as shown in the following screenshot. To create new dictionary entry click **New** button:

Dictionary Entries- List View

Performing Core Configuration and Management Tasks

5. After clicking **New**, you will able to see configuration page as shown in the following screenshot:

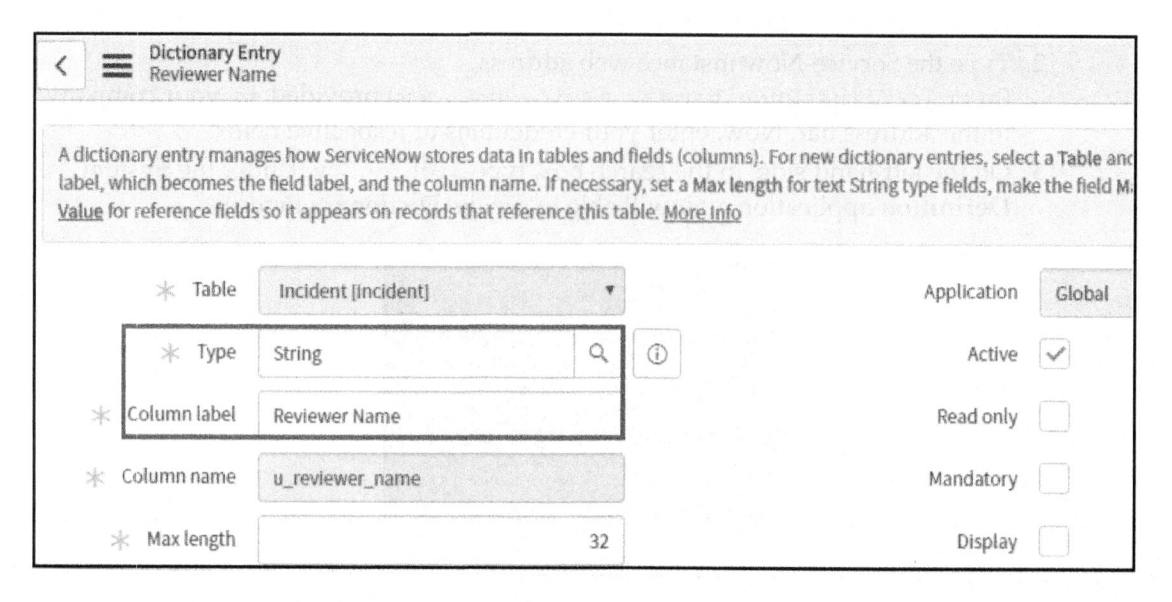

Dictionary Entry
Reviewer Name

A dictionary entry manages how ServiceNow stores data in tables and fields (columns). For new dictionary entries, select a Table and label, which becomes the field label, and the column name. If necessary, set a Max length for text String type fields, make the field M Value for reference fields so it appears on records that reference this table. More Info

* Table	Incident [incident]	Application	Global
* Type	String	Active	✓
* Column label	Reviewer Name	Read only	
* Column name	u_reviewer_name	Mandatory	
* Max length	32	Display	

New dictionary entry

6. Click **Submit** button to save **Reviewer Name** on incident form.
7. You can also access dictionary through incident form as shown in the following screenshot:
   1. Go to the incident application.
   2. Click on **Create New module**.

[116]

8. Right click on Incident Form's header and hover the mouse over **Configure** option and at last select **Dictionary** option as shown following:

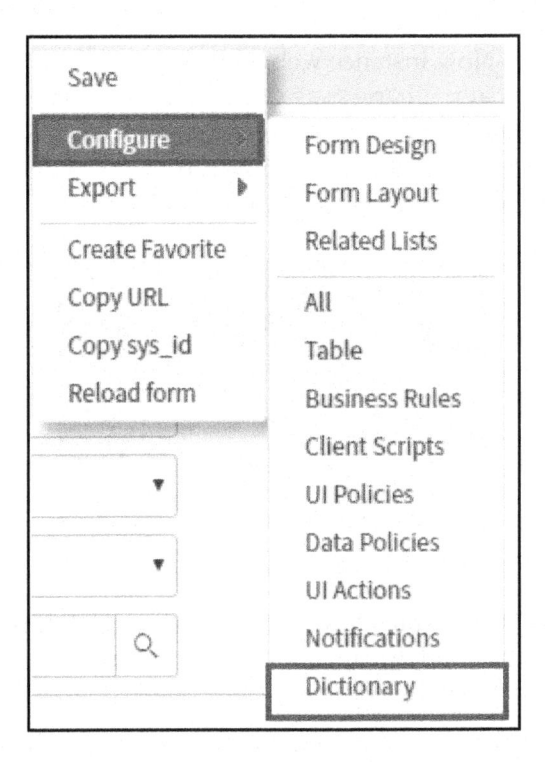

Access "Dictionary" through Service-Now form

Understanding the Service-Now tables schema

Service-Now is an enterprise-level system and it has its own data mode. Through the schema map, you can understand tables and their relationships in a visual manner.

Getting ready

To step through this recipe, you should have active an Service-Now instance, valid credentials, and admin role.

How to do it...

1. Open any standard web browser.
2. Type the Service-Now instance web address (`https://{instance_name}.service-now.com`) provided by your company in the address bar. Now, enter your credentials in respective fields.
3. On the left-hand side, in the search box, type `tables`, and Service-Now will search for **Tables & Columns**, as shown here:

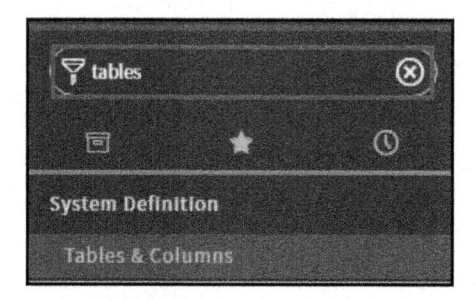

Tables & Column module

4. Under **System Definition**, click on the **Tables & Columns** module. After clicking on it, you will able to view the following screen, where you will able see all the tables and columns of the system:

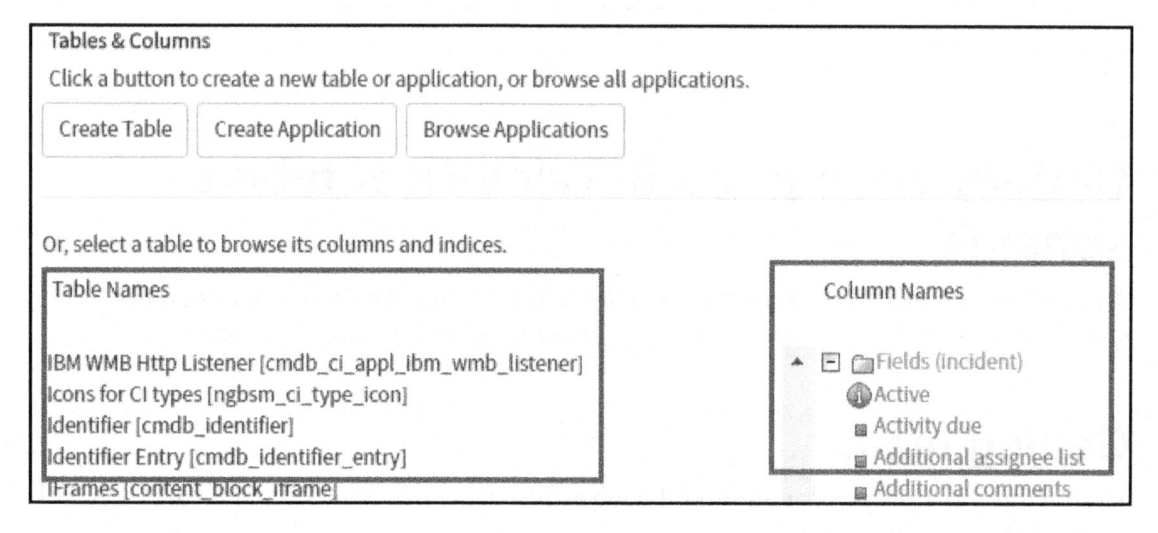

Tables and column module's sections

Chapter 2

5. If you click on any column name field, you can even see **Column Attributes**, as shown here:

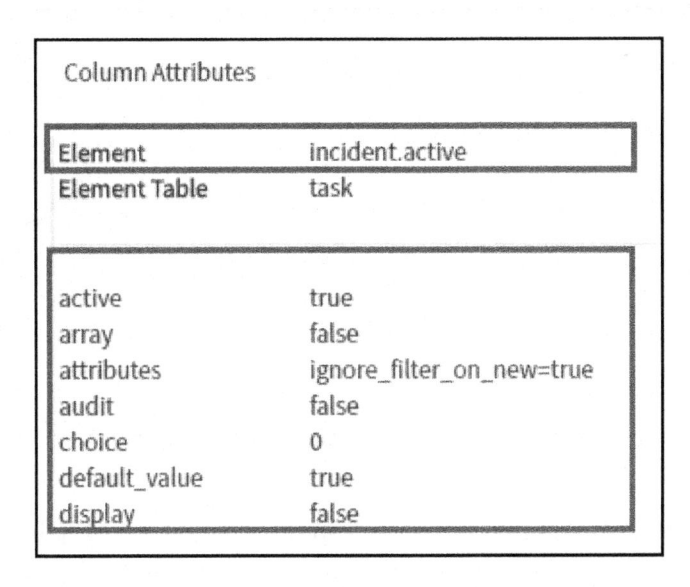

Column Attributes	
Element	incident.active
Element Table	task
active	true
array	false
attributes	ignore_filter_on_new=true
audit	false
choice	0
default_value	true
display	false

Column attributes

6. If you want to view the schema map of any table, say, the `Incident` table, scroll down and select the table as **Incident** and click on the **Schema map** button:

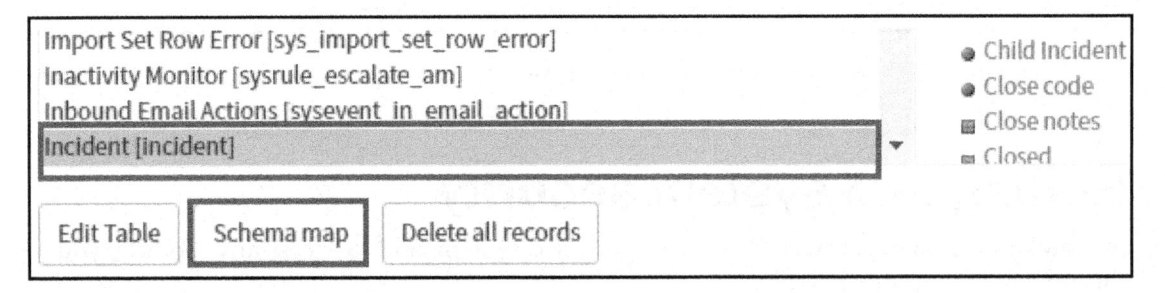

Schema map of incident table

[119]

Performing Core Configuration and Management Tasks

7. After clicking on **Schema map**, you will able to see the following screenshot:

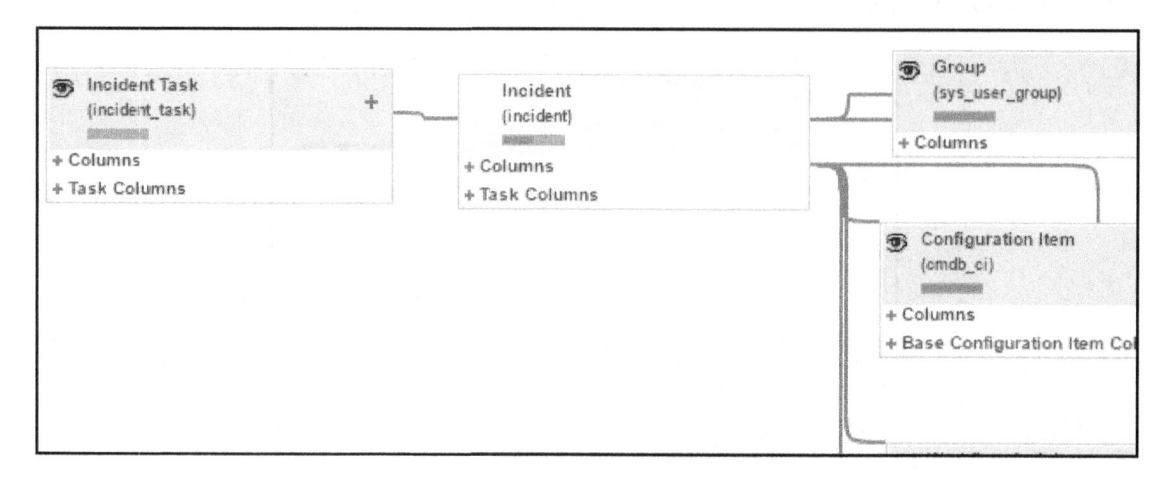

Schema Map

8. It is important to mention that you can filter the relationship by unchecking the check box:

Schema Map filter

Getting into system security

As you know by now, Service-Now is a role-based system, and to access any module, you should have the respective role.

Getting ready

To step through this recipe, you should have an active Service-Now instance, valid credentials, and an admin or security admin role.

How to do it...

1. Open any standard web browser.
2. Type the Service-Now instance web address (`https://{instance_name}.service-now.com`) provided by your company in the address bar. Now, enter your credentials in respective fields
3. On the left-hand side, type `system security` in the search box, and Service-Now will search for the module for you:

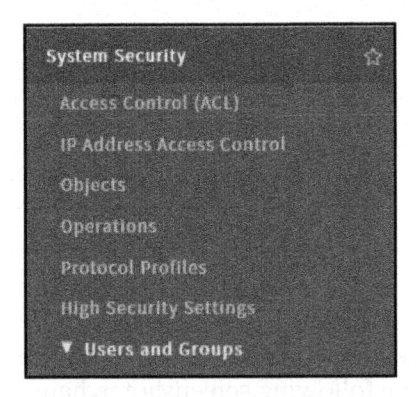

System security module

4. To create a new role, you need to type the `role` in the search box, and Service-Now will search the module for you. Click on the **Roles** module:

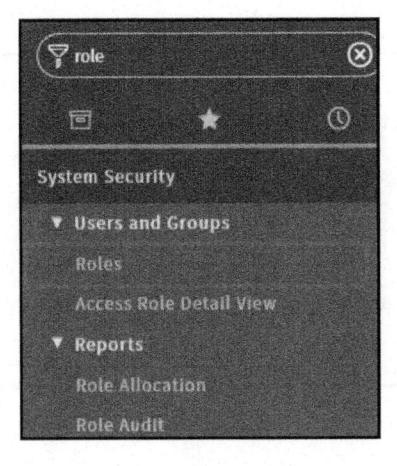

Roles Module

5. **Roles** module acts as a central repository of all system and custom roles. After clicking on the **Roles** module, you will be able to see all roles as given here, where you need to click on the **New** button:

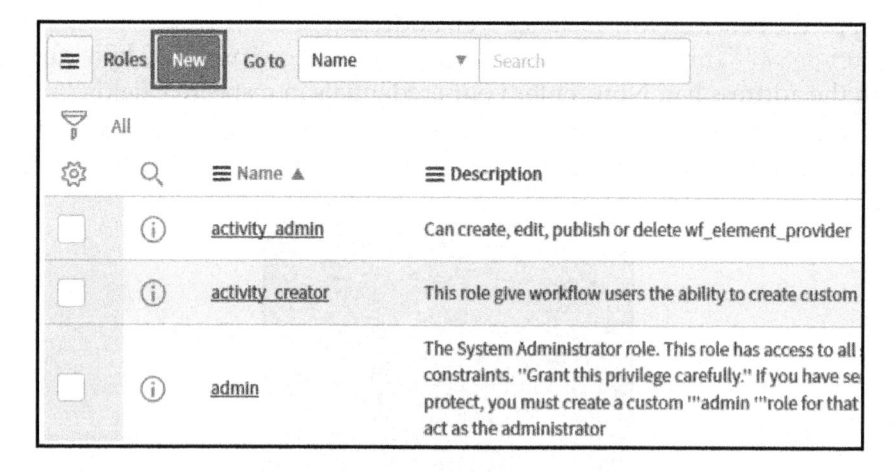

Name	Description
activity_admin	Can create, edit, publish or delete wf_element_provider
activity_creator	This role give workflow users the ability to create custom
admin	The System Administrator role. This role has access to all constraints. "Grant this privilege carefully." If you have se protect, you must create a custom '"admin '"role for that act as the administrator

Create new role

6. After clicking on the **New** button, you will be able to see the role configuration page, as shown in the following screenshot, where you need enter necessary configuration details as shown following:

- **Name:** `ipad_request`
- **Description:** `Only managers can request an iPad for employee`

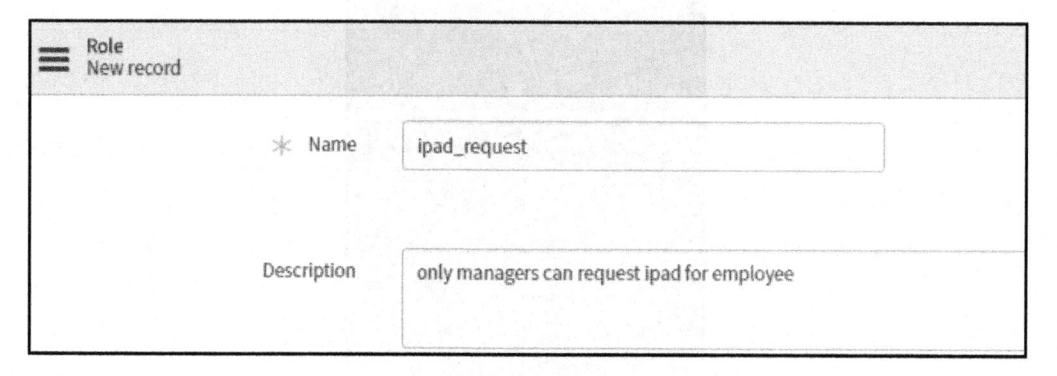

Name	ipad_request
Description	only managers can request ipad for employee

New role configuration

[122]

7. Now click on **Submit** button and the **ipad_request** role is created and added to the roles list as shown following:

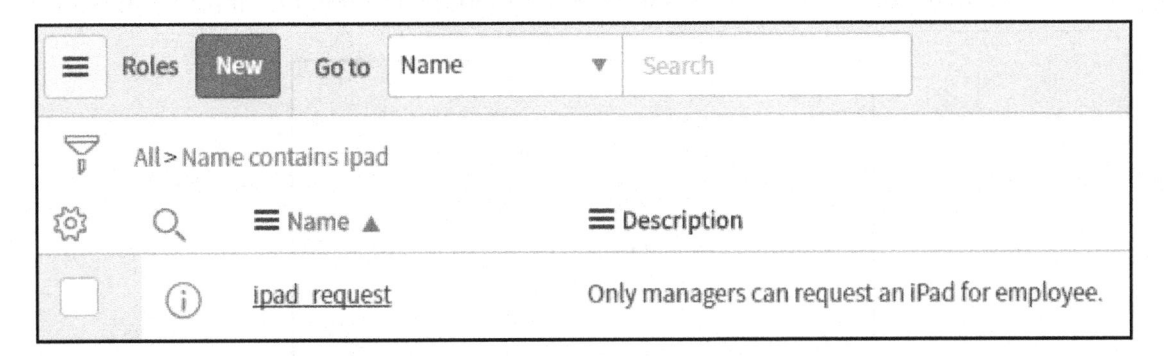

≡ Name ▲	≡ Description
ipad_request	Only managers can request an iPad for employee.

All > Name contains ipad

8. Until the new role (`ipad_request`) is assigned to any module or catalog item, there is no use for it. On many occasions, you may come across a situation where you have to modify a current system role or create new roles in a Service-Now instance. If you edit any system role, then you must have the **security_admin** role, which you add in your profile because of admin. To elevate a role, you need to click on your profile and then on **Elevate Roles** option:

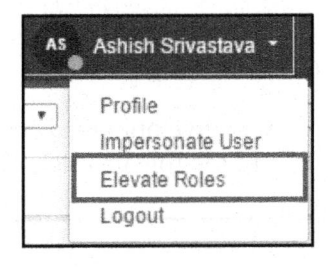

Elevate role to get access

[123]

Performing Core Configuration and Management Tasks

9. After selecting **Elevate Roles**, a pop up window will come on screen as shown following and you need to check **security_admin** box and click on **OK** and after that you will have **Access Control (ACL)** module which holds all role restrictions:

Elevated role security admin

The user gets access to a specific module, application, or catalog if all following are true:

The user has one of the roles specified in the role list or the list is empty. Conditions in the `Condition` field evaluate to true, or conditions are empty.

The script in the `Script` field (advanced) evaluates to true, sets the variable answer to true, or is empty.

10. For an example, If you want to give only read-only access for tasks, then you can find that specific role and add the role in, as shown in the following screenshot:

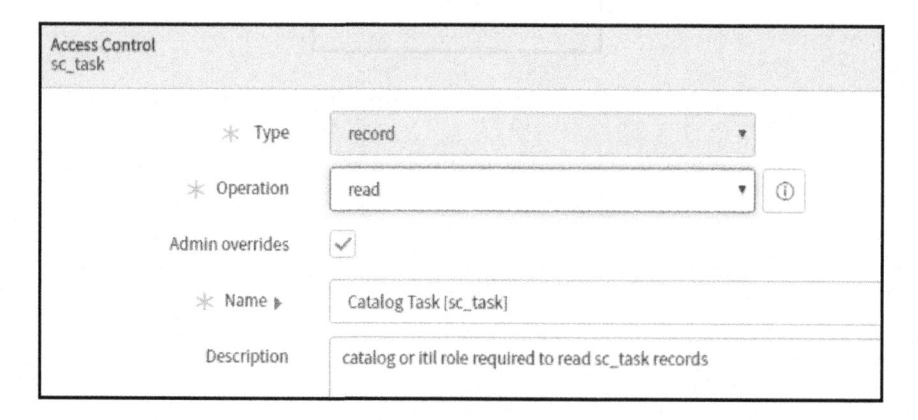

Current role with read operation

[124]

11. Now add your new role **ipad_request** which will facilitate user to view IPad related task well:

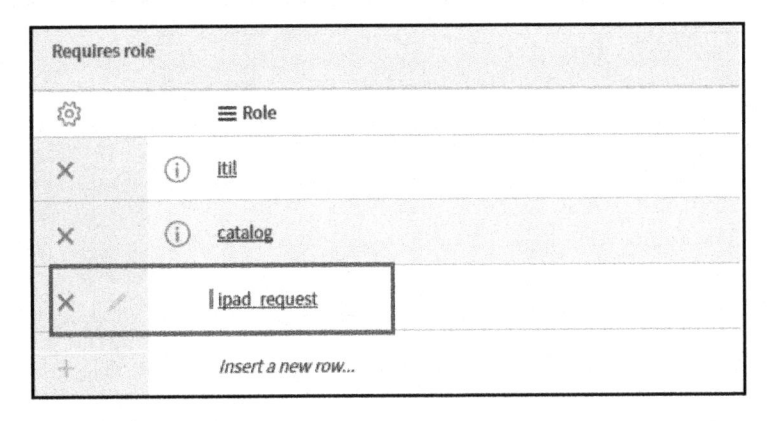

New role added

There's more...

It is important to note that if you mark Elevated **privilege** check box on role configuration page then user needs to elevate to high security to setting to access any item.

3
Building Data-Driven Application

In this chapter, we will cover the following recipes:

- Starting a new application
- Getting into new modules
- Getting into the client script
- Getting into the server-side script
- Understanding team development plugin
- Understanding web services
- Understanding development best practice

Introduction

Service-Now provides a great platform to developers. It is important to note that it provides its own functions and classes to support a new development.

Starting a new application

Out of the box, service-now provides many applications for facilitating business operations and other activities in an IT environment, but if you find that the customer's requirements are not fitting into the system's applications boundaries then you can think of creating new applications. In these recipes, we will build a small application which will include table, form, business rules, client script, ACL, update sets and deployment.

Building Data-Driven Application

> **TIP**
> For the bonus chapter on web services you can refer at `https://github.com/PacktPublishing/ServiceNowCookbook`.

Getting ready

To go through this recipe, you must have an active Service-Now instance, valid credentials, and an admin role.

How to do it...

1. Open any standard web browser and type the instance address.
2. Log in to the Service-Now instance with the credentials.
3. In the search box on the left-hand side, type `Local Update Sets` and Service-Now will search out the module **Local Update set module** for you:

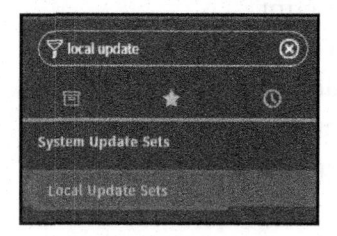

Local update set for a new application

4. Now, you need to click on **Local Update Sets** module under System Update Sets application to create a new update set so that you can capture your entire customization in the update set:

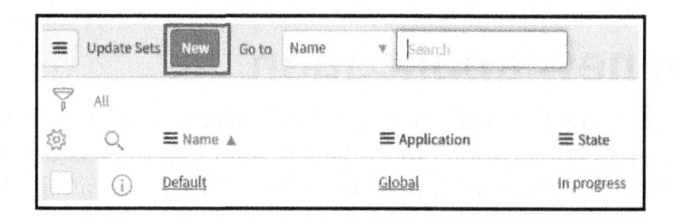

Create a new update set

5. On clicking, you need to configure the update set to capture the development items as follows:
    1. **Name:** `Book registration application`
    2. **State:** `In progress`
    3. **Description:** `Book registration application development items`

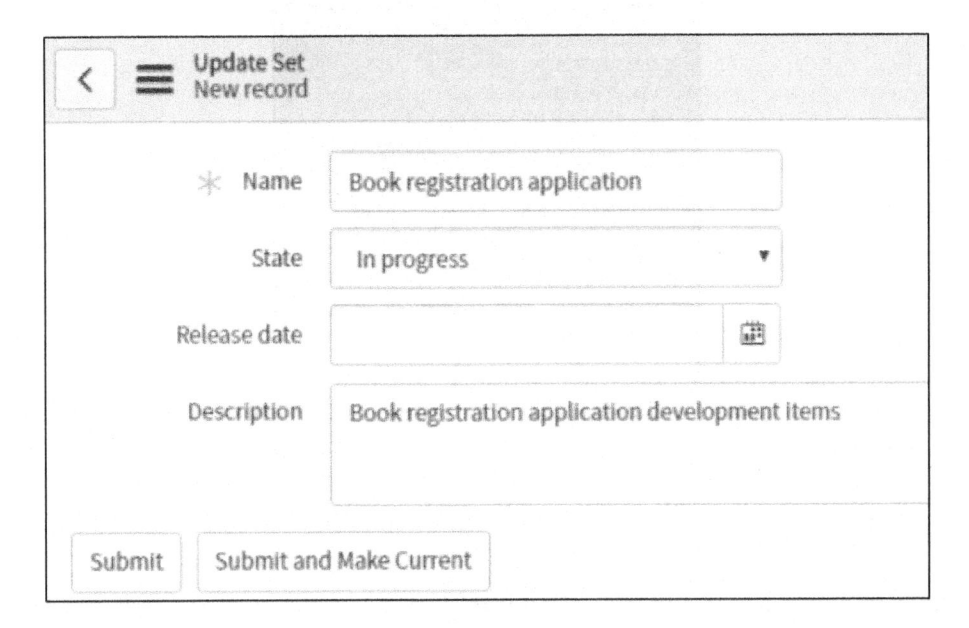

The local update set–book registration application

6. Now click on **Submit and Make Current** Button on update set.
7. Now you will able to see the **Book registration** application update set next to your profile, which means you are ready to create a new application and all development items will be captured in this update set only:

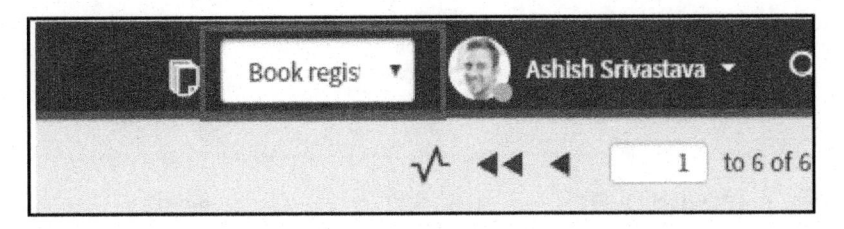

The current update set

Building Data-Driven Application

8. On the left-hand side in the search box, type `system definition` and click on the **Application Menus** module under system definition application:

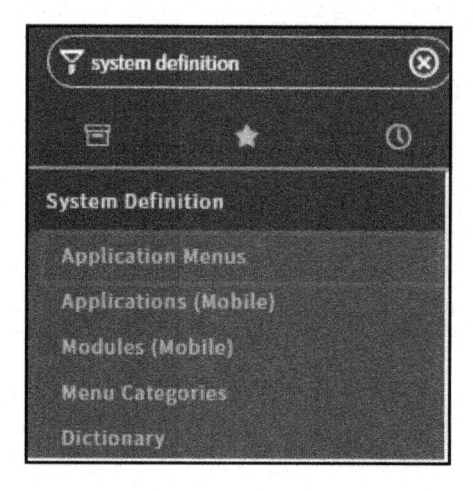

system definition

System Definition

Application Menus
Applications (Mobile)
Modules (Mobile)
Menu Categories
Dictionary

The application menu to create a new application

9. After clicking on **Application Menus module,** you will able to all application as follows. To make this recipe, you should have some better understand how applications look like in service-now environment. To understand better, you can click on any application menu as shown here; where you can see the application and associated modules:

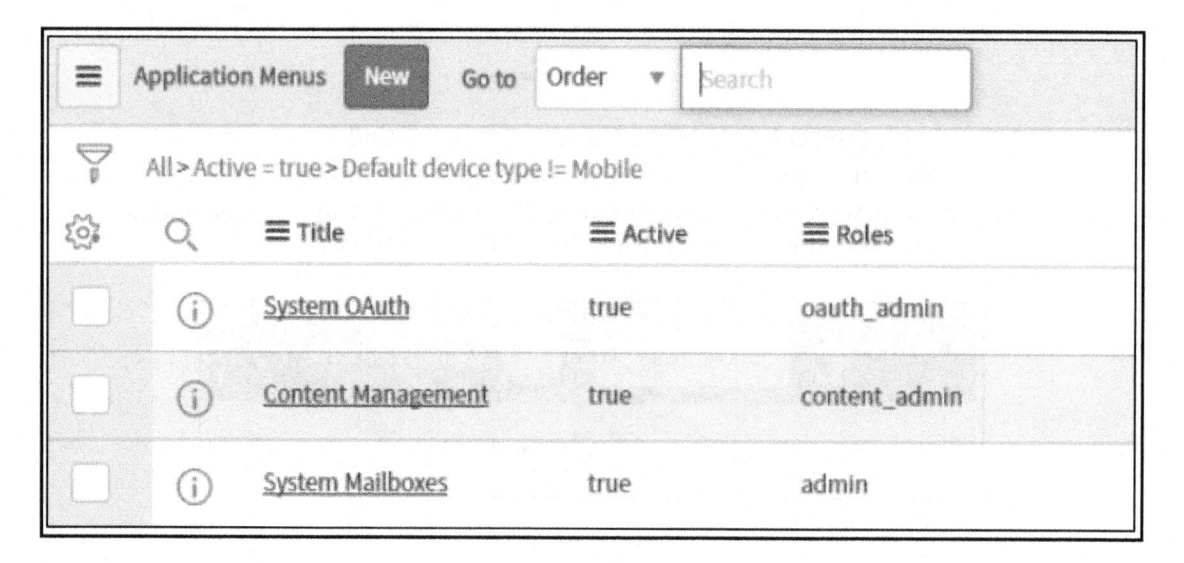

Title	Active	Roles
System OAuth	true	oauth_admin
Content Management	true	content_admin
System Mailboxes	true	admin

All > Active = true > Default device type != Mobile

[130]

Application Menus records

10. But for now let's suppose you have clicked on **Self-Service** application menu as follows:

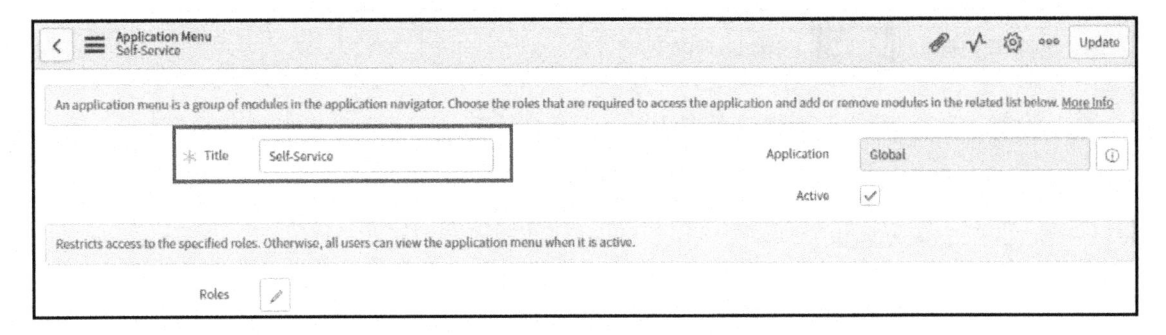

Self-service application

11. Now to see the associated modules with Self–Service application, you need to scroll down as shown here, and if you want to add new module in application then click on **New** button:

Title	Table	Order ▲
Homepage		50
About		100
Service Catalog		100
Knowledge	label [service_knowledge]	110

Self-service application's modules

Building Data-Driven Application

12. By now you should have a better understanding of how applications look within the service-now environment. So, to make a new application, you need to click on the New button on the **Application Menus** page:

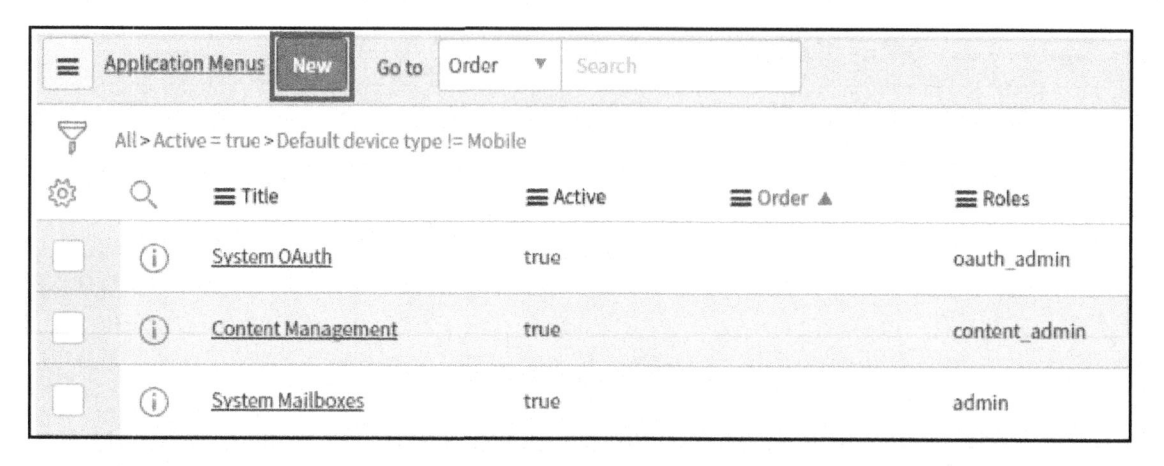

		Title	Active	Order ▲	Roles
☐	ⓘ	System OAuth	true		oauth_admin
☐	ⓘ	Content Management	true		content_admin
☐	ⓘ	System Mailboxes	true		admin

The applications repository

13. After clicking on the **New** button, you will able to see the **Application Menu** configuration page. To understand better, let's consider this example. For instance, you are creating a `Book Registration` application for your customer with the following configuration:

- **Title**: `Book Registration`
- **Role**: Leave Blank
- **Application**: `Global`
- **Active**: `True`
- **Category**: `Custom Applications` (you can change it as per your requirement)

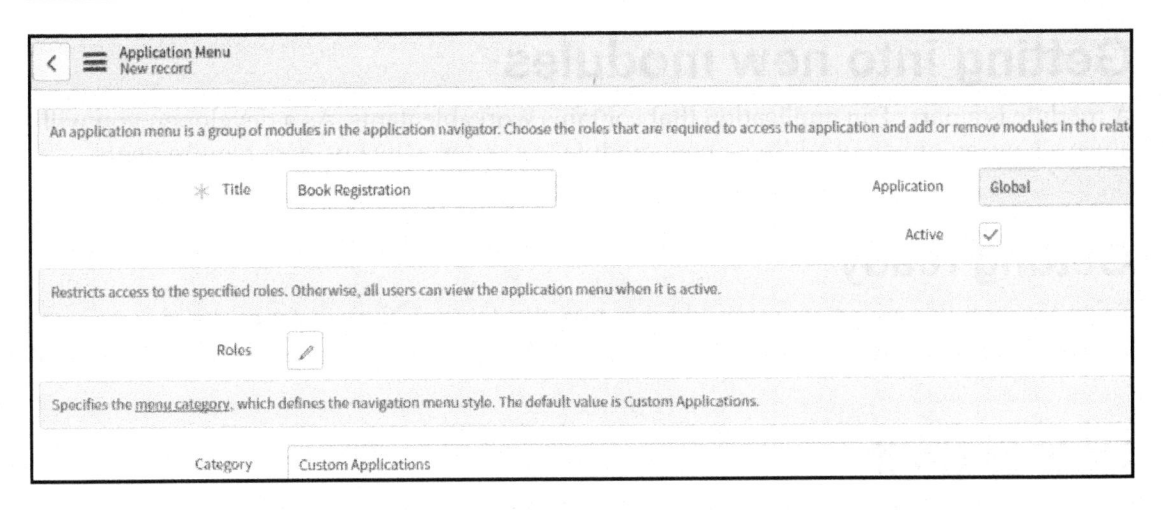

< ≡	Application Menu New record				

An application menu is a group of modules in the application navigator. Choose the roles that are required to access the application and add or remove modules in the relat

* Title	Book Registration		Application	Global
			Active	✓

Restricts access to the specified roles. Otherwise, all users can view the application menu when it is active.

Roles	✎

Specifies the menu category, which defines the navigation menu style. The default value is Custom Applications.

Category	Custom Applications

Book registration configuration

14. Click on the **Submit** button. After some time, a new **Book Registration** application menu will be visible under the application menu:

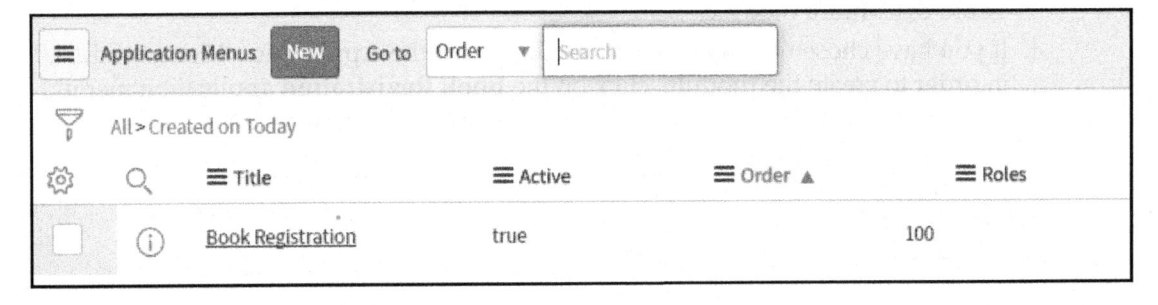

≡	Application Menus	New	Go to	Order ▼	Search	
▽	All > Created on Today					
⚙	🔍	≡ Title		≡ Active	≡ Order ▲	≡ Roles
☐	ⓘ	Book Registration		true	100	

Book registration

Getting into new modules

A module is a part of an application that contains workable items. As a developer, you will always have an option of adding a new module to support new business requirements.

Getting ready

To go through this recipe, you should have an active Service-Now instance, valid credentials, and an admin role.

How to do it...

1. Open any standard web browser and type the instance address.
2. Log in to the Service-Now instance with the credentials.
3. Service-Now gives you many options to create a new module. You can create a new module from the **Application Menu** module or you can go through the **Table & Column** module.
4. If you have chosen to create a new module from the **Application Menu** module, in order to create the module, click on the **Book Registration** application menu and scroll down. To create a new module, click on the **New** button:

Creating a new module

Chapter 3

5. After clicking on the **New** button, you will able to see a Module configuration screen where you need to configure the following fields:

- **Title**: `Author Registration`
- **Application Menu**: `Book Registration`

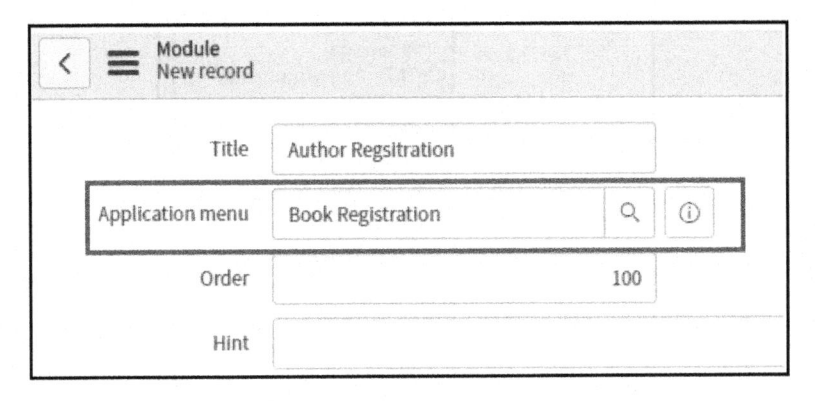

The Author Registration module registration under the Book Registration menu

6. Now, in the **Link Type** section, you need to configure the new module, rather I would say, you need to define the base line regarding what your new module will do-whether the new module will show a form to create a record or it will show a list of reports from a **Table** or execute some of the reports. That's why this is a critical step:

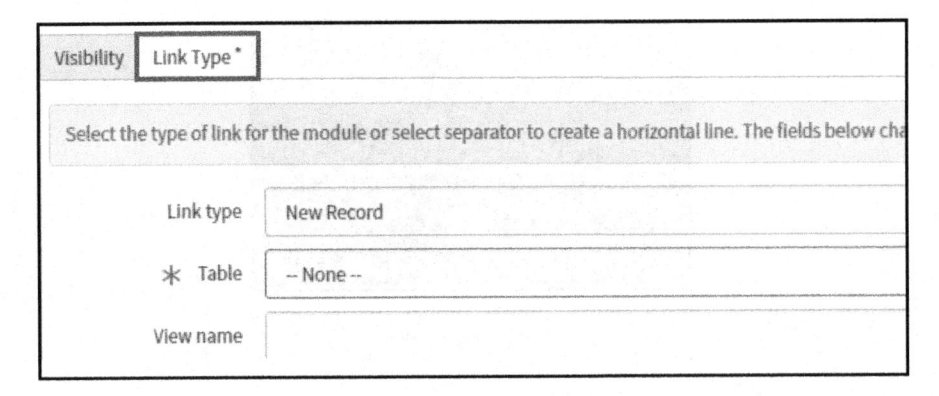

Link type to create a new module and select a table

[135]

Building Data-Driven Application

7. **Link type** gives you many options to decide the behavior of the new module:

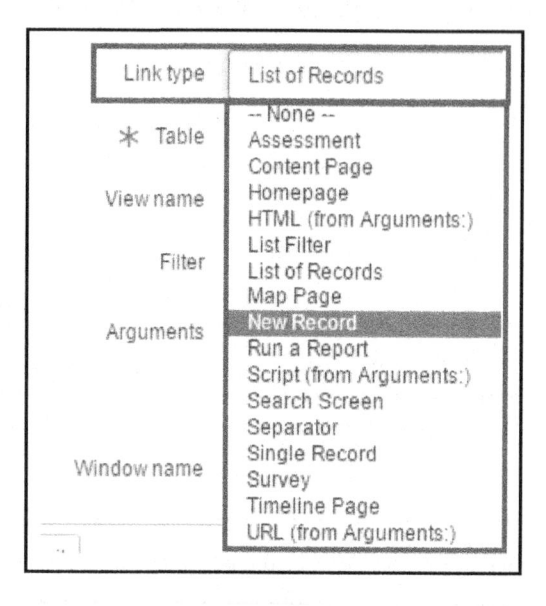

Link type options

8. Now, let's take a different approach to create a new module. On the left-hand side, type `Column` and Service-Now will search the **Tables & Columns** module for you. Click on the **Tables & Columns** module:

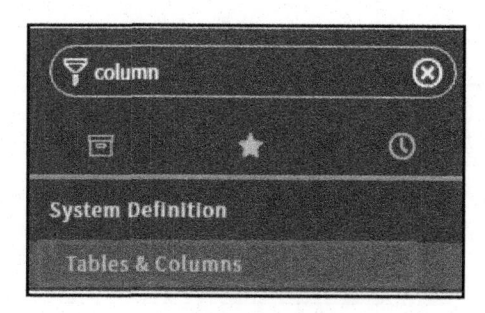

The Tables & Columns module

9. Now, you will see the configuration page, as shown, where you need to click on the **Create Table** button. Note that by clicking on **Create Table**, you can create a new table:

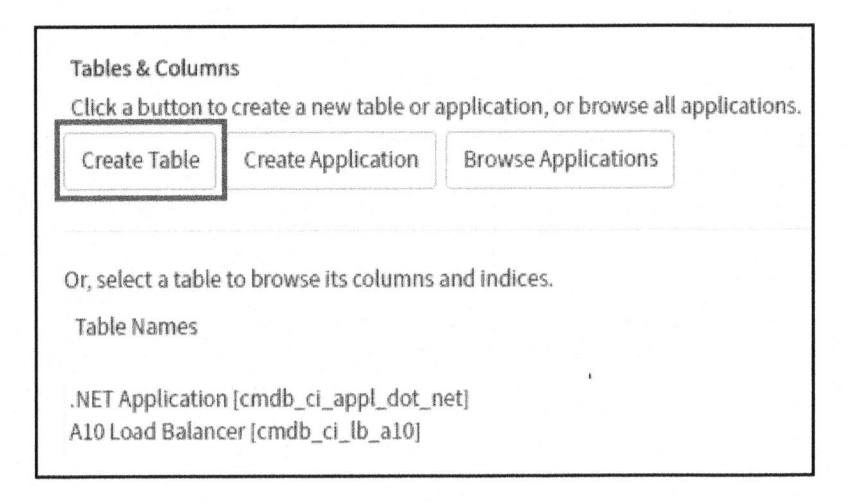

Tables & Columns–Create a new table

10. After clicking on the **Create Table** button, you will see the configuration page, as illustrated, where you need to configure the following fields:

- **Label:** Author Registration (module name)
- **Name:** Auto populate
- **Extends table:** Task (by extends, your module will incorporate all fields of the base table, in this scenario, the Task table)

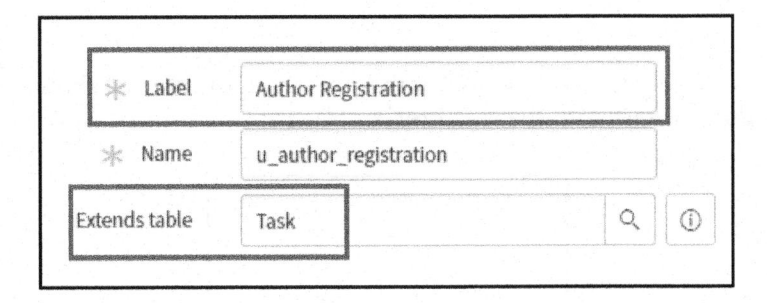

Module Configuration

[137]

Building Data-Driven Application

11. To create a new module through table, check the **Create module** checkbox, and to **Add module to menu** under your application, select the application name:

Add module in application

12. **Controls** is a critical section as Service-Now gives an option to auto-create a number. For an incident, INC is the prefix or for a change ticket CHG is the prefix; here, you are also allowed to create your prefix for a new module record:

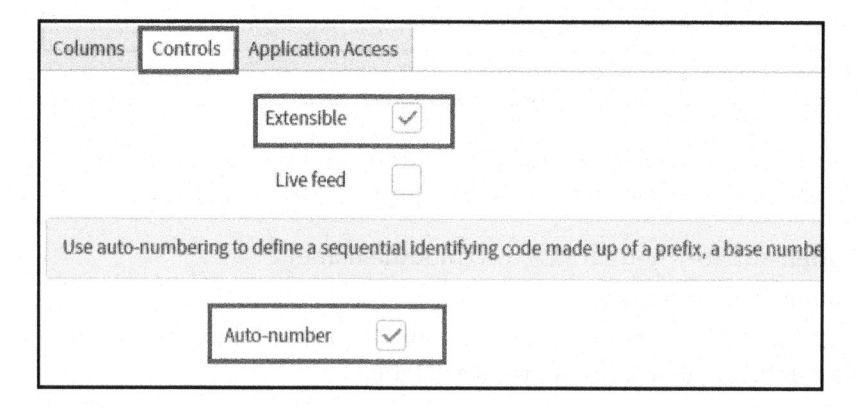

Configure the new module Controls section

13. Now, you will be able to auto number the configuration, as shown; your new records will start with the AUT **Prefix**:

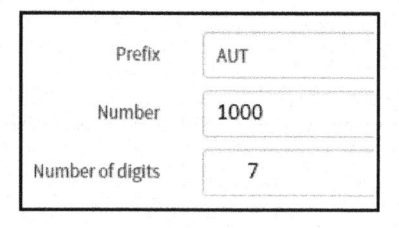

New module auto numbering

14. Click on **submit**.
15. After submission of the form, Service-Now will automatically create a role for the new module, as shown. Only the `u_author_registration_user` role holder will be able to view the module. So, whenever a request is generated, you will need to go into that particular user's profile from the user administration module to add a role:

Role created for module

16. Your module is created, but there are no fields. So, for rapid development, you can directly add a column to the table by clicking on **Insert a new row…**:

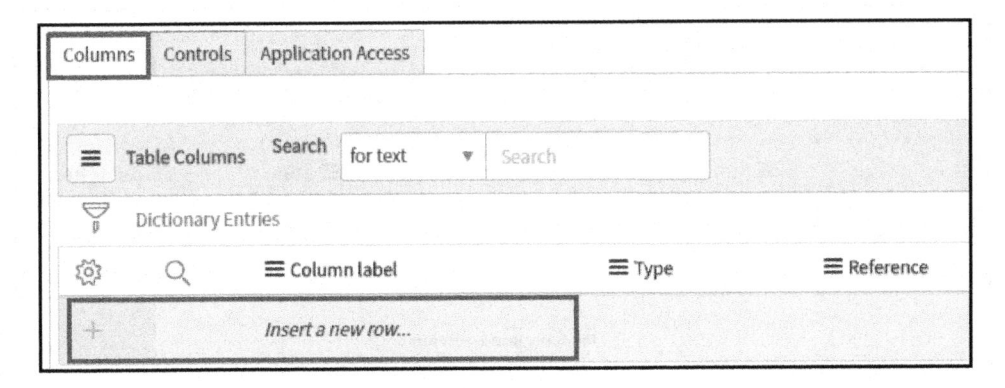

The Insert field in the form

Building Data-Driven Application

17. As an output, you will see that a new **Author Registrations** module is added under the **Book Registration** application:

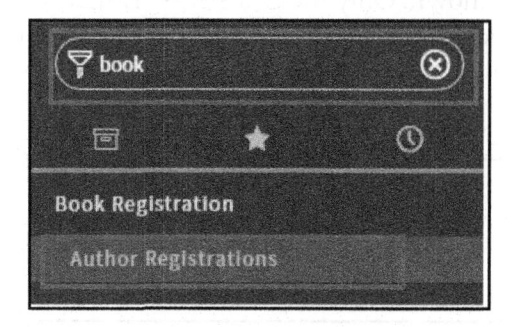

Search the newly created module

18. Now, if you click on the **Author Registrations** module, you will see the following page:

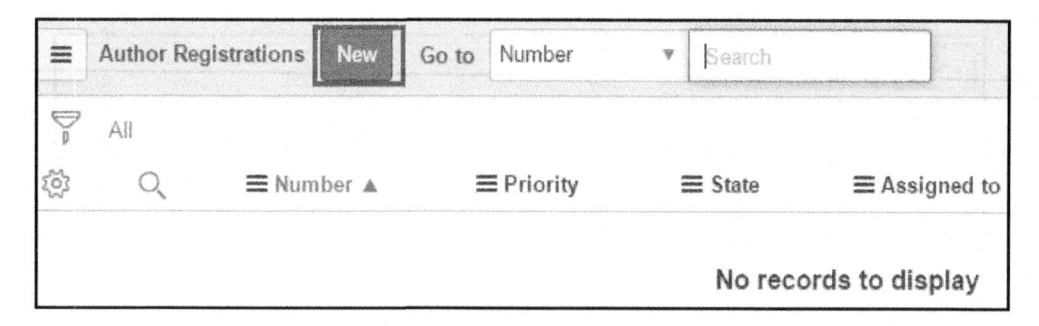

The Author Registrations page

Chapter 3

19. After clicking on the **New** button, you will see the form, as shown. Note that you have not added any field on the `u_author_registration` table, but the table extends to the `TASK` table. That's why you are able to see fields on the form, but they are coming from the `TASK` table:

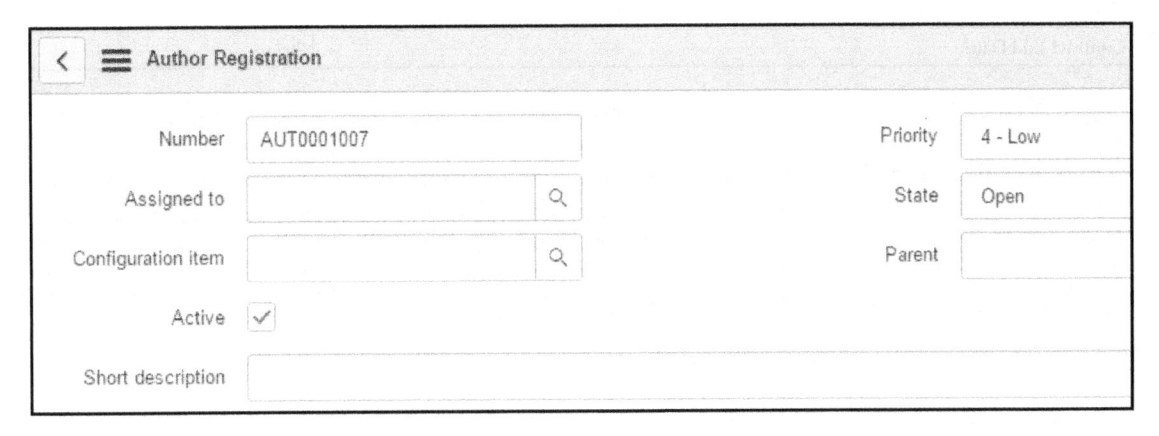

Author registration form without new fields

20. If you want to add new fields to the form, you can do so by performing the following steps:

    1. Right-click on the banner.

    2. Select **Configure.**

    3. Click on **Form Layout.**

21. Now, in the create new field section, you can enter the desired Field Name and Type, as shown:

Form Fields	Field Type
Author Name	String
Author Primary E-mail Address	String
Author Secondary E-mail Address	String
Author Mobile Number	String
Author Permanent Address	String
Author Temporary Address	String
Country	India
USA	
UK	

[141]

Building Data-Driven Application

Australia	
Author Experience	String
Book Type	Choice
Book Title	String
Contract Start Date	String
Contract End Date	String

Author registration form fields

1. Click on **Add** and **Save**.
2. After saving the form, the new fields are added to the **Author Registration** form:

Author registration form

3. To create a new form section in the form view, click on the **Create new section** option and **add** the name:

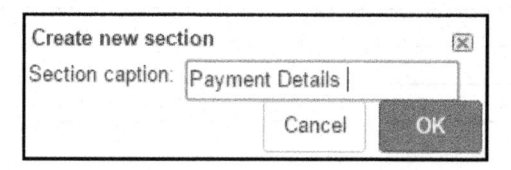

Create a new section

4. After creating the new `Payment Details` section, you can add fields under this section:

Form Fields	Field Type
Country	String
Preferred Payment Currency	Currency
Bank Name	String
Branch Name	String
IFSC Code	String
Bank Address	String

Payment Details section fields

5. As an output, you will see the following screen fields under **Payment Details** on **Author Registration form**:

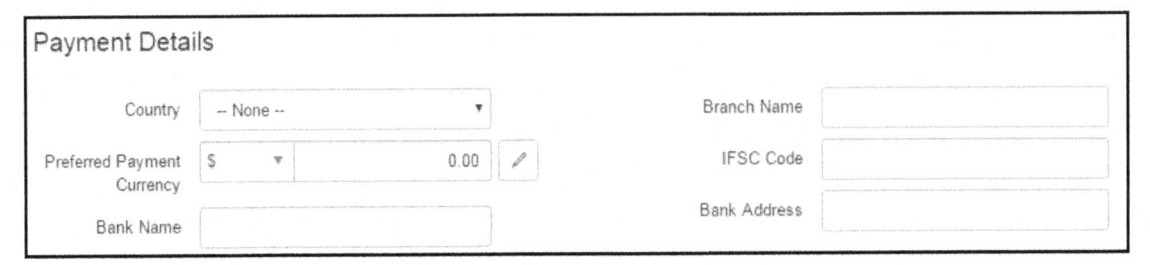

Author registration Payment Details form section

6. As an output, your Author Registration form ready for users.

Getting into the client script

Client scripts run on the browser side and use JavaScript as native. Click on `https://www.codecademy.com/learn/javascript` to read more about javascript. Client scripts can be used to put validation on a Service-Now form and for customization of Service-Now behavior, such as making any field read-only, mandatory, or hidden. Note that it's not advisable to use a client-side script to customize the behavior of a form as it impacts the form performance. Out of the box, Service-Now provides many client-side functions to perform operations.

Building Data-Driven Application

Getting ready

To go through this recipe, you should have an active Service-Now instance and valid credentials with an admin role.

How to do it...

1. Open any standard web browser and type the instance address.
2. Log in to the Service-Now instance with the valid credentials.
3. On the left-hand side, type `Author Registration`, click on the right module on the header, as shown, and select **Client Scripts**:

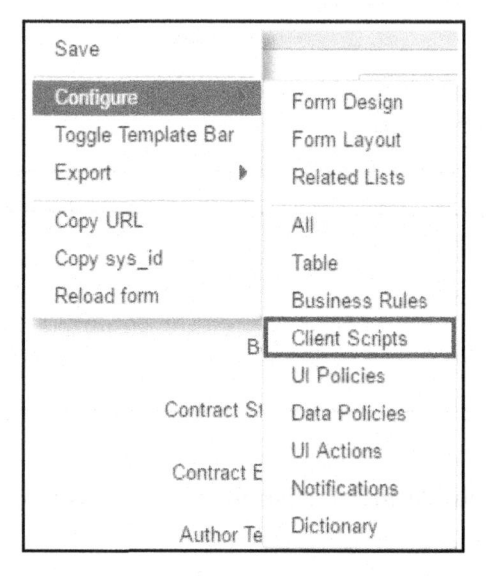

Client scripts

4. Now you will able to see client scripts records in the following page, where you will need to click on the **New** button to create client script:

Create a new client script

5. Out of the box, Service-Now provides the following types of **Client Scripts**:
   - `onLoad`: Use the `OnLoad` script when you want to perform when the form is loaded, like set value on the Service-Now form. Note that once the type is selected, Service-Now will automatically bring out the `onLoad` function for you in the script box.
     - **Name**: `author registration onload`
     - **Type**: `onLoad`
     - **Table**: Author Registration

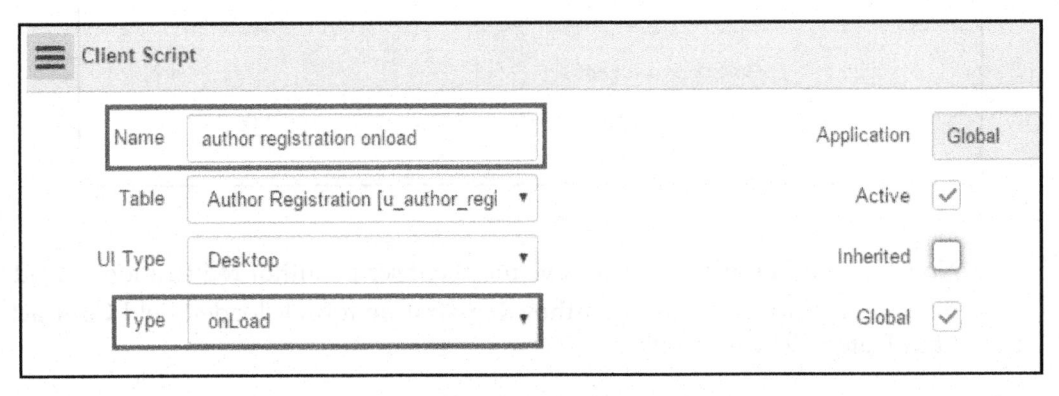

On load client script

   - `g_form`: This is the global variable that is provided by Service-Now to manipulate the field value on the client side.

Building Data-Driven Application

6. Now, the requirement is to make the **Contract Start Date** read-only on **Author Registration form** as it will be entered by other another department..
7. To get the variable name, go to the **Contract Start Date** field of the form, as shown here, to get the `Show -'u_contract_start_date'` field name, which is the name of the variable. So, if you want to access a field, you will have to use its variable name:

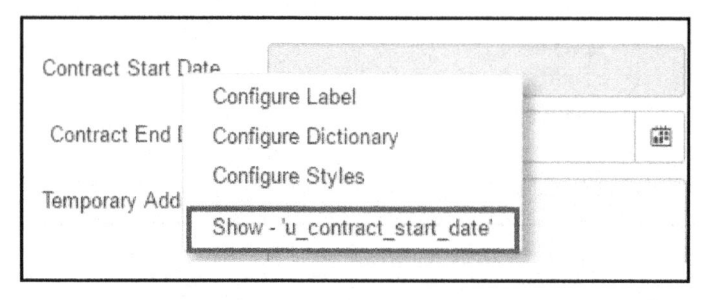

Form variable name

8. Now, add the following script to the script box:

```
Function onLoad()
{
    g_form.setReadonly ('u_contract_start_date',
  true);
}
```

On load script

- Now click on **Submit** button to save the client script author registration onload.
- Now as an output whenever **Author Registration** form is loaded field **Contract Start Date** will be read only.

9. The **on Change script** can be used when any field changes the value and, based on that field change, you can manipulate the behavior of the form. Note that to run the **on Change script**, you need to select the **Field name** field and on change of **Field Name** option **Author Registration** form will change the behavior.

10. OnSubmit is used to submit any form within the Service-Now environment. A **submit** button is available on the form out of the box. You can use onSubmit when you want to perform any action during the submission of a record. The OnSubmit **Client Script** configuration is shown here:
    - **Name:** author registration onSubmit
    - **Table:** Author Registration[u_author_regi]
    - **Type:** onSubmit

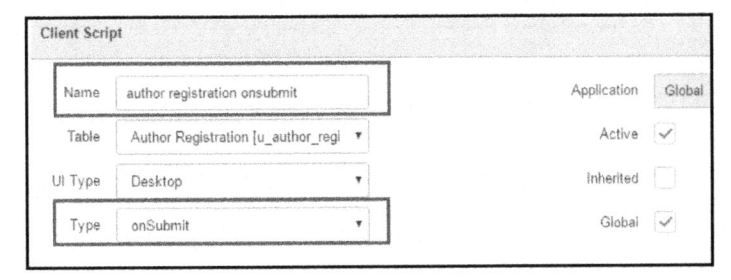

    The OnSubmit client script

11. If you want to put a validation on **Author Registration Form** submission that contract end date can't be less than contract start date, run the following code:

    ```
    function onSubmit()
    {
       // get contract end date
       var con_end =
    g_form.getValue('u_contract_end_date');
       // get contract start date
       var sat_date =
    g_form.getValue('u_contract_start_date');
       // check if contract end date is earlier than
    start date

       if(sat_date > con_end)
          {
             // alert for user
             alert("Please select valid contract
    end date.
                Contract end date cannot be in
    past");
             // highlight necessary field on form
             g_form.flash("u_contract_end_date",
    "#FF0000", 10);
             // don't allow submission of form
    ```

```
                return false;
        }
}
```

```
function onSubmit()
{
    // get contract end date
    var con_end = g_form.getValue('u_contract_end_date');

    // get contract start date
    var sat_date = g_form.getValue('u_contract_start_date');

    // check if contract end date is earlier than start date

    if(sat_date > con_end)

        {
            // alert for user
            alert("Please select valid contract end date. Contract end date cannot be in past");

            // highlight necessary field on form
            // flash color - RED FF0000

            g_form.flash("u_contract_end_date", "#FF0000", 10);

            // don't allow submission of form
            return false;
        }
}
```

The OnSubmit Client Script

12. As an output, you will see that if the `Contract end date` value is less than the `Contract start date` value, then Service-Now will pop up an error and highlight the relevant field in red, as shown:

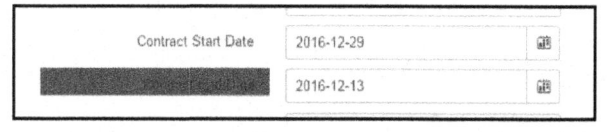

Validation on the form field

Getting into the server-side script

The server-side script runs on Service-Now server-side. Out of the box, Service-Now provides many ways to interact with **Business Rules** and **Script Includes**. **Business Rules** are like a **Data Manipulation Language** (**DML**) command, which helps to manipulate the form field, and **Script Includes** are like a central repository of code, where you place all your code and call from the client side.

Getting ready

To go through this recipe, you should have an active Service-Now instance and valid credentials with an admin role.

How to do it...

1. Open any standard web browser and type the instance address.
2. Log in to the instance using valid credentials.
3. To make recipe let's understand some basics out of the box, Service-Now provides predefined variables, which you can use globally:
    - `current`: The `current` variable refers to the Service-Now form, which is currently being displayed
    - `Previous`: This is the record before any changes were made. This variable is available on delete or update, but not available for the async business rule
    - `g_scratchpad`: The scratchpad object is available on the display **Business Rule** only, which is used to pass information to the client side
4. When a current record is being referenced, there may not be a current record when a business rule runs, which means that the `current` variable will be null. You should check for null before using the variable:

    ```
    if (current == null )
       return;
    ```

5. The types of business rules are as follows:
    - `Before`: You can use this business rule when you want to perform any action, but the `Before` data is stored in Service-Now tables.
    - `After`: You can use this business rule if you want to update related records that you want to display immediately.
    - `Display`: Performance of the Service-Now form is very important and you should always bear this in mind. By the display business rule, you can have server-side object access on the client side.
    - `Async`: You can use this business rule when you want to update information on related records that don't need to be displayed immediately.

Building Data-Driven Application

6. On the left-hand side in the search box, type **author registration** and service-now will search out **Author Registration** module for you. Now click on it to view the **Author Registration form**.
7. Now right click on the header of **Author Registration form**, as shown here and select **Business Rules**:

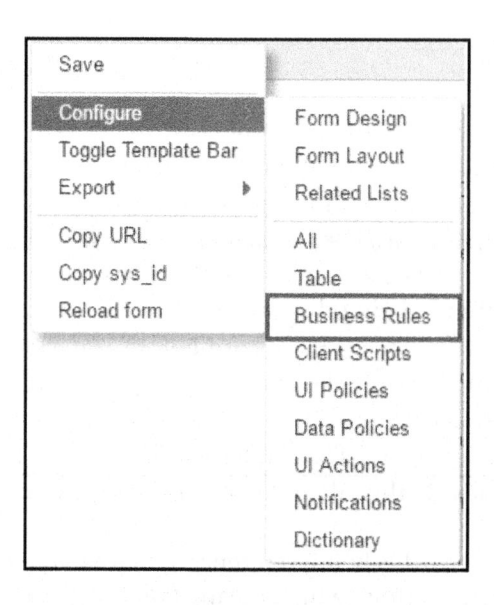

8. Now, you will be able to see the business rules record in following page, where you will need to click on the **New** button to create a new business rule:

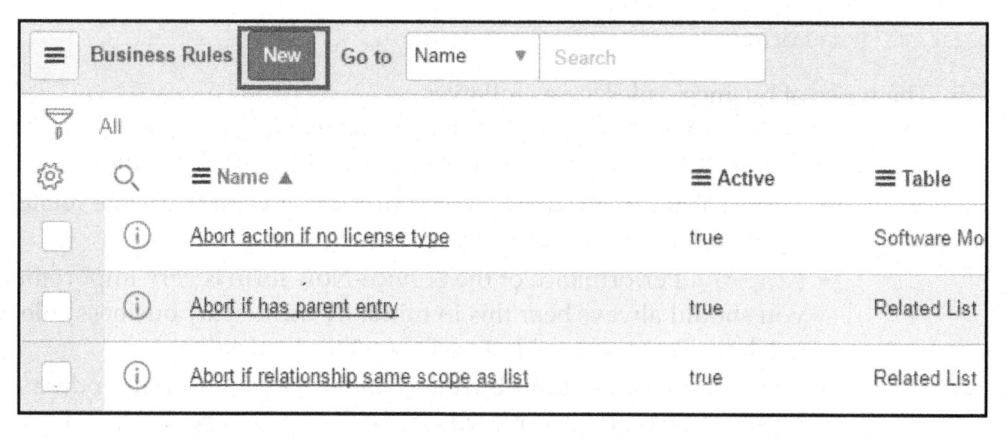

Create a new business rule

9. After clicking the **New** button, you will see the configure page, as shown, which needs to be configured as follows:
   - **Name:** create task for australia finance dep.
   - **Table:** Author Registration [u_author_registration]
   - **Advanced:** True

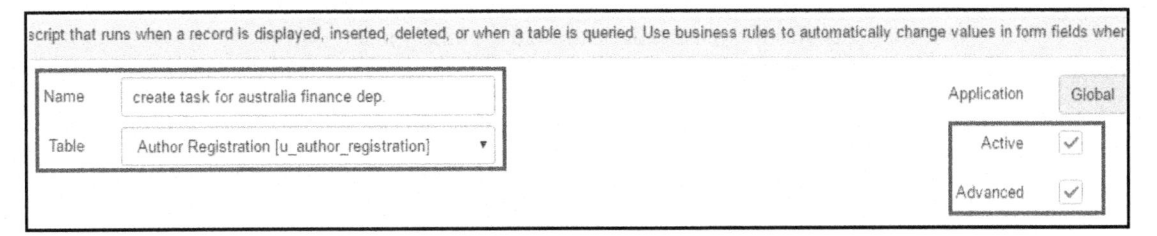

Business rule configuration

10. Now, you need to configure the condition for the business rule, as given:
    - **When:** after
    - **Country:** Australia
    - **Insert:** True

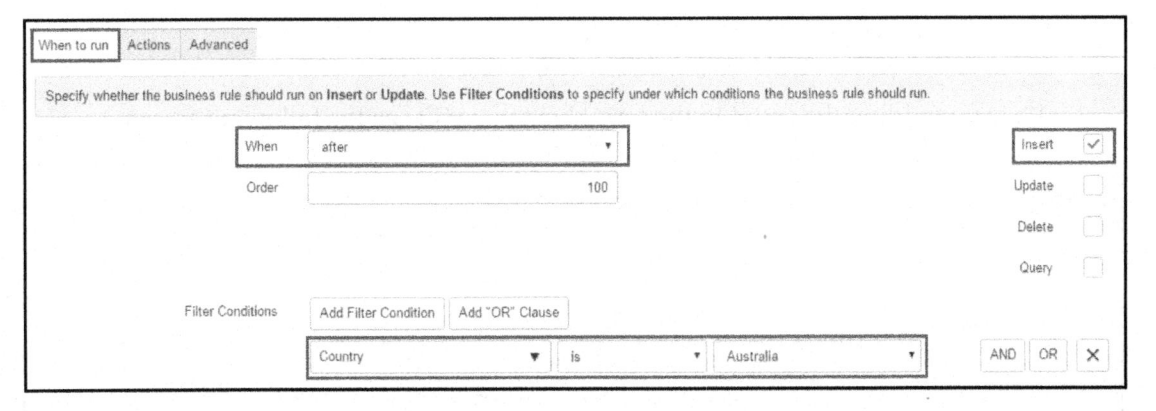

Business rule condition configuration

Building Data-Driven Application

11. Let's understand the basic difference between **Insert** and **Update**. For instance, if you have marked the **Insert** checkbox, then the business rule will be executed only once, but if you have marked the **Update** checkbox, then the business rule will be executed whenever a record is updated. If you have checked the **Advanced** field, then the **Advanced** form section will be visible on the form to add the following script:

    ```
    var aus_finance = new GlideRecord("task");
    aus_finance.short_description =
    current.short_description;
    aus_finance.u_country = current.description;
    aus_finance.u_currency =
    current.u_preferred_payment_currency;
    aus_finance.u_bank = current.u_bank_name;
    aus_finance.u_author = current.u_author_name;
    aus_finance.sys_domain = current.sys_domain;
    var sysID = aus_finance.insert();
    current.rfc = sysID;
    var mySysID = current.update();
    gs.addInfoMessage("Task"+ " " + aus_finance.number
      + " "+
                    "created for Australia finance
                     department" );
    action.setRedirectURL(aus_finance);
    action.setReturnURL(current);
    ```

12. After adding the script in the script box, you will see the following screen:

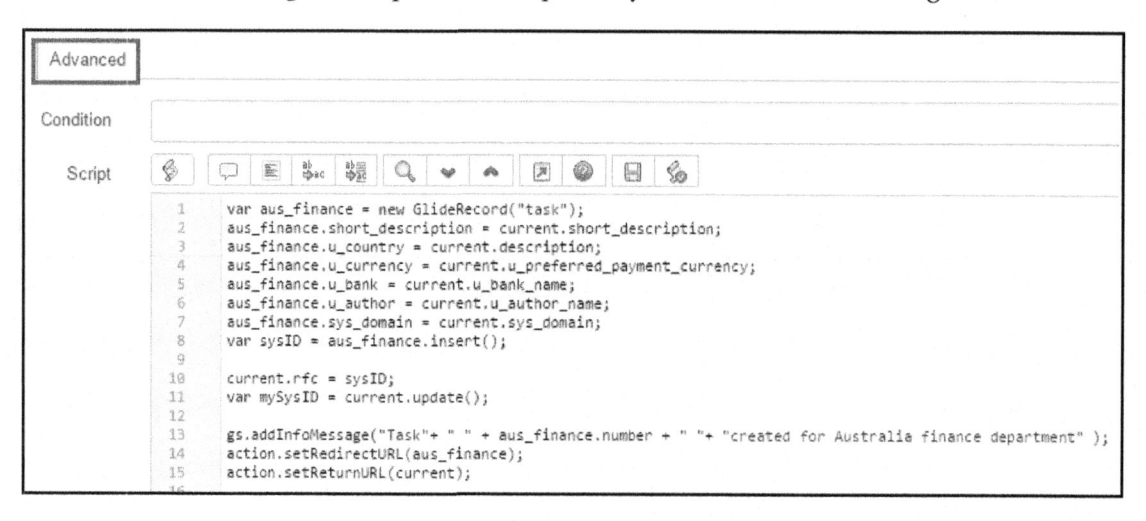

After business rule Script

[152]

13. Once the **Author Registration** form is submitted, you will see a message on the top of the form `Task TASK0020009 created for Australia finance department`, as shown:

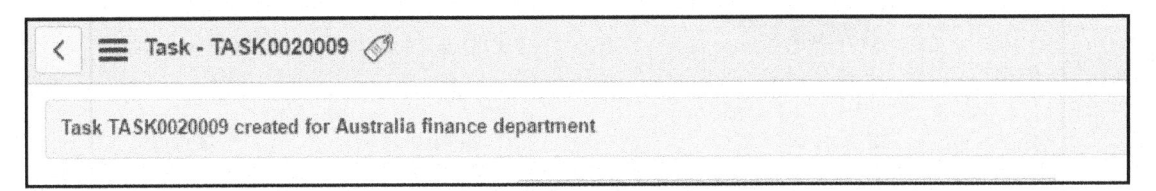

> Task - TASK0020009
>
> Task TASK0020009 created for Australia finance department

Task created for finance department

14. The **Script Includes** repository stores classes and functions to be used by a server script and run when it is called by a side script or client side script. It's a very efficient way to get information from the server-side without affecting performance.
15. To create **Script Includes**, type `script includes` in the search box on the left-hand side and Service-Now will search the modules for you. Click on **Script Includes** in the **System Definition** application, as shown:

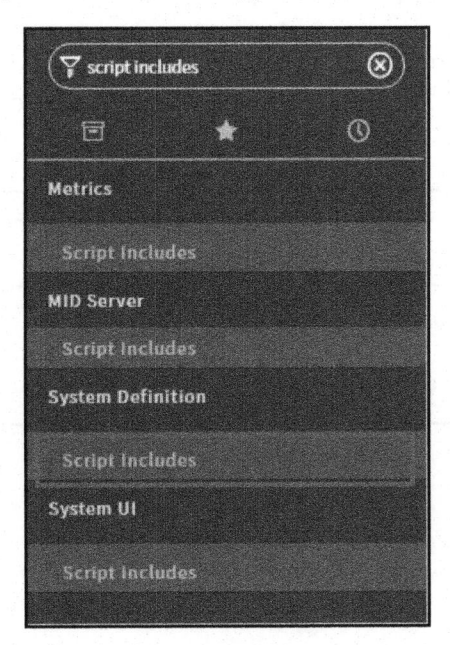

The Script include module

[153]

Building Data-Driven Application

16. Now, you will be able to see the **Script Includes** records page. To create a new script include, click on the **New** button:

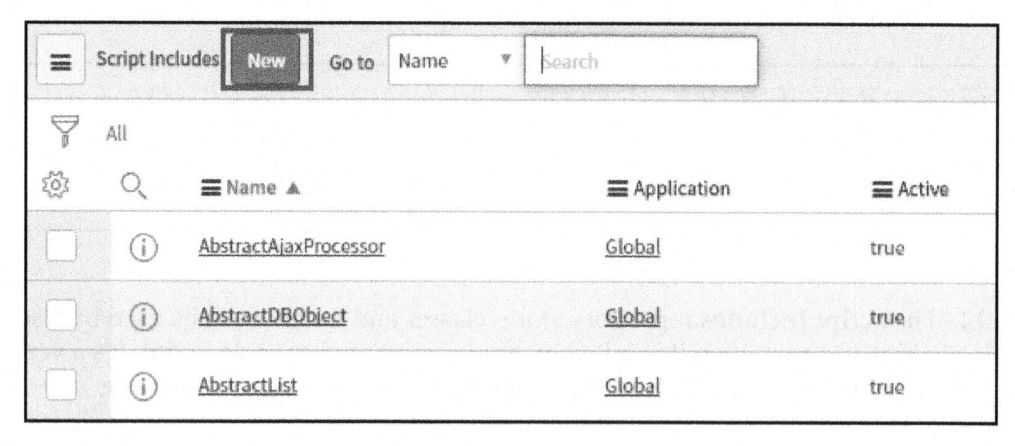

Create new Script Includes

17. Now you will see the configuration page, as shown, which needs to be configured as follows:

- **Name**: `AuthorRegistration`
- **API Name**: `global.AuthorRegistration` (**Auto populate**)
- **Client callable**: `True`

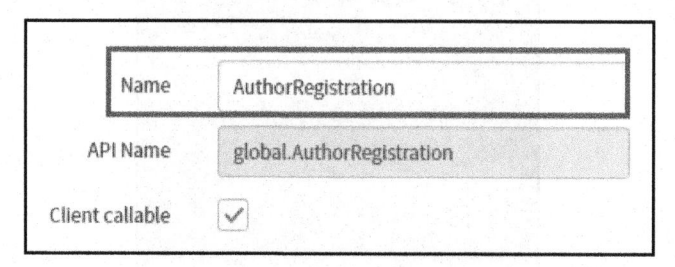

Script Includes configuration part 1

[154]

18. On the same page, you will be able to see the following screenshot:

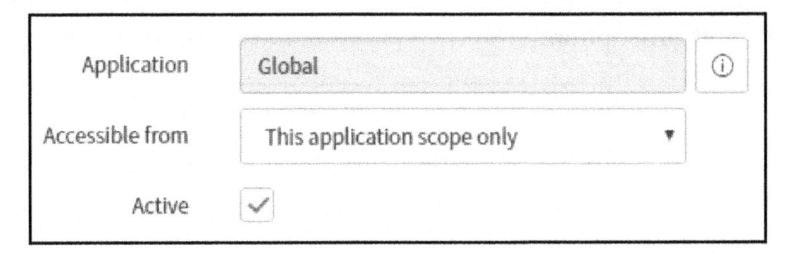

Script Includes configuration part 2

19. In the script box on the **Script Includes**, you can type the **Script**, as shown:

20. You can type the following script in the script include script box:

```
var AuthorRegistration = Class.create();
AuthorRegistration.prototype =
Object.extendsObject(AbstractAjaxProcessor,
  {
    AuthorRegistrationAlert:function()
      {
        // return value of contract end date to
confirm from user
        return "Please Confirm End Date is" + " " +
    this.getParameter('sysparm_contract_end');
      }
  }
);
```

Building Data-Driven Application

21. Now open the **Author Registration Form** again by Author registration module, On **Author Registration Form** right-click on the **header**, and select **Client Scripts** from **Configure** option:

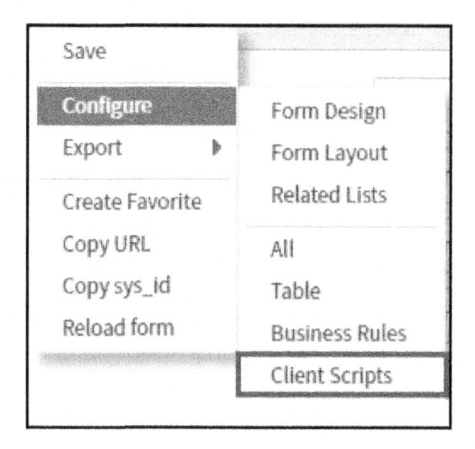

Create onChange script

22. Now, click on the **New** button and configure the client script, as given:

    - **Name:** GlideAjax - On Change Script
    - **Type:** onChange
    - **Field name:** Contract End Date
    - **Active:** True

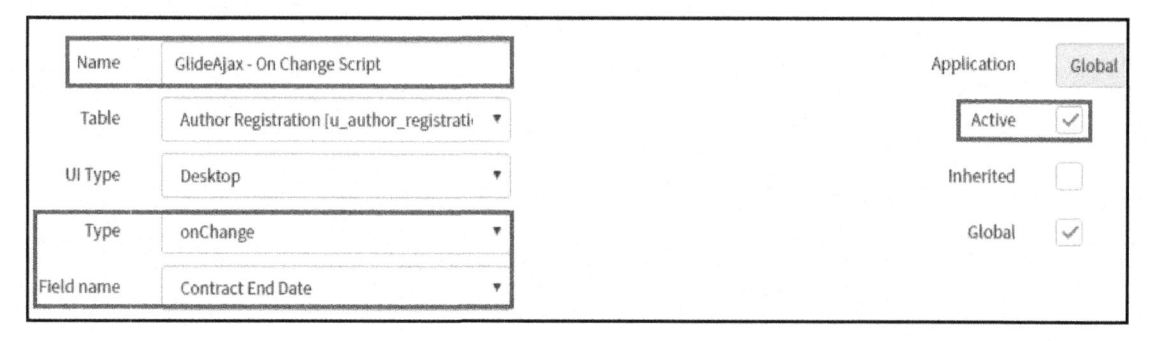

Client Script – onChange

23. Now, type the following script in the client script box:

```
function onChange(control, oldValue, newValue,
isLoading)
  {
```

```
      if (isLoading)
      {
       return;
      }
      // get value in con_end variable
       var con_end =
    g_form.getValue('u_contract_end_date');
      // call script include from client
       var ga = new GlideAjax('AuthorRegistration');
      //call function from script include
   ga.addParam('sysparm_name','AuthorRegistrationAlert');
      // pass contract end value to script include
       ga.addParam('sysparm_contract_end',con_end);
      //define function to get response from server
       ga.getXML(AuthorRegistrationParse);
      function AuthorRegistrationParse(response)
       {
          var answer=
   response.responseXML.documentElement.getAttribute
       ("answer");
       alert(answer);
      }
   }
```

```
function onChange(control, oldValue, newValue, isLoading)
{
  if (isLoading)
  {
  return;
  }
    // get value in con_end variable
    var con_end = g_form.getValue('u_contract_end_date');
    // call script include from client
    var ga = new GlideAjax('AuthorRegistration');
    //call function from script include
    ga.addParam('sysparm_name','AuthorRegistrationAlert');
    // pass contract end value to script include
    ga.addParam('sysparm_contract_end',con_end);
    //define function to get response from server
    ga.getXML(AuthorRegistrationParse);

    function AuthorRegistrationParse(response)
    {
        var answer= response.responseXML.documentElement.getAttribute("answer");
        alert(answer);

    }
}
```

OnChange client script

24. As an output, a dialog window will pop up when you enter `contract end date`:

> Please Confirm End Date is 2016-12-16
>
> ☐ Prevent this page from creating additional dialogs.
>
> OK

Alert box from GlideAjax

Understanding the team development plugin

The **Team Development** module is available out of the box, which is designed for developers only. For instance, if you are assigned to a big Service-Now development team where multiple developers are working on one application, then maintaining the entire development work is very difficult. The **Team Development** module provides many features that facilitate ease of development work management.

Getting ready

To go through this recipe, you must have an active Service-Now instance and valid credentials to log in with an admin role. Keep in mind that if you have a code reviewer in your team, then the reviewer must have the `teamdev_code_reviewer` role.

How to do it...

1. Open any standard web browser and type the instance address.
2. Log in to your Service-Now instance using the credentials.
3. If the **Team Development** module is not installed, then you can activate it by going to the plugin module, where you can search for it.

4. Once the module is activated, you can for search it by typing `team development` in the search box, as shown:

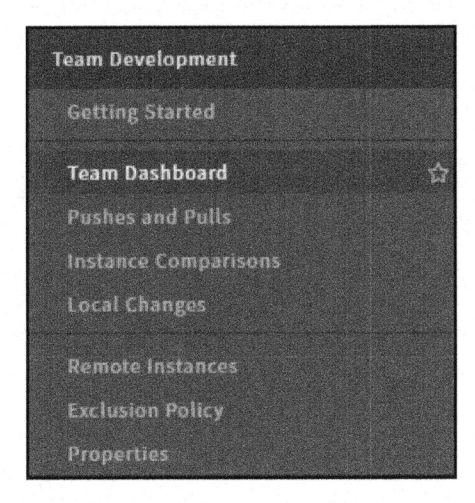

The team development module

5. In very big development project environments where multiple teams are working on one application, you can request sub development instances, but the parent will be your development instance only. For instance, if you want to set up three sub development instances, then you must do as shown:

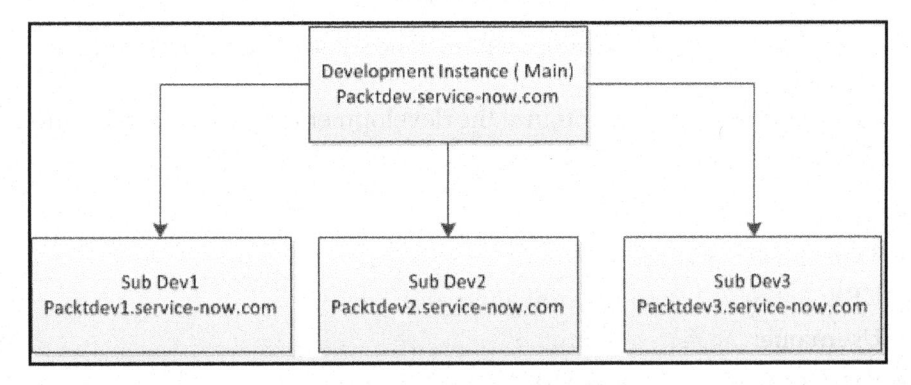

Instance classification for the team development module

6. Here, you should bear in mind that an additional subdevelopment instance may incur an additional charged by Service-Now.

Building Data-Driven Application

7. Click on the **Team Dashboard** module. You will see the following configuration page:

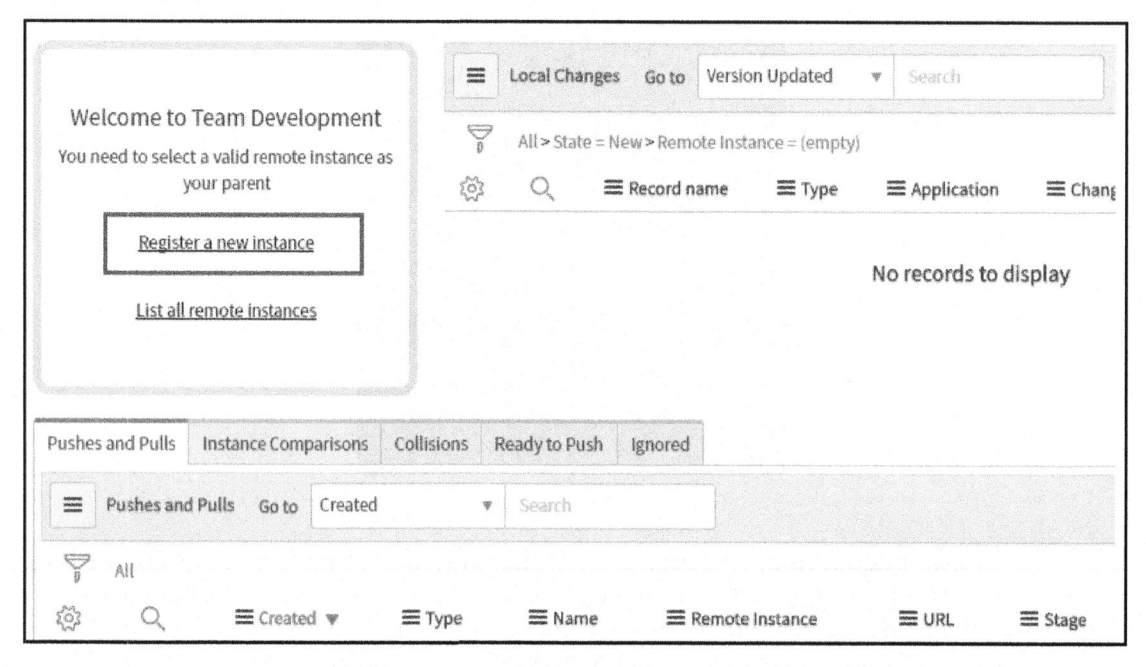

Team development

8. To register a new subdevelopment instance, you need to click on **Register a new instance**.
9. As an admin, you can configure the development instance's subinstances, as follows:

- **Name**: `SubDev1`
- **Type**: `Development`
- **URL**: `Subdevelopment instance URL`
- **Username**: `Admin account`
- **Password**: `Admin password`
- **Test connection**: Click on **Test Connection** and **Submit**:

[160]

Team development configuration page

10. After submission of the form, you will see the following page where you can **Push** and **Pull** items from and to parent instances:

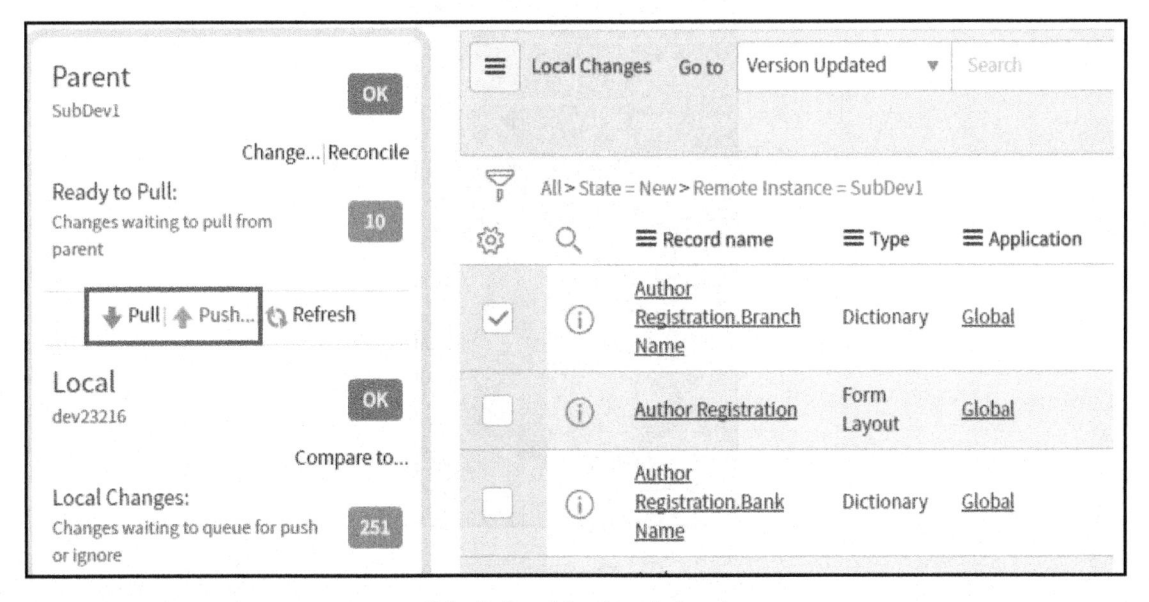

Push and pull records through team development

Understand web services

Out of box, service-now provide channels to communicate with outside world. Service-now is capable enough to communicate over HTTP based web services. It's is advisable to use MID (Management, Instrumentation, and Discovery) to communicate to outside world as MID server communicate over HTTP to communicate to service-now instances.

Building Data-Driven Application

Getting ready

To step through this recipe, you should have active instance and valid credentials with admin/web services role.

How to do it...

1. Open any standard web browser and type instance address.
2. Login in service-now instance with valid credentials.
3. On left hand side in search box, type `web services` and service-now will search out module for you as shown following:

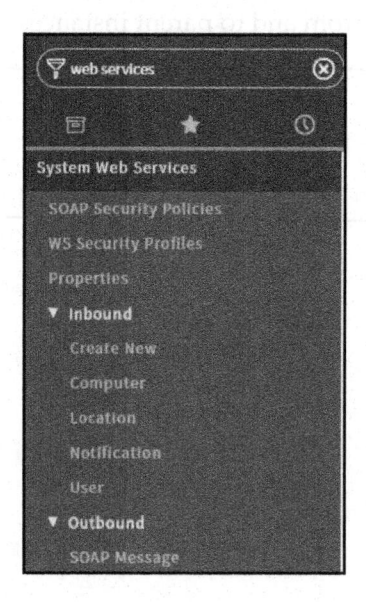

Web services

4. Out of box, service-now provides following types of web services.
   - **Publisher**: By publishing the web services, you can provide data to external sources to consume. Each service-now table has potential to publish its data to external system.
   - Click: **Create New** under **Inbound** to create new inbound web services

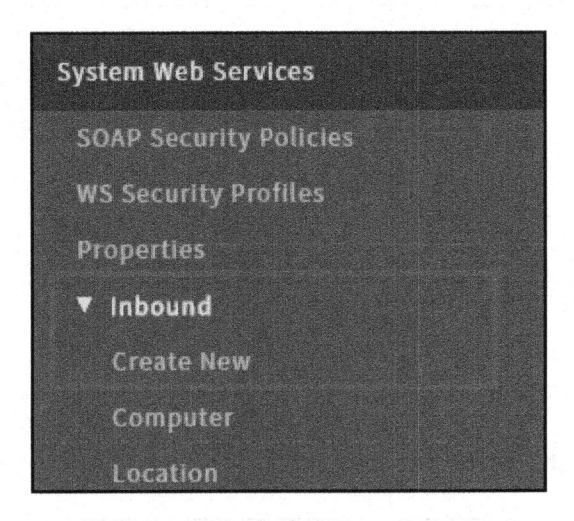

   Inbound web services

5. After clicking, you will able to see web service configuration page where you need to enter following fields:
   - **Label**: incident table publish
   - **Name**: u_incident_table_publish (auto populate)

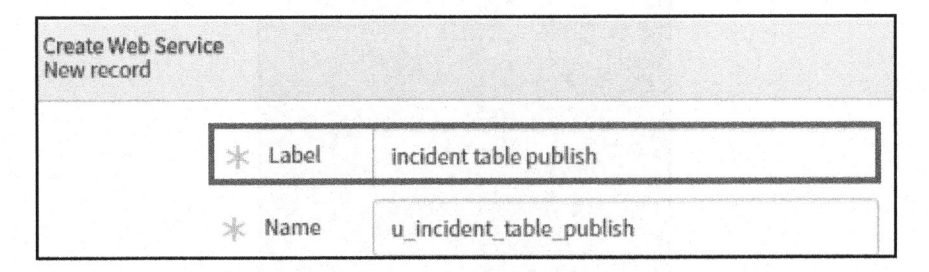

   Inbound web service configuration part 1

[163]

Building Data-Driven Application

6. After configuring basic fields, you will need to enter target table from which fields will be published:
     - **Target table**: Incident
     - **Copy fields from target table:** true

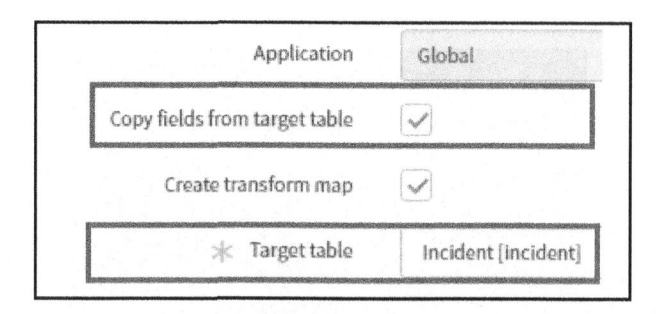

Inbound web service configuration part 2

7. Click **Create** button to create new web service.
8. After clicking **Create** button. A new web service **incident table publish** will be added in **System Web Services** as shown following:

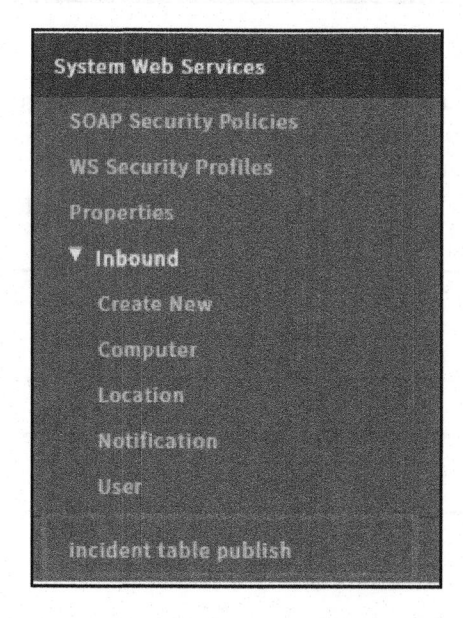

New web service incident table publish created

9. Once web service is created and added in **System Web Services**. You will able to view WSDL of your inbound web service. Through web services's **WSDL** you can access incident's table fields which will be available inn XML format:

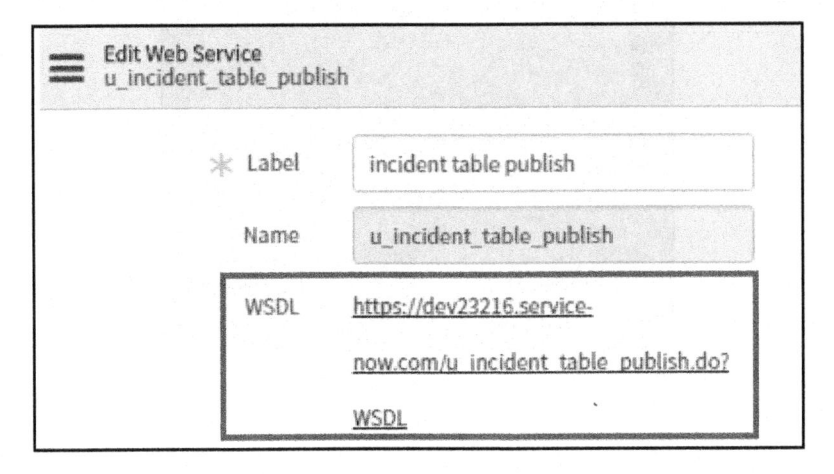

Edit Web Service
u_incident_table_publish

* Label	incident table publish
Name	u_incident_table_publish
WSDL	https://dev23216.service-now.com/u_incident_table_publish.do?WSDL

Inbound email WSDL

10. In additon, you will able to see all your fields from target tables as shown following from incident table:

Web Service Fields

		Label	Name ▲
✕	ⓘ	Active	active
✕	ⓘ	Activity due	activity_due
✕	ⓘ	Additional assignee list	additional_assignee_list

Web services fields

- **Consumer**: By creating outbound message. you can create, read, update or delete records through 3rd party web services and also invoke web services

11. Now click on **SOAP Message** module under Outbound section to create new **SOAP Message** as follows:

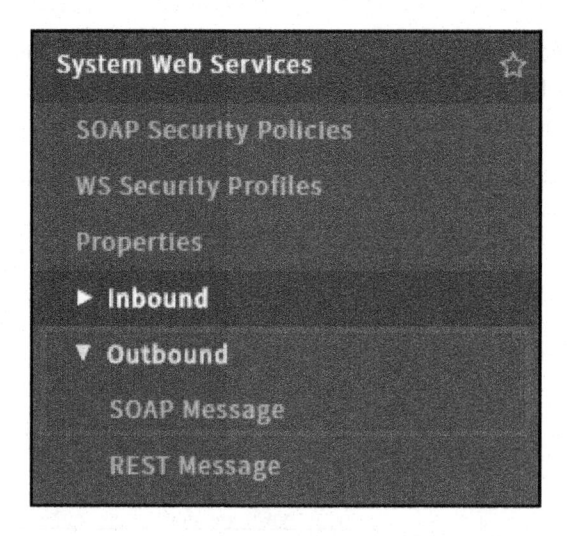

Outbound web service

12. Now you will able to see all SOAP messages in following screen where you need to click on **new** button to create **SOAP Messages**:

Outbound SOAP messages

13. Now, you can configure the SOAP message as following:
    - **Name** : `Outbound web service`
    - **WSDL** : `https://dev23216.service-now.com/u_incident_table_publish.do?WSDL`

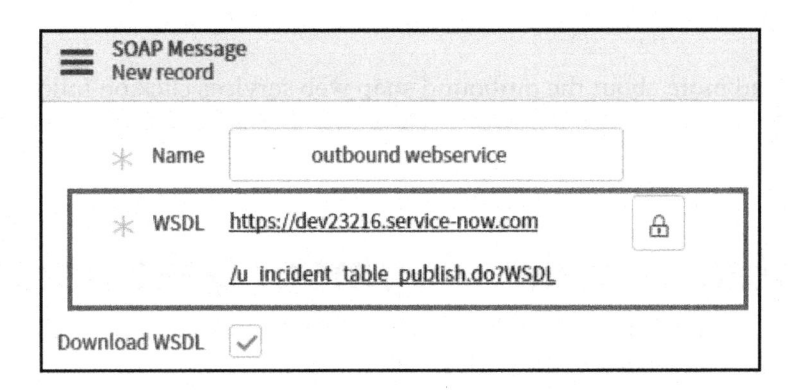

Add WSDL in outbound web services

14. Click on **Submit** button.
15. Now after submission, you can see all the functions which are available for integration purpose:

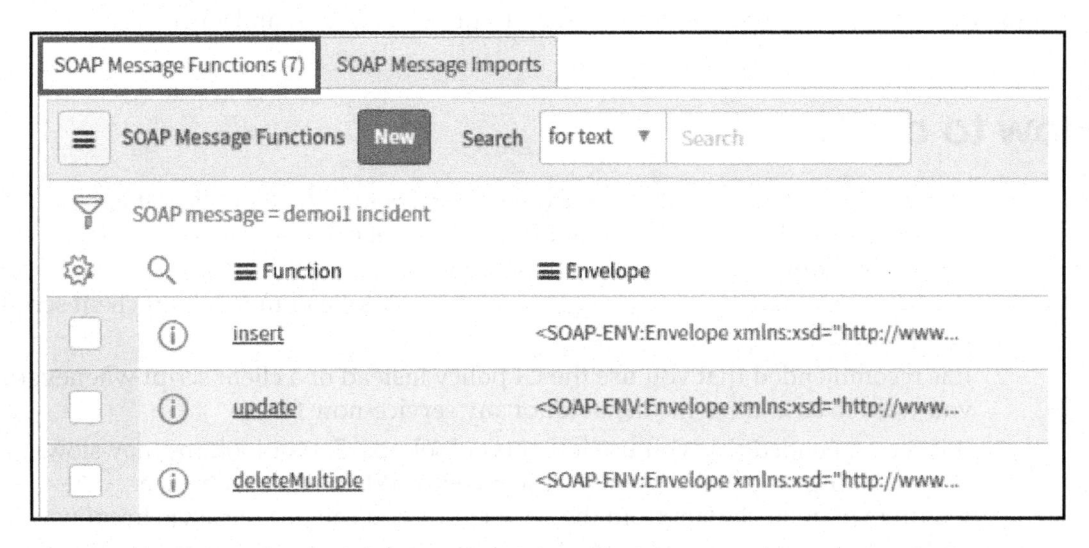

SOAP Message Functions

[167]

16. Now after successful authentication, you can use for **insert**, **update**, **deleteMultiple**, and so on actions in business rules and scripts.

See also

- To read more about the outbound soap web services click on following link `http://wiki.servicenow.com/index.php?title=Outbound_SOAP_Web_Service#gsc.tab=0`

Understanding development best practice

Service-now recommends that you follow the product development best practices for rapid development and for enhancing the performance.

Getting ready

Getting the desired result is not very difficult, but getting the desired result by following the best practices is a challenge in itself. If development works were not done by following the best practices, you may face performance issues, frequent incidents, and so on.

How to do it...

1. The client script loads on the service-now form before the UI policy. It is recommended that you use a minimum number of client scripts as the client script slows down the form Please follow `http://wiki.servicenow.com/index.php?title=Client_Script_Best_Practices` link to read more about client script best practices.
2. It is recommended that you use the UI policy instead of a client script whenever you want to customize the behavior of any service-now form.
3. It is recommended that you use less server lookups. Server lookups may slow down loading or lock the form for few seconds. Whenever you have a requirement to fetch data from the server side, you can use the asynchronous glide ajax function, which doesn't lock the form as compared to the synchronous glide ajax function.

4. Business rules are like your database operation commands. When you want to insert/delete/update any record, you can use business rule, but while setting up business rule conditions remember that a record can be inserted only time, but updates may happen multiple times. Please follow `http://wiki.servicenow.com/index.php?title=Business_Rules_Best_Practices` link to read more about best practices of business rule.

It is not recommended that you create a global business rule. Instead of a global business rule, you can create script includes, which behave like your central repository of functions and you can call them on the client side. Note that by selecting a table as global, you are allowed to create a global business rule.

4
Configuring Alerts and Notifications

In this chapter, we will cover the following recipes:

- Understanding the Service-Now system mailbox
- Creating a new e-mail notification
- Creating an e-mail template
- Creating an e-mail notification script
- Setting up an inbound e-mail action
- Inbound e-mail action – new
- Inbound e-mail action – forward
- Inbound e-mail action – reply
- E-mail notification by event registry
- E-mail notification troubleshooting

Introduction

Communication and notification are two essential pillars of the IT service management application. Therefore, Service-Now has an inbuilt functionality to send or receive e-mails from mailboxes or user accounts like other enterprise applications. To send an e-mail notification from a Service-Now instance, you will have to configure the e-mail notification to trigger end users. In many cases, customers ask for a functionality to log a ticket via e-mail, but you should not worry as Service-Now provides this functionality out of the box.

Understanding the Service-Now system mailbox

Microsoft Outlook is widely used by many individuals and corporate houses for e-mail communication. If you have worked on Microsoft Outlook, then you will be able to correlate the Service-Now system mailbox effortlessly. This recipe will show you how to check incoming or outgoing of Service-Now e-mails for troubleshooting purposes.

Getting ready

Service-Now has built-in mailboxes called **System Mailboxes**, which facilitate e-mail communication regardless of inbound or outbound e-mail. To step through this recipe, you should have an active Service-Now instance, valid credentials, and the admin role.

How to do it...

1. Open any standard web browser and type the Service-Now instance address.
2. Log in to the Service-Now instance using your credentials.
3. On the left-hand side in the search box, type `system mailbox`:

Search the Service-Now system mailbox

4. You will be able to see the **System Mailbox** application on the left-hand side:

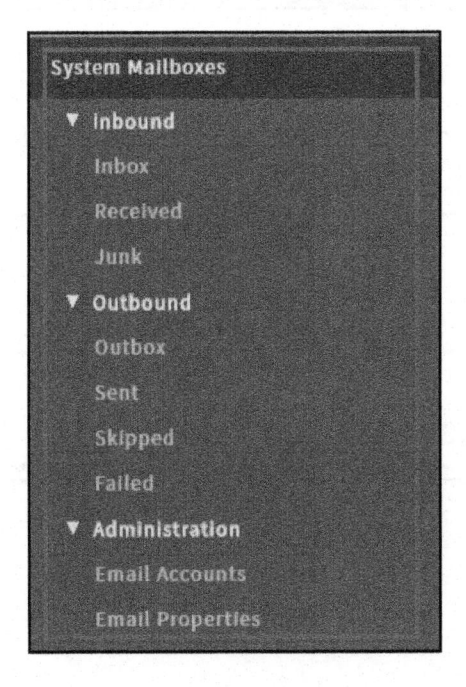

The System Mailbox application

Configuring Alerts and Notifications

5. Before going further, you should understand the background of **System Mailboxes.** The Service-Now system mailbox application is divided into the following parts:
    - The **Inbound** part of **System Mailboxes** is dedicated to incoming e-mail with respect to the Service-Now instance. So, for instance, if you compare the system mailbox with Microsoft Outlook, then you will be able to correlate it with your e-mail inbox, which stores all the e-mails regardless of who sends them:

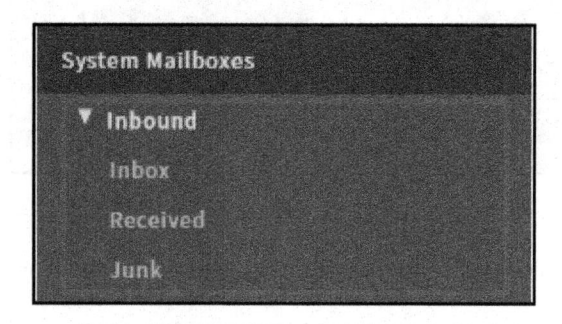

System mailbox – Inbound part

    - If you click on **Inbox**, you will be able to see incoming e-mails in the inbox, as shown in the following screenshot:

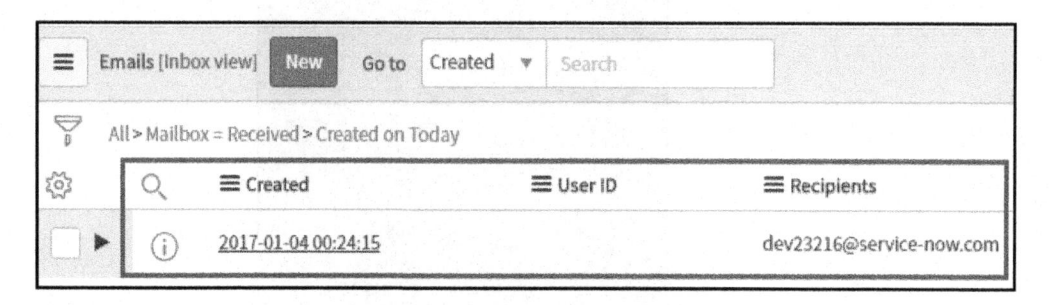

System mailbox – Inbox view

- The **Outbound** part of the system mailbox is dedicated for all outgoing e-mails. So, for an example, if you again compare the system mailbox with Microsoft Outlook, then you will be able to correlate it with your outbox or sent e-mail. For better understanding, ideally when any incident is created or updated an e-mail notification is triggered to end user so you will be able to see a log in the **Sent** module, which verifies that service-now has sent an e-mail to the end user:

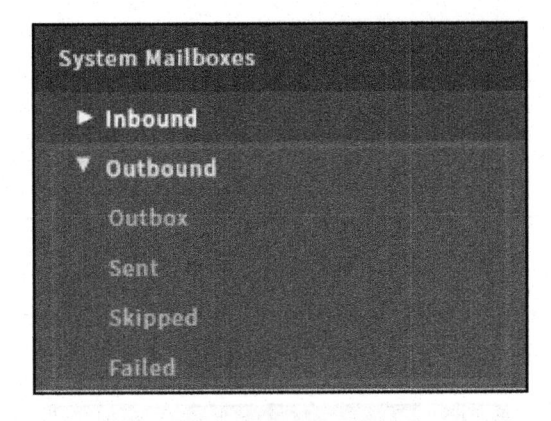

System mailbox – Outbound part

- If you click on the **Sent** module, then you will be able to see all the e-mails that have been sent from the Service-Now instance, as follows:

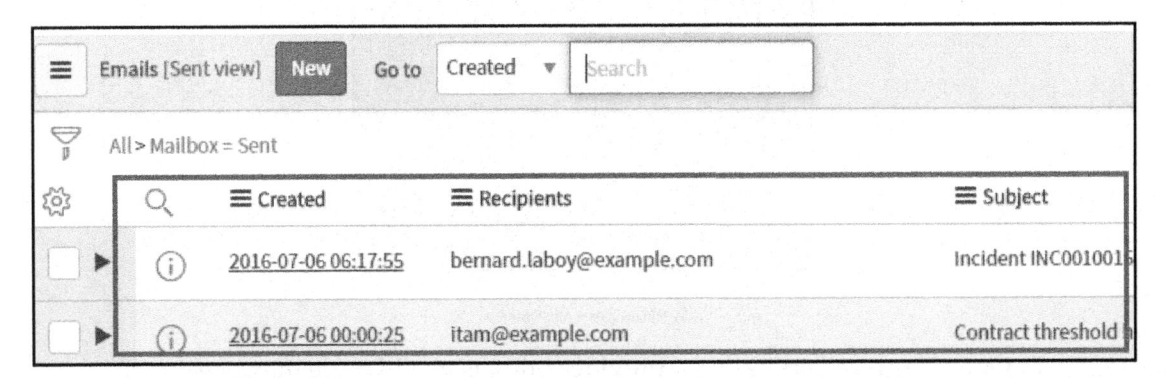

System mailbox – Sent view

Configuring Alerts and Notifications

- If you click on the **Outbox** module, then you will be able to see all the e-mails that are pending or in the process of being sent out from the Service-Now instance:

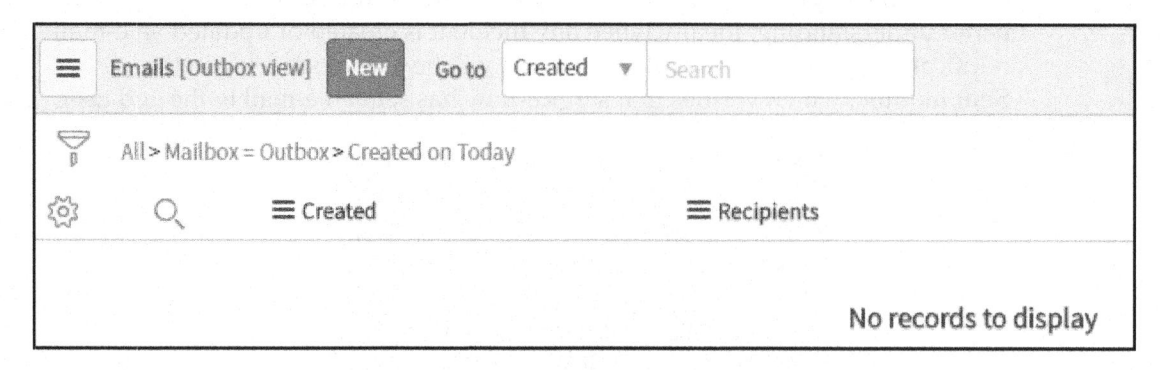

System mailbox – outbox view

6. The **Administration** module is part of the Service-Now **System Mailboxes** application, which includes many key features for troubleshooting:

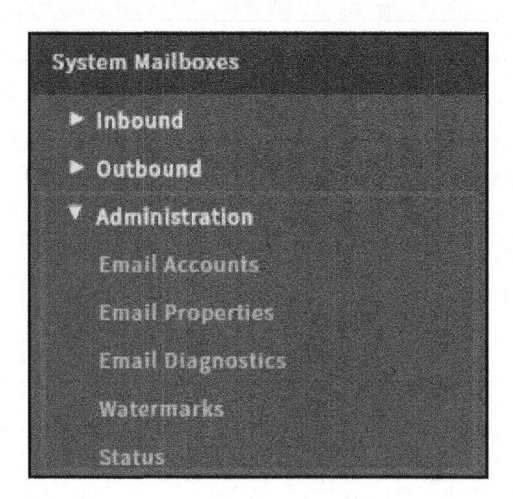

System mailbox – Administration

7. Out of the box, Service-Now provides options to add more than one e-mail account (incoming or outgoing) apart from system mailboxes. It is important for you to know that Service-Now supports **SMTP**, **POP3**, and IMPS account types. While implementing this, keep in mind that there can be only one outgoing **SMTP** server for sending e-mail from Service-Now:

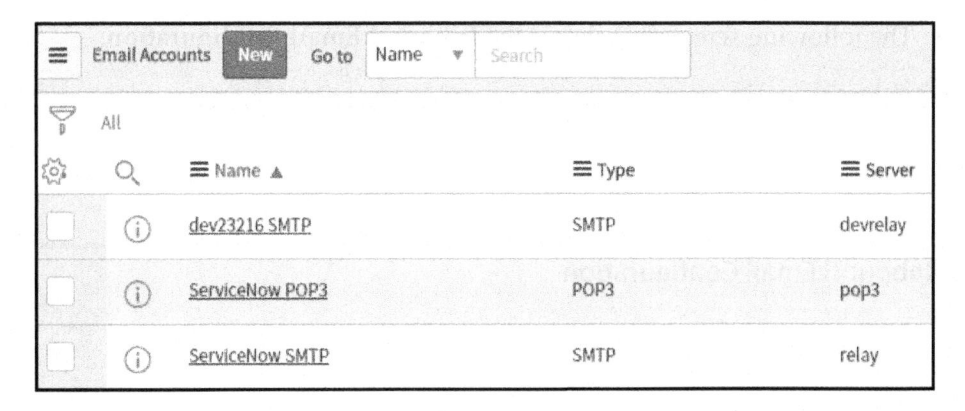

	Name ▲	Type	Server
ⓘ	dev23216 SMTP	SMTP	devrelay
ⓘ	ServiceNow POP3	POP3	pop3
ⓘ	ServiceNow SMTP	SMTP	relay

Email Accounts – List View

8. The **Email Properties** module is the heart of e-mail notifications. From here, you will be able to decide whether you want to send or receive an e-mail notification or not. So, if you want to send an e-mail notification to an end user, check the **Email sending enabled** box, or if you want to receive e-mails from the end user, then check **Email receiving enabled**. The following screenshot shows the outbound e-mail configuration properties:

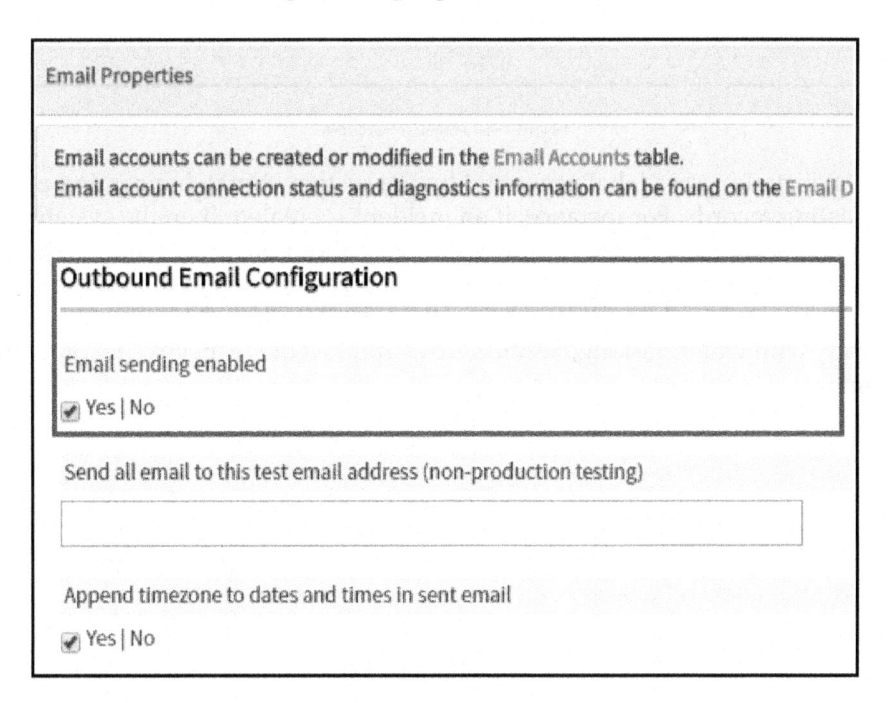

Outbound Email properties configuration

9. The following screenshot shows the **Inbound Email Configuration**:

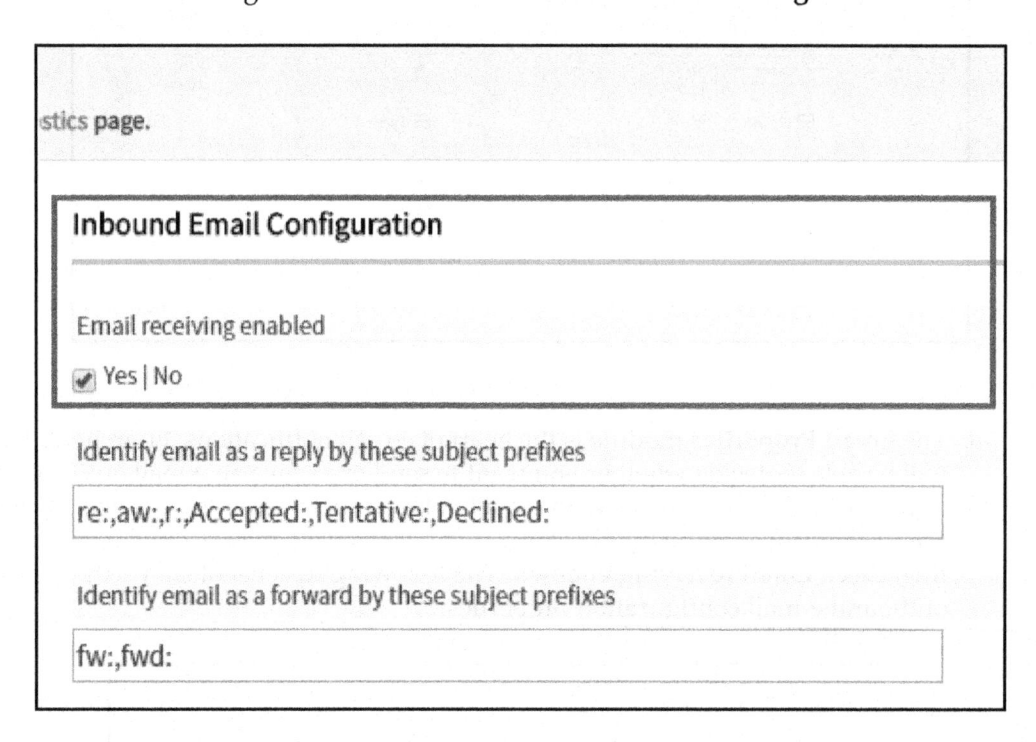

Inbound e-mail properties configuration

10. Watermarking is a label generated by the system to match incoming e-mail to existing records. For instance, if an incident is created, then the system triggers an e-mail notification to the end user to notify about incident details. The end user has two options to provide comments on the incident: On the Service-Now instance, or by adding comments in the e-mail itself and sending it back. In this way, with watermarking, Service-Now updates the respective records via e-mails:

Chapter 4

> **Preview email**
>
> Click here to view Request: REQ0010001
>
> Number: REQ0010001
> Due date: 2015-07-25 23:47:41 PDT
> Opened: 2015-07-23 23:47:42 PDT
> Approval: Approved
>
> Requested items:
> RITM0010001: Apple iPad 3, Stage: Fulfillment
>
> `Ref:MSG0000012`   Watermark

Watermark in an e-mail notification

On many occasions, customers don't want watermarks in e-mail notifications for a better look and feel, so in such scenarios, you also can hide watermarks globally:

1. In the search box, type `[sys_properties.list]`.
2. Add a new property called `[glide.email.watermark.visible]` and set it to `false`.

Creating a new e-mail notification

Standard communication is necessary for the end user. This recipe will show you how to create a new e-mail notification for end users, IT staff, stakeholders, and so on.

Getting ready

To step through this recipe, you should have an active Service-Now instance, valid credentials, and the admin role.

How to do it...

1. Open any standard web browser and type the instance address.
2. Log in to the Service-Now instance using the credentials.
3. On the left-hand side in the search box, type `system notification`:

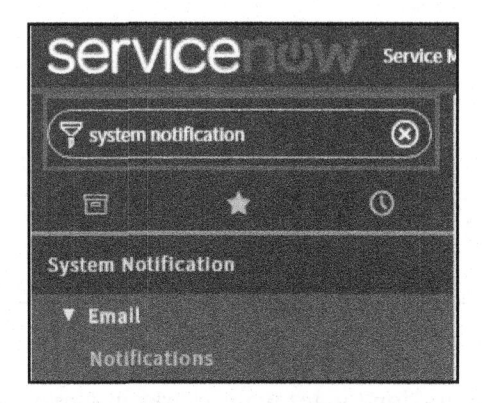

The search system notification application

4. Now you will be able to see the **System Notification** application on the left-hand side:

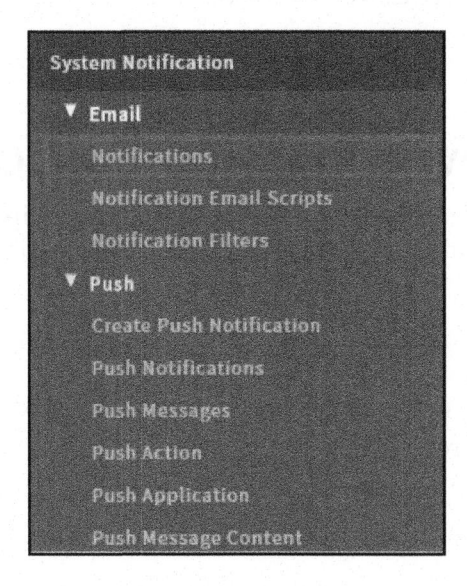

The System Notification application

5. Click on the **Notification** module. You will be able to see all the out-of-the-box notifications provided by Service-Now:

System notification configuration records – List View

6. In order to create a new notification, click on the **New** button. You will be redirected to the notification configuration page and you can configure it as follows:

- **Name**: Incident P1
- **Table**: Incident [incident]

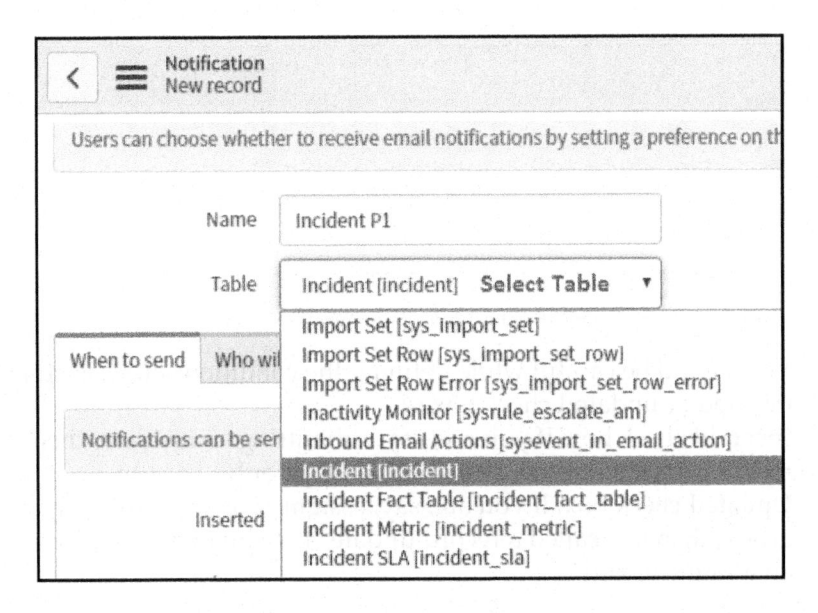

Select the table for e-mail notification configuration

Configuring Alerts and Notifications

7. After configuring, you will be able to see the following screen. After selecting the **Tables** and entering the notification name, you need to define the conditions:

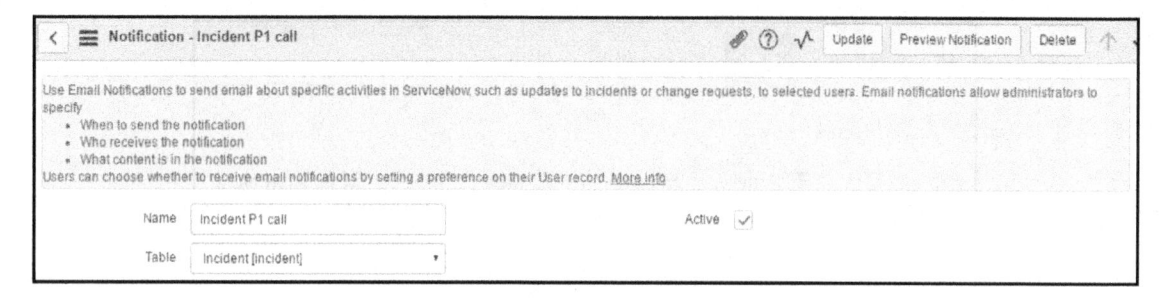

The Configure Email Notification page

8. The **When to send** section is for configuring the conditions. I have defined a condition that "If the incident priority is P1", send out a notification; likewise, you will need to define a condition to send notifications according to your business requirement:

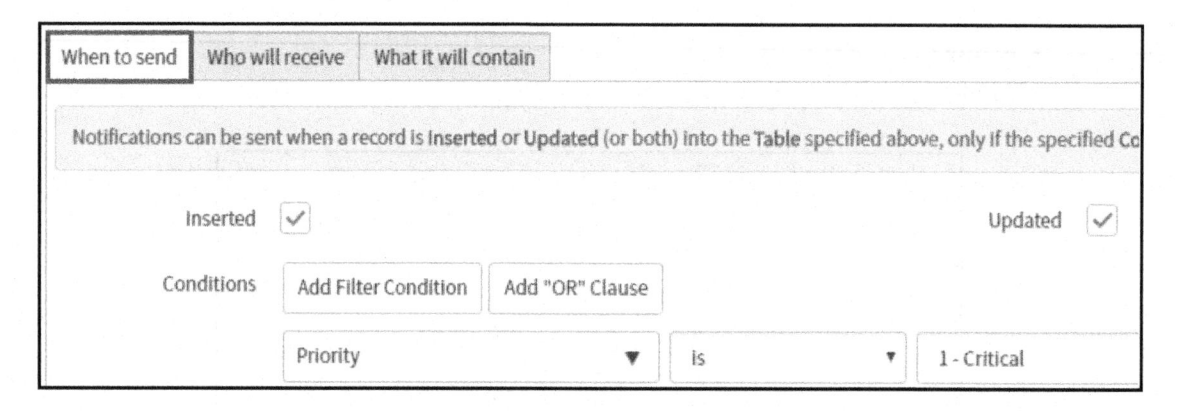

The Configure Email Notification – the When to send section

You should be careful while defining the conditions and selecting the inserted or updated check boxes:

Inserted check box: If you are, say, submitting an incident, then it is called record insertion, so there will be one insert only

Updated check box: If you are, say, assigning an incident to the resolver group, then it is called a record update, so there may be multiple updates on a single record

[182]

Chapter 4

9. The **Who will receive** section is for the recipient's configuration. Service-Now provides the feature of including user name, field name, and group name out of the box. If you want to include the name of any user directly in the e-mail notification, you can do so:

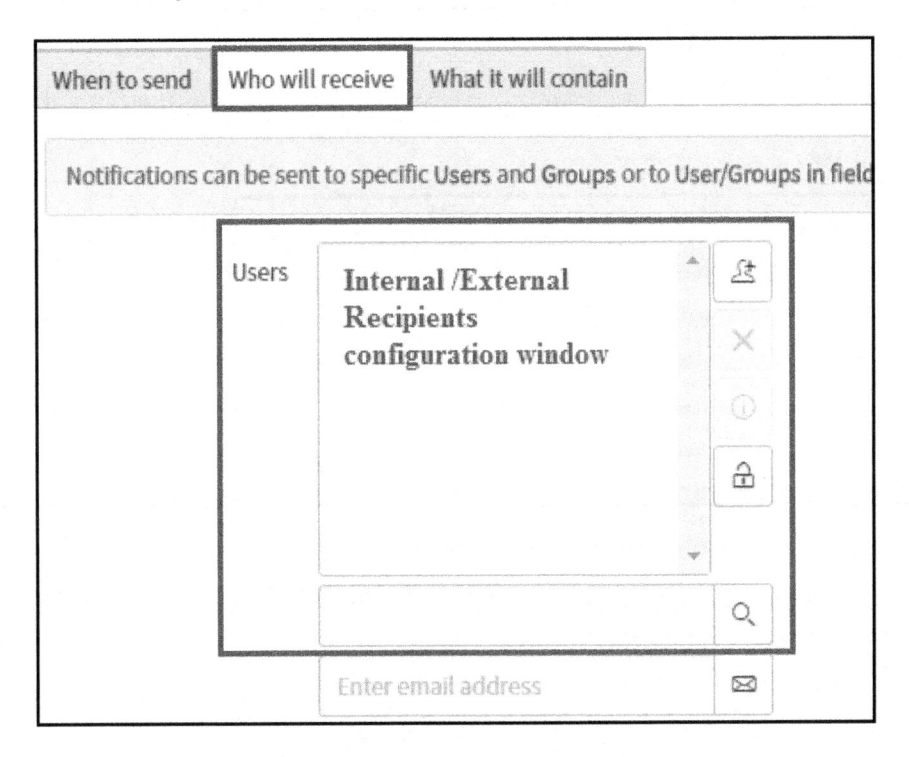

```
When to send | Who will receive | What it will contain

Notifications can be sent to specific Users and Groups or to User/Groups in field

Users    Internal /External
         Recipients
         configuration window


         Enter email address
```

Configure Email Notification – the Who will receive section part 1

> It's not recommended to include user names in e-mail notification configurations, as by doing this, a restriction is put on the reusability of the e-mail notification.

Configuring Alerts and Notifications

10. By selecting the **incident** table, you get access to the incident fields in e-mail notifications. So in the **User/Groups in fields** field, you can select more than one field to send out notifications:

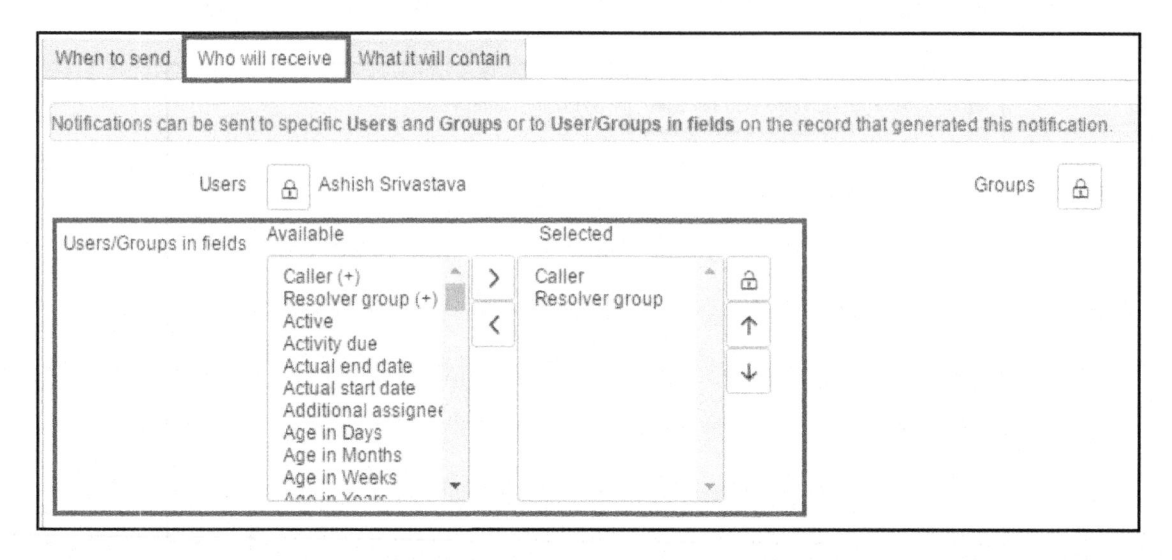

Configure Email Notification – the Who will receive section part 2

> If you want to send out notifications to the caller and resolver group, then you can select them.

11. As an output, You will be able to see the following:

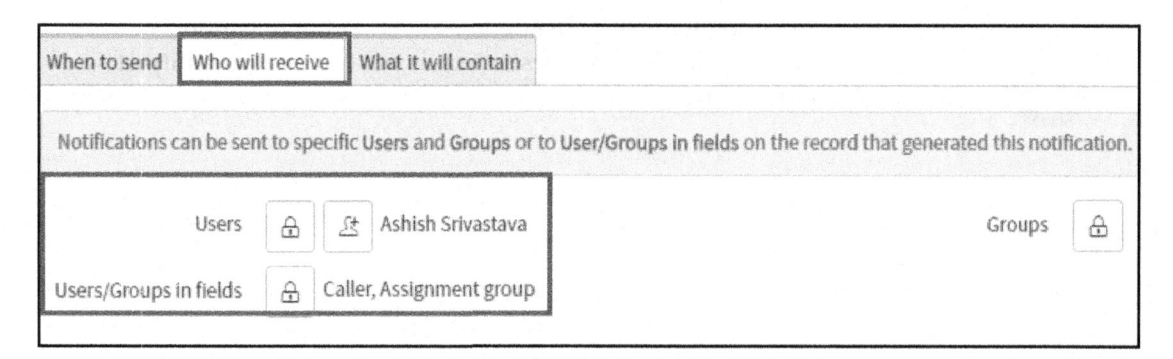

The Configure Email Notification – the Who will receive section part III

[184]

12. Now you need to configure the look and feel of e-mail notifications. There are two ways to do it: either you can configure them here, in **What it will contain** section or you can use e-mail templates. However, the advantage of **Email template** is that it is reusable components that can be used by more than one e-mail notification:

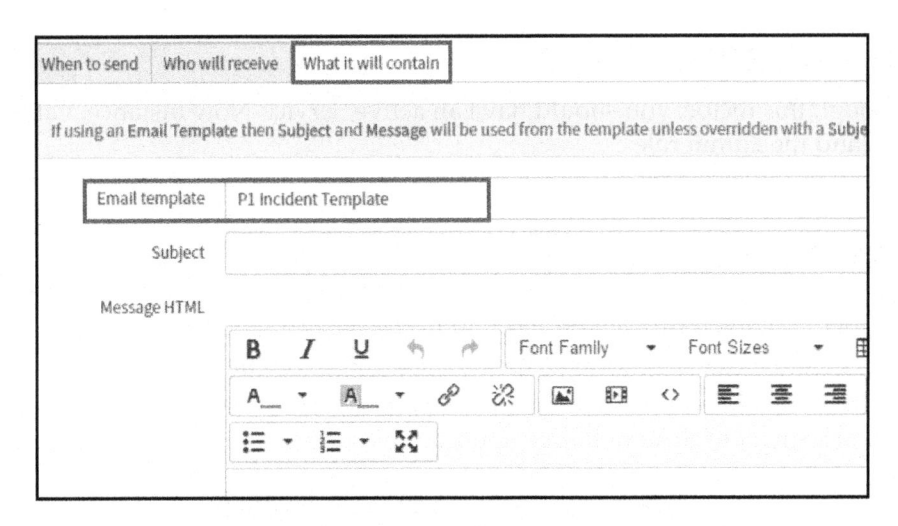

Configure Email Notification – the What it will contain section

13. Now click on the **update** button, and your e-mail notification configuration is ready, as shown here:

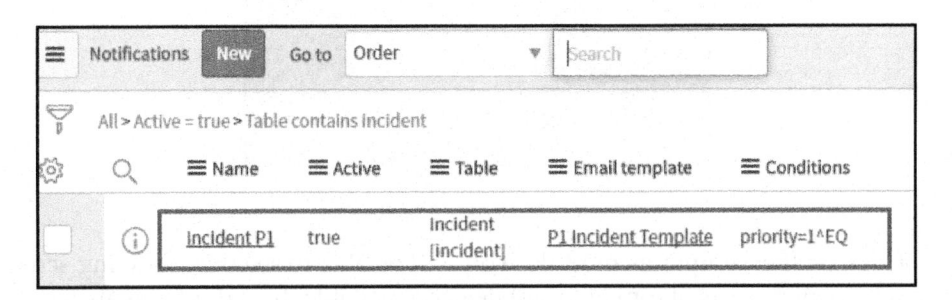

Output

14. As an output, if incident priority is critical then email notification **Incident P1** will be triggered by using **P1 Incident Template**.

Creating an e-mail template

An e-mail template is a reusable component that may be used with more than one e-mail notification to maintain the look and feel of the e-mail notification of the organization.

Getting ready

To step through this recipe, you should have an active Service-Now instance, valid credentials, and the admin role.

How to do it...

1. Open any standard web browser and type the instance Web address.
2. Log in to the Service-Now instance using the credentials.
3. On the left-hand side in the search box, type `System Policy` and service-now will search out **System Policy** application for you:

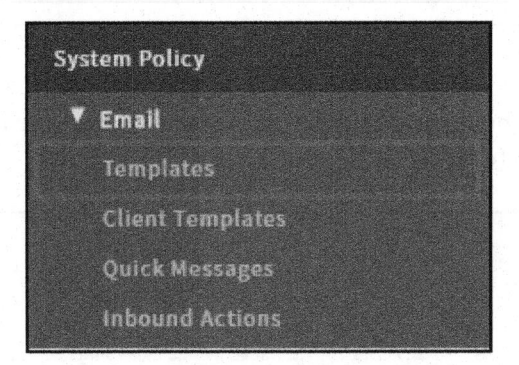

The System Policy Application for Email Template

4. Click on the **Templates** module. You will be able to see the following screen, where all records of e-mail templates are available. In order to create a new e-mail template, you need to click on the **New** button:

Chapter 4

≡ Email Templates **New** Go to Name ▼ Search

All

	≡ Name ▲	≡ Subject
▶ ⓘ	change.calendar.integration	SPECIAL CASE TEMPLATE -- Push changes in...
▶ ⓘ	change.calendar.integration.remove	SPECIAL CASE TEMPLATE -- Push changes in...

Email template configuration records – List View

5. In **Email Templates**, you will need to configure fields as mentioned in the next few steps:
    1. In the **Name** field, enter the desired name by which you want to recognize this e-mail notification; I've made it `P1 Incident Template`.
    2. In the **Table** field, you will need to select a table name to which you want to apply this e-mail template; I have selected **Incident** because I want to apply this template to the incident table's e-mail notification:

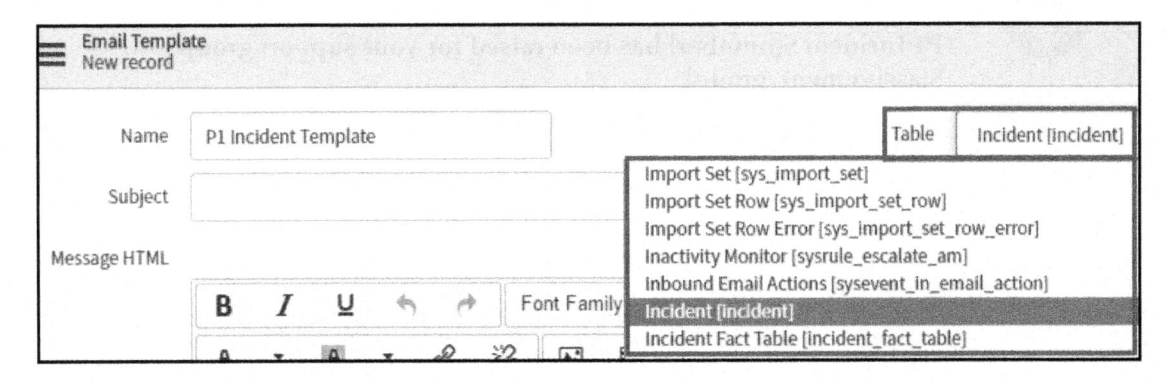

Email Template New record			
Name	P1 Incident Template	Table	Incident [incident]
Subject		Import Set [sys_import_set]	
		Import Set Row [sys_import_set_row]	
		Import Set Row Error [sys_import_set_row_error]	
Message HTML		Inactivity Monitor [sysrule_escalate_am]	
		Inbound Email Actions [sysevent_in_email_action]	
	B I U ↶ ↷ Font Family	**Incident [incident]**	
		Incident Fact Table [incident_fact_table]	

The Email Template table section

[187]

6. The **Subject** is the most critical part of an e-mail notification. You can add any meaningful subject in the **Subject** field:

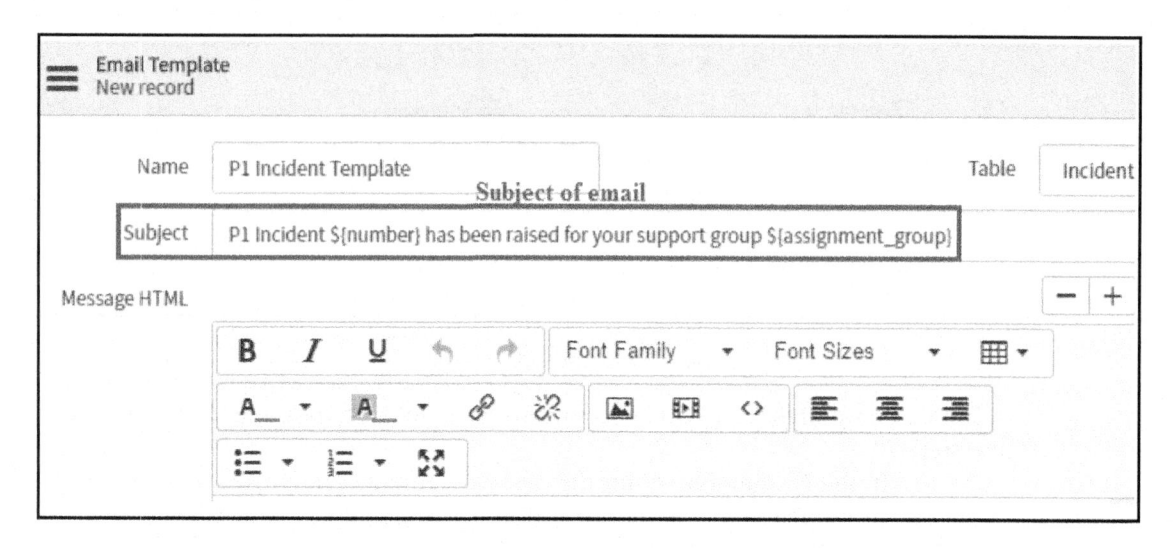

Email template configuration part 1

> You can also access incident form field values using `${variable_name}`. For example, if you want to include the incident number and assignment group name in the e-mail subject, then you can use the following:
>
> **P1 Incident ${number} has been raised for your support group ${assignment_group}**

7. Now you need to design the look and feel of the e-mail notification for end users. The Service-Now **Message HTML** field supports HTML, so you can design the look and feel according to your requirements:

Email Template – Editing tools

8. You can make an e-mail template like the following one, but you need to make sure whether a label is referring to a field; if it is, then it should have a field value you can access using `${field_name}` from the table:

Packt Service Desk			
System notification – Call Id ${number}			
If necessary, please contact us and quote the reference number. e-mail: ServiceDesk@packt.com			
Call details			
Id:	${number}	Type:	INCIDENT
Status:	${state}	Category:	${category}
Priority:	${priority}	Sub-Category:	${subcategory}

Email template configuration part 2

9. As an output of this, whenever any P1 incident is created, the e-mail notification will use **P1 Incident Template** e-mail template to send out the e-mail notification to end users.

Creating an e-mail notification script

On many occasions, the required information which is stored in another table or related tables, and in such cases, an e-mail notification script is recommended to be used to fetch relevant information from related tables, such as getting the requester's e-mail address which is in user table of Service-Now.

Getting ready

To step through this recipe, you should have an active Service-Now instance, valid credentials, and the admin role.

How to do it...

1. Open any standard web browser and type the instance Web address.
2. Log in to the Service-Now instance using your credentials.
3. On the left-hand side in the search box, type `Notification Email Scripts`, and Service-Now will search out the module for you as follows:

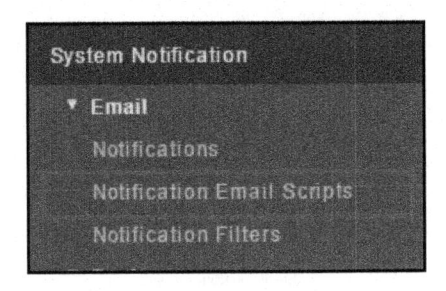

Notification E-mail Scripts

4. Click on the **Notification Email Script** module. Now you will be able to see, out-of-the-box **Email Scripts** on the screen. In order to create a new e-mail script, click on the **New** button:

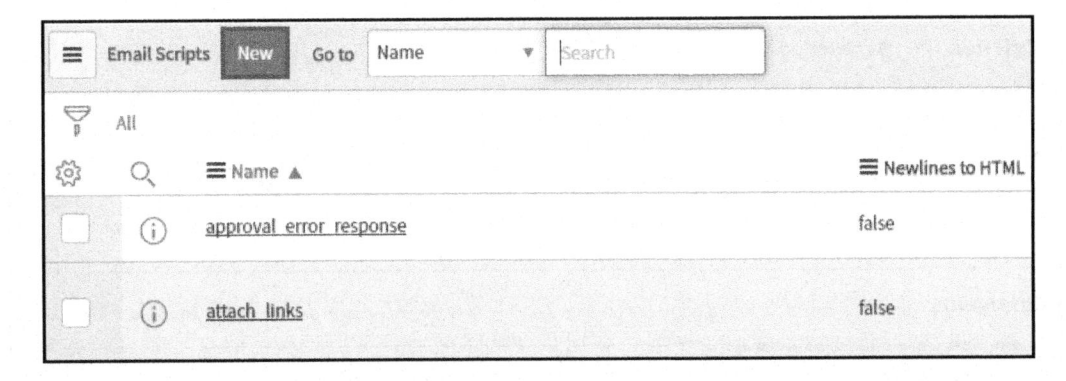

E-mail script configuration – List View

5. The e-mail notification script is a reusable component, so to define new, you have to configure below field:

    - **Name** is critical as you will be able to call notification; you will be able to call a notification script only by its name such as `addcomments`.

Configuring Alerts and Notifications

- In the **Script** section, you will need to make a script, but keep in mind that to show the output, you will need to add the `template.print()` function as follows:

Email notification script

6. To call the e-mail notification script in e-mail notifications, you will need to use the `${mail_script:notification_script_name}` syntax like `${mail_script: addcomments}` as follows:

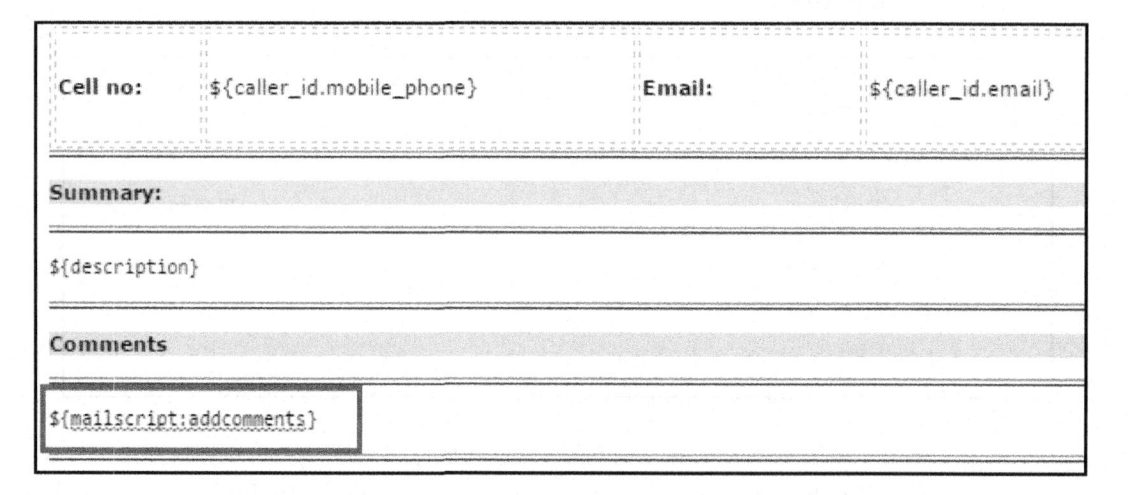

Add e-mail notification script in e-mail notification

7. Now as an output journal field is added in email notification template **P1 Incident Template** which will be used by email notification **Incident P1**.

Setting up an inbound e-mail action

E-mails are very convenient for users. Many end users like to send an e-mail rather than using a helpdesk application. Service-Now provides an out-of-the-box functionality: an inbound e-mail action for processing incoming e-mails to Service-Now.

Getting ready

To step through this recipe, you should have an active Service-Now instance, valid credentials, and the admin role.

How to do it...

1. Open any standard web browser and type the instance Web address.
2. Log in to the Service-Now instance using the credentials.
3. On the left-hand side, type `inbound action`, and Service-Now will search out the **Inbound Action** module for you:

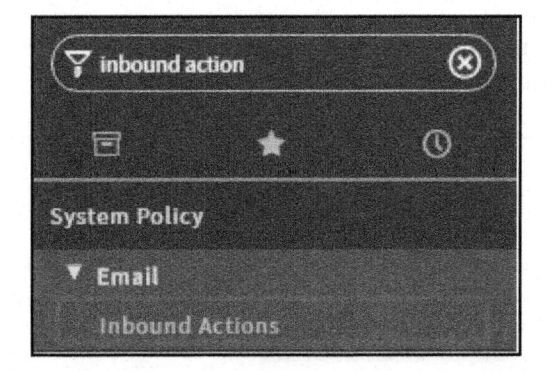

Inbound action

Configuring Alerts and Notifications

4. Click on the **Inbound Email Actions** module; you will see the following screen:

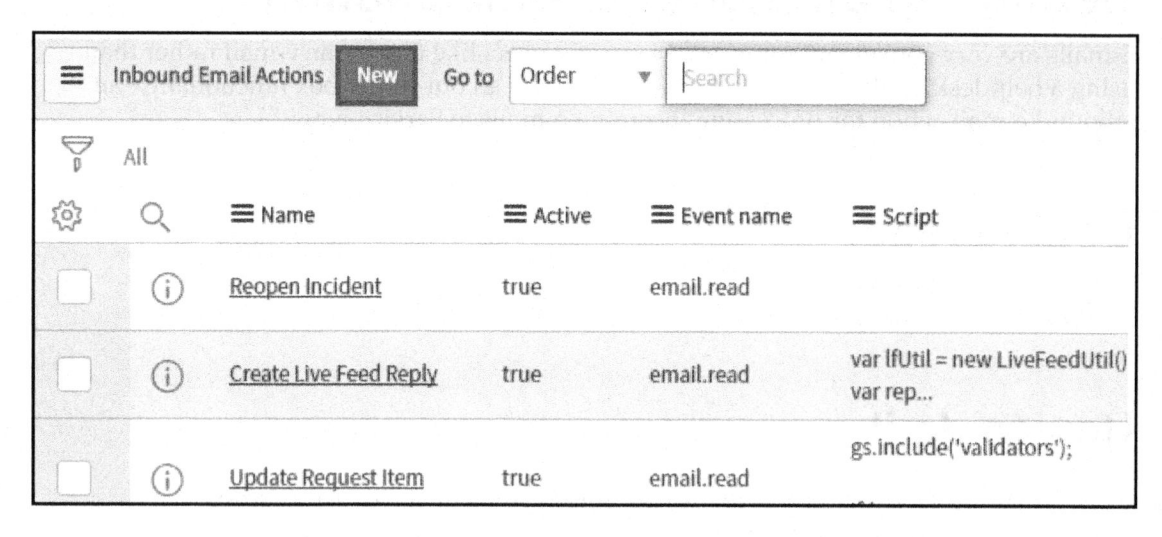

Name	Active	Event name	Script
Reopen Incident	true	email.read	
Create Live Feed Reply	true	email.read	var lfUtil = new LiveFeedUtil() var rep...
Update Request Item	true	email.read	gs.include('validators');

Inbound Email Action – List

5. To create a new inbound e-mail action, click on the **New** button. You will be able to see a configuration page and you can configure it as follows:

   - **Name**: In this field, you can provide any desired name, like I've used **Inbound integration**:

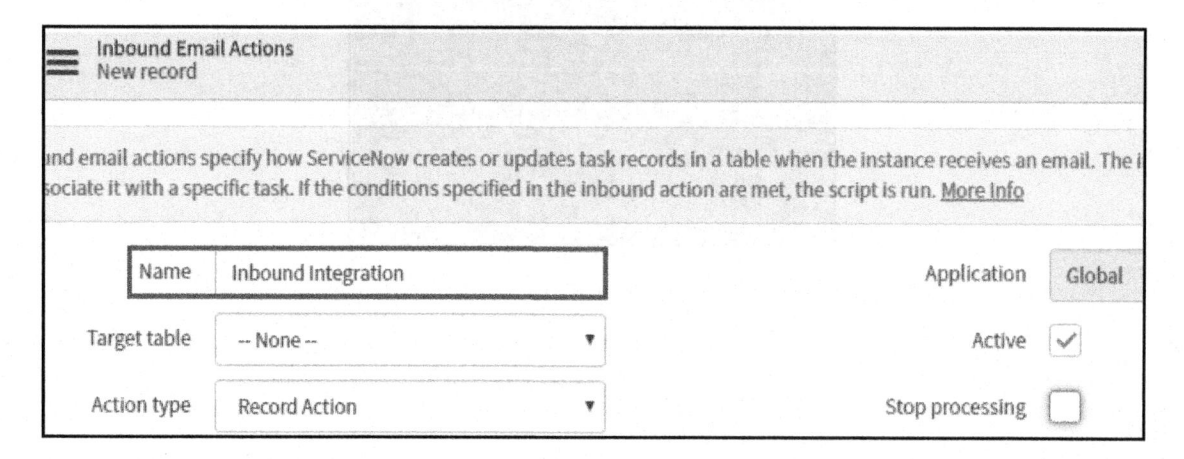

Inbound Email Actions – New record

...nd email actions specify how ServiceNow creates or updates task records in a table when the instance receives an email. The i...sociate it with a specific task. If the conditions specified in the inbound action are met, the script is run. More Info

Name	Inbound Integration		Application	Global
Target table	-- None --		Active	✓
Action type	Record Action		Stop processing	☐

The Inbound Email Action configure page

- **Active**: If you select this check box, it indicates that integration is active, and if the check box is unchecked, it indicates that integration is inactive.
- **Target table**: This field includes system tables and custom tables as well. For processing incoming e-mails or for what action should be taken by Service-Now instance for incoming e-mails, you must select a table:

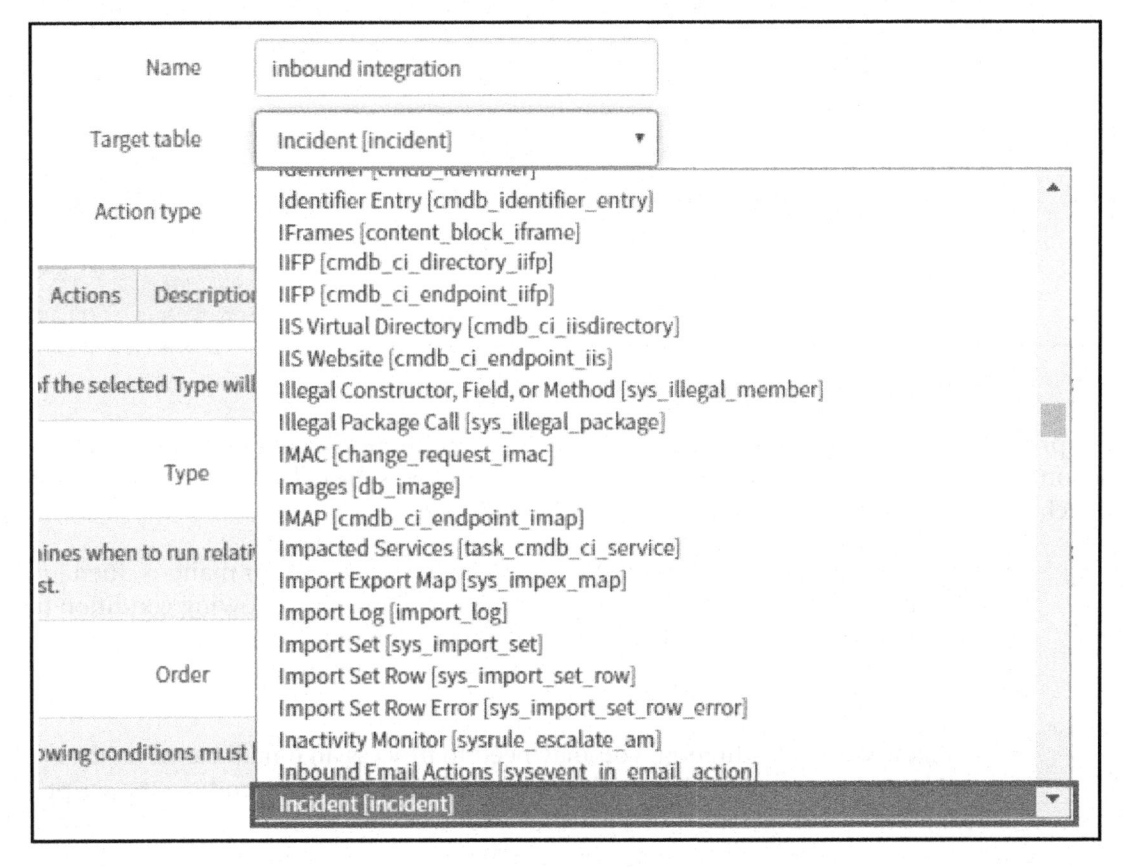

Inbound Email Action – select table

Configuring Alerts and Notifications

After selecting the **Target table**, you need to configure the **When to run** section, where you need to define the type of action. For better understanding, let's compare the Service-Now mailbox with Microsoft Outlook. Usually, many professionals create different folders for managing incoming/outgoing e-mails by e-mail rules; likewise, you need to create a rule for processing incoming e-mails:

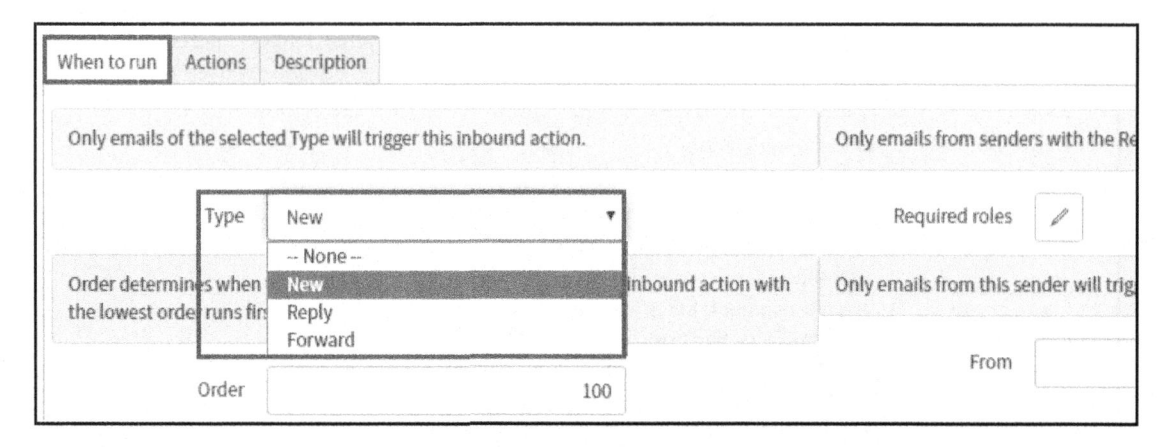

Inbound e-mail action – e-mail processing condition

For processing incoming e-mails, you need to define conditions for every inbound e-mail action regardless of whatever prefixes are included with the subject line. So if the condition matches, then the script that will run `else` will be skipped.

- If you want to integrate Service-Now with an Exchange Server mailbox, then while defining the inbound e-mail action, you can use the following condition for processing e-mail by **e-mail subject** in the condition box:

    ```
    email.subject.indexOf("New Author> 0)
    ```

- In a more complex situation, you may need to process an e-mail based on the e-mail body; to process such e-mails, you can use the following code in the script box:

    ```
    if(email.body_text.indexOf("Bank of America") > 0)
    ```

> Often, many organizations prefer e-mail integration of Service-Now with external systems. In such a case, it is advisable to create a mailbox on Exchange Server and create a forward rule on Exchange to forward all e-mail to Service-Now to create support tasks.

Inbound e-mail action – new

For processing new e-mails that don't contain a prefix, a new inbound action should be created with the New type so that the Service-Now mailbox can take appropriate action for the incoming e-mails. For instance, if users want assistance from the service desk of an organization, they have two choices: either they can log in to a Service-Now portal or they can send an e-mail to the service desk mailbox for handling incoming e-mail.

Getting ready

To step through this recipe, you should have an active Service-Now instance, valid credentials, the admin role and an e-mail box on Exchange Server.

How to do it...

1. Open any standard web browser and type the instance Web address
2. Log in to the Service-Now instance using your credentials.
3. On the left-hand side, type `inbound email action`, and Service-Now will search out the module for you.
4. Click on the **Inbound Email Actions** module, and then click on the **New** button.
5. Now configure the main section as follows:
    - **Name**: `Inbound integration new`
    - **Target table**: `Incident`
    - **Active**: Mark true

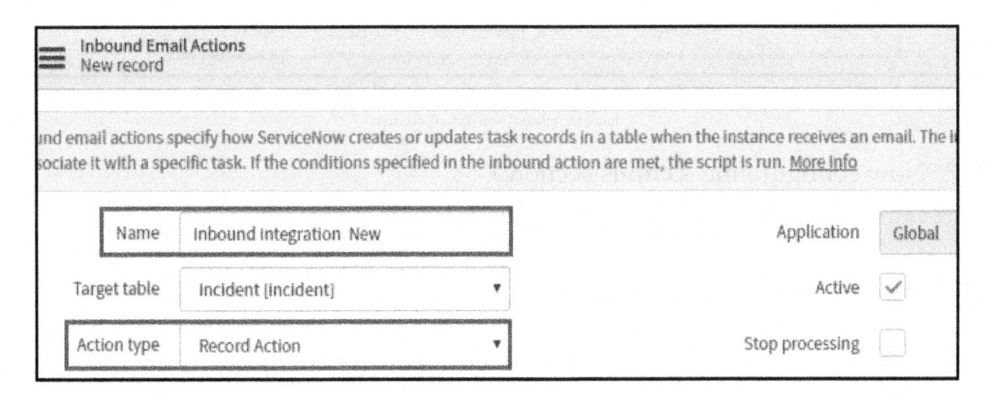

Inbound Action – New record

Configuring Alerts and Notifications

6. Now configure the **When to run** section as follows:
   - **Type:** New
   - **Condition**:
     `email.from.index.Of("packt.document@packt.com") >=0`

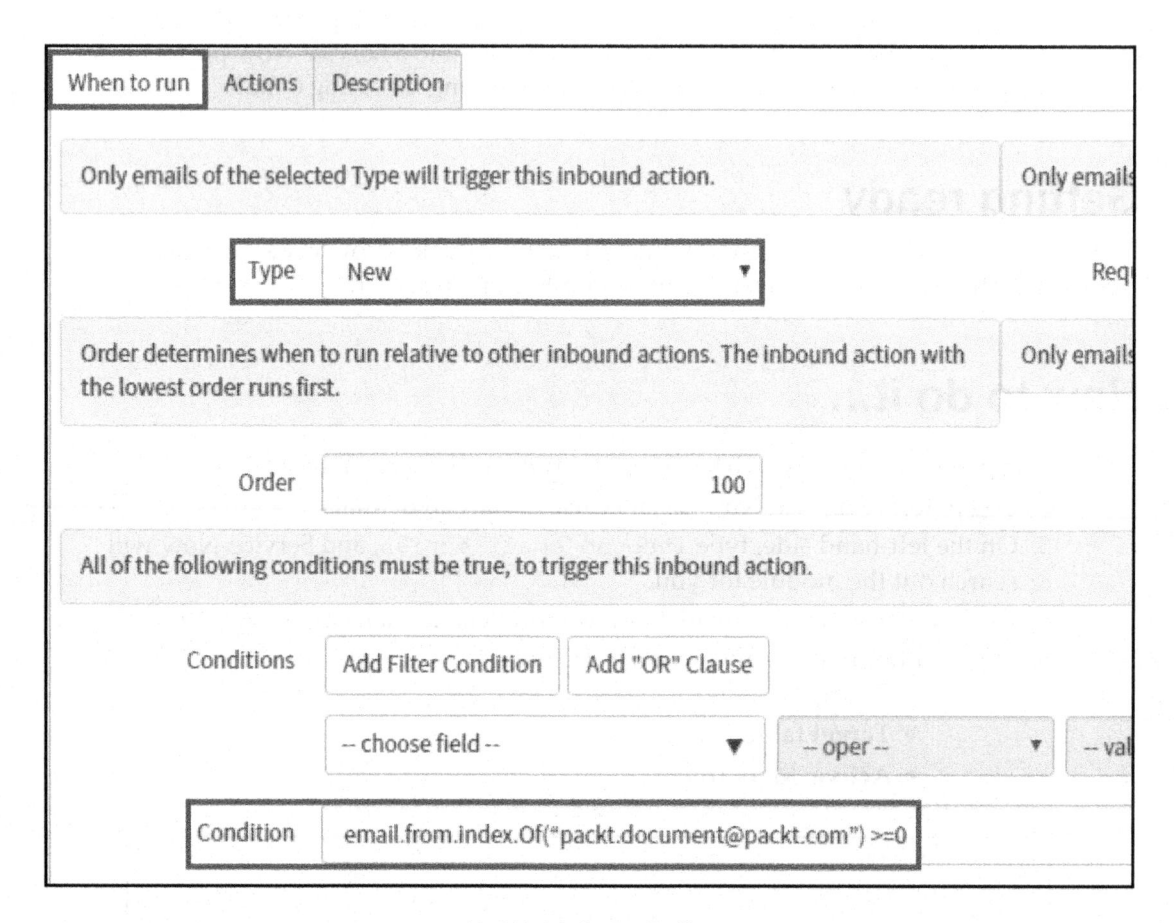

Inbound Action – New Type Condition

7. Now configure the **Actions** section.

Chapter 4

8. In the script box, add the following script:

```
//Insert Caller fields on incident form.

current.caller_id = gs.getUserID();

// Insert comments fields on incident form from email
  body.

current.comments = "received from: " +
email.origemail + "\n\n"
+ email.body_text;

// Insert short description field of incident form to
email
  subject

current.short_description = email.subject;

// Set category field on incident form to
"PACKT
  Document"

current.category = "PACKT Document";

// Set Subcategory field on incident form to
"Author
  Query"

current.subcategory = "Author Query";

// set business services on incident form to
Author
Document.
Business service is a reference field that's why
we are
getting
display value of field.

current.u_business_services.setDisplayValue('Author
    Document ');

// Set assignment group on incident form to document
    reviewer
  team. Sysid is being used to reference field
```

[199]

```
    current.assignment_group =
    "9a94569ddb3fd280568eb58dbf96199b";

    //set state field on incident form to New

    current.incident_state = 1;

    // Set Impact field on incident to "3-Low"

    current.impact = 3;

    // Set contact type field on incident form to
email.

    current.contact_type = "email";

    // Set priority field on incident to "3-
Moderate"
     current.priority = 3;

    // checking if body of email contains
    "serviceNOw"

    if(email.body_text.indexOf("ServiceNow") >= 0)

     {

      // if condition is true then set author field
      on
       incident to "Ashish Srivastava"

       current.u_author = "Ashish Srivastava";

     }

      // checking if body of email contains
    "Informatica"

      else if(email.body_text.indexOf("Informatica")
    >= 0)

     {

       // if condition is true then set author field
on
incident to "J Gorge"

       current.u_author = "J Gorge";
```

```javascript
    }
    // if any condition do not match
    else
    {
    // set author field on incident to "Any Other"
    current.u_author= "Any Other";
    }
    // checking if email body contains "Bank of America" or
    "Bank of Scotland"
    if (email.body_text.indexOf("Bank Of America ") >= 0 ||
    email.body_text.indexOf("Bank of Scotland") >= 0
    )
    {
    // if condition is true then "sub sub category will be
        set is "author's
    payment will process in 7 working days".
    current.u_sub_subcategory = "Payment Would Process In 7
    Working Days";
    }
    else
    {
    // if condition is false then "sub sub category will be
    set is " Payment
    Would Process In 3 Working Days".
    current.u_sub_subcategory = "Payment Would Process In 3
    Working Days ";
```

Configuring Alerts and Notifications

```
    }

    // insert new record by using supplied values which have
       been set for current
       record.

    current.insert();

    // stop inbound email action rule after process.

    event.state="stop_processing";
```

```
 1  current.caller_id = gs.getUserID();
 2  current.comments = "received from: " + email.origemail + "\n\n" + email.body_text;
 3  current.short_description = email.subject;
 4  current.category = "PACKT Document";
 5  current.subcategory = "Author' Query";
 6  current.u_business_services.setDisplayValue('Author Document ');
 7  current.assignment_group = "9a94569ddb3fd280568eb58dbf96199b";
 8  current.incident_state = 1;
 9  current.impact = 4;
10  current.notify = 2;
11  current.contact_type = "email";
12  if(email.body_text.indexOf("ServiceNow") >= 0)
13  {
14      current.u_author = "Ashish Srivastava";
15  }
16  else if(email.body_text.indexOf("Informatica") >= 0) {
17      current.u_author = "J Gorge";
18  }
19  else {
20      current.u_author= "Any Other";
21  }
22  if (email.body_text.indexOf("Bank Of America ") >= 0 || email.body_text.indexOf("Bank of Scotland") >= 0 )
23  {
24      current.u_sub_subcategory = "Payment Would Process In 7 Working Days";
25  }
26  else
27  {
28      current.u_sub_subcategory = "Payment Would Process In 3 Working Days";
29  }
30  current.insert();
31  event.state="stop_processing";
```

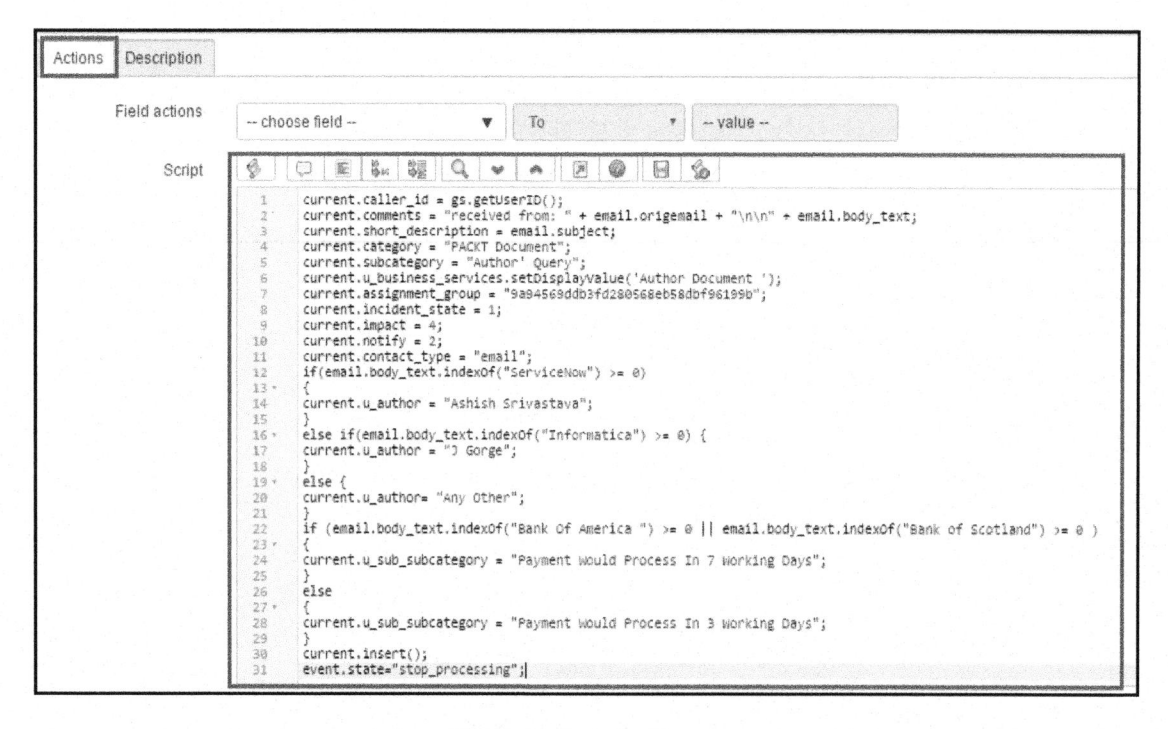

Inbound Action – New type condition script

9. Click on **Submit or Update**.
10. Now as an output whenever any end user is sending a new email to packt.document@packt.com e-mail box then an incident will be created on service-now application.

Inbound e-mail action – forward

For processing an e-mail that begins with forward prefixes, a new inbound action with the `Forward` type should be created so that the Service-Now mailbox can take appropriate action against forwarded e-mails.

Getting ready

To step through this recipe, you should have an active service-now instance, valid credentials, an admin role and an email box on Exchange Server.

How to do it…

1. Open any standard web browser and type the instance Web address
2. Log in to the Service-Now instance using your credentials.
3. On the left-hand side in the search box, type `inbound email action`, and Service-Now will search out the module for you.
4. Click on the **Inbound Email Actions** module and then click on the **New** button.
5. Now configure the main section of inbound e-mail action as follows:
    - **Name**: `Create Incident - Forward`
    - **Target table**: `Incident`
    - **Active**: Mark true

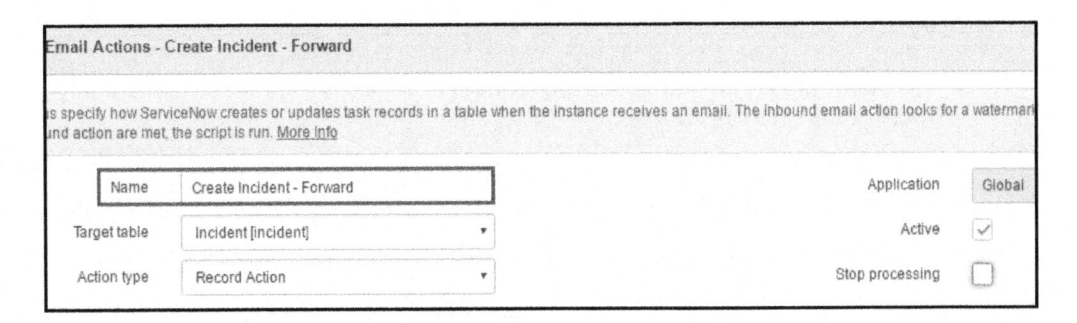

Inbound Action – Forward type

6. It is important to note that in this recipe, instead of putting condition in condition box, we are putting condition in script body.

Configuring Alerts and Notifications

7. Now configure the **When to send** section as follows:
   - **Type**: Forward
   - **Condition**: leave empty (no condition)

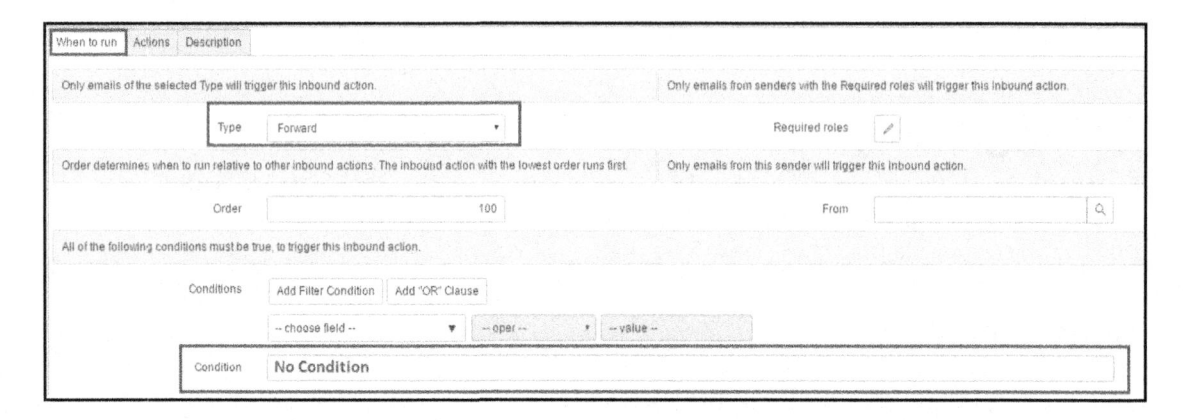

Inbound Action – Forward type condition

8. Now configure the **Actions** sections as follows:
   - **Field Action**: Leave empty
   - **Script**: In the script box, add the following script:

```
/*

If organization's email box is integrated with service-now then
the  following code will be useful for you.

*/

// take email in varibale to convert in lower case to avoid any
case sensitivity issue.


var emailTo=email.to;

emailTo=emailTo.toLowerCase();

//guest user sysID is 5136503cc611227c0183e96598c4d906

//if the person who sent email is not part of oragnization's AD
server then opened by field will be set as guest user

if (current.opened_by == "5136503cc611227c0183e96598c4d906")
```

```
        {
            current.u_external_sender = email.from;
        }
        // if email was forwarded to "authortechquery@packt.com" (
        which reside on organization's exchnage server ) then a copy of
email
        //will be sent to service-now instance to create a support ticket.
        if (emailTo.indexOf("authortechquery@packt.com") >= 0)
        {
        // set caller id field on incident form
        current.caller_id = gs.getUserID();
        // set comments field on incident form to email body.
        current.comments = "forwarded by: " + email.origemail + "\n\n" +
email.body_text;
        //set short description field in incident form to email subject
        current.short_description = email.subject;
        //set category field on incident form to "Author Query"
        current.category = "Author Query";
        // set subcategory on incident form to "Technical Query"
        current.subcategory = "Technical Query";
         // set sub subcategory field on incident form to " Other"
        current.u_sub_subcategory = "Other";
         // set business services on incident form as "Technical Book"
        current.u_business_services.setDisplayValue('Technical Book');
        // Set state field on incident form as "New". New
        =1
```

Configuring Alerts and Notifications

```
    current.incident_state = 1;

    // Set Notify field on incident form as 2
    current.notify = 2;

    // set contact type field on incident form as
    "email"

    current.contact_type = "email";

    // insert the record in table

    current.insert();

    // stop inbound email action rule after
processing.

    event.state = "stop_processing";

}
```

```
1   var emailTo=email.to;
2   emailTo=emailTo.toLowerCase();
3   //5136503cc611227c0183e96598c4d906 guest user sysID
4   if (current.opened_by == "5136503cc611227c0183e96598c4d906")
5   {
6       current.u_external_sender = email.from;
7   }
8
9   if (emailTo.indexOf("authortechquery@packt.com") >= 0)
10  {
11      current.caller_id = gs.getUserID();
12      current.comments = "forwarded by: " + email.origemail + "\n\n" + email.body_text;
13      current.short_description = email.subject;
14
15      current.category = "Author Query";
16      current.subcategory = "Technical Query";
17      current.u_sub_subcategory = "Other";
18      current.u_business_services.setDisplayValue('Technical Book');
19      current.incident_state = 1;
20      current.notify = 2;
21      current.contact_type = "email";
22
23  current.insert();
24  event.state = "stop_processing";
25
26  }
```

Inbound Action – Forward type condition script

9. Click on **Submit** button now.

10. Now as an output whenever any end user is forwarding an email to authortechquery@packt.com e-mail box then an incident will be created on Service-Now application.

Inbound e-mail action – reply

Replies to inbound e-mail actions are primarily for updating support tickets, such as incident tasks, problem tasks, and change tasks. For processing an e-mail that begins with Reply prefixes, a new inbound e-mail action should be created with the Reply type so that the Service-Now mailbox can take appropriate action for the incoming (replied) e-mail. For instance, if a support group member is replying on a supporting ticket, then comments will be updated as additional comments in the Service-Now.

Getting ready

To step through this recipe, you should have an active Service-Now instance, valid credentials, and the admin role.

How to do it...

1. Open any standard web browser and type the instance Web address.
2. Log in to the Service-Now instance using your credentials.
3. On the left-hand side, type `inbound email action`, and Service-Now will search out the module for you.
4. Click on **Inbound Email Actions**, and then click on the **New** button.
5. Configure the main section of the inbound e-mail action as follows:

- **Name**: `Create incident by mailbox`
- **Target table**: `incident`

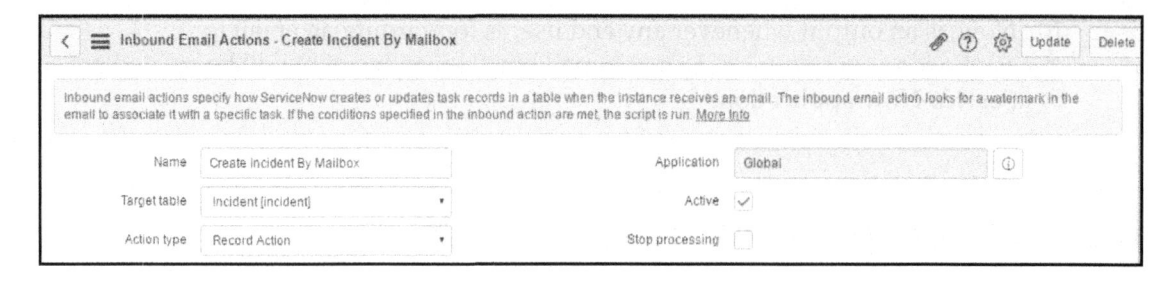

Inbound Email Action – Reply

6. Configure the **When to run** section as follows:

   - **Type**: `Reply`
   - **Condition**: `email.to.indexOf("IT.Support@packt.com" || email.to.indexOf(IT.Support@PACKT.com))>=0;`

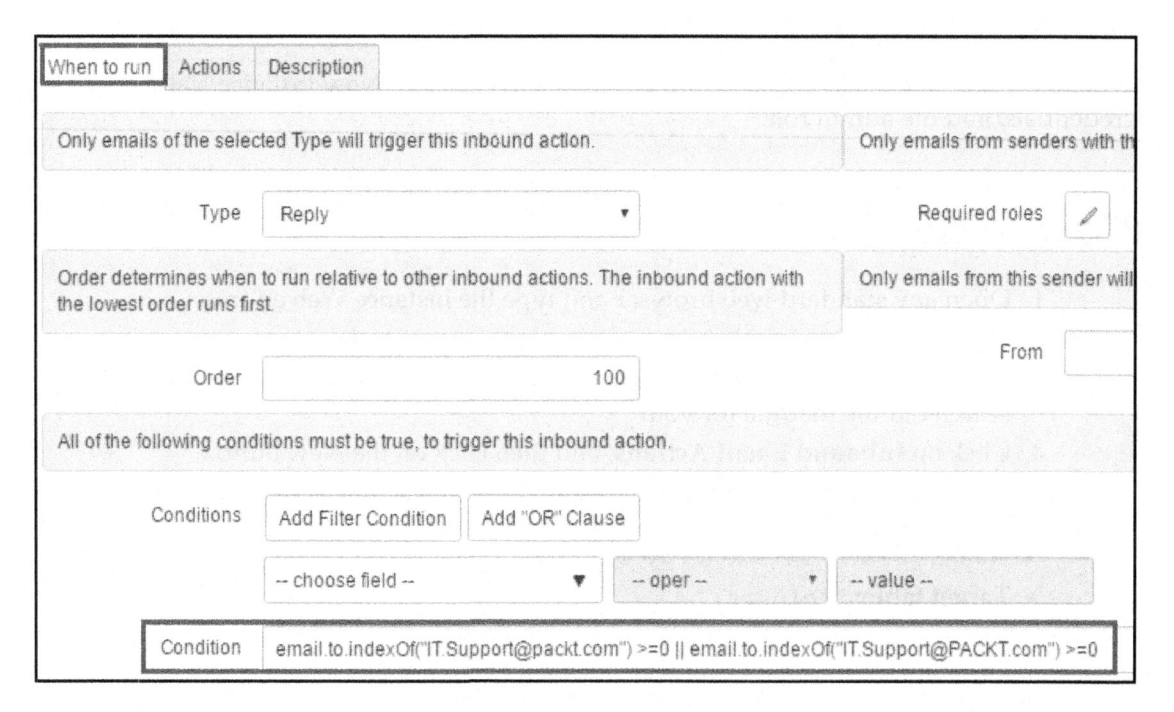

Inbound Email Action – Reply type condition

7. Configure the **Actions** section.
8. In the script box, add the following script:

```
// convert email in lower case avoid any case sensitivity
   issue.
var emailTo=email.to;

emailTo=emailTo.toLowerCase();

//guest user = "5136503cc611227c0183e96598c4f706" sysID.
If email
id does not recognize by service-now then it will mark
user is
guest user

if (current.opened_by ==
"5136503cc611227c0183e96598c4f706")

{

//set external field on incident form as email address of

current.u_external_sender = email.from;

}

// if email was sent to IT.Support@packt email box then
exchange
will send copy to service-now mail box for processing.

else if (emailTo.indexOf("IT.Support@packt.com") >=
0)

{

// set caller field on incident form

current.caller_id = gs.getUserID();

// set comments fields on incident form from body of
email.

current.comments = "Replied from: " + email.origemail
+
"\n\n" +
```

Configuring Alerts and Notifications

```
email.body_text;

// set short description field on incident form from email subject

current.short_description = email.subject;

// set category fields on incident as "book"

 current.category = "Book";

// set category fields on incident as "Technical Book"

 current.subcategory = "Technical Book";

// set sub subcategory on incident form as "Other"

 current.u_sub_subcategory = "Other";

// set business services on form as "Author Query"

 current.u_business_services.setDisplayValue('Author Query');

// set state field on form as "New"

 current.incident_state = 1;

// set contact type on incident form as "email"

 current.contact_type = "email";

// insert record with values

 current.insert();

// stop inbound email action rule after process.

 event.state = "stop_processing";

}
```

```
    Actions    Description

ld actions   -- choose field --           ▼    To              ▼   -- value --

   Script

         1    var emailTo=email.to;
         2    emailTo=emailTo.toLowerCase();
         3    if (current.opened_by == "5136503cc611227c0183e96598c4f706"){
         4        current.u_external_sender = email.from;
         5    }
         6    if (emailTo.indexOf("IT.Support@packt.com") >= 0) {
         7        current.caller_id = gs.getUserID();
         8        current.comments = "Replied from: " + email.origemail + "\n\n" + email.body_text;
         9        current.short_description = email.subject;
        10        current.category = "Book";
        11        current.subcategory = "Technical Books";
        12        current.u_sub_subcategory = "Other";
        13        current.u_business_services.setDisplayValue('Author Query');
        14        current.incident_state = 1;
        15        current.notify = 2;
        16        current.contact_type = "email";
        17
        18        current.insert();
        19        event.state = "stop_processing";
        20    }
        21
        22
```

Inbound Email Action – Reply Type Condition Script

9. Click on **Submit** button.
10. As an output whenever any user is replying the e-mail and marking e-mail box IT.Support@packt.com in the **TO** field of email then a copy will be sent to service-now for creating an incident.

There's more…

Likewise, you can create a support task in Service-Now for other tables as well. You can even trigger the catalog item workflow from the inbound email action.

E-mail Notification by event registry

By default, Service-Now provides e-mail notifications and events, but if existing e-mail notifications or events don't fulfill your requirements, then you can create your own events to send out notifications for specific changes of Service-Now records. It's important to note that a business rule needs to be created for new events.

Getting ready

To step through this recipe, you should have an active Service-Now instance, valid credentials, and the admin role.

How to do it...

1. Open any standard web browser and type the instance Web address.
2. Log in to the Service-Now instance using your credentials.
3. On the left-hand side, type **REGIS** and Service-Now will search out module for you. Under **System Policy** application, you need to select the **Registry** module:

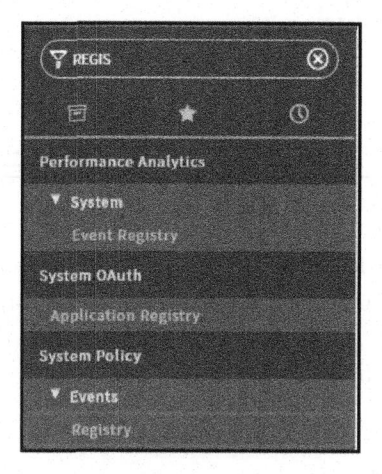

System Policy – Event Registry

4. Now you will see all systems the event registries. In order to create a new event registry, click on the **New** button:

Chapter 4

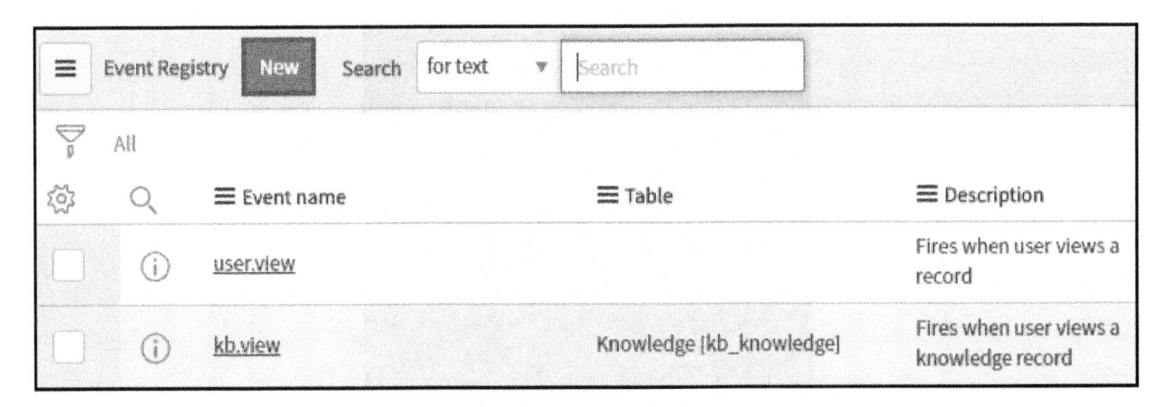

		Event name	Table	Description
		user.view		Fires when user views a record
		kb.view	Knowledge [kb_knowledge]	Fires when user views a knowledge record

Event Registry – Records

5. On the event registration configuration page, configure the following:
    - **Event name**: `Take.Ownership`
    - **Table**: `Incident [incident]`
    - **Fired by**: `Fired by take ownership business rule`

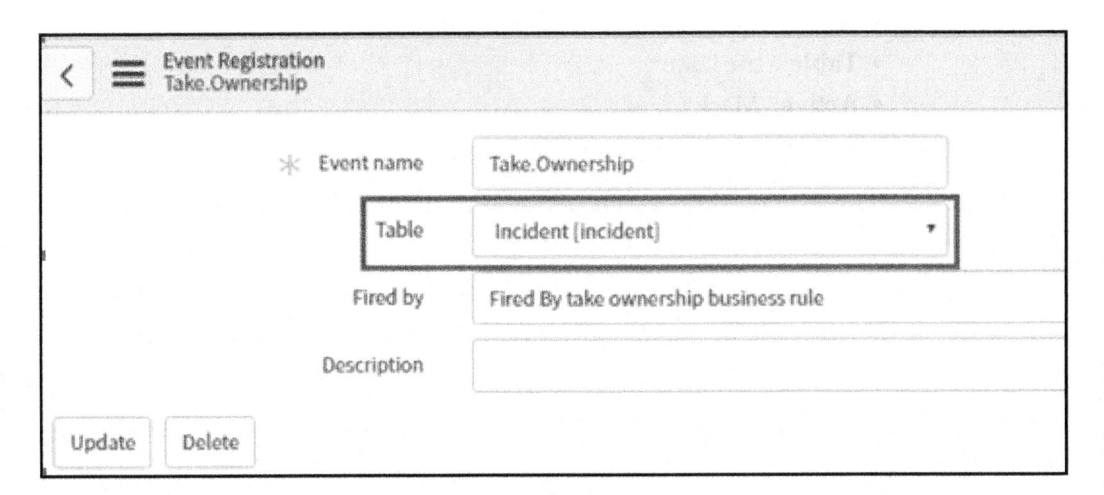

Event Registry – Take ownership

6. Click on **Submit** button.

7. On the left-hand side in the search box, type `Business Rule`, and Service-Now will search out the **Business Rule** module for you. Under **System Definition**, select **Business Rules**:

[213]

Configuring Alerts and Notifications

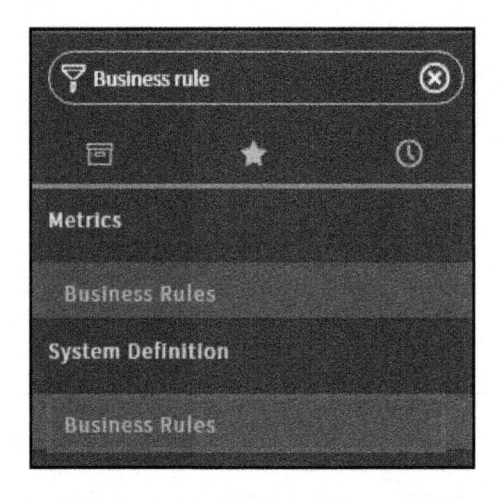

The Business Rules module

8. Click on the **Business Rules** module, and click on **New** on the **Business Rules** list record page.
9. Configure the main section of Business Rule as follows:
    - **Name**: `Ownership`
    - **Table**: `Incident`
    - **Active**: Mark `true`
    - **Advanced**: Mark `true`

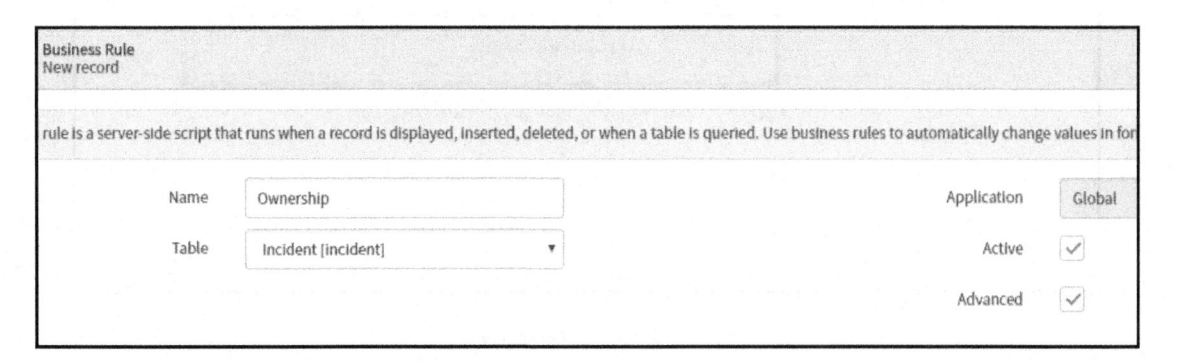

Business Rule of Event

10. Configure the **When to run** section of the ownership business rule as follows:
    - **When**: `After`
    - **Insert**: Mark `true`
    - **Update**: Mark `true`

[214]

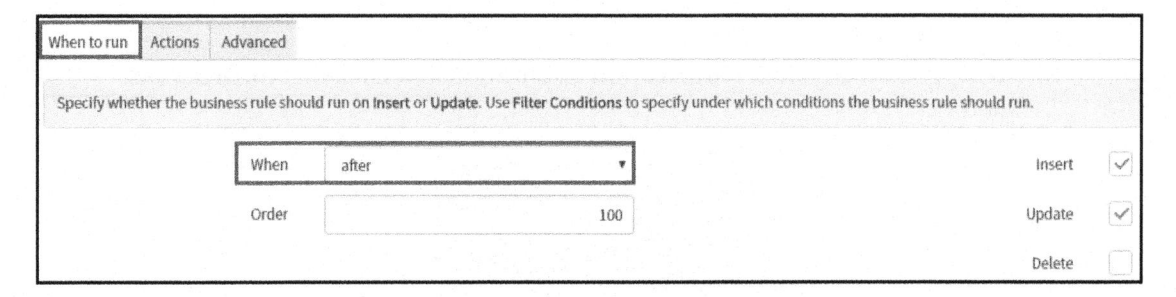

The business rule condition of event

11. Configure the **Advanced** section of the ownership business rule:
    - Condition: Leave blank
    - Script: In the box, write the following script:

```
// test for current "assignment to" field on incident form

if (!current.assigned_to.nil() && current.assigned_to.changes())
{
    // add email event in scheduler
    gs.eventQueue("Take.Ownership", current,
    current.assigned_to.getDisplayValue() ,
    previous.assigned_to.getDisplayValue());

}
```

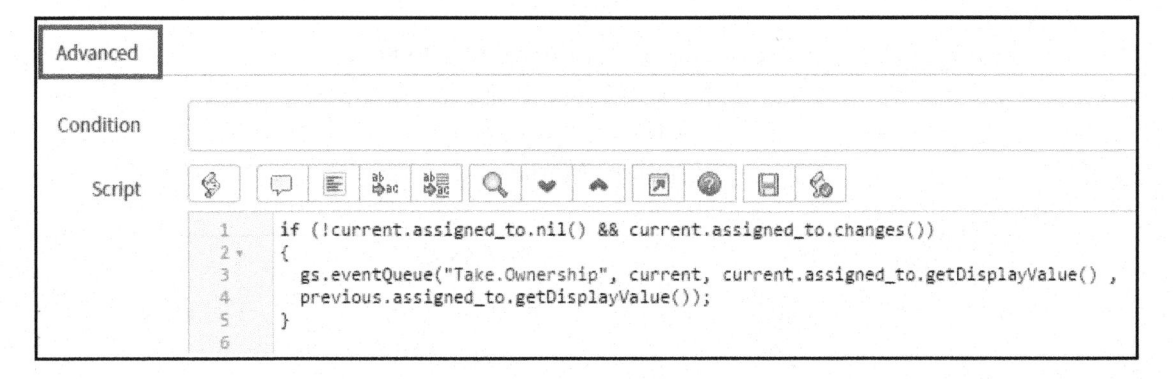

The business rule script of event

[215]

Configuring Alerts and Notifications

12. Click on **Submit** button.
13. Now, go to the **System Notification** application and click on **Notifications** module:

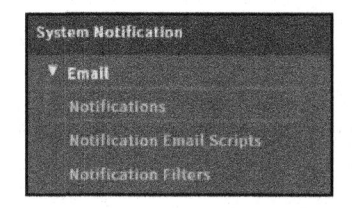

System Notification

14. To create a new notification, click on the **New** button:

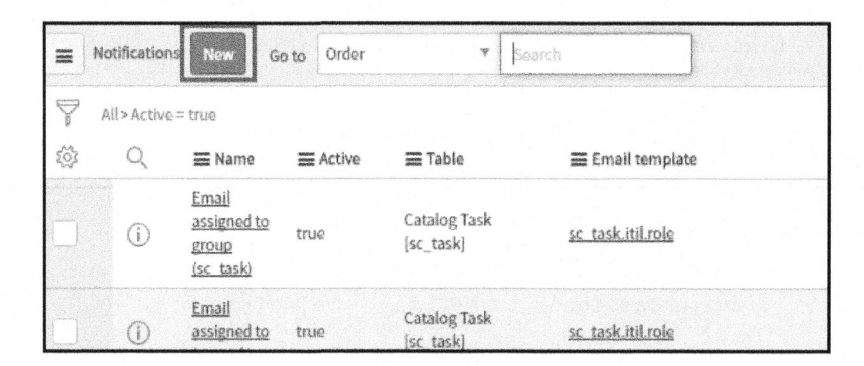

Notification for event

15. Configure the main section of the notification as follows:
    - **Name**: `Take Ownership`
    - **Table**: `Incident`
    - **Active** : Mark `true`

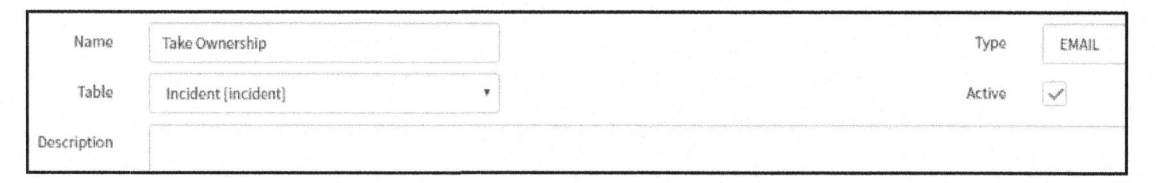

E-mail Notification

16. Click on the **Advanced view** button to view the **When to send** section:

[216]

Chapter 4

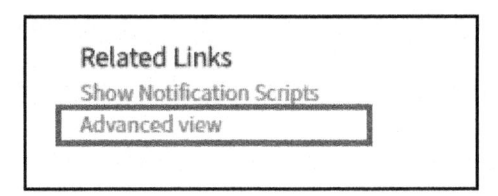

The Advance view to view the Send when field

17. Now, configure the **When to send** section of the notification as follows:

    - **Send when:** `Event is fired`
    - **Event name:** `Take.Ownership`
    - **Conditions:** `Assigned to` field `changes`

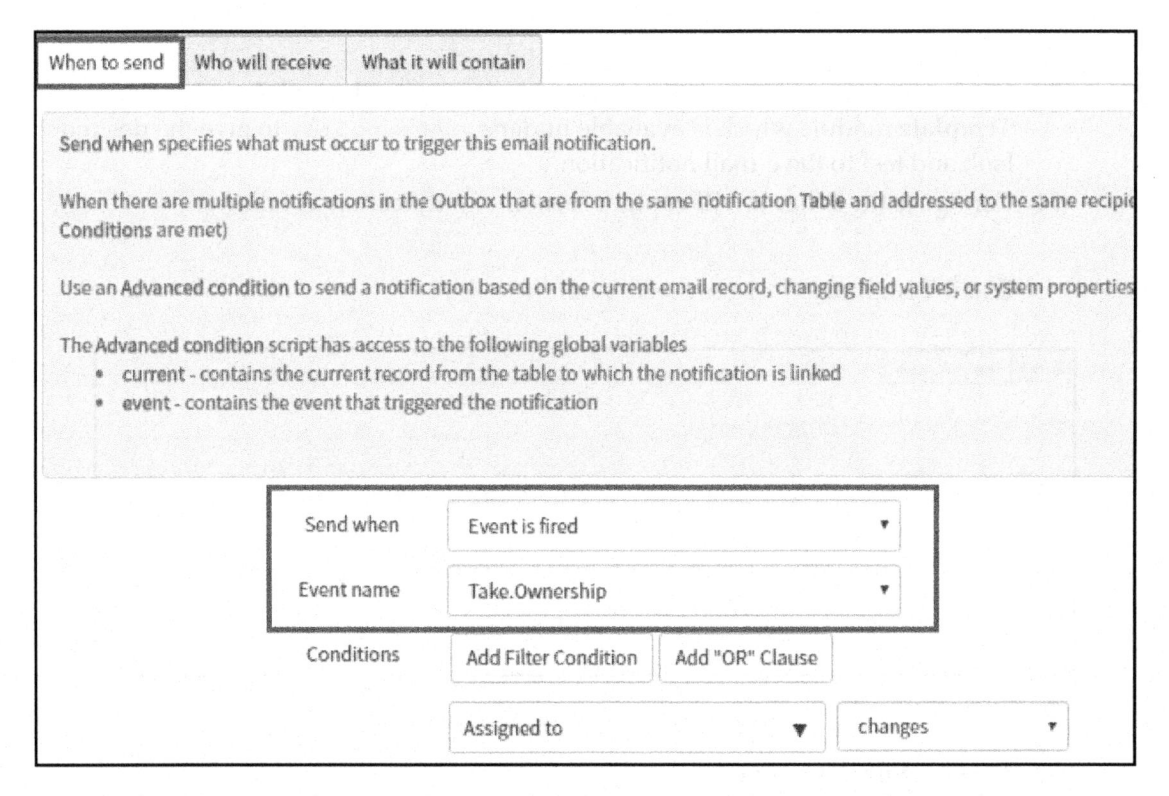

E-mail notification condition of event

18. Configure the **Who will receive** section of the notification as follows:

[217]

19. **Users/Groups in fields**: Set this to **Assigned to, Assignment group**:

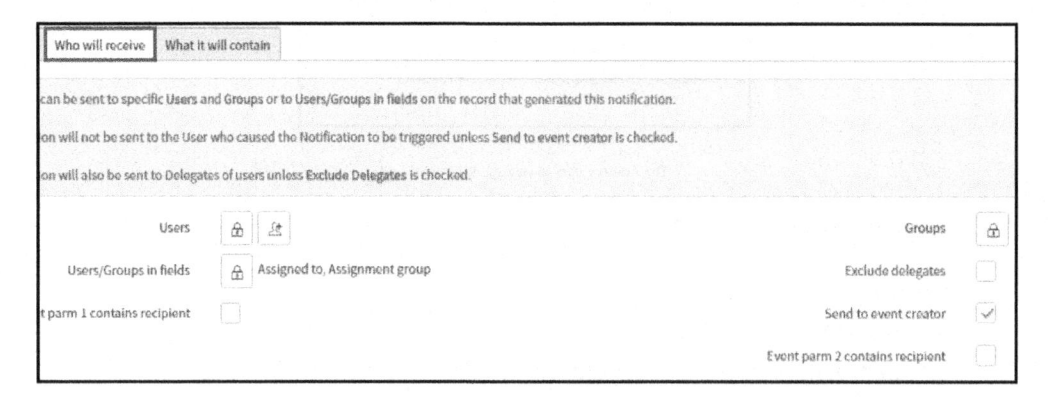

E-mail notification: the Who will receive section of event

20. Create a new e-mail template `incident.ownership` through **Email Template** module which is available under `system policy` to give the desired look and feel to the e-mail notification.
21. Configure the **What it will contain** section of notification as follows:

- **Email Template:** `Incident.ownership`

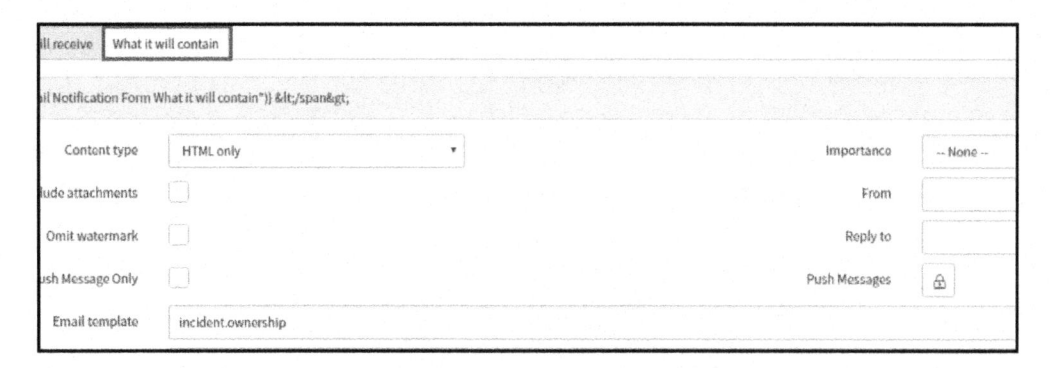

E-mail notification – the What it will contain section of event

22. Click on **Submit** button.
23. As an output an email notification `Take.Ownership` will be created through new event `Take.Ownership`.

E-mail notification troubleshooting

In the Service-Now operational environment, a support team faces many issues related to e-mails. In this recipe, you will see how to troubleshoot them.

Getting ready

To step through this recipe, you should have an active Service-Now instance, valid credentials, and the admin role.

How to do it...

1. If there is e-mail integration between mailboxes by Exchange Server, then often admins face looping issues of e-mail, which creates many support tickets just with replies.

    In such cases, you need to create a condition to not process these autoreply e-mails:

    ```
    if(email.from.indexOf("noreply@externalsystem.com")
    >= 0 ||
        email.from.indexOf("salessuport@packt.com ") >=
        0
            {
             event.state="stop_processing";
            }
    ```

2. If your organization is using Service-Now for external communication purposes, then the instance e-mail address (that is, `dev23216@service-now.com`) will be exposed to the outer world. In many cases, external mailboxes (that is, `sales@externalsystems.com`) start sending e-mail to the direct Service-Now e-mail address, which creates an unnecessary support tasks. To resolve such issues, follow these steps:
    1. On the left-hand side, type `email properties`, and Service-Now will search out the **Email Properties** module for you.

2. Under **System Properties**, click on **Email Properties**:

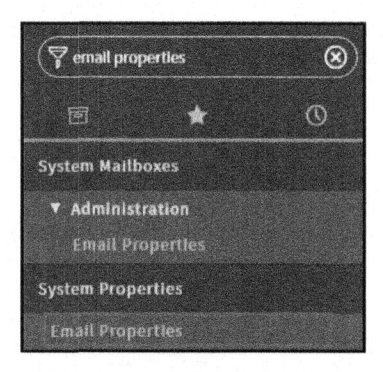

Email properties

3. Under the **Inbound Email Configuration** section, in **Ignore email from these senders**, use the name before the @ sign. In the (comma-separated) field, add unwanted e-mail addresses (that is, `sales@externalsystems.com`):

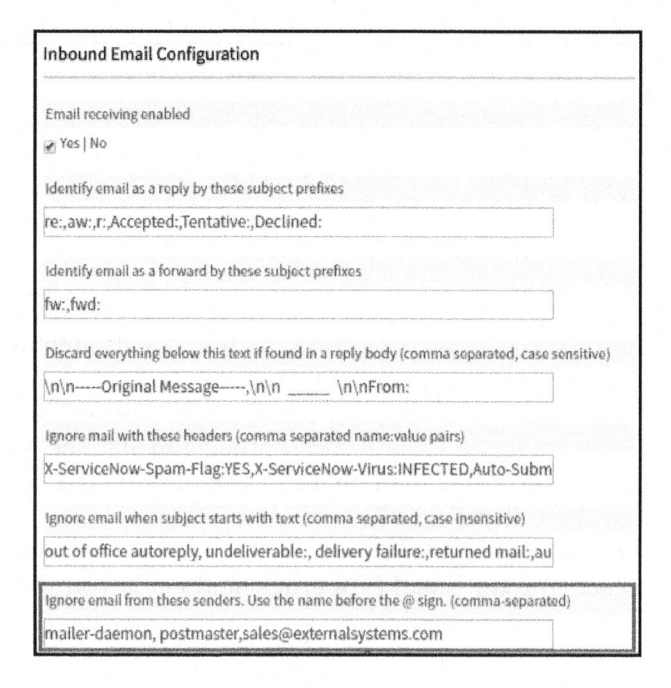

Email Properties – Update

4. Click on **Save** button.

5. The inbound e-mail condition is skipped.

- Mailbox e-mail addresses are case sensitive, so let's take an example. `IT.Support@packt.com` and `IT.Support@PACKT.com` are two different addresses from a Service-Now e-mail integration point of view, which can cause skipping of the inbound action's condition. To resolve such an issue, it's a good practice to convert e-mail addresses into lower case:

    ```
    var emailTo=email.to;
    emailTo=emailTo.toLowerCase();
    ```

5
Building and Configuring Reports

This chapter covers the following recipes:

- Viewing and running reports
- Creating new reports
- Scheduling reports
- Sending multiple reports in one e-mail
- Creating a table-specific report module
- Creating a dashboard
- Including the date in a report's e-mail notification
- Working with the report's header and footer template
- Working with the report sources
- Working with the report range
- Creating a database view

Introduction

Reports are an essential part of any enterprise application. On many occasions, managers and business executives request reports. From the previous chapters, you understood that Service-Now provides small applications for dedicated process, and for the purpose of reporting, Service-Now provides a dedicated reporting application, which can be accessible by admins, ITIL, the report administrator, the global report user, the group report user, or the report publisher. In this chapter, you will see how you can view the report, schedule the report, report templates, and so on.

Viewing and running reports

Service-Now can provide reports in Excel, PDF, and image formats, but regarding business reporting, where business heads, managers, or executives ask for reports, Service-Now reporting seems to be weak. It is worth including a few scenarios here: Every company has their own format or reporting template, which may include a logo, styles, color combination, or reports on different report sheets in the same Excel workbook; this kind of reporting is not feasible from Service-Now. In this recipe, you will see how to view and run already existing reports in the Service-Now environment.

Getting ready

For this recipe, you need an active Service-Now instance and valid credentials or a valid role. If you have a role as an admin, ITIL, report group, or group admin, then you can access Service-Now reports.

How to do it...

1. Open the standard browser and type web address of Service-Now.
2. Log in to service-now using your credentials.
3. In the search box, type `reports`, and Service-Now will search **Report Application** as follows:

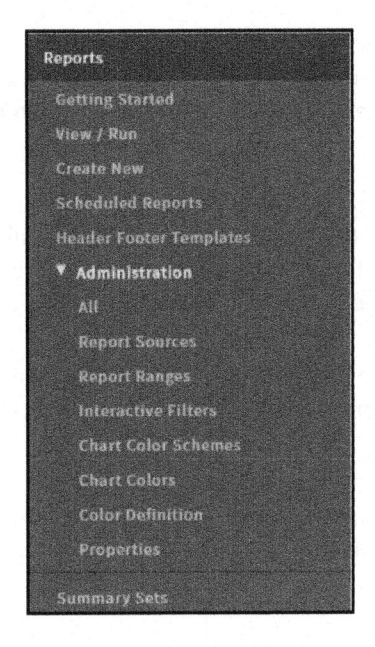

Service-Now reporting module

4. If you want to view or run a report, then click on **View** or **Run**. You will be redirected to the following screen:

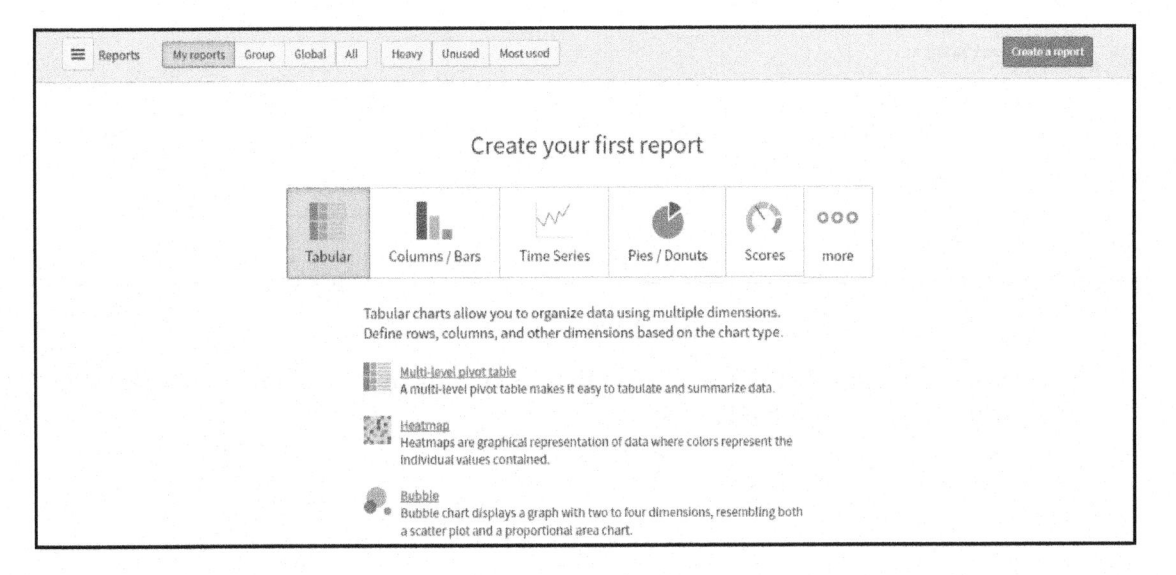

Service-Now report view or run page

Building and Configuring Reports

> Service-Now reports are role-based; so if you have an admin, ITIL, report group, or report admin role then can you access reports.
> Connecting this feature with business, you can create either a global report or a group report, depending on reporting requirement.

5. Service-Now has designed the report page very logically and in an easy-to-use manner. If you know the report name, then you can use filter as well as highlighted in red in the next screenshot. You only need to type name of the report in the search box and press *Enter* key and Service-Now will search for the report for you.

6. Out of the box, on the **Reports** page of Service-Now provides a few options such as **My reports**, **Group**, **Global**, or **All** are for filtering the reports only based on access level of report.

7. If you click on the **Global** report button, then you will able to see all global reports which are available for all users. To view the global report click on **Open Incident by Assignment**:

	Type	Title	Table	Scheduled	Last run	↑ Runs
★		Open Items by Escalation	Task [task]		2016-07-12 04:51:48	14
★		Users by Location	User [sys_user]		2016-07-12 04:51:18	7
★		KPI - Average Work Effort for Resolving Incidents by Category	Incident Time Worked [incident_time_worked]		2016-07-12 04:51:08	2
☆		My Incidents by State	Incident [incident]		2016-06-20 02:25:01	1
★		Open Incidents by Assignment	Incident [incident]		2016-07-12 04:52:48	1

Service-Now Global Report Page

8. Now you will able to view report **Open Incidents by Assignment** in bar format which is shared with all users:

[226]

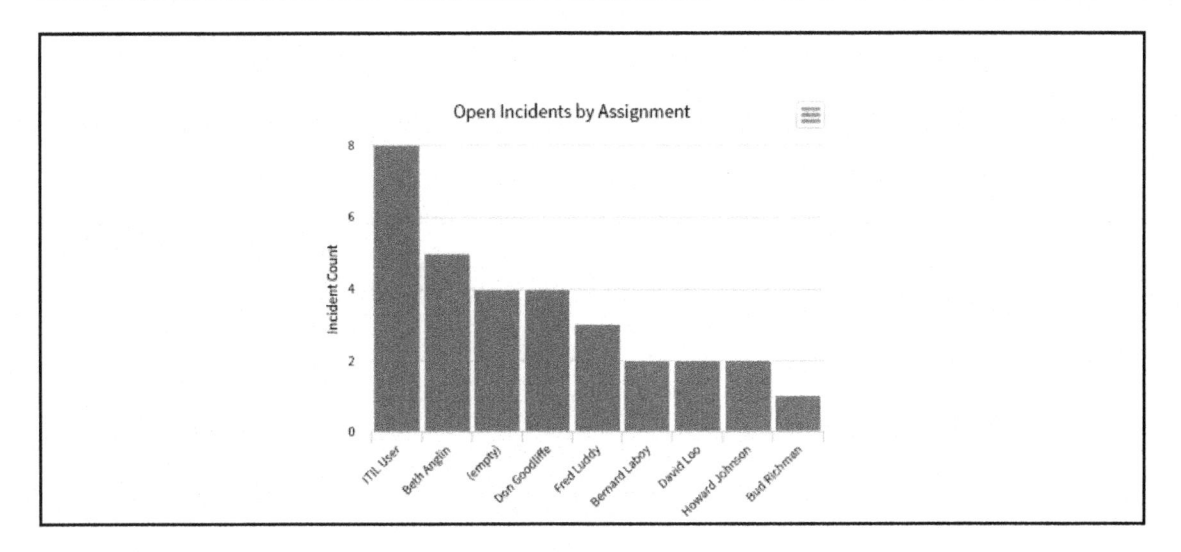

Open incidents by assignment report

Creating new reports

By default, Service-Now provides the View/Run module to view the existing report or create new report. In this recipe, you will learn how to create new reports within the Service-Now environment.

Getting ready

For this recipe, all you need is an active Service-Now instance, valid credentials and a role (admin, report admin, or report Group).

How to do it…

1. Open a web browser (Google Chrome, Firefox, Safari, or Internet Explorer).
2. Type the instance web address in the address bar.
3. Log in to the Service-Now instance using the credentials.
4. Type `Report` in the search bars (left-hand side).

Building and Configuring Reports

5. Now, Click on **Create View/Run** module under report application.
6. Now configure the report as follows.
7. After click, you will able be able to view selected columns in **section 3** as shown in following screenshot:

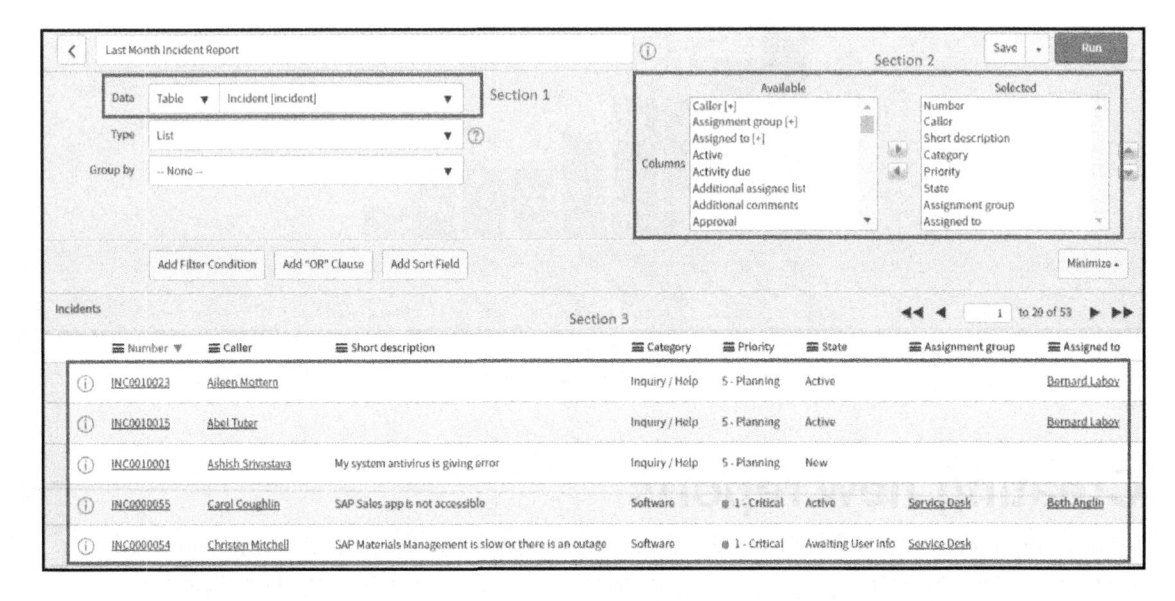

Service-Now Create New Report

8. If you click on the **section 1** drop-down menu, you will able to view all the tables (system/custom) from which you can generate the desired report in either the list or other graphical formats. From the region marked **Section 1** in the preceding screenshot, select the table from which you want to generate the report, and enter the name for the report by which it will be available to the users.
    - **Name**: Last Month Incident Report
    - **Data**: Table - Incident

9. By default, the incident table has lots of fields which are not necessary to include in the report, or do not make sense for the end user or management. So, from the region marked **Section 2** in the preceding screenshot, you can move whatever field you want in the report from the **Available** column to the **Selected** column as follows.
    - Number
    - Caller
    - Short Description

- Category
- Priority
- Assignment group
- Assigned To

10. By default, Service-Now doesn't put any filters or conditions on the report. That's why you will be able to see all the records of a table. It completely depends on your reporting requirement. To add a filter in the report click on **Add Filter Condition** button let's understand this by an example if you want to generate an incident report of specific period like 3rd September 2016 to 15th October 2016 and assignment group are `Database Atlanta` and `Database San Diego` then you can create following filter conditions:

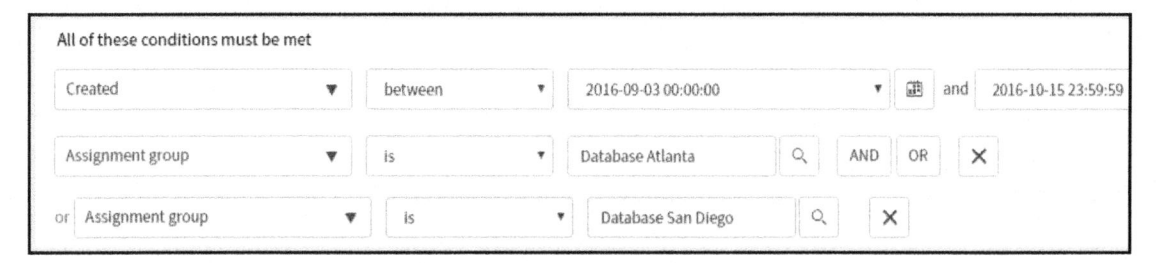

11. Now click on **Run** button to generate the report.
12. Now you can save your report by clicking on **Save** button as shown following, but by just saving, it will be available only to you which mean only you are allowed to view the report and will be added under **My reports**:

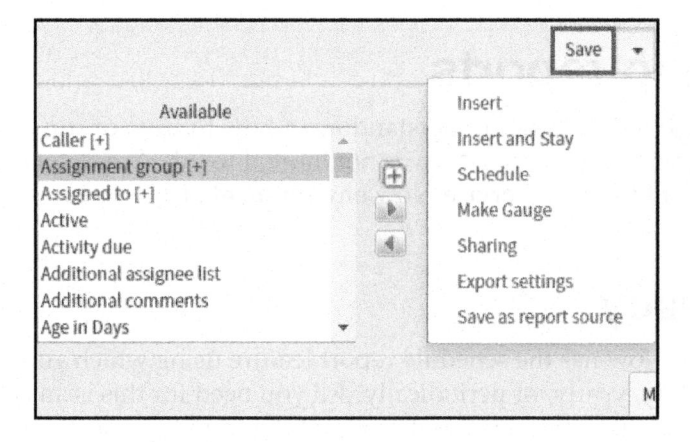

Service-Now Report Saving

Building and Configuring Reports

13. Now if you want to share the created report **Last Month Incident Report** with other users/group, and then click on **sharing** button. After clicking on Sharing button a pop up window **Sharing setting** will be appear on screen and you can add any group in the Groups section as follows:

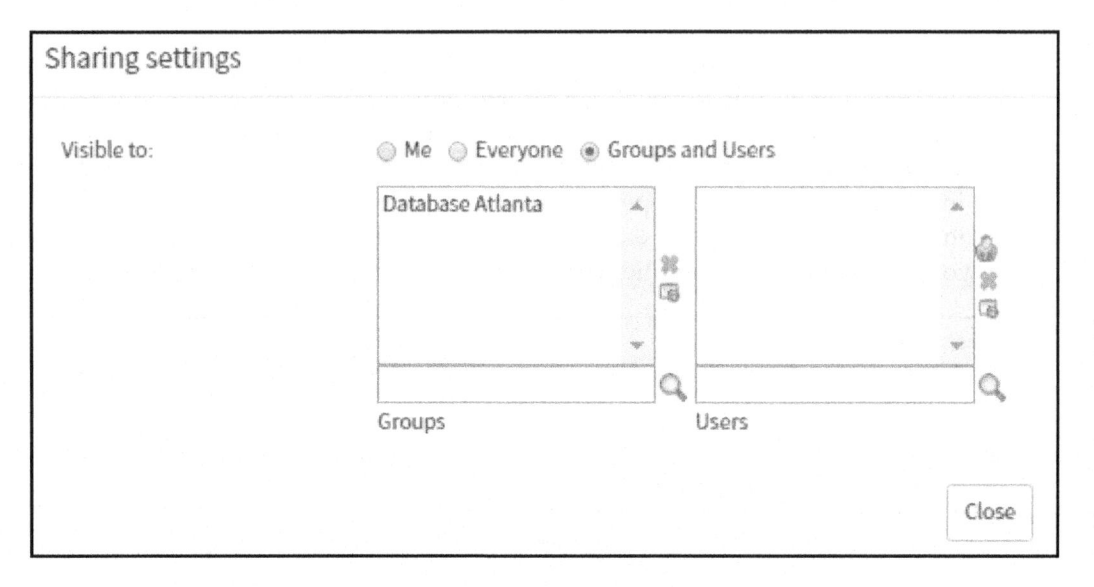

Service-Now share reports

14. As an output your **Last Month Incident Report** is created and shared with Database Atlanta group.

Scheduling reports

By now, you should have a better understanding of how to view or run an existing report and create new reports, but Service-Now is not limited to this. You can even schedule reports to be sent out from the Service-Now environment at any time.

Getting ready

By default, Service-Now has the schedule report feature using which you can schedule a report daily, monthly, yearly, or periodically. All you need for this is an active Service-Now instance, valid credentials, and a role (admin, report admin, or report group).

How to do it…

1. Open a web browser (Google Chrome, Firefox, Safari, or Internet Explorer).
2. Type the instance web address in the address bar.
3. Log in to the Service-Now instance using the credentials.
4. Type the `Report` in the search bar (left-hand side).
    - Click on **View** or **Run** module under report application, as now you can see a newly created report.
5. **Last Month Incident Report** as shown in following screenshot:

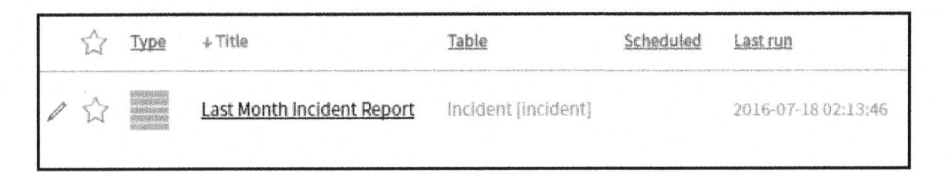

Service-Now newly created report

6. Click on the **Last Month Incident Report** again.
7. Click on the **Save** button(down arrow) and again click on **Schedule** button:

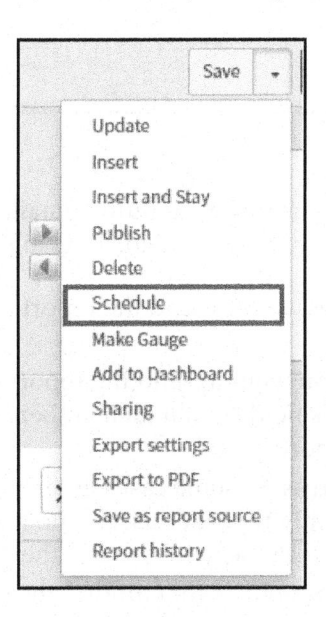

Service-Now report schedule button

Building and Configuring Reports

8. After clicking on the **Schedule** button, you will be redirected to the following screen, where you can see the report name in the **Report** field and the name of the report in the **Name** field, which you can modify at your convenience:
    - **Name**: `Schedule execution of Last Month Incident Report`
    - **Report**: `Last Month Incident Report`

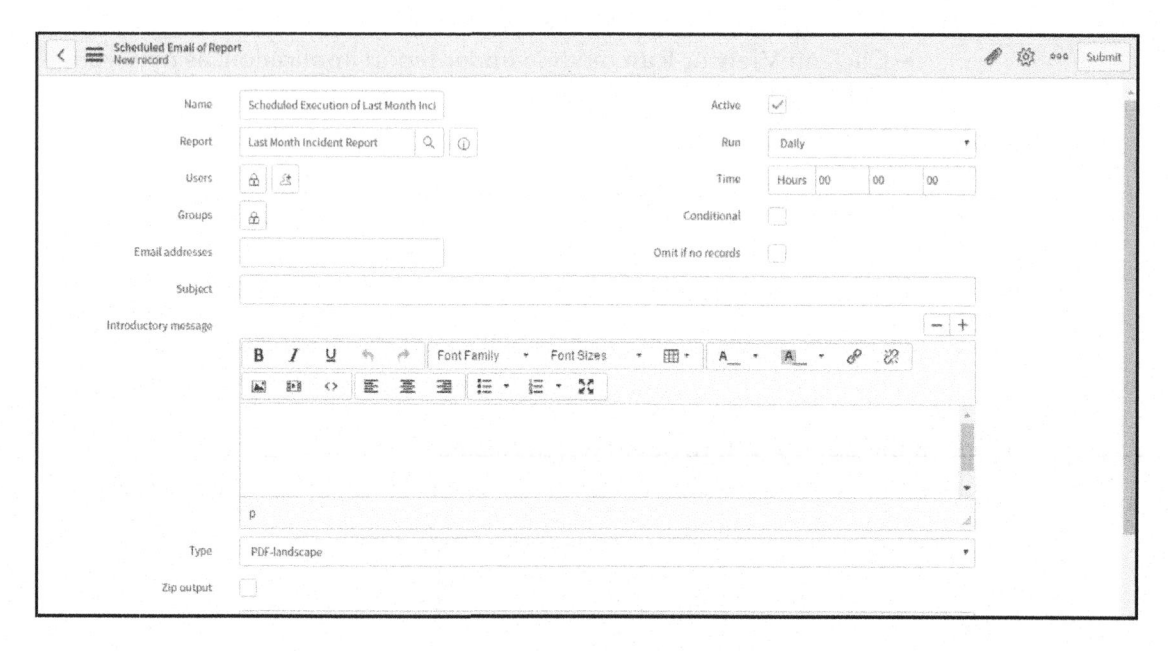

Service-Now schedule report screen

9. Now we need to configure the **Scheduled email of report** page for monthly report. The description of various fields is as follows:

    - **Users**: If you want to send the report to individuals, then you can add users here.
    - **Group**: If you want to send the report to a group, then you can add the group in this field so that all members of that group will receive the monthly report.
    - **E-mail address**: In some cases, there may be a business requirement to send a monthly report to users who are not in the Service-Now user table. In such a case, you can add the e-mail addresses of those users.
    - **Subject**: This field is for entering the subject for the monthly report by which it will be delivered in users' mailboxes.

- **Run**: This field is very important; here, we decide when the report should be delivered to the user's mailbox. If you want to send a daily report, then select daily; similarly, you can select monthly, weekly, and periodically.
- **Omit if no record**: If there is no record in the table, then by default, Service-Now generates the report in a defined format and sends it to the user as an e-mail notification. So, to prevent this you can select this option so that Service-Now does not send an empty file to the user.
- **Introduction message**: Many organizations use a specific format to send reports to end users, so if your organization has a predefined format, then you can use that, or you can write a nice introduction in the e-mail.
- **Type**: This is the report format in which you want to send the report file to end users. By default, Service-Now can send reports in Excel, image, PDF, and CSV formats:

10. Now configure the **Schedule Email of Report** as follows:

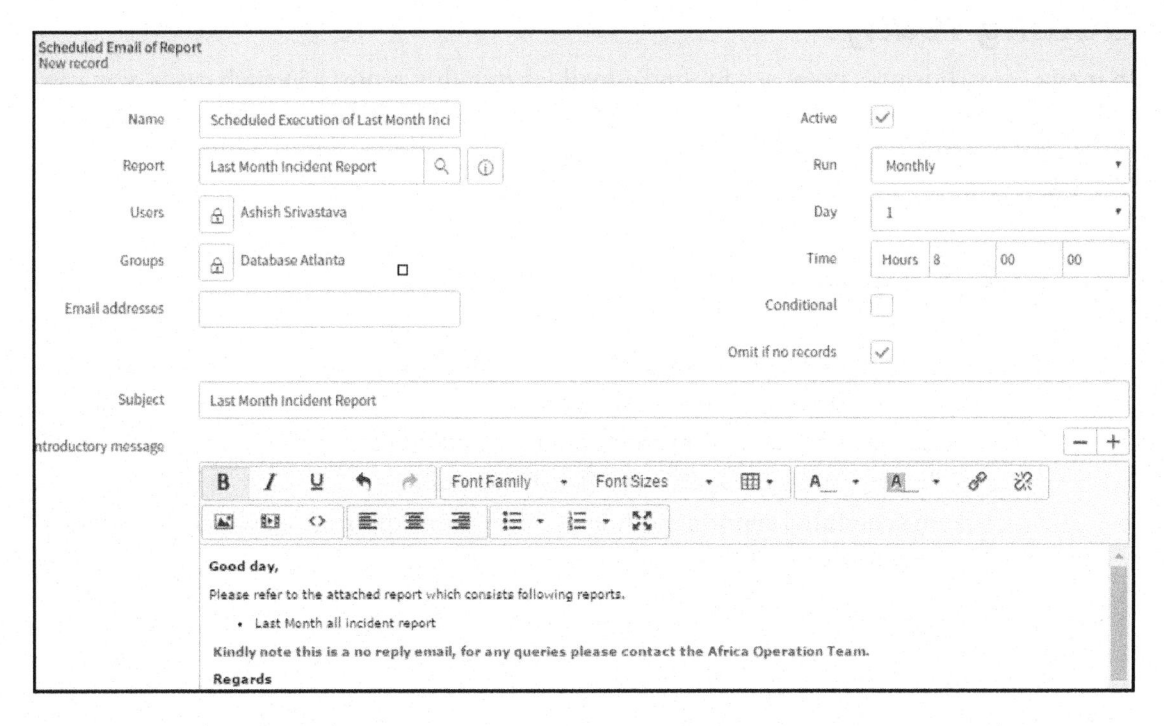

Service-Now schedule report (filled form) screen

Building and Configuring Reports

11. After configuration click on **Submit** button and after submission it will be added in **Scheduled Reports** module under **Reports Application** and based on time field it will be executed.

There's more...

You can view all schedule jobs in which is going to run today in **Today's Scheduled Jobs** module under **System Scheduler Application.**

Sending multiple reports in one e-mail

If you had sent a few reports after the previous recipe, would your client have been happy with your multiple e-mails? Perhaps not, so in this recipe we see how to schedule multiple reports in one e-mail.

Getting ready

In many cases, business users ask for one e-mail for monthly reports; in such cases, you can include more than one report in the same e-mail. For this recipe, all that you need is an active Service-Now instance, valid credentials, and a role (admin, report admin, or report group).

How to do it...

1. Open a web browser (Google Chrome, Firefox, Safari, or Internet Explorer).
2. Type the instance URL in the address bar.
3. Log in to the Service-Now instance using the credentials.
4. Type the Report in the search bar (left-hand side).
5. Click on **scheduled reports** module under reports application, which acts as a repository of all scheduled reports:

Chapter 5

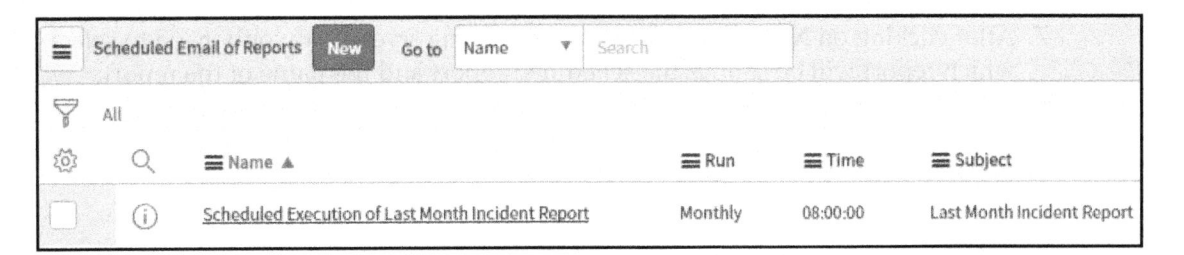

≡	Scheduled Email of Reports	**New**	Go to	Name ▼	Search			
▽	All							
⚙	🔍	≡ Name ▲				≡ Run	≡ Time	≡ Subject
☐	ⓘ	Scheduled Execution of Last Month Incident Report				Monthly	08:00:00	Last Month Incident Report

Service-Now Scheduled Report screens

6. Click on **Scheduled Execution of Last Month Incident Report** and scroll down, in the **Included in Email related list**, click on **New**:

Reports – Included in Email section

[235]

Building and Configuring Reports

7. After clicking on **New**, you will see the following screen. You only need to select which report will be sent as the scheduled report and the name of the report:

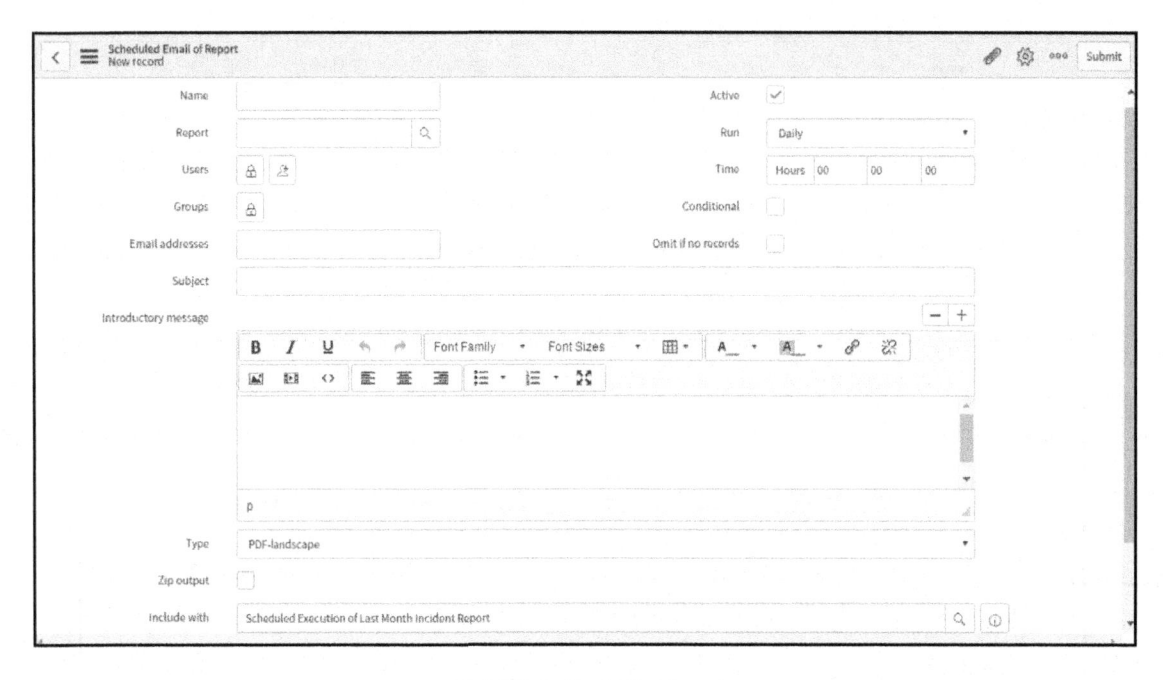

Included in Email section Blank form

8. Enter the **Name** of the report as `Last month breach report`, select the `breached SLAs by Type` **Report** field, change the run field value to on demand, and submit the form. It's also worth noting that you can change the report format as well:

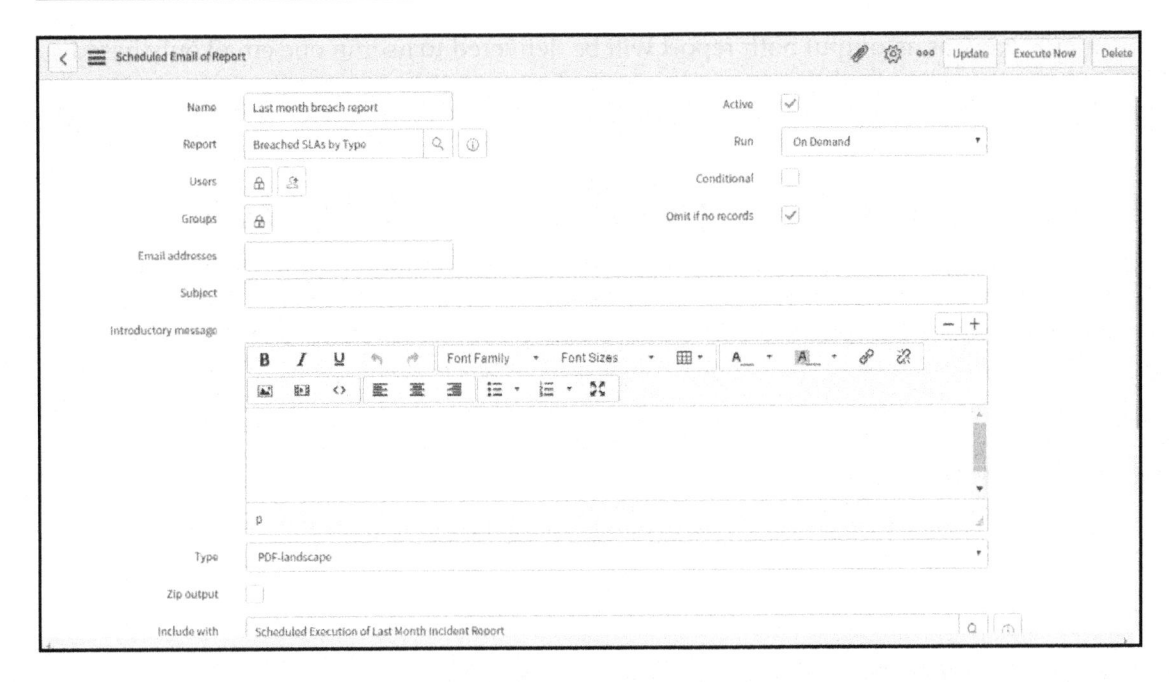

Included in Email section filled form

9. Now in the following screen, you can see that the newly created schedule report has been added with the original report:

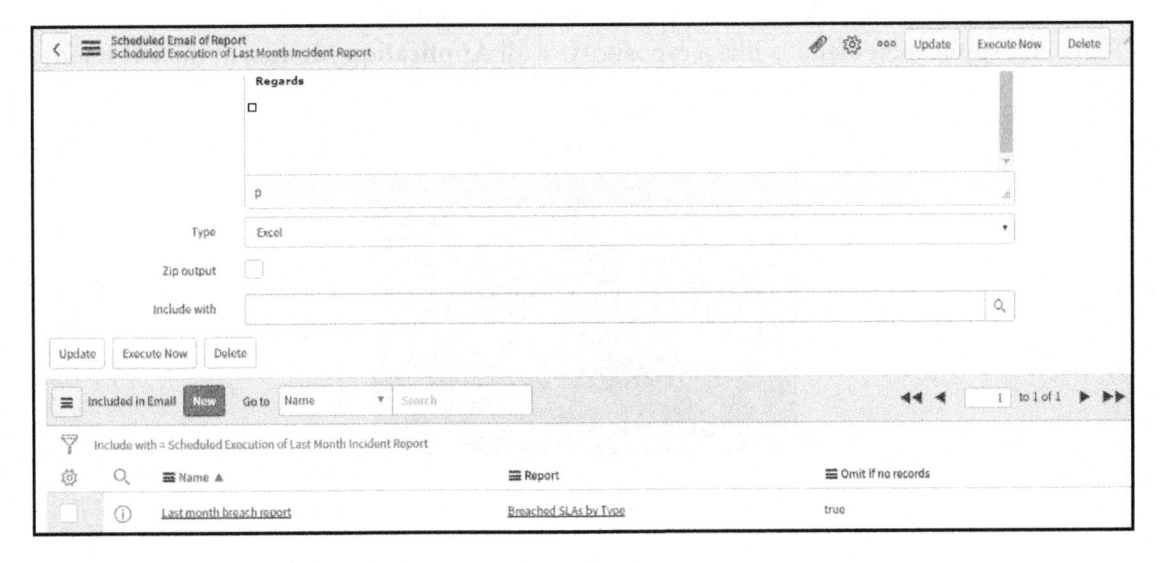

Output – Last Month Incident Report added in report schedule

10. Now as an output both report will be delivered to user in one email only based on report schedule.

Creating a table-specific report module

On many occasions, business users want access to the report module, but as the system admin or because of security reasons we don't wish to give them access. So, for business users, we can create a report module where they can view or run their own report. In this recipe, you will see how to create a dedicated module for reporting.

Getting ready

All you need is an active Service-Now instance and valid credentials to log in to Service-Now and an admin role.

How to do it...

1. Open a web browser (Google Chrome, Firefox, Safari, or Internet Explorer).
2. Type the instance web address in the address bar.
3. Log in to the Service-Now instance using the credentials.
4. Application menu is like a repository of all **Application Menus**. In the left-hand search box, type application menus and service-now search out application menu module for your:

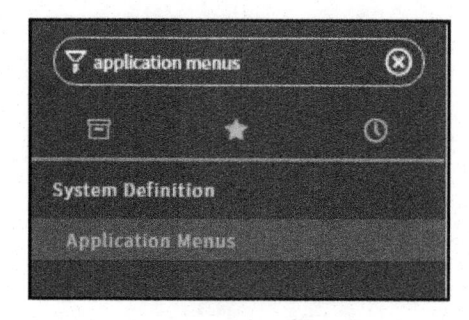

Application menus

5. Click on **Application Menus**, after that you will able to see the following screenshot where you can see all application of service-now:

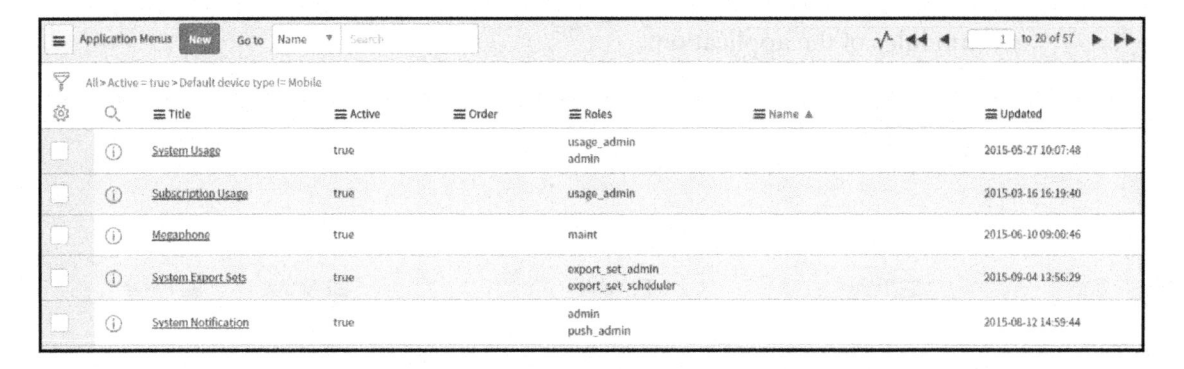

Service-Now application menu

6. Click on the **filter** of **Application Menus**, add the following condition in the **filter:** `active is true and Name contains self`:

Service-Now application menu filter condition

Building and Configuring Reports

7. Now you will able to see the self-service module. We are adding new a reporting module under **Self-Service** (`itil_self_service`), so click on it.
8. After clicking on **Self-Service** (`itil_self_service`), you will able to view all the modules of the application:

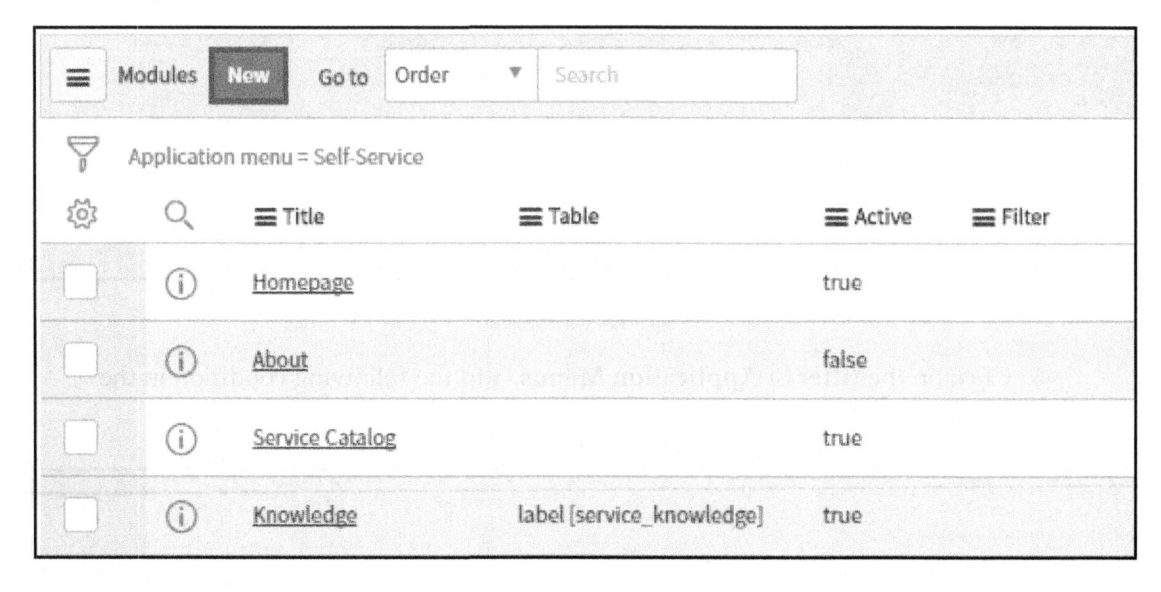

		Title	Table	Active	Filter
		Homepage		true	
		About		false	
		Service Catalog		true	
		Knowledge	label [service_knowledge]	true	

Modules | New | Go to Order | Search
Application menu = Self-Service

Service-Now self-service application module list

[240]

9. Click on **New** (module) to create a new module under the **Self-Service** application. In the new module form, enter the following details:
    - **Title**: View Last Month Incident Report (name of the module)
    - **Order**: 700 (position of the module in the application)
    - **Visibility**: Leave the role blank (if there is no role, then all users will able to view this module)

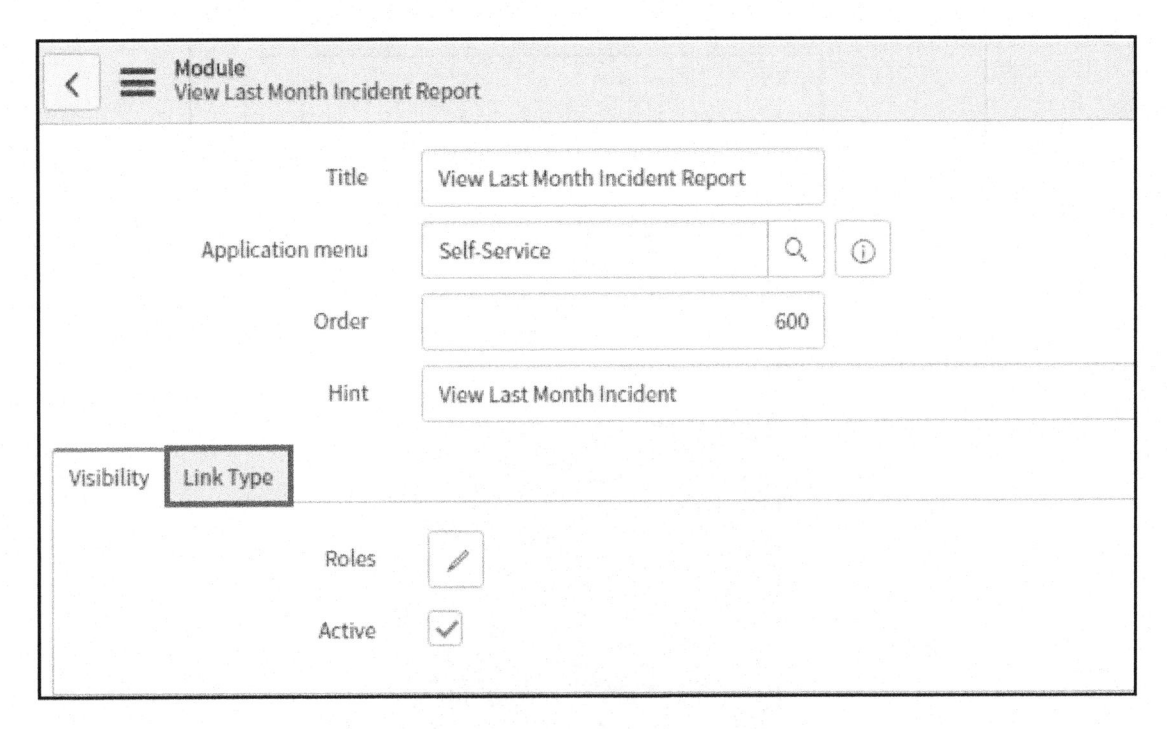

Reporting module configuration Part I

Building and Configuring Reports

- Click on the **Link Type** section. In the **Link type** field, select `Run a Report` and in the **Report** field, select `Last Month Incident Report` and **Submit** the form:

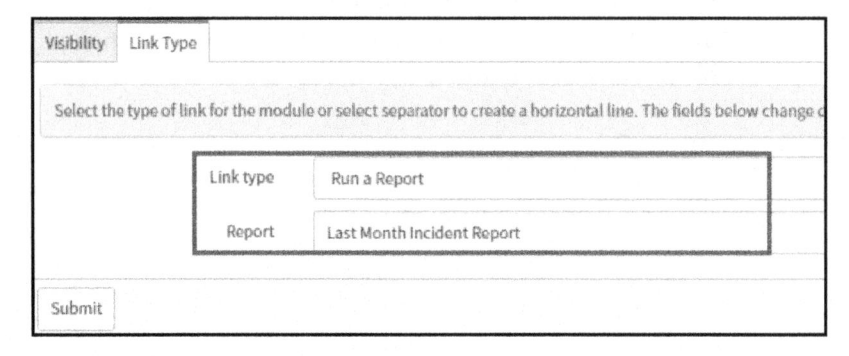

Reporting module configuration Part II

10. Now, the new reporting module **View Last Month Incident Report** has been added to the self-service module:

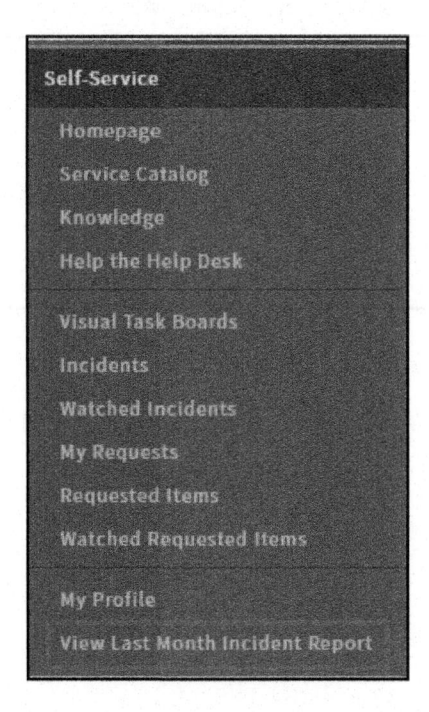

Self-service application with new module

[242]

11. Now as an output end user will able to use this new module View Last Month Incident Report in Self Service Application.

Creating a dashboard

Dashboards are the key to determining the overall status of a team, a senior management, or middle management executive's request for a dashboard. In this recipe, we will see how to create a dashboard.

Getting ready

For this recipe, all you need is an active Service-Now instance, valid credentials, and an admin role.

How to do it...

1. Open a web browser (Google Chrome, Firefox, Safari, or Internet Explorer).
2. Type the instance web address in the address bar.
3. Log in to the Service-Now instance using the credentials.
4. Type `Homepage` in the search bar (left-hand side) and click on **Homepage module**:

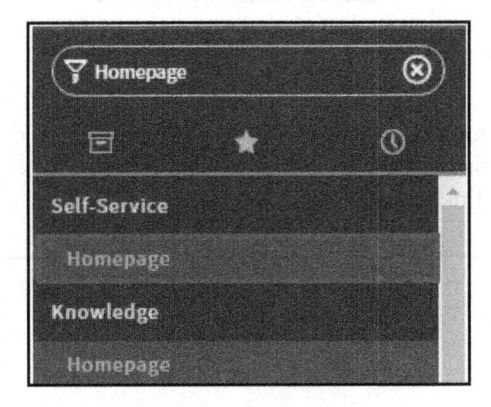

Self Service – Homepage

Building and Configuring Reports

5. After clicking on **Homepage**, you will be redirected to the **System Administration** home page. From the system administration page, click on **Switch to page:**

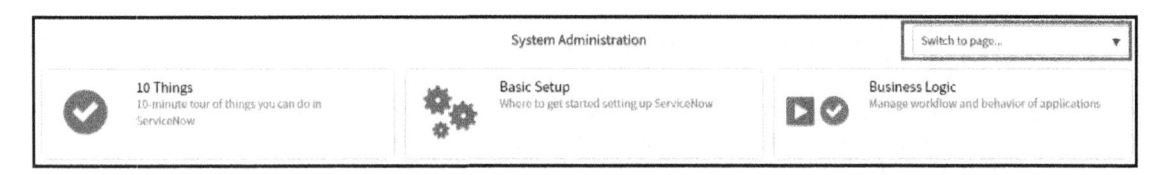

Homepage – Switch to page...

6. Click on **New page** option under Switch to page and Service-Now will automatically create a new home page named `My HomePage` for you, but you will have to configure the new homepage:

New Home Page

7. Now you need to configure **My Homepage 1**. It depends on the business requirement as to what data you want to show on the dashboard and which data makes sense to business users, such as last month's open tickets, breached tickets, about to breach tickets, and so on:

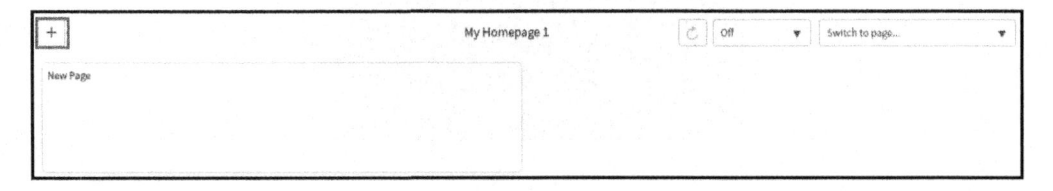

New home page configuration

Chapter 5

8. We have configured the dashboard, but we still have one challenge; that this new home page will only be visible to you. So, to make it visible to all users, go to **Homepage Admin** and select **Pages**:

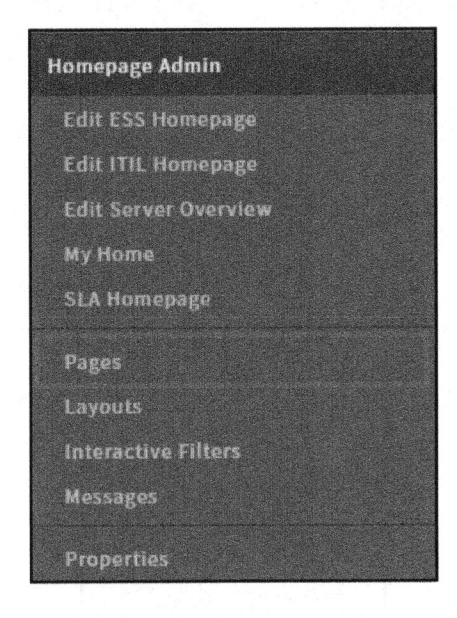

Homepage Admin module – Home Pages

9. Now search for the home page by title and open it. After that mark check **Selectable** field, click on the **Update** button. Now other users will also able to view the home page:

Make the Home Page visible to others

Building and Configuring Reports

10. Now other users are able to view our new dashboard, but it will be blank for all users as you have not added any content on the dashboard. So, now go to the report module and again open **Last Month Incident Report**, click on the **Save(down arrow)** button, and select **Add to Dashboard** option:

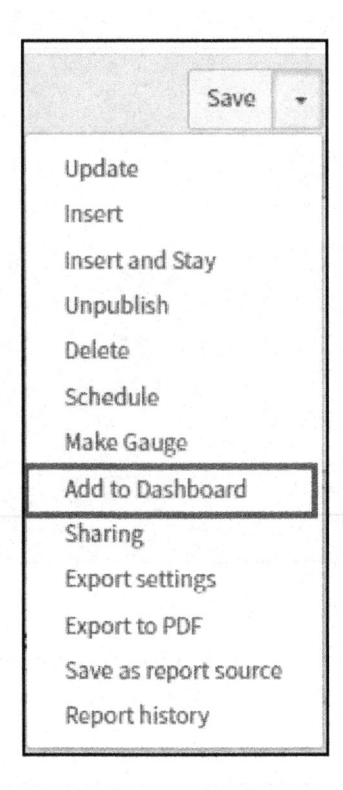

Add report to Dashboard

11. Once the **Add to Dashboard** option has been selected, a window will pop up to indicate the home page name, report position, and report name, you only need to select the position of the report by clicking on the region marked **Section 2** in the following screenshot:

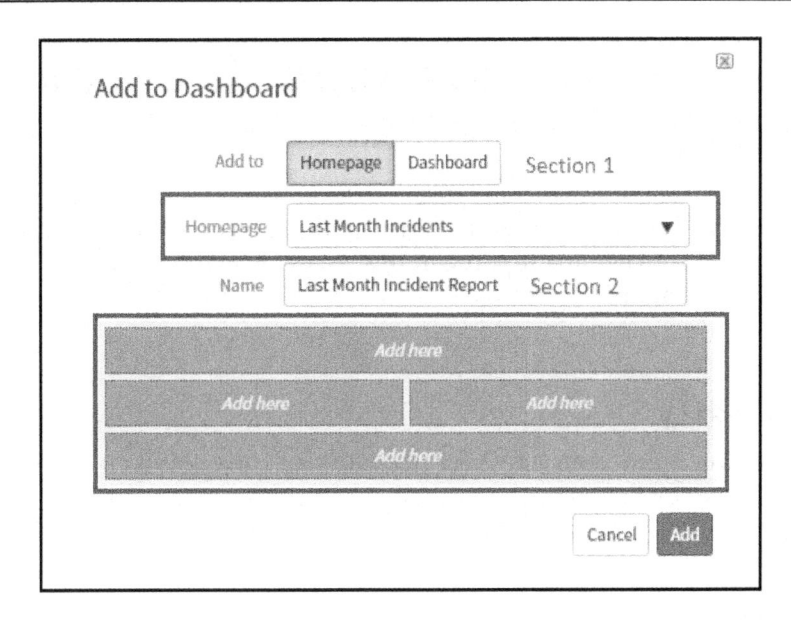

Add report to the dashboard popup

12. Once the position of report is selected, a report will be added on the home page **Last Month Incidents**. Now any user can check this home page and make the necessary decision for calls:

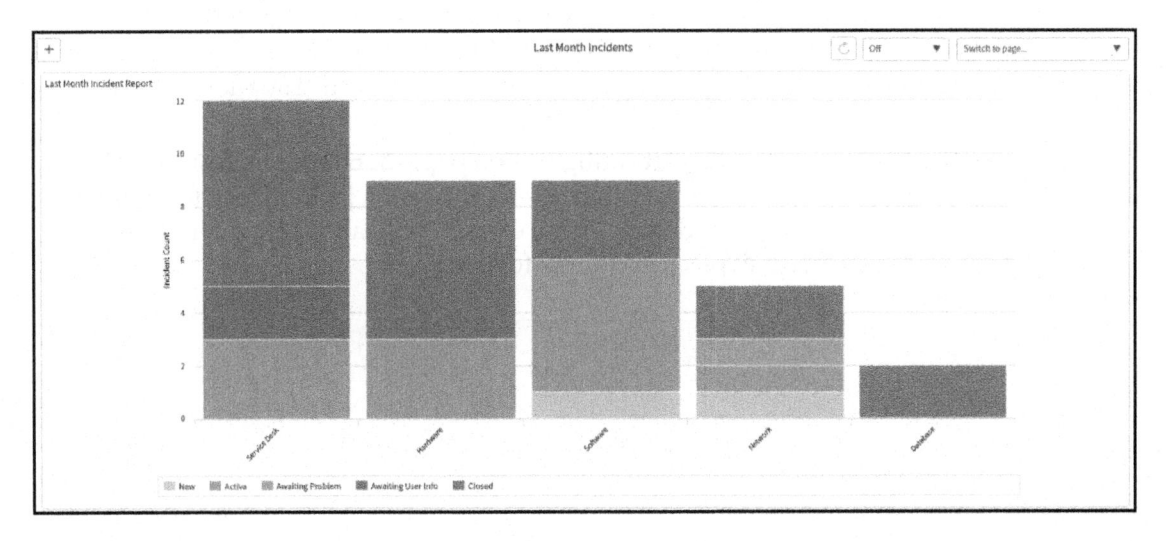

Last month incident report on the home page

Including the date in a report's e-mail notification

By default, Service-Now doesn't include dates in the subject of an e-mail notification. That's why many clients ask for the date to be included in the subject of e-mail notifications so that they can differentiate between the reports. In this recipe, we will learn to include the date in a report's e-mail notification.

Getting ready

For this recipe, all you need is an active Service-Now instance, valid credentials, and an admin role.

How to do it...

1. Open a web browser (Google Chrome, Firefox, Safari, or Internet Explorer).
2. Type the instance web address in the address bar.
3. Log in to the Service-Now instance using credentials.
4. On the left-hand side search box, type reports in the search box and select **Scheduled Report** module under **Reports Application**.
5. Now open the `Scheduled Execution of Last Month Incident Report` record.
6. The **Schedule Email of Report** configuration page–`Subject` field supports javascript that's why we can also include a declaration javascript in the subject line. So if we want to include date in the e-mail notification of the report e-mail, then you can and small piece of code as follows:

Chapter 5

Report date in e-mail notification

Subject: `javascript :"Last month incident report" + gs.now();`

7. As an output, you will able to view the date in the subject of the report in your emails:

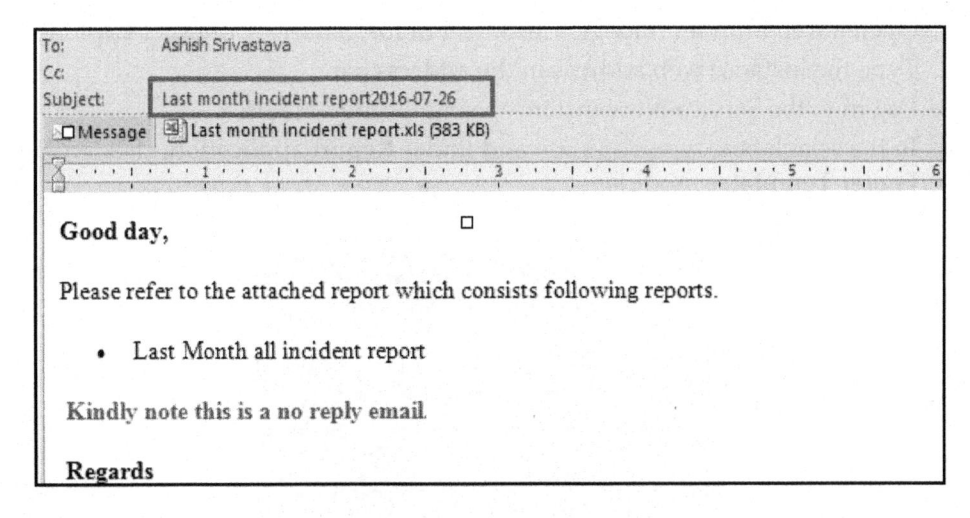

Date in subject of report e-mail

[249]

Working with the report's header and footer template

Many companies have their own many format style. Service-Now can generate reports in Excel, PDF, JPEG, and PNG formats. Header and footer templates are useful when you want to download or schedule in PDF format and you can't enforce header and footer template features in other formats. In this recipe, you will learn to work with the report's header and footer template.

Getting ready

For this recipe, you need an active Service-Now instance and valid credentials and an admin role.

How to do it...

1. Open a web browser (Google Chrome, Firefox, Safari, or Internet Explorer).
2. Type the instance web address in the address bar.
3. Log in to the Service-Now instance using the credentials.
4. In the search box, type `reports` and under **Report** application, click on **Header Footer Templates** module:

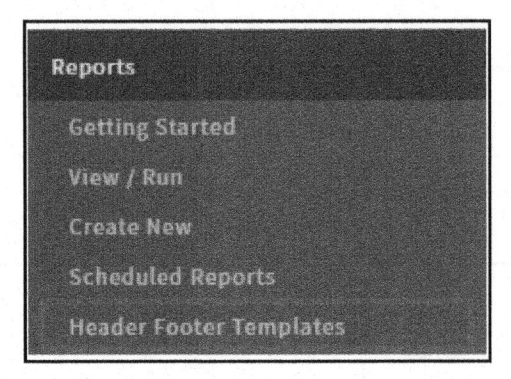

Reports Header and Footer

5. After clicking on **Header Footer Templates**, you will be redirected to the following page where you can view the default template which is provided by Service-Now. So you have two options, either you can make changes in the default template or you can create a new header and footer. To create a new header and footer you can click on **New Button**:

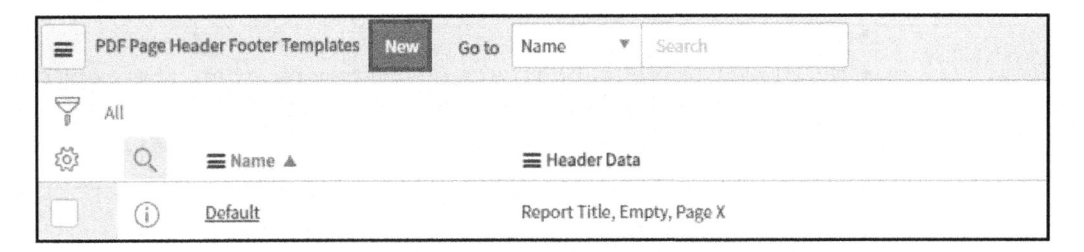

Reports – header and footer page

6. After clicking on the **New** button, you will be redirected to the following page. You will need to configure the footer and header which are in different sections (**Header Configuration** and **Footer Configuration**):

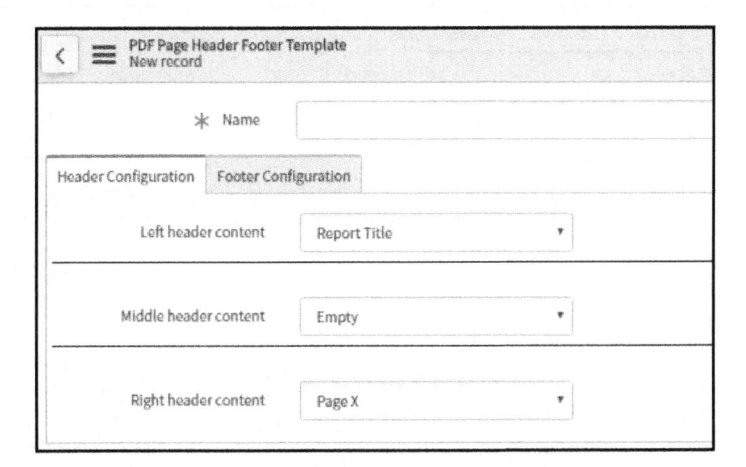

Header and footer template configuration template

7. In the **Name** field, you can give any desired name to remember the template and apply it while generating reports in the PDF format. Now, we need to configure the header and footer of the PDF which has three parts (left, center, and right) and in all three sections, Service-Now provides the following options:
   - `Page X`
   - `Page X of Y`

Building and Configuring Reports

- `Report Title`
- `Run by`
- `Run date and time`
- `User specified text`
- `Image`
- `Empty`
- My client gave a business requirement that the report should be e-mailed.
- On the left side of the header, the logo of the company
- In the middle of the header, the title of the report
- On the right side of the report, data and time

8. For that business requirement, you will have to select **Left header content** as `Image`, after which an image upload option will come up where you need to update the logo of the company. Select **Middle header content** as `Report Title` option and finally, **Right header content** as `Run Date and Time` option:

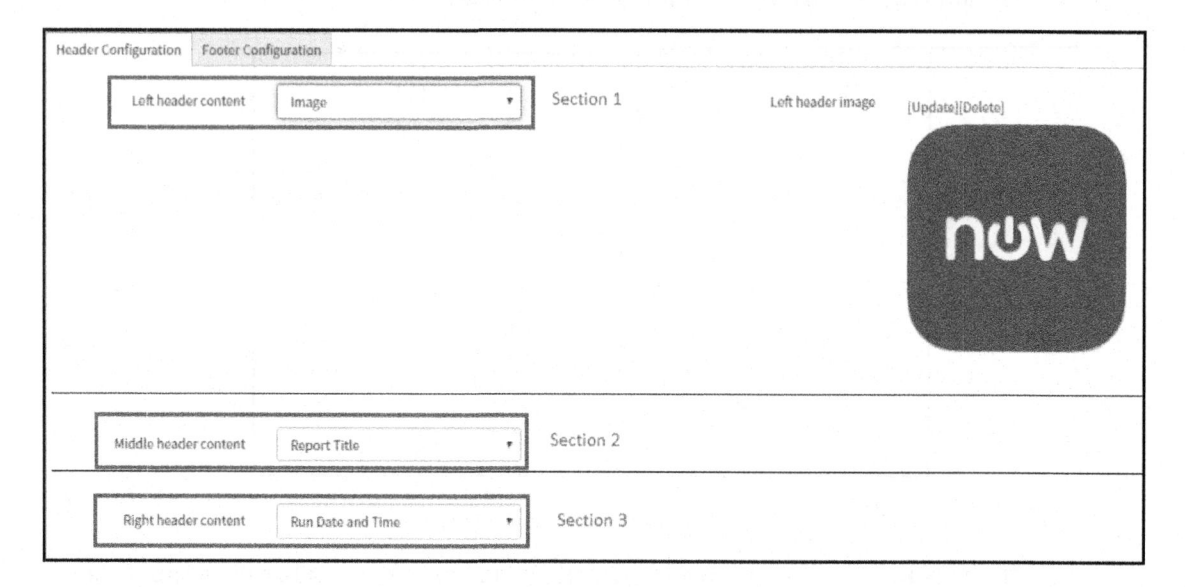

Report header and footer configuration

9. After configuring the header, you will need to configure the footer. So now my client wants the report footer in the following format:
    - On the left side of the footer, a monthly report text

[252]

- In the middle of the footer, page number
- On the right side, total pages

10. You need to click on the **Footer Configuration** section. You need to select **Left footer content** as `User Specified Text`, once you select it a Left Footer Text field will pop up and in that field, you can type the desired text such as `Monthly Report`. In **Middle footer content** select `Page X` so that page numbers can appear on the middle of the footer. Finally, select footer content as `Page X of Y` so that current vs. total pages come on the right side of the footer of the report:

Report footer configuration

11. After configuring this, click on **Submit**. Now you can see the newly created template in the header and footer page:

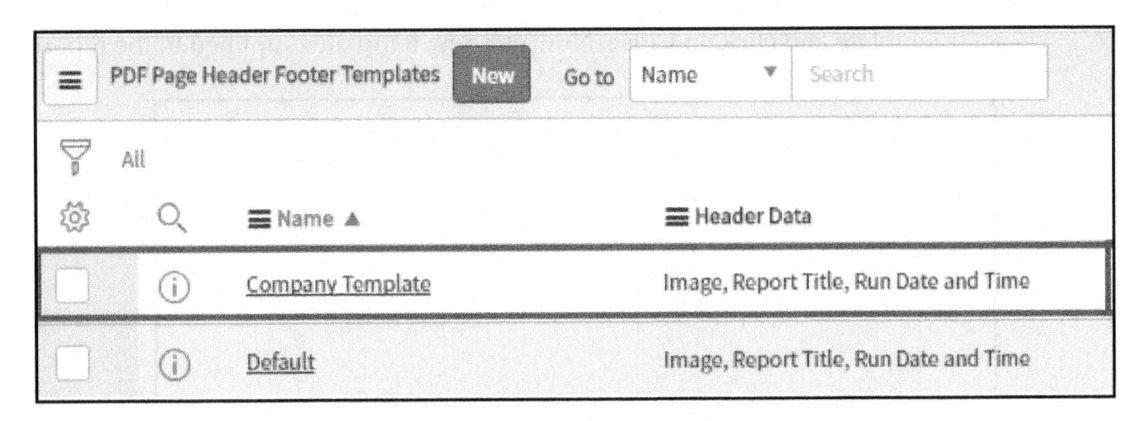

New header and footer added in list

Building and Configuring Reports

12. Our work is not done yet as we need to apply this template in the report as well. To apply a template in reports, go to the report **Last month incident report** and click on the small arrow beside the save button to view all the options. From the options, you need to select **Export Settings**:

Report export setting

13. Once you click on **Export Settings**, a popup appears where you need to select your template and click on **Close**. Now our new template is applied to the report:

Export settings pop-up window

[254]

14. Now return to the options from the save button and click on the Export to PDF option. A popup appears again to confirm orientation and delivery. If your report has many columns, then select **Landscape**, and if you want to download the report to the local system, then click on **Generate now**. You can also e-mail the report directly from here:

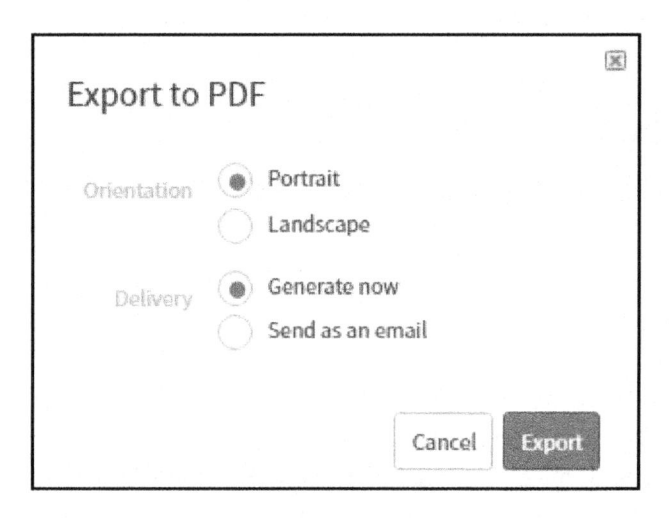

Export to PDF

15. As an output, you can view the report with the configured header:

PDF report header

16. As an output, you can view the report footer as shown in following screenshot:

PDF report footer

Working with the report sources

Report filters are very useful for a system administrator. Very often, we come across a situation where we need to refine the report filter to meet the business requirement. So, to avoid rework we can define a report source as a reusable component. In this recipe, we will learn to work with report sources.

Getting ready

For this recipe, you need an active service-now instance, valid credentials and an admin role.

How to do it...

1. Open a web browser (Google Chrome, Firefox, Safari, or Internet Explorer).
2. Type the instance web address in the address bar.
3. Log in to the Service-Now instance using the credentials.
4. Type the `report` in the search bar (left-hand side).
5. Under the reports application, from the administration section, click on **Report Sources**:

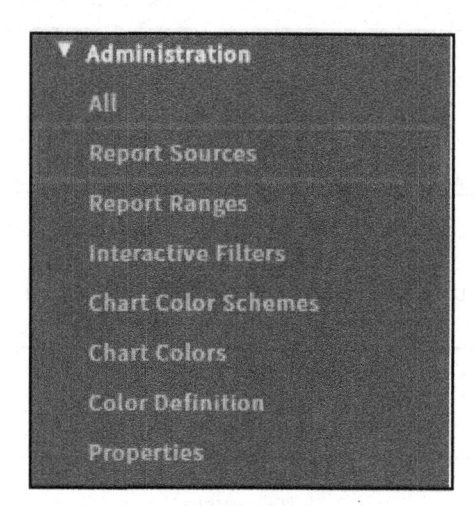

▼ Administration
All
Report Sources
Report Ranges
Interactive Filters
Chart Color Schemes
Chart Colors
Color Definition
Properties

6. You will be redirected to the following page, where you can view the predefined **Report Sources**. If you want to create a new data source, then click on **New** button:

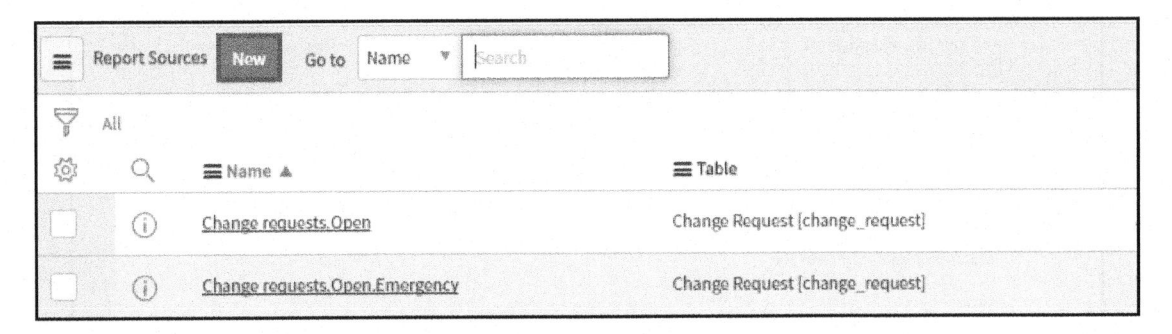

Name	Table
Change requests.Open	Change Request [change_request]
Change requests.Open.Emergency	Change Request [change_request]

Report source

7. Now we need to configure our Report source page. Data source configuration completely depends on the business requirement because it's the business requirement alone that will let us know for which table we should make data source and with what conditions:

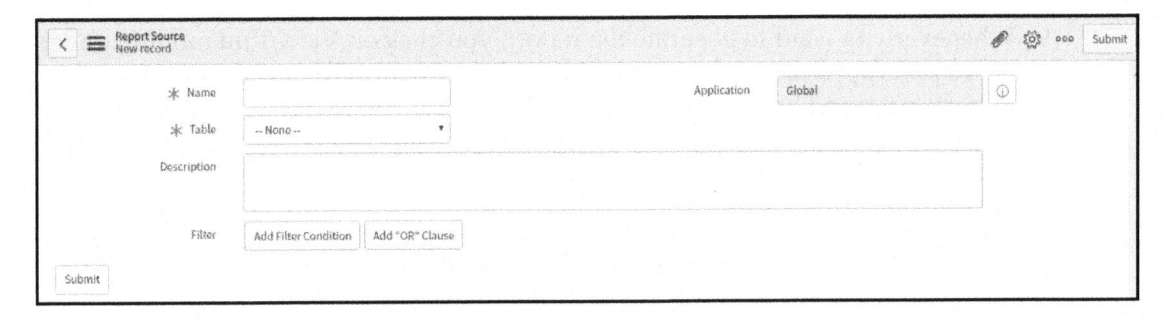

Report source configuration page

Building and Configuring Reports

8. Since it's an admin's module, admins can decide the report source creation based on the reporting request. If any request comes frequently, then admins can create a report source to save the efforts:

Report source configuration

9. Whenever you want to generate the report, you click on View/Run module under the Reports application. After that you click on **Create a Report** button on Reports page and by default service-now redirects you to the report page where you need to select table, type, columns, group by and filters but to apply report source you need to change `Data` Field from `Table` to `Report Source` as shown in following screenshot:

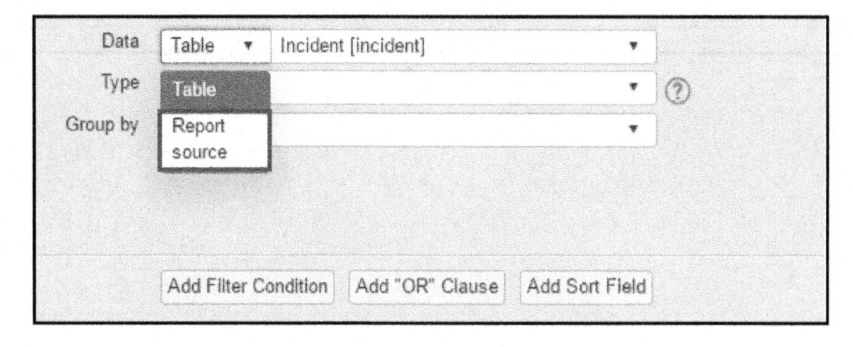

Select report source

[258]

Chapter 5

10. Now you need to select your **Data** field as **Report Source**. We have created a new data source, `Monthly Report Open Incident`. So, now you need to select it from the reference field:

New report configuration

11. Since we have just applied data sources in the report, you don't need to apply the same filter again in report sources. If your business requirement is to filter the record more, such as with a specific location record or a particular date, then you can filter the report further. In the following reports, I have filtered the report further with `Assignment group` and the `Closed` field:

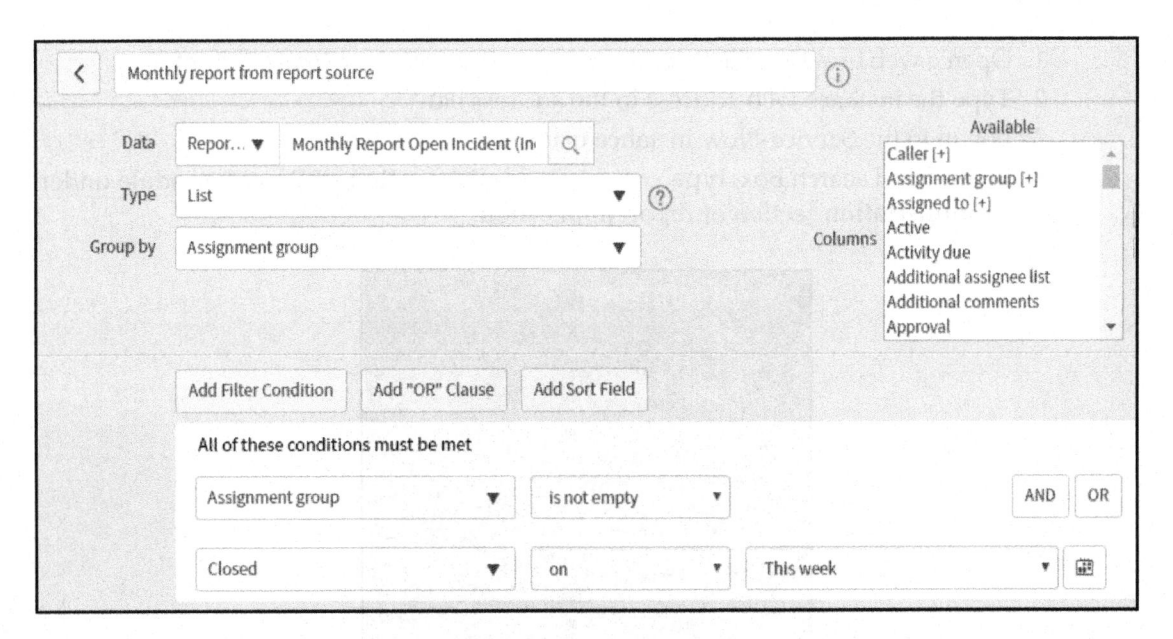

Report configuration via report source

12. As an output you will able to see a report which is combination of a data source and direct report filters as well.

[259]

Working with the report range

The report range feature is applied to only those dates which are very helpful in filtering the reports. On multiple occasions, clients request for a dashboard where they want to see first half (all incident which were create in last 4 hours. Let's understand this by an example so for an instance if a standard business day is from 8.00 AM to 4.30 PM then we can consider first half from 8.00 AM to 12.00 PM) call/tasks details with other parameter such as monthly or quarterly. This recipe will teach you to work with a report range.

Getting ready

For this recipe, all you need is an active Service-Now instance, valid credentials, and a role (admin or report admin).

How to do it...

1. Open a web browser (Google Chrome, Firefox, Safari, or Internet Explorer).
2. Type the instance web address in the address bar.
3. Log in to the Service-Now instance using the credentials.
4. In left-hand search box, type `reports` and click on **Report Ranges** module under **Administration** section of report application:

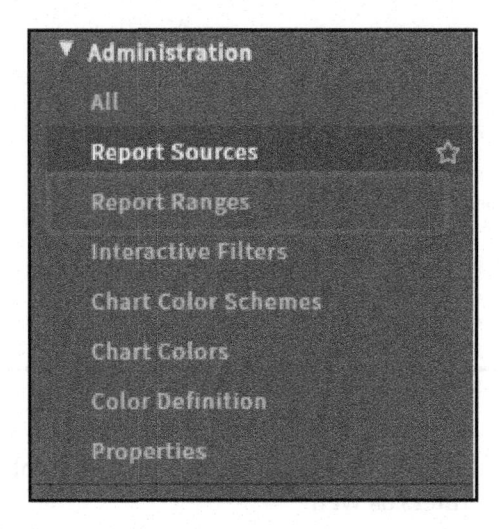

Create report range

5. Now you need to configure the report range. The report range form has the following fields which must be configured properly:
    - **Label**: Here you can give any name which you want your client to recognize, such as the `First Half` (calls in the last four hours). In the **Label** field you can give any desired name but please note that the name should be easy to understand for your customer or client.
    - **Name**: This contains the entire system table list where you can select any table. If you want to make a report range for a specific table, then you can select that table as well.
    - **Upper value duration**: This field defines a high value in range from 0, so if you want to filter reports from 0th hour to 3.59th hours as the first half, then you can enter it in this field:

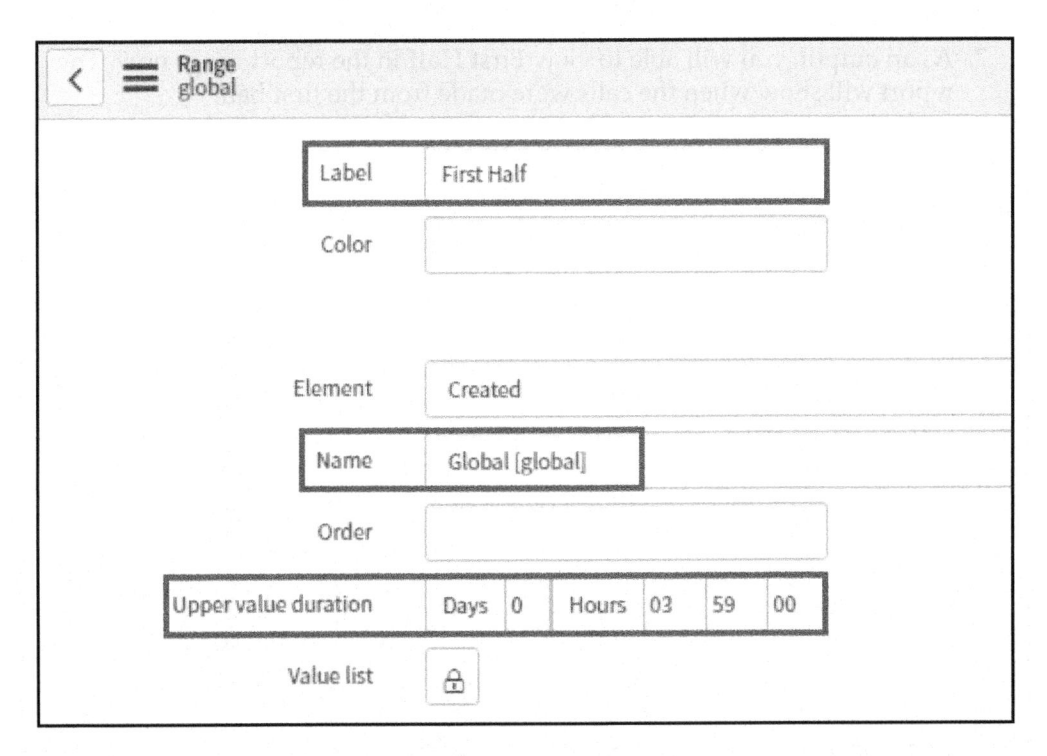

Report range configuration

- After selecting the Name (Global), select **Element as Created** and submit the rage configuration page.

Building and Configuring Reports

6. Go to the **View** and **Run** option where you will able to see **Last Month Incident Report**. Click on the **report** and change **Type** to Bar, **Group by** to Created, and **Stacked by** to State:

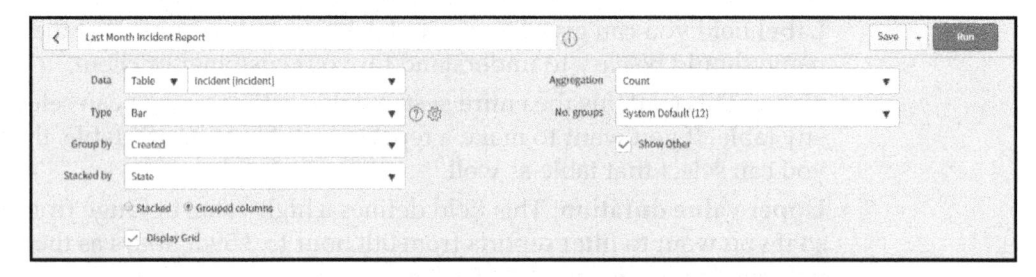

Report configuration for report range

7. As an output, you will able to view **First Half** in the report range now. This report will show when the calls were made from the first half:

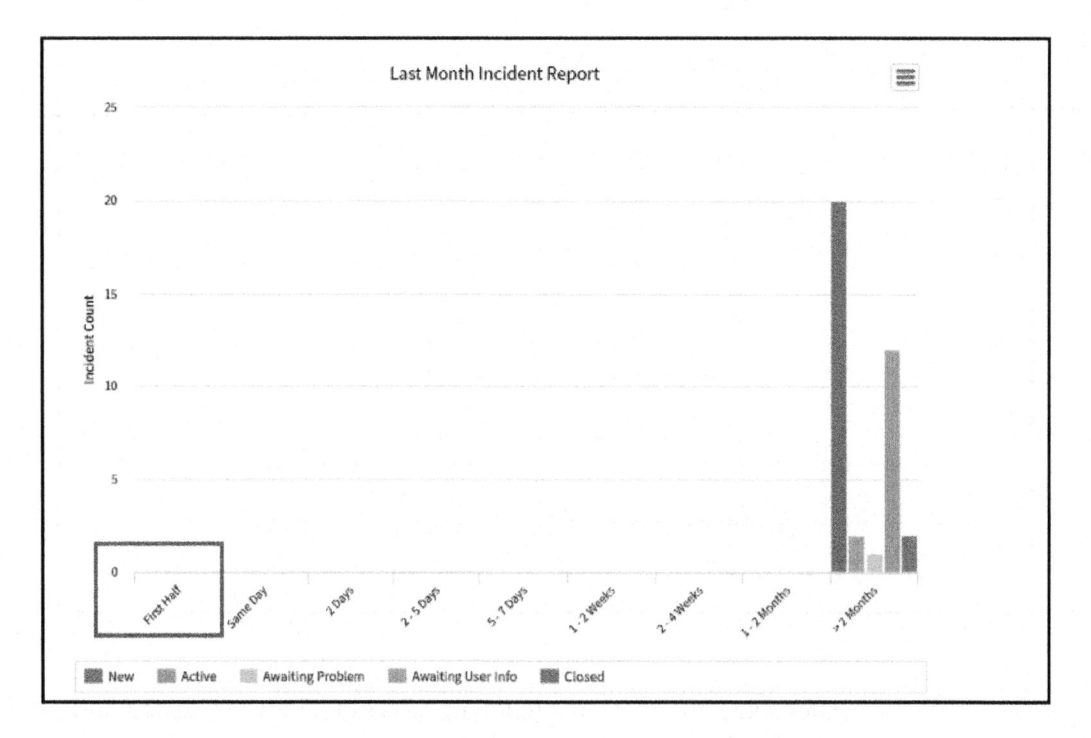

New report range

[262]

Creating a database view

Service-now provides system tables in which the data is stored and the product also provides a facility to create a custom table for a custom application, but it is worth to note that most of tables refer to each and other. On many occasions, clients ask for reports which are hard to get from a single table or a reporting module. In such a case, you can use the database view to connect more than one table to get the desired report. In this recipe, you will learn to create a database view.

Getting ready

For this recipe, you need an active service-now instance, valid credentials, and an admin role.

How to do it...

1. Open a web browser (Google Chrome, Firefox, Safari, or Internet Explorer).
2. Type the instance web address in the address bar.
3. Log in to the Service-Now instance using the credentials.
4. In the left-hand search box, type `database view` but **Database Views** module is not available under the reporting module and only available for admins. Click on **Database views** module under the **System Definition Application**:

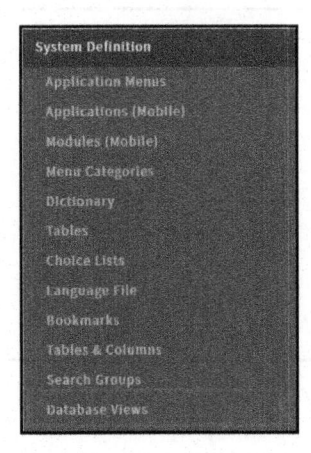

Database View Module

Building and Configuring Reports

5. Having clicked on **Database Views**, you will able to see the following screen where all the system database views are available. You need to click on the **New** button to create new database views:

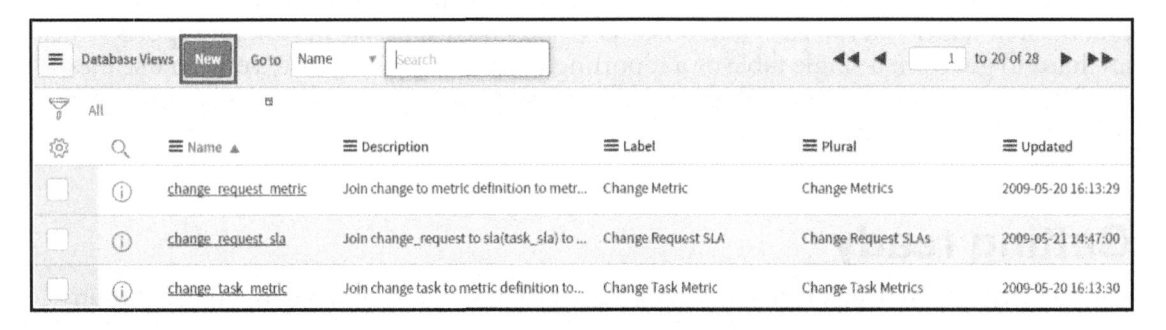

Name	Description	Label	Plural	Updated
change_request_metric	Join change to metric definition to metr...	Change Metric	Change Metrics	2009-05-20 16:13:29
change_request_sla	Join change_request to sla(task_sla) to ...	Change Request SLA	Change Request SLAs	2009-05-21 14:47:00
change_task_metric	Join change task to metric definition to...	Change Task Metric	Change Task Metrics	2009-05-20 16:13:30

New Database View Creation

6. After clicking on the **New** button, you will able to see the following screen where you need to give the name and label of your database view:
   - **Name**: `u_join_tables`
   - **Description**: `Joining two tables`

> **Database views** are available as a table in the report module.

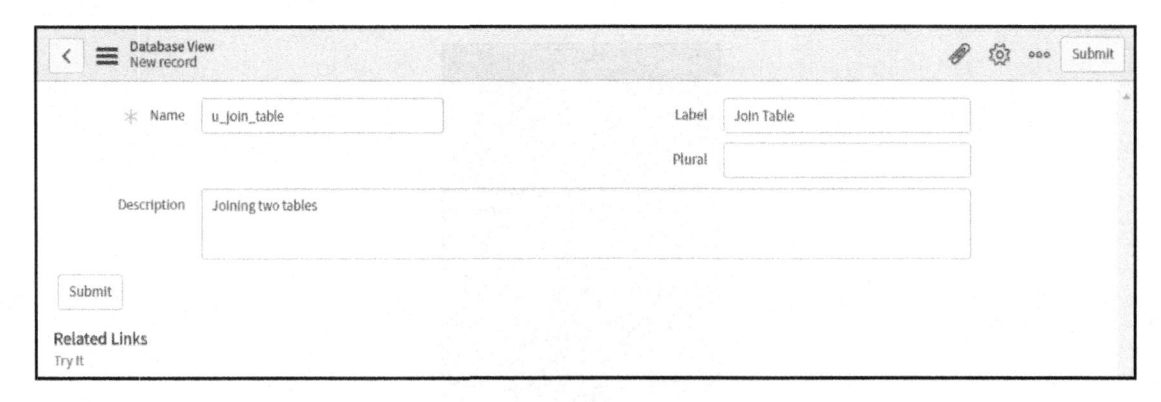

Define database view

[264]

7. Now, click on **View Tables** (New button) to add tables in database view. There are two tables which are being joined to produce the desired report. For instance, if you are creating a change ticket from an incident, then for the change ticket, the incident ticket will be the parent. To access the database view table, you will have to create variable prefixes which are just a variable to connect incident and change request table:

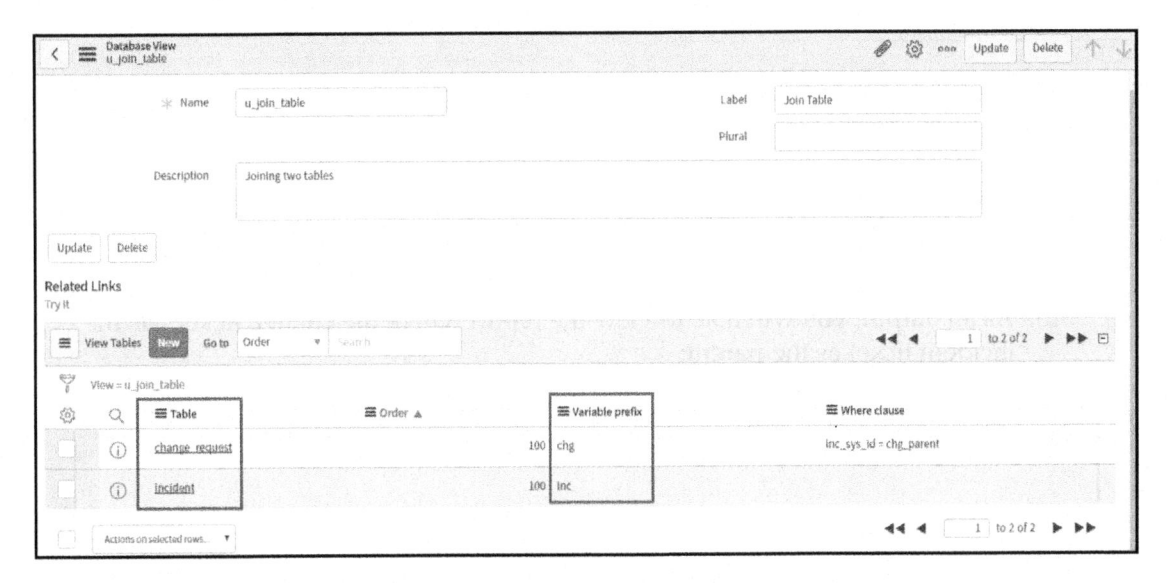

Database view tables

8. Now, it's very important to understand how you want to connect the two tables. As in this case, incident is the parent of the change ticket, so in the `Where` clause, we need to join tables using the parent field of change and `sys_id` of incident record.

Building and Configuring Reports

9. Now click on **Related Links Try It** to view the database view result:

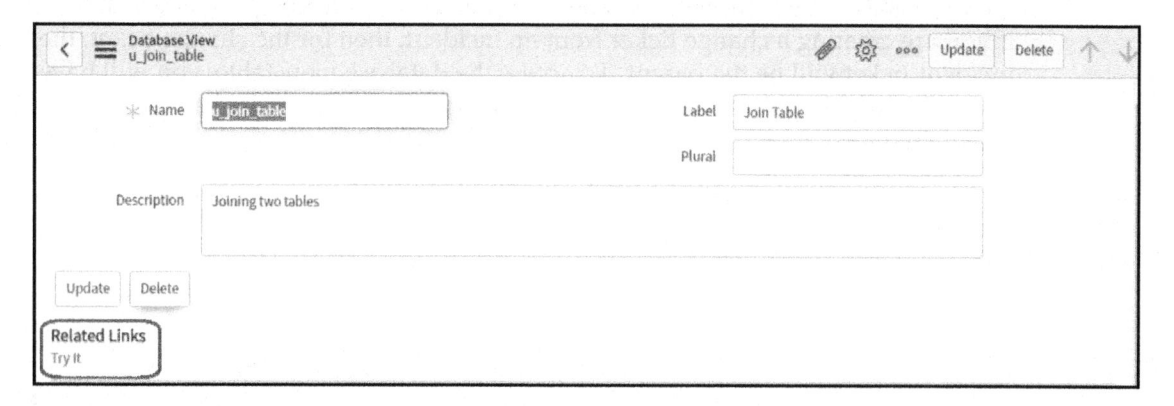

Database view

10. As an output, you will able to view the report where the change ticket has the incident ticket as the parent:

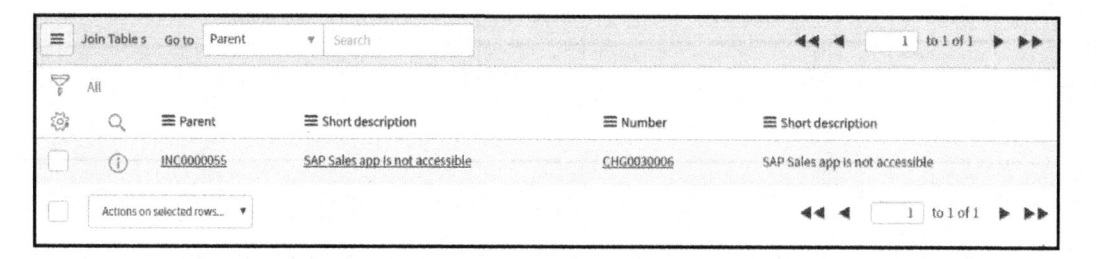

Database view result

11. If you want to show limited fields from the change request, then you will have to add the fields in the view field. I have added the **number**, **short description**, and **parent** fields in the table:

Add fields in the change request view table

12. If you want to show limited fields from the incident table, then you will have to add the fields in the view field. I have added short description and `sys_id` in the table:

Add fields in the incident view table

13. For non-admins, database view will be available as a table in the **view/run** module of reports application. To use Database Views, non-admins need to click on the view/run and after that **Create New Report button** to view reporting page, now select table as `Join Table(u_join_table)` database views:

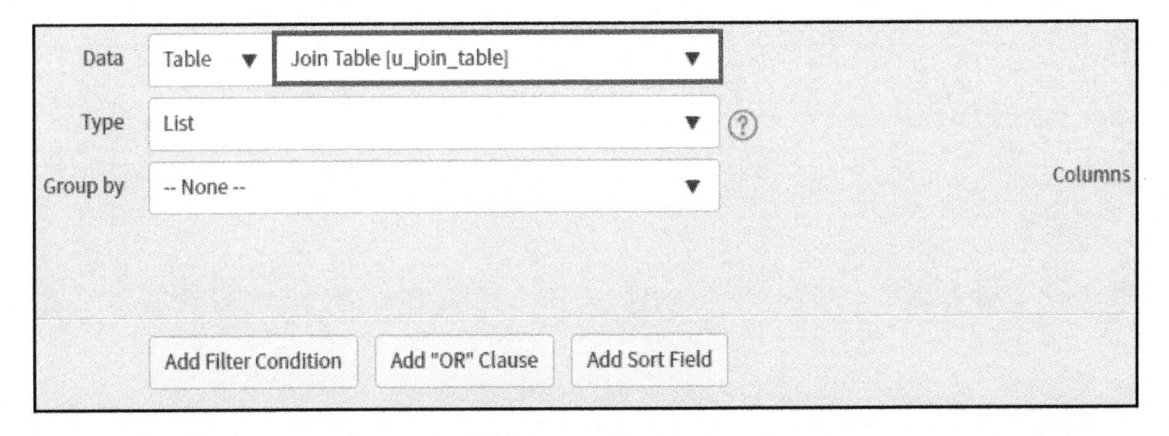

Report Module – Database View table

14. Now, click **Run** button to generate the report.

6
Creating and Configuring Workflow Activities

In this chapter, we will cover the following recipes:

- Understanding the Service-Now workflow
- Attaching a workflow with the service catalog
- Attaching workflows with current/new modules
- Workflow troubleshooting
- Setting up an approval activity
- Working with condition activities
- Working with task activities
- Working with workflow utilities
- Setting up e-mail notifications from workflows
- How to configure a timer in workflows
- Understanding the approval engine

Introduction

If I say workflows are the soul of Service-Now, then probably it won't be incorrect. Process management is critical in the IT service management domain and maintaining a process within an organization is very challenging as well. Service-Now has a built-in workflow engine and module which is extremely helpful in defining and maintaining a process.

Understanding the Service-Now workflow

E-commerce websites are very popular these days. So, for instance, if you are ordering any item from any e-commerce website, then there are certain processes which need to be followed, such as selecting the desired item, adding it to the cart, adding the address, making the payment shipment of item and so on. Likewise, if any request is raised, then the approval of the manager is required, for procurement of any item finance team approval is required and so on.

Getting ready

To step through this recipe, you should have an active Service-Now instance, valid credentials, and an admin role.

How to do it...

1. Open any standard web browser and type the instance address.
2. Log in to the Service-Now instance using the credentials.
3. On the left-hand side, type `workflow` and Service-Now will search out `workflow` application for you, as shown in following screenshot:

Chapter 6

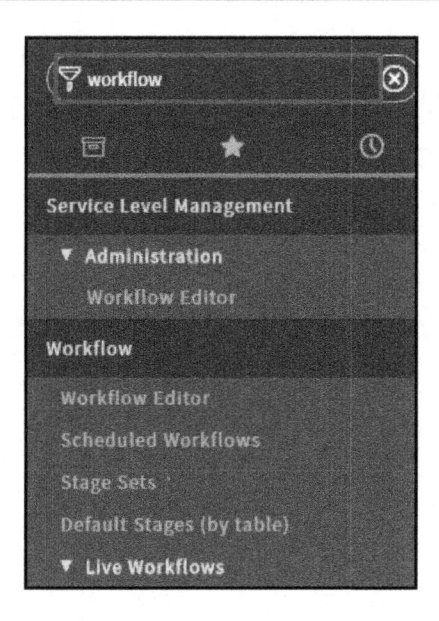

The Service-Now Workflow

4. Under `workflow` application, the **Workflow Editor** module is the repository of all workflows and the graphical editor as well. If you want to view any workflow within Service-Now, then you can click on the **Workflow Editor** module, after which you will see the following screen:

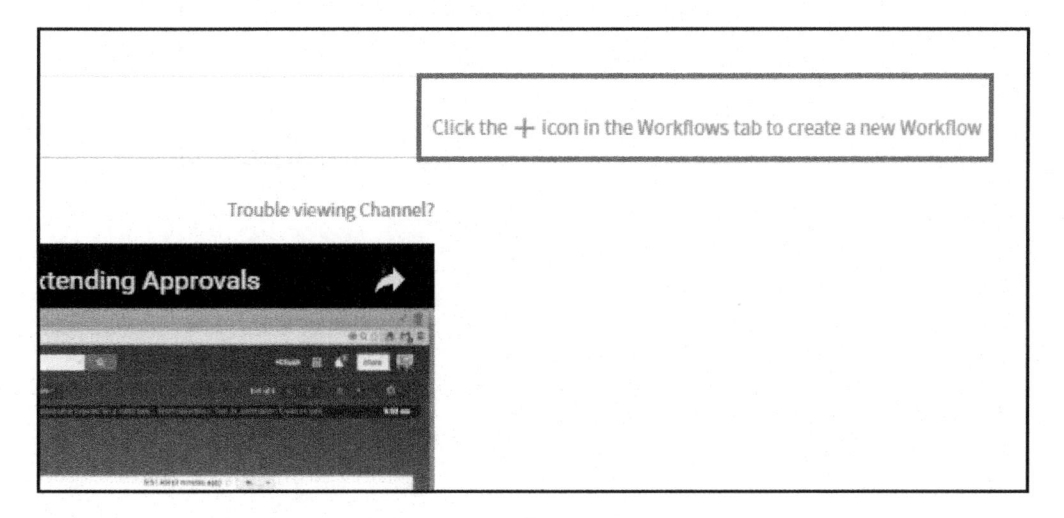

The Workflow Editor module

[271]

Creating and Configuring Workflow Activities

5. If you want to search any workflow, then you can search it by name in the **Workflows** section:

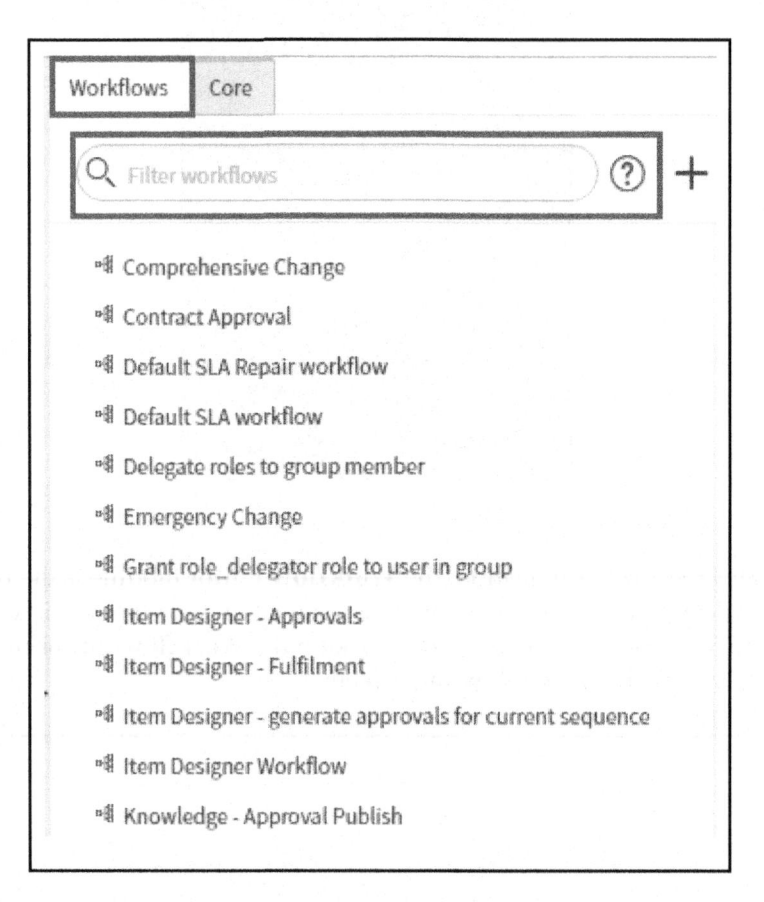

```
Workflows    Core

 Q  Filter workflows                      ?  +

  ▪ Comprehensive Change
  ▪ Contract Approval
  ▪ Default SLA Repair workflow
  ▪ Default SLA workflow
  ▪ Delegate roles to group member
  ▪ Emergency Change
  ▪ Grant role_delegator role to user in group
  ▪ Item Designer - Approvals
  ▪ Item Designer - Fulfilment
  ▪ Item Designer - generate approvals for current sequence
  ▪ Item Designer Workflow
  ▪ Knowledge - Approval Publish
```

Search the workflow

6. If you want to edit the behavior of a workflow, then you can use a system-defined workflow activity. Out of the box, Service-Now provides many activities in the **Core** Section such as the `switch` condition, user approvals, group approval, tasks, catalog task, `If` conditions and so on as follows:

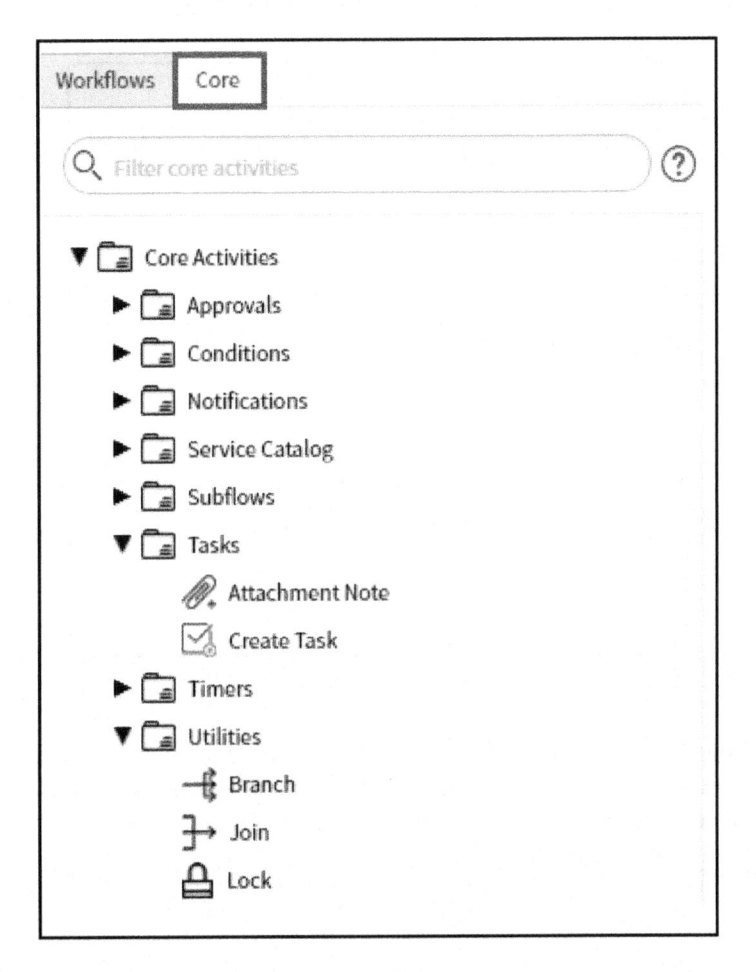

Workflow activities

7. It is important to note that there are two states of a workflow:

   - **Checkout**: If you want to edit or modify any published workflow, then you can click on the **Checkout** button. Only after clicking on **Checkout** button, will Service-Now will allow you to modify the workflow:

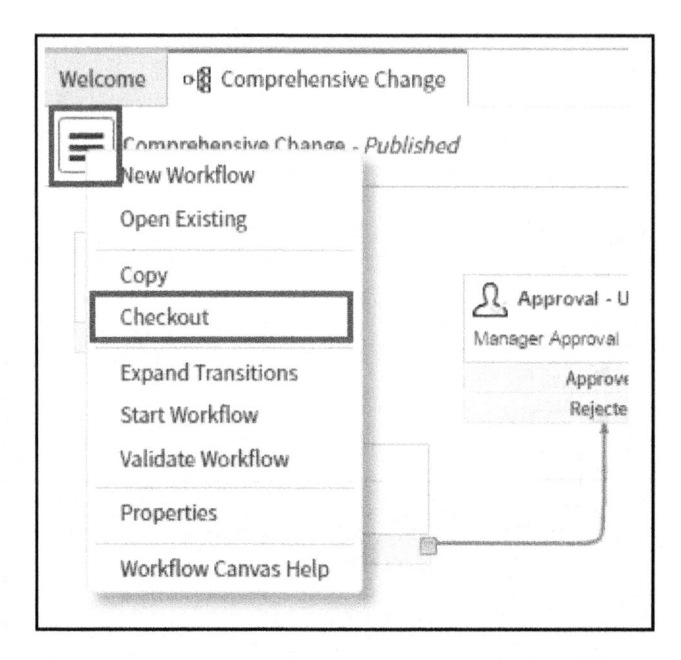

   Edit workflow

   - **Published**: If your workflow is ready then you can click on Publish which will capture workflow in update set as well. It is important to note that **Publish** and **Checkout** options will not be available at the same time:

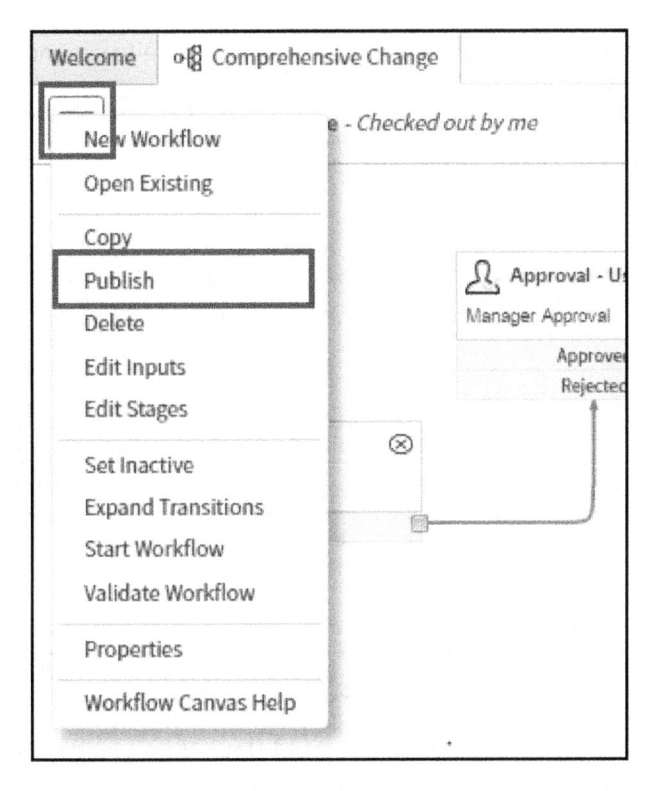

Publish workflow

8. If you want to know more information about the workflow such as conditions, application, schedule and so on then you can click on the information button as given here:

Workflow information

Creating and Configuring Workflow Activities

9. After clicking on **information** button, you will able to see more information about the workflow as follows:

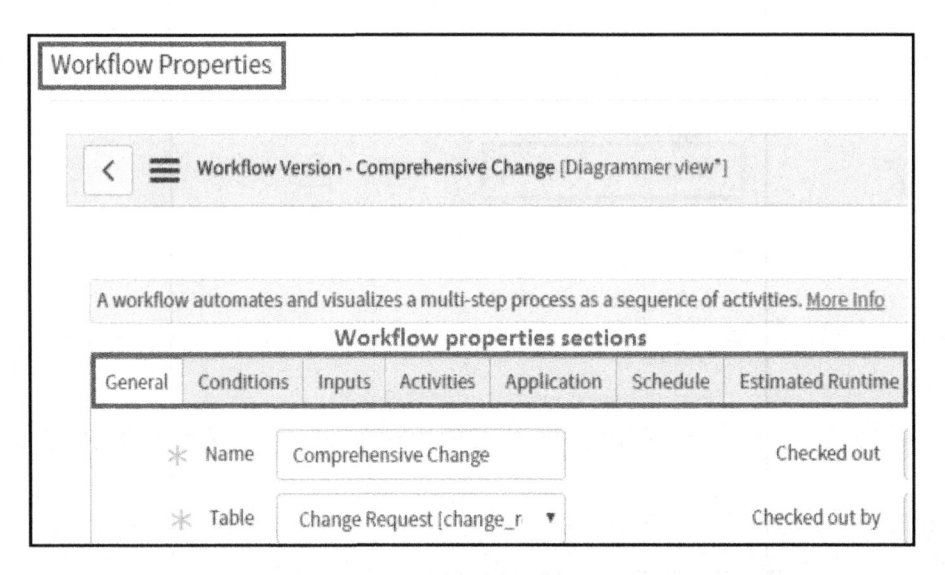

Workflow information with sections

10. Finally, if you want to create a new workflow, then you can click on the **+** button, as shown in the following screenshot:

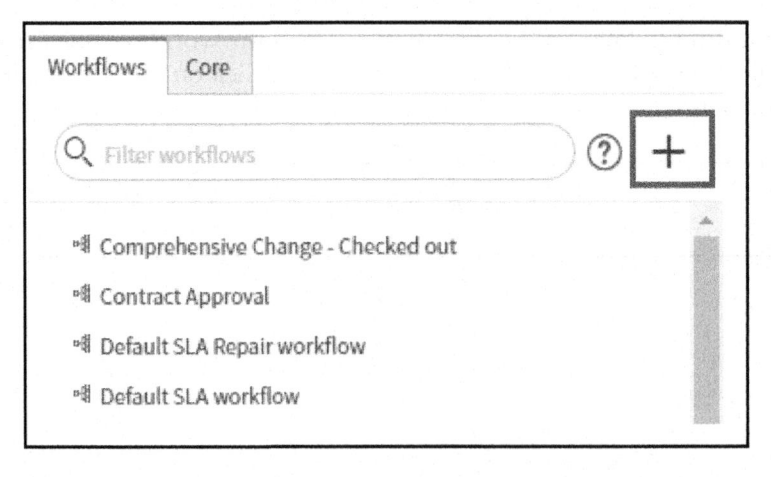

Create new workflow

[276]

11. Once you click the **+** button, a **New Workflow** window appears and you need to configure it as follows:
    - **Name**: You can give any desired name such as `Custom Workflow`
    - **Table**: This field contains all system-defined tables and custom tables as well, where you need to select a table on which the workflow will run as the `Task` table
    - **Description**: This is just a free text box for adding a meaningful description

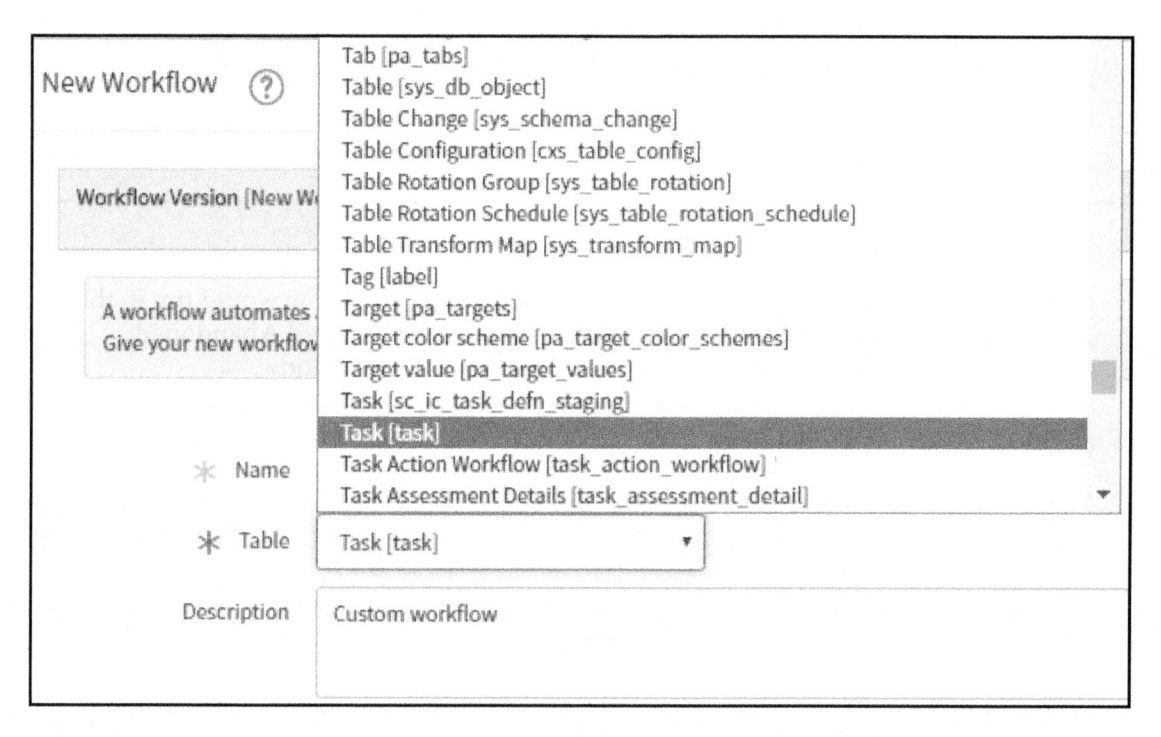

New workflow configuration

12. You need to understand that every workflow within the Service-Now environment triggers at certain conditions. That's why, for running your custom workflow, you need to configure the conditions. As I am running the workflow in the `Task` table, I can choose any field which belongs to the `Task` table or a related table:

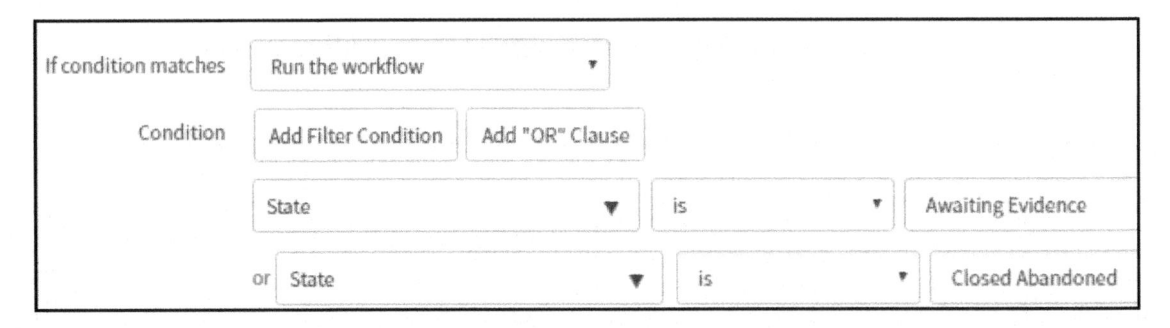

Workflow condition

13. Let's summarize the workflow configuration. This workflow would run in the Task table when the state is **Awaiting Evidence**, and **Closed Abandoned**:
    1. Click on **Submit** button on **New Workflow** window.
    2. Now a whole new blank canvas will be available for you to configure, as shown here:

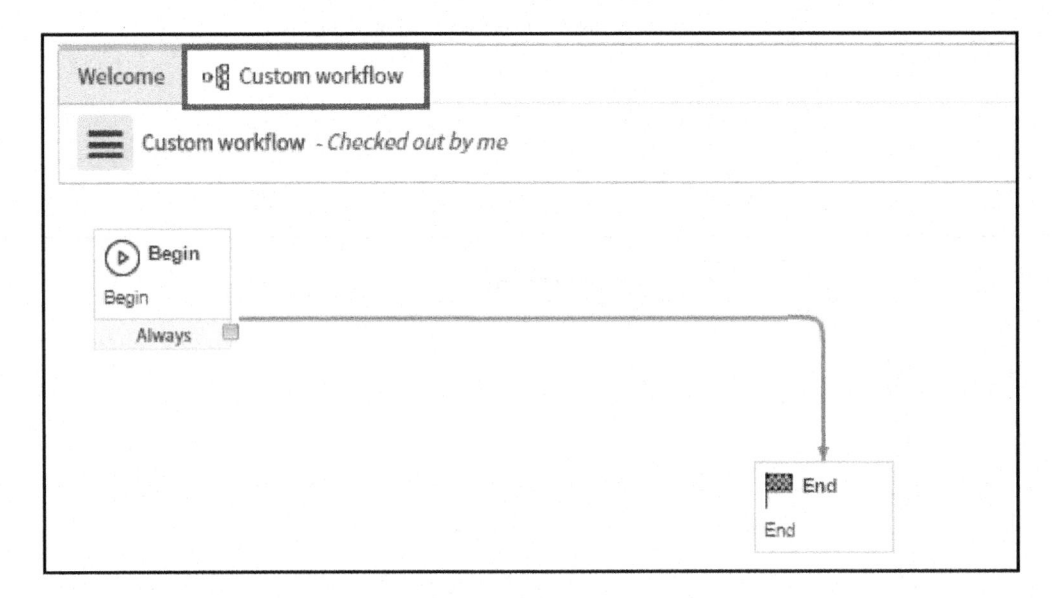

Custom workflow blank canvas

3. After clicking on **Submit**, a newly created workflow **Custom Workflow** will be added to the Workflows section as well:

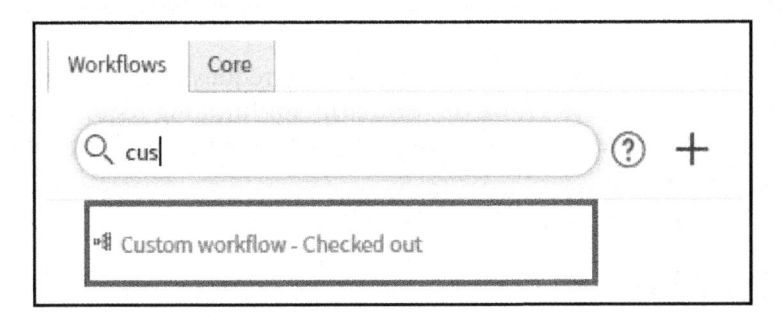

New workflow added in the Workflows section

> Activities follow the drag and drop rule; you can drag and drop any activity on the canvas. If you want to add any activity between two activities, then you should drag the activity and drop it when the connecting wire turns **blue**:

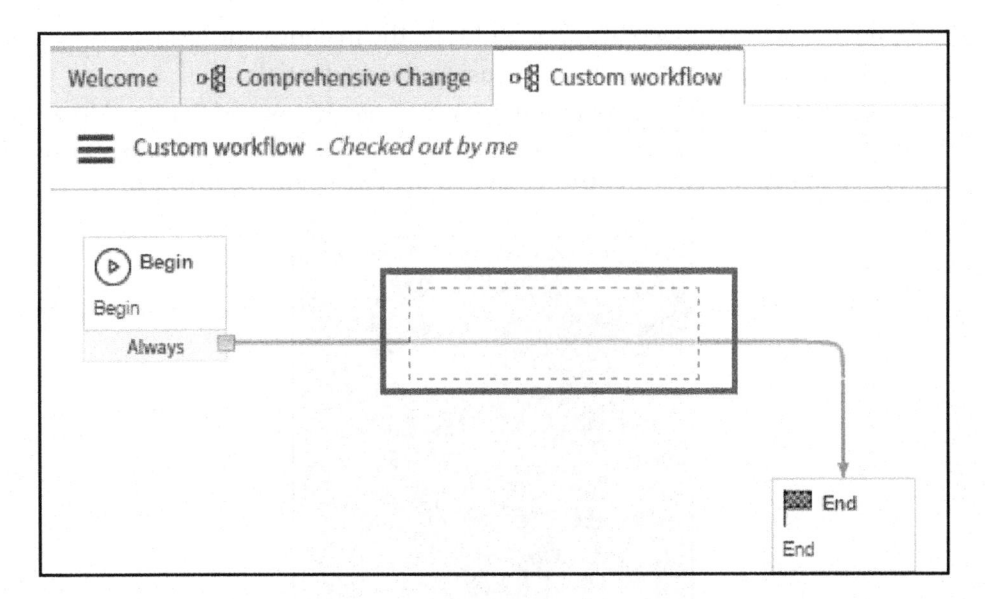

Workflow drag and drop

Attaching a workflow with the service catalog

You should know that there are three ways to raise any request: By the service catalog, record producer, or order guide. However, primarily for fulfilling request requirements, the service catalog should be used. For maintaining a process in the service catalog, a workflow is attached with it.

Getting ready

To step through this recipe, you should have an active Service-Now instance, valid credentials, and an admin role.

How to do it...

1. Open any standard web browser and type the instance address.
2. Log in to the Service-Now instance using the credentials.
3. On the left-hand side, types maintain in the search box and Service-Now will search **Maintain Items** module for you now under **Service Catalog application** select **Maintain Items** module as give in the following screenshot:

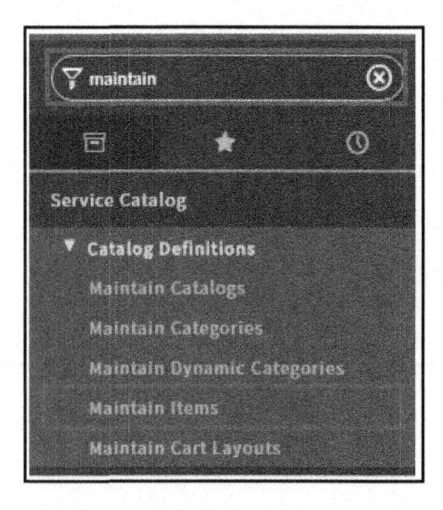

Service Catalog Maintain Items

4. You will now see a list of catalog items. If you want to attach a new workflow with the catalog item, then you can click on any **catalog item** but for now let support **Apple iPad3** catalog item, as shown in following screenshot:

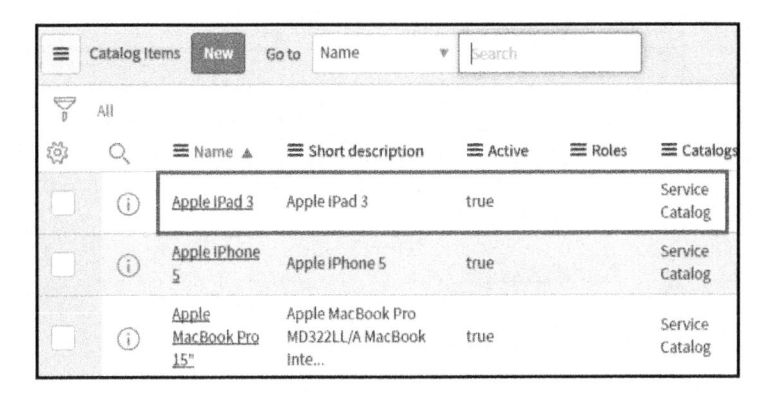

Catalog item

5. Now open the **Apple iPad3** catalog item and if you want to change the workflow of it, then you can go on the **Workflow** field, as shown in the following screenshot and select the new relevant workflow. Please note, **Workflow** is a reference field which refers to the `wf_workflow` table (it holds all the workflows of Service-Now). Here in the **Workflow** field, `Procurement Process Flow - Mobile` is selected, which means after the submission of the `Apple iPad3` catalog item form, Service-Now will attach this workflow with request items but now, if due to any business reason, you want to add a new workflow with the `Apple IPad 3` process, then you can attach a new workflow as well:

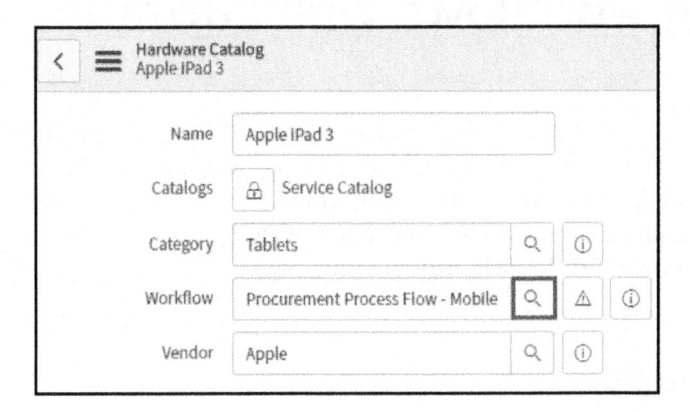

Catalog item workflow

6. After clicking on the **reference** icon (marked in red), you will now see the following screen which contains all the workflows of Service-Now:

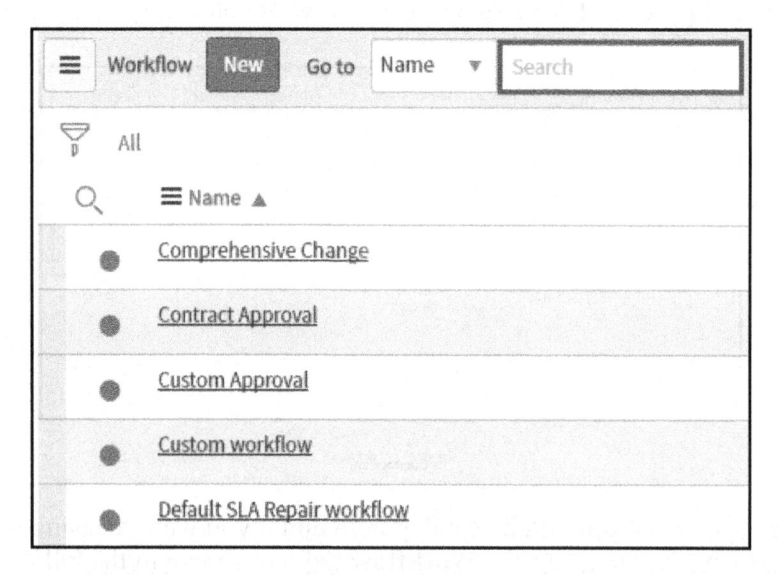

Workflow records

7. From the popup box, you can search and select your new workflow **Custom Workflow**. After selecting it will be attached with catalog item **Apple iPad3**.
8. Now click on Update button to save the new workflow with catalog item.

Attaching workflows with current/new modules

On many occasions, apart from service catalog, many existing or new modules need to follow certain processes of organization. Let's take an example of contract management. A typical contract management application should have contract center approval, finance department approval, auto renewal of contract, notification of expiry, and so on. So, to maintain such process workflow should be attached.

Getting ready

To step through this recipe, you should have an active Service-Now instance, valid credentials, and an admin role.

How to do it...

1. Open any standard web browser and type the instance address.
2. Log in to the Service-Now instance using the credentials.
3. On the left-hand side in the search box, type `workflow` and under **Workflow**, click on **Workflow Editor**.
4. If you want to modify the process of existing module or application, then you can add your conditions to the existing module's workflow. So let's understand this by an example. Out of the box, service-now provides workflow for managing the change management process, contract management and so on but every organization might have its process. So, service-now gives privilege to modify existing workflows as well.
5. If you want to attach a new workflow with module, then you need to set conditions only, and if these conditions are matched, then the workflow will start automatically. Let's understand this by an example; if you want to add a new workflow with problem management application then you can configure workflow as follows:
    1. **Name**: `Problem Management`
    2. **Table**: `Problem`
    3. **Description**: `Problem management process`

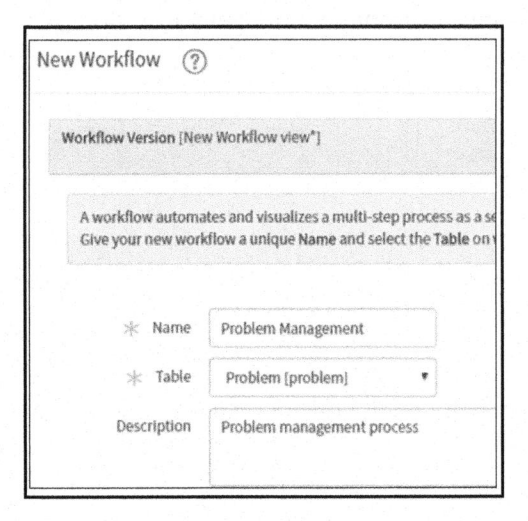

Problem management workflow configuration

4. Now, add the condition in **Problem Management Workflow** as follows:

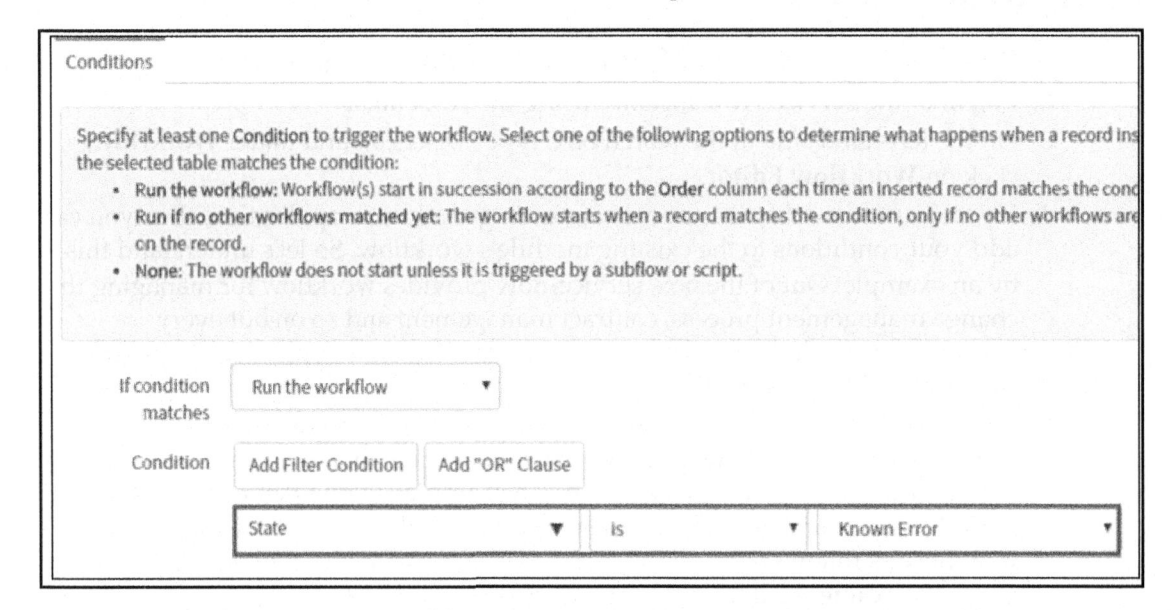

```
Conditions

Specify at least one Condition to trigger the workflow. Select one of the following options to determine what happens when a record ins
the selected table matches the condition:
  • Run the workflow: Workflow(s) start in succession according to the Order column each time an inserted record matches the cond
  • Run if no other workflows matched yet: The workflow starts when a record matches the condition, only if no other workflows are
    on the record.
  • None: The workflow does not start unless it is triggered by a subflow or script.

If condition       [ Run the workflow        ▼ ]
matches

Condition          [ Add Filter Condition ] [ Add "OR" Clause ]

                   [ State          ▼ ] [ is      ▼ ] [ Known Error     ▼ ]
```

Problem management condition

5. Now click on **Submit** button.
6. Now, add activates in problem management as follows:

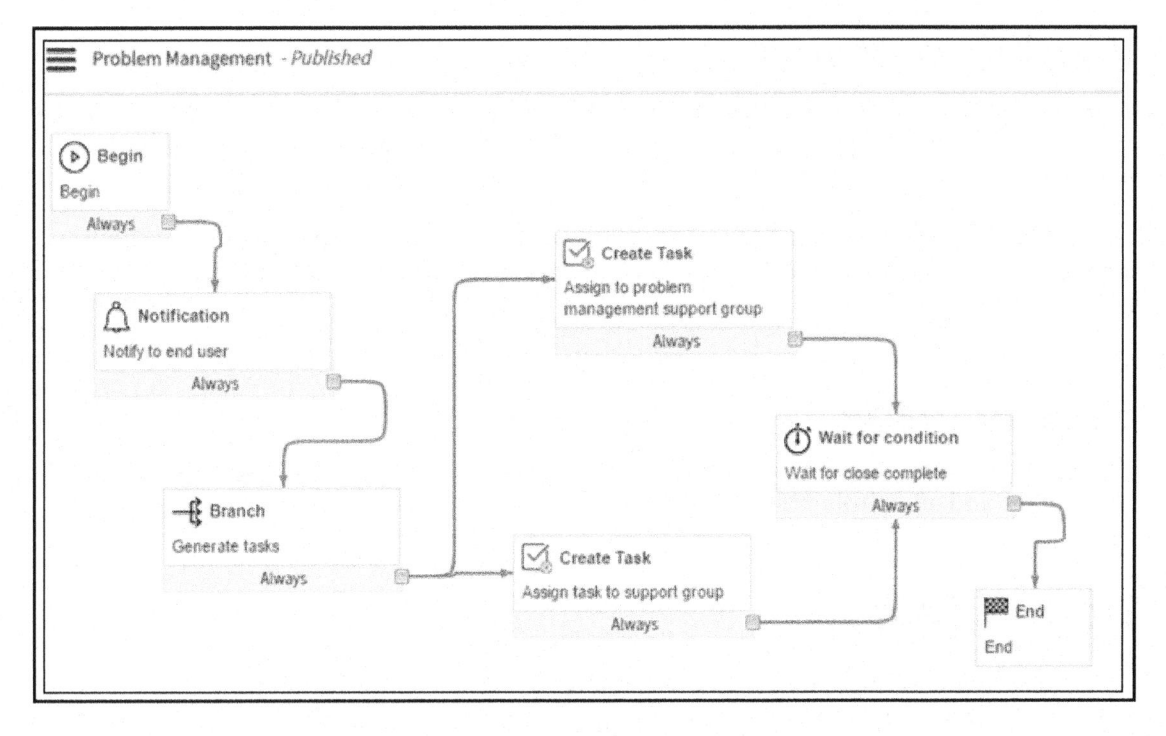

Problem management workflow

7. Now click on **Publish** button.
8. As an output, **Problem management workflow** will trigger when problem task status is **Known Error.** Now whenever this kind problem is reported workflow will send a email notification to end user and after that two catalog task will be created for support group and problem management support group and once both tasks are completed , problem ticket will be closed.

There's more...

Now similarly, you can checkout any existing workflow of module and modify as per your business requirements.

Workflow troubleshooting

A workflow may be considered as a tracker of a process. You can get to know the status of a request or any other item such as a contract management request or change management request.

Out of the box, in some modules, you are allowed to view the workflow using the **show workflow** button, but in some cases, you need to go through a different approach to view the status of request or task.

Getting ready

To step through this recipe, you should have an active Service-Now instance, valid credentials, and an Admin role.

How to do it…

1. Open any standard web browser and type the instance address.
2. Log in to the Service-Now instance using the credentials.
3. On the left-hand side, type `workflow` and under **Workflow** application. Now let's understand some basics:

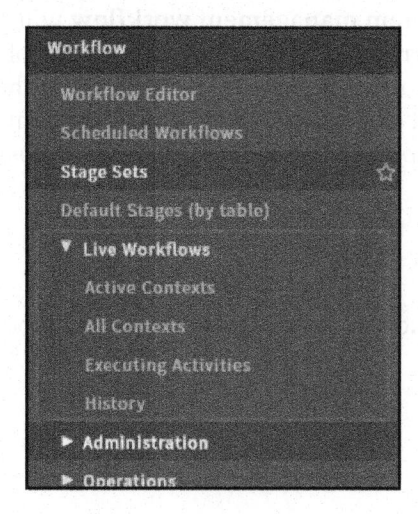

Workflow troubleshooting

- **Active Contexts**: This module is helpful to understand active workflows, so whatever workflow is being run in the system it would be available here.
- **All Contexts**: This module stores all active and inactive workflows. You can consider this as a repository of all the workflows which are under process and which are completed as well.
- **Executing Activities**: Note that you should know that a workflow without an activity or blank canvas is meaningless. So, with this module, you can get to know which activity is being run in the active workflow. It's is more focused on the activity level.
- **History**: This module stores all completed workflows.

4. If you are working in a large development team environment, then you may come across a situation where you are not able to check out the published workflow. You can troubleshoot in the following ways:
    1. First let's understand the root cause of an issue by an example: For instance, imagine you are working in team where two more developers (Ryan and Prince) are working with you. If Ryan has checked out the workflow `Procurement Process Flow - Mobile` of the **Apple IPad3** catalog item, then you are not allowed to check out the workflow of the item. You are able to see the workflow `Procurement Process Flow - Mobile` in the **Published** state but the **Checkout** option will not be available:

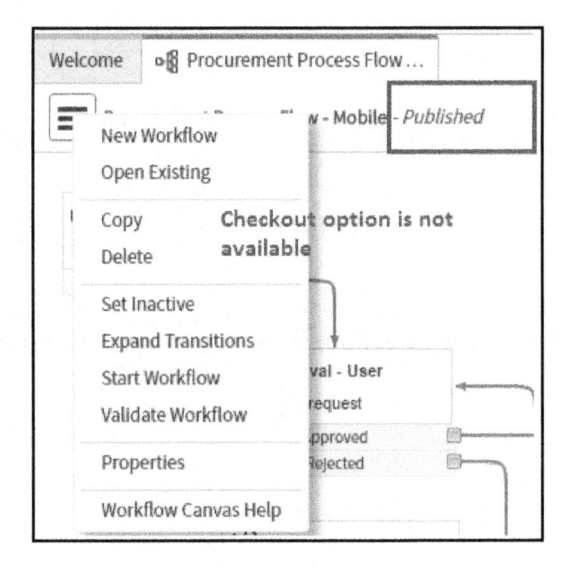

Locked workflow

Creating and Configuring Workflow Activities

- To resolve such an issues, you have the following options:
- **As option 1**: **Ryan** should check out the workflow, you can impersonate him and publish the workflow and after publishing the workflow service-now will allow you to check out the workflow.
- **As option 2**: You can ask to check out and publish the workflow to **Ryan**. Once Ryan is done with the task, you will able to see **Force Checkout** options as shown in following screenshot:

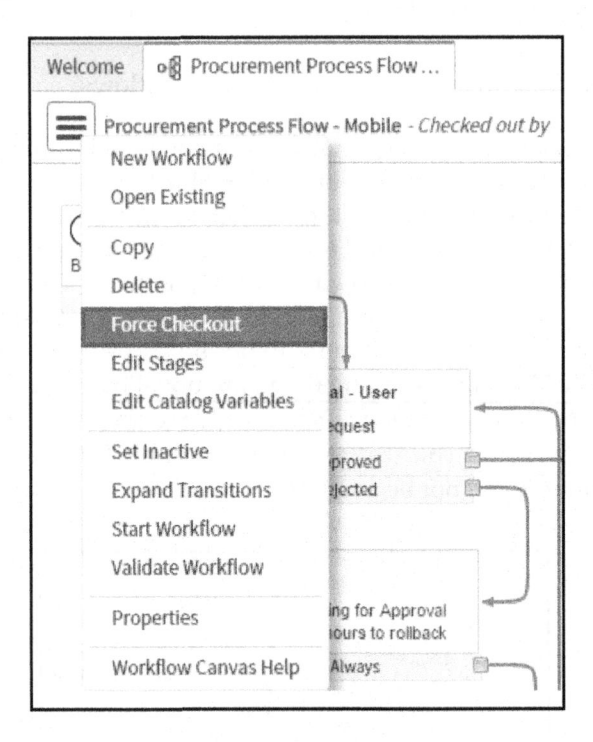

Force Checkout workflow

2. After clicking on **Force Checkout** button, you are allowed to make modification in workflow.

Setting up an approval activity

Approvals are a very critical part of any process. For instance, if you need a laptop, phone, or data card to work from home for your company, then an approval is mandatory from your reporting manager, but if your company is procuring a new laptop then an approval from your company's finance department would be mandatory.

Getting ready

To step through this recipe, you should have an active Service-Now instance, valid credentials, and an admin role.

How to do it...

1. Open any standard web browser and type the instance address.
2. Log in to the Service-Now instance using the credentials.
3. On the left-hand side, type `workflow` and under **Workflow**, click on **Workflow Editor**.
4. Out of the box, service-now provides following activities for **Approvals** so let's understand some basics first:

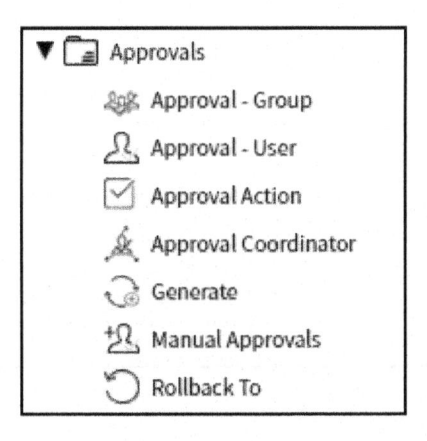

▼ Approvals
- Approval - Group
- Approval - User
- Approval Action
- Approval Coordinator
- Generate
- Manual Approvals
- Rollback To

Workflow approval activity

Creating and Configuring Workflow Activities

- **Approval Group**: This activity is dedicated for group approval, so let's better understand this activity from an example. So, for instance, if your organization is procuring new laptops or new server for IT department, then an approval from the finance department is mandatory. The finance department may have many users, so a dedicated approval group should be made for them.
- It's is very important to configure the `wait for` condition for group approval. In business scenarios, sometimes an approval from a member is enough, but in some cases, all group members are supposed to approve the request, so you should choose the wait condition very carefully:

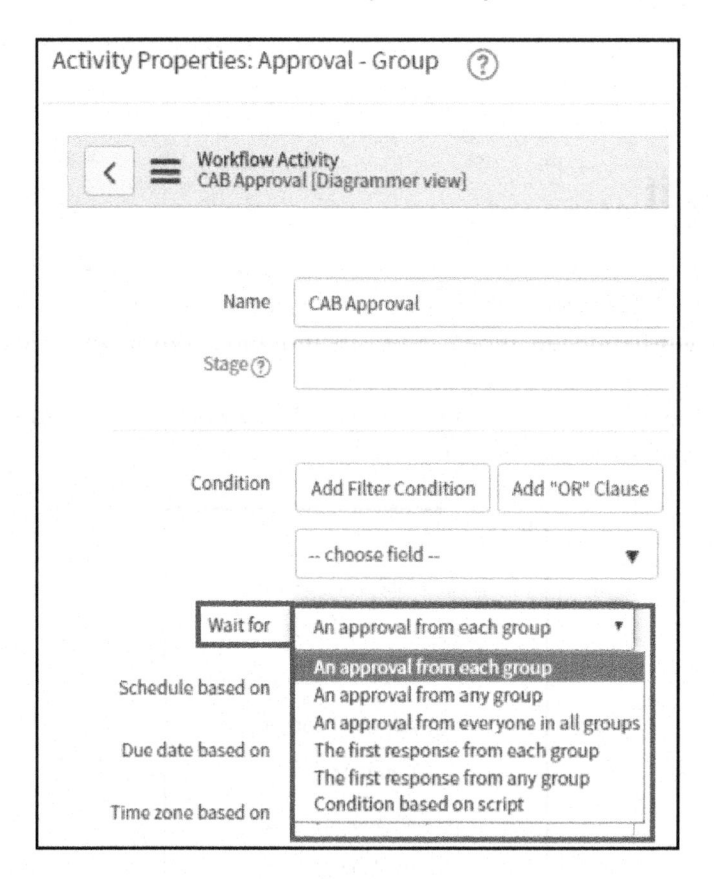

Group approval wait condition

5. After configuring the **wait for** condition for a group, you need to select the approval group. Here, you can directly select any group as the group field refers to the `sys_user_group` table where all groups are stored:

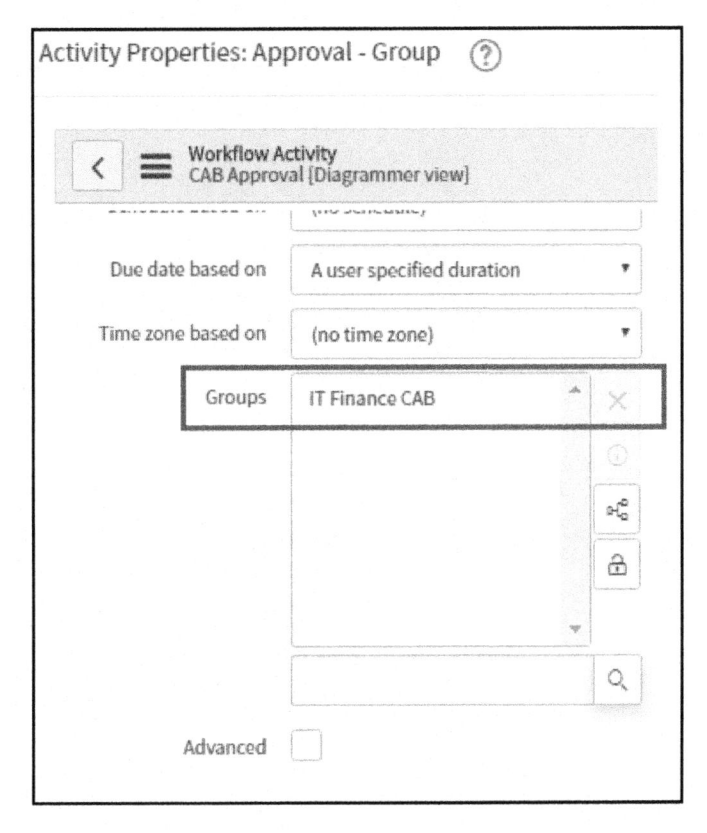

Add group approval

6. Now click on **Submit** button to add activity in workflow.

Creating and Configuring Workflow Activities

- **Approval – User**: This activity is dedicated for individual approvals. If you want to add specific user, then you can directly add them in the workflow, but from the maintenance aspect it is not a good practice because if any approval is changed then you will have to modify workflow again:

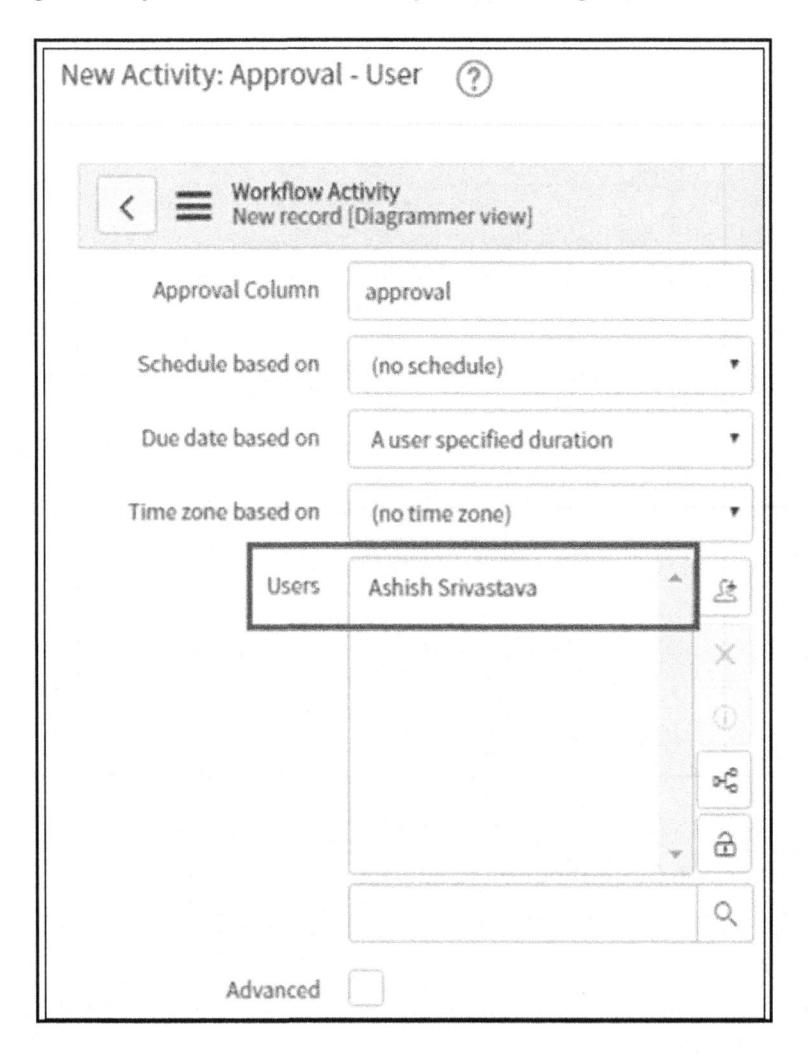

Individual approver

- It is important to note that you can add more than one user for request approval in a workflow.

- You can write small pieces of code in the user field to avoid a regular effort of maintenance. `${requested_by.manager}` which mean approval request will go to user's manager always:

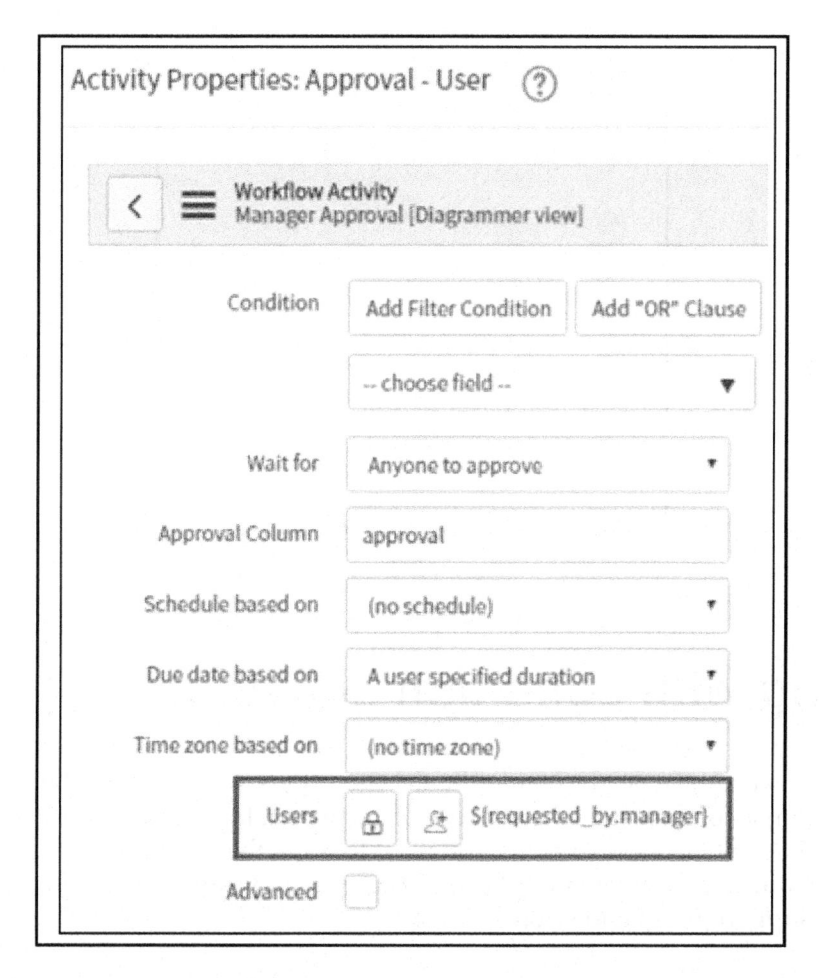

Dynamic approver

7. Now Click on **Submit** button to add activity in workflow.

- **Approval Action**: As an output of any user or group approval, you can use this activity to set the request stage as approved/rejected.

- **Approval coordinator**: This activity is very useful when there is more than one approval regardless of group or individual or manual approval. You can configure group or users or manual approval, as shown in following screenshot:

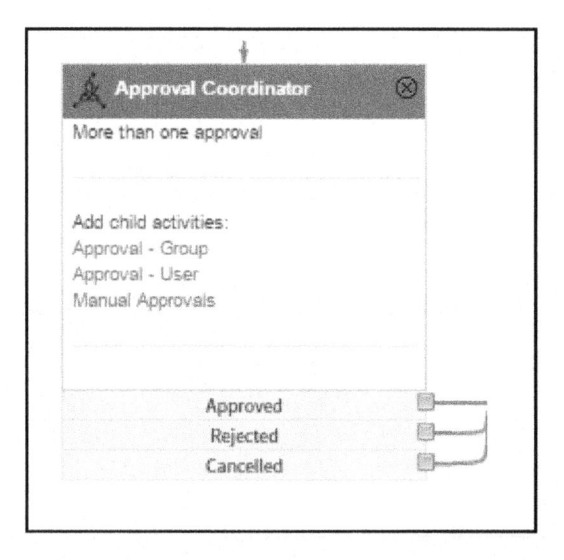

Approval Coordinator approval

Working with condition activities

Conditions are very essential part of any workflow. You may come across a situation multiple times where you need to configure the conditions in a workflow. Let's understand this by an example for an instance if you have catalog item for business software access and based on selection of business software you want to route the task to different support group as SAP business software to SAP support group, service-now business software to service-now support group and so on.

Getting ready

To step through this recipe, you should have an active Service-Now instance, valid credentials, and an admin role.

How to do it...

1. Open any standard web browser and type the instance address.
2. Log in to the Service-Now instance using the credentials.
3. On the left-hand side, type `workflow` and under **Workflow**, click on **Workflow Editor**.
4. Out of the box, Service-Now provides condition activities, as shown following so let's understand the basics first:

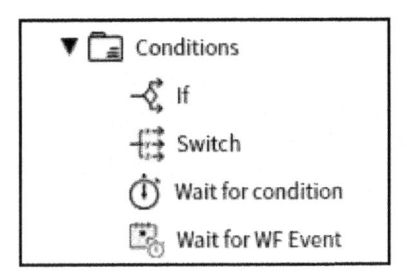

Workflow conditions

- **If** : On many occasions, you may be required to get variables or field value from the user's form. Let's take catalog item **Business Software Access** for better understanding as shown in following screenshot:

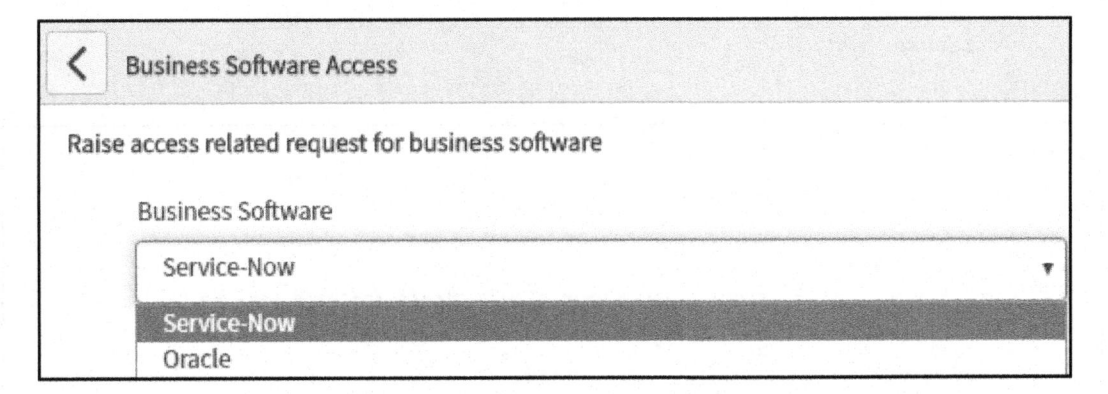

Select business software

- Now if you want to perform different actions based on the **Business Software** selection, then you will have to write a small script in the `If` activity of the workflow:

```
//returning fucntion value

answer = ifScript();

// create fucntions or use can ifScript function as well which is provided by Service-Now by default

function ifScript()
{
  //check for business software value which is available on request form
  //current : it is a predefined global variable which is provided by Service-Now.
  //variable_pool : catalog items contains many fields/variables.Please keep in mind that variable reside in variable_pool and to access catalog item's field value you need to variable_pool.
  //u_business_software.name : it is the variable name which is available in request item name. Here we are taking value of u_business_software and comparing it so the form which is submitted by user contains "your options == "Service-Now"" then "if" activity will return yes for further processing.
  if (current.variable_pool.u_business_software.name == "your_options")
  {
        return 'yes';
    }
    return 'no';
  }
```

```
answer = ifScript();

function ifScript()
{
    if (current.variable_pool.u_business_software.name == "Service-Now")
    {
        return 'yes';
    }
    return 'no';
}
```

If condition script

- You should make the **If** activity with the name **Check if form options**, where you can put the preceding script to check the business software field options on the catalog item. If the options are matched then It will set the task to the service-now support group:

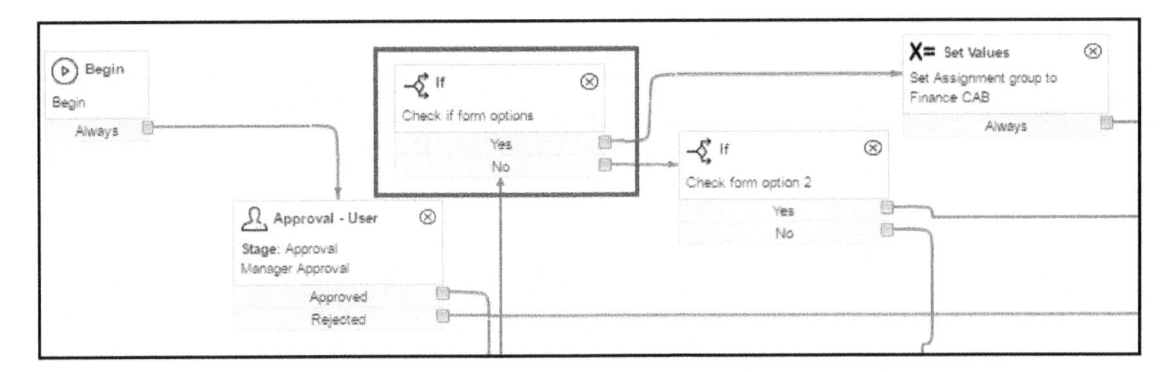

Workflow If conditions

- If you want set a short description of catalog task based on the **Business Software** field of **Business Software Access** catalog item without using `If activity`, then you can also configure in catalog task activity:

```
//u_business_software : This is name of variable of "Business Software"
field
//task : This is variable by which you can set values in task table.
//variable_pool : catalog items contains many fields/variables. Please keep
in mind that variable reside in variable_pool and to access catalog item's
field value you need to variable_pool

// If Service-Now is selected on "Business Software Access" catalog item
then task's short description will be Access request for Service-Now
business software
if(current.variable_pool.u_business_software == "Service-Now"")
   {
    task.short_description = "Access request for Service-Now business
software";
   }
// If oracle is selected on "Business Software Access" catalog item then
task's short description will be Access request for Access request for
Oralce business software
else if (current.variable_pool.u_business_software == "Oracle")
   {
    task.short_description = "Access request for Oralce business software";
   }
```

Creating and Configuring Workflow Activities

```
//If no options is selected on Business Software Access" catalog item then
task's short description will be No business software is selected
else
   {
     task.short_description = "No business software was selected";

   }
```

```
Advanced script
1    if(current.variable_pool.u_business_software == "Service-Now")
2    {
3        task.short_description = "Access request for Service-Now business software";
4
5    }
6
7    else if (current.variable_pool.u_business_software == "Oracle")
8    {
9
10       task.short_description = "Access request for Service-Now business software";
11   }
12
13   else
14   {
15       task.short_description = "No business software was selected";
16
17
18   }
```

Set task description by workflow

5. Click on **Submit** button to add activity in workflow and as an output, when a **Business Software Access** request is raised and if business service field is selected as Service-Now then after manager's approval, catalog task short description will be set as **Access request for Service-Now business software** or if business service field is selected as Oracle then catalog task short description will be set as **Access request for Oracle business software** and so on.

- **Wait for condition**: This activity is commonly when you want to wait for certain condition such as **close complete** in the workflow. Let's take an example for better understanding. If there is more than one task are running in parallel and you want that request should be closed once both tasks are completed. So in such a situation, you can use the wait for condition activity for the closure of the original request.

6. Now, you need to configure the wait for condition. You have access to all the variables of the table and you can choose any one of them as per your requirement same as I have set status field to Closed Complete so all task should reach to close complete status in order to complete the request:

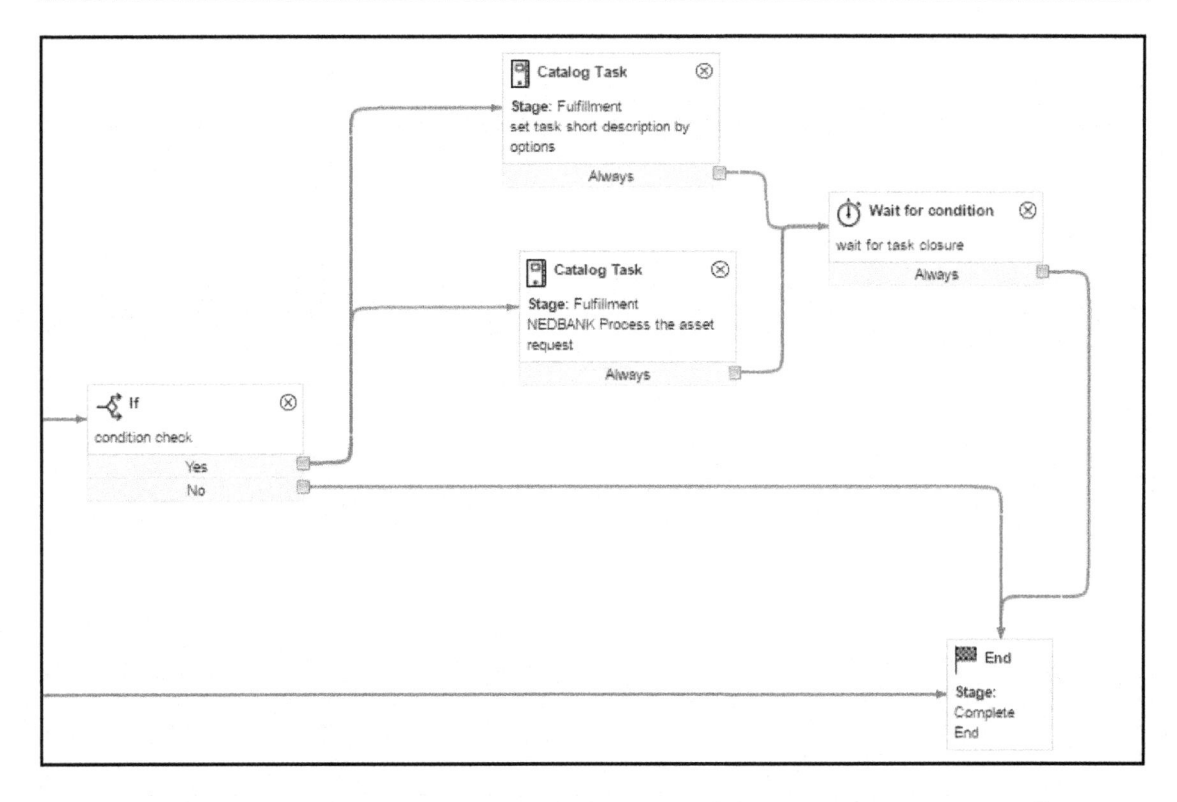

Chapter 6

[Workflow diagram showing: condition check (If) with Yes branch leading to two Catalog Task boxes — "Stage: Fulfillment, set task short description by options" and "Stage: Fulfillment, NEDBANK Process the asset request" — both flowing (Always) to "Wait for condition: wait for task closure" and then to End (Stage: Complete End). The No branch flows directly to End.]

7. Now you need to configure the **Wait for condition**. You have access to all the variables of the table and you can choose any one of them as per your requirement as I have set status field to Closed Complete so all task should reach to close complete status in order to complete the request:

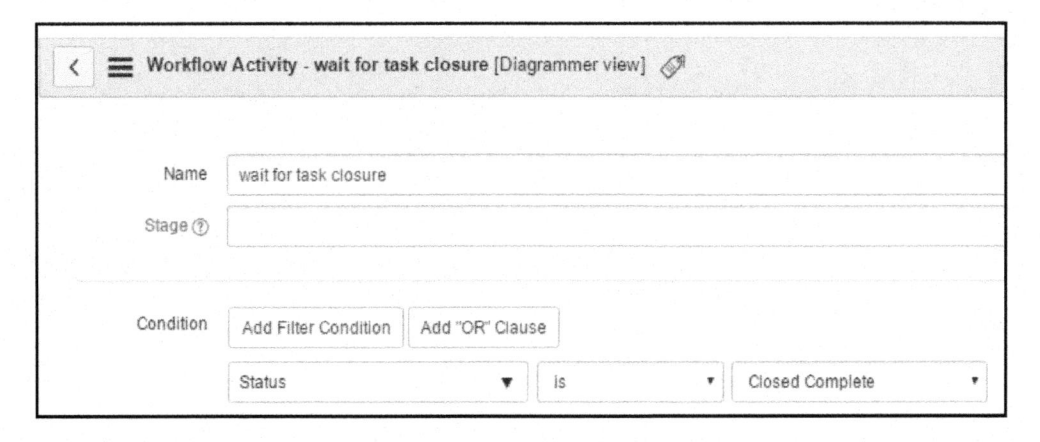

[Screenshot of Workflow Activity - wait for task closure [Diagrammer view]. Name: wait for task closure. Stage: (empty). Condition: Status is Closed Complete.]

Wait for close complete status

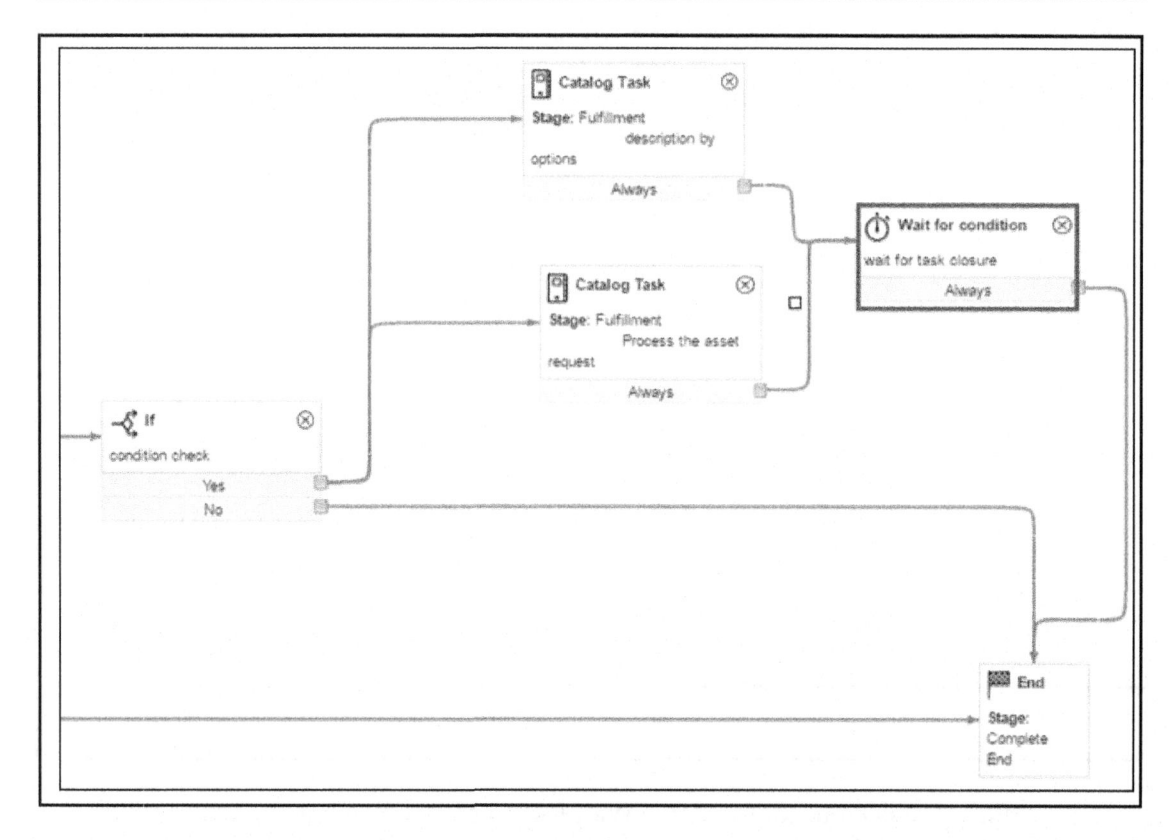

Creating and Configuring Workflow Activities

Wait for condition activity

- As an output, when both tasks are closed complete, the request will be completed.

Working with task activities

Tasks are an integral part of service-now and for each and every IT staff effort a task should be created so that they can account the work against their name. Task activity creates and modifies the workflow tasks. It is important to note that you are allowed to create task activity when workflow is running on table which extends Task table. There are two activities related to tasks and we will take a look at these activities in this recipe.

Getting ready

To step through this recipe, you should have an active Service-Now instance, valid credentials, and an admin role.

How to do it...

1. Open any standard web browser and type the instance address.
2. Log in to the Service-Now instance using the credentials.
3. On the left-hand side in the search box, type workflow and under workflow application, click on workflow editor module.
4. Out of the box, service-now provides following activities for **Tasks** in the workflow:

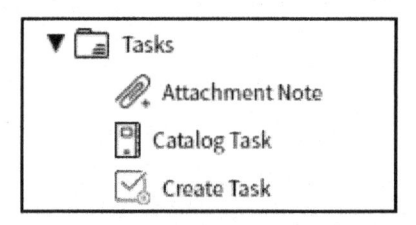

Workflow task activity

- **Catalog Task**: This activity creates a catalog task record only. It is important to note that catalog task activity is available for service catalogs only:

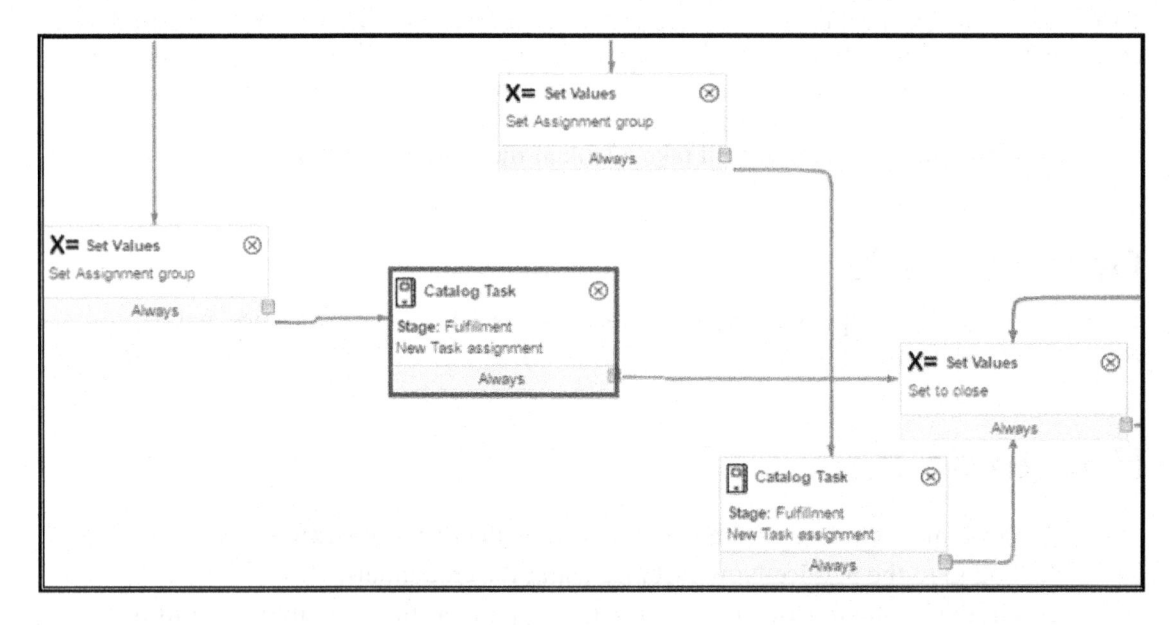

Workflow catalog task

5. If you are using **Set Values** activity then you can directly set assignment group of catalog task **New Task assignment** through it but if on request item form assignment group field is available then by following script you can set assignment group:

Chapter 6

![Activity Properties: Catalog Task - Workflow Activity - New Task assignment [Diagrammer view] - Advanced script:]

```
task.assignment_group = current.assignment_group;
```

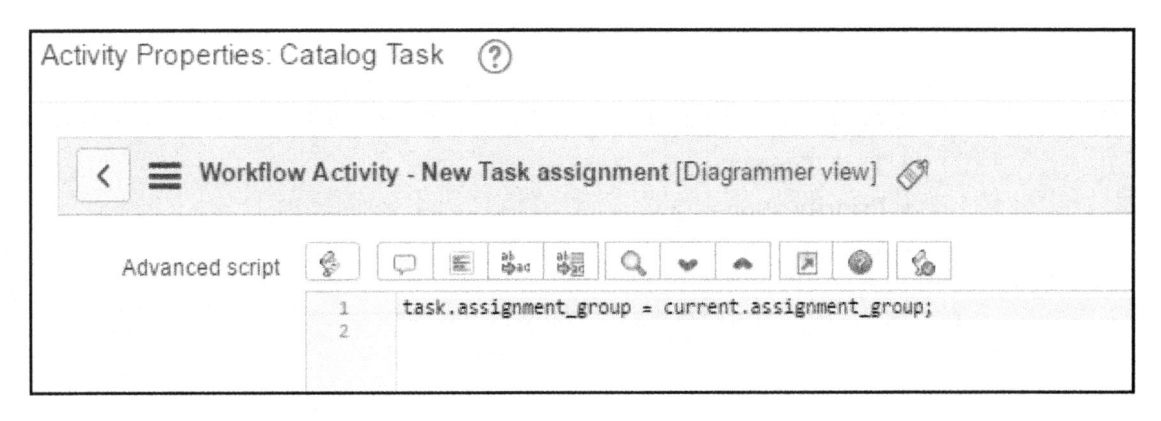

Assign task assigned to request item assignment group

Script:
`task.assignment_group = current.assignment_group;`

- **Create Task**: This activity is available for all tables which extends task table and you can create any task from this activity as an enhancement task, problem task, feature task and so on. So for better understanding, let's see an example. For instance, if you want to create an enhancement task from service request, then to create from **Create task** activity as follows:

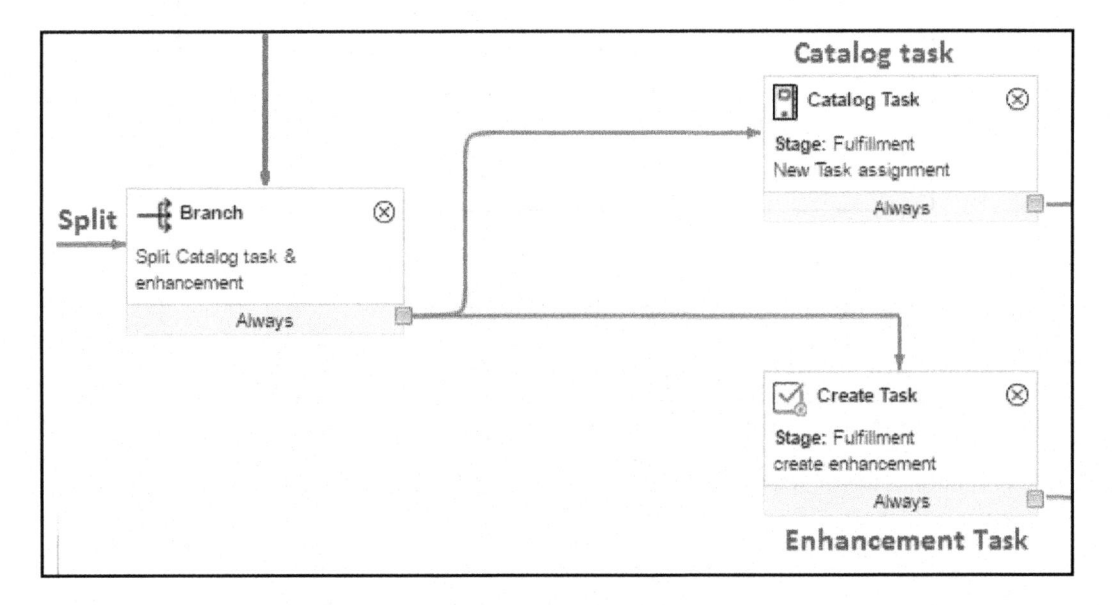

Split task

[303]

Creating and Configuring Workflow Activities

6. Here we are trying to create an enhancement task from catalog item as follows:
   - **Name** : Create enhancement
   - **Stage** : Fulfillment
   - **Task Type** : Enhancement
   - **Priority** : None
   - **Wait for completion** : True

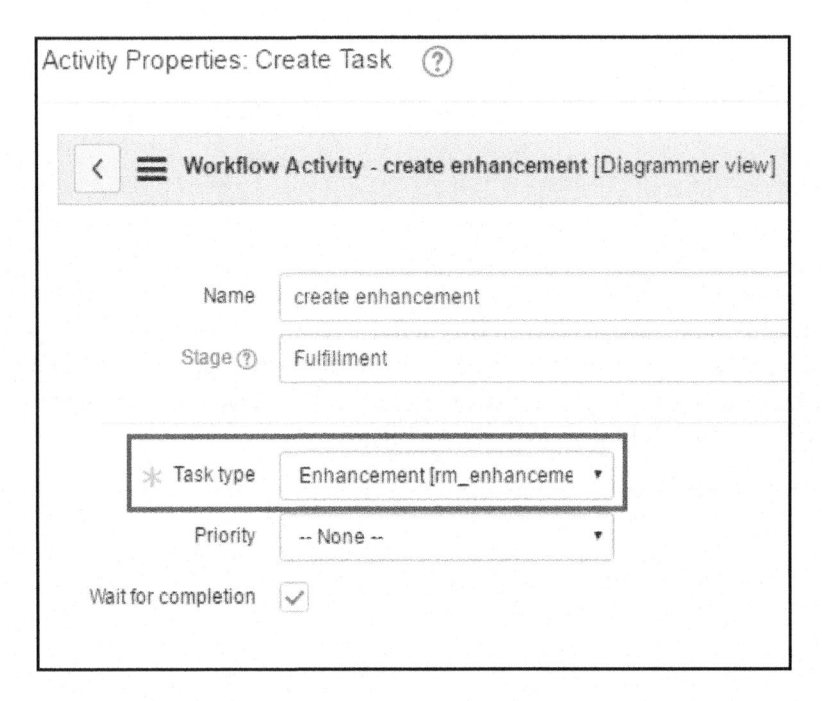

Enhancement task

7. Now add the following script advance script box:

```
// Here we are creating enhancement task from service catalog.
On enhancement form we have created new fields where data is being pushed.
// set request item number to enhancement name

task.u_enhancement_name = current.number;

// set enhancement short description
// current.number = pull request item number
// current.variable_pool.u_business_software.getDisplayValue() = For an
instance, if business software is a reference field then to retrieve it's
text value you need to use getDisplayValue() function which is provided by
```

Service-Now.

```
task.short_description = current.number + " "+ "For" + " "+
current.variable_pool.u_business_software.getDisplayValue()+" " +"Business
Software";

// set enhancement's task assignment group = request item assignment group

task.assignment_group = current.assignment_group;

// set enhancement's cmdb_ci field from catalog item form
task.cmdb_ci = current.variable_pool.u_business_software.u_select_asset;
```

//set enhancement's portfolio field to IT. Please keep in mind that portlofio field is reference field that's why you are allowed to use sysId of "IT" by passing sysID youc can get text value of record.

```
task.u_portfolio = "30e14b3beb131100b749215df106fe0f";

//set enhancement's description field from catalog item
task.description = current.variable_pool.u_description;

//set enhancement's description field from catalog item

task.u_requested_by = current.variable_pool.u_requested_by;

//set enhancement's description field from catalog item
task.requested_for = current.variable_pool.u_requested_by;

//set enhancement's description field from catalog item
task.u_business_software = current.variable_pool.u_business_software;

//set enhancement's priority to Not Provided
task.priority = 6;

////set enhancement's state NEW

task.state = 3;
```

Creating and Configuring Workflow Activities

```
Advanced script

1   task.u_enhancement.name = current.number;
2
3   task.short_description = current.number + " "+ "For" + " "+
4
5   current.variable_pool.u_business_software.getDisplayValue()+" " +"Business Software";
6
7   task.assignment_group = current.assignment_group;
8
9   task.cmdb_ci = current.variable_pool.u_business_software.u_select_asset;
10
11  task.u_portfolio = "30e14b3beb131100b749215df106fe0f";
12
13  task.description = current.variable_pool.u_description;
14
15  task.u_requested_by = current.variable_pool.u_requested_by;
16
17  task.requested_for = current.variable_pool.u_requested_by;
18
19  task.u_business_software = current.variable_pool.u_business_software;
20
21  task.priority = 6;
22
23  task.state = 3;
24
```

Enhancement task script

8. As an output, whenever a request is created and workflow triggers it create one catalog task and another enhancement task. Let's take an example for better understanding, suppose there is catalog item **Enhancement request for business Software** with **enhancement business software** workflow on service-now portal which facilitates enhancement request of business software then process will run as shown in following screenshot:

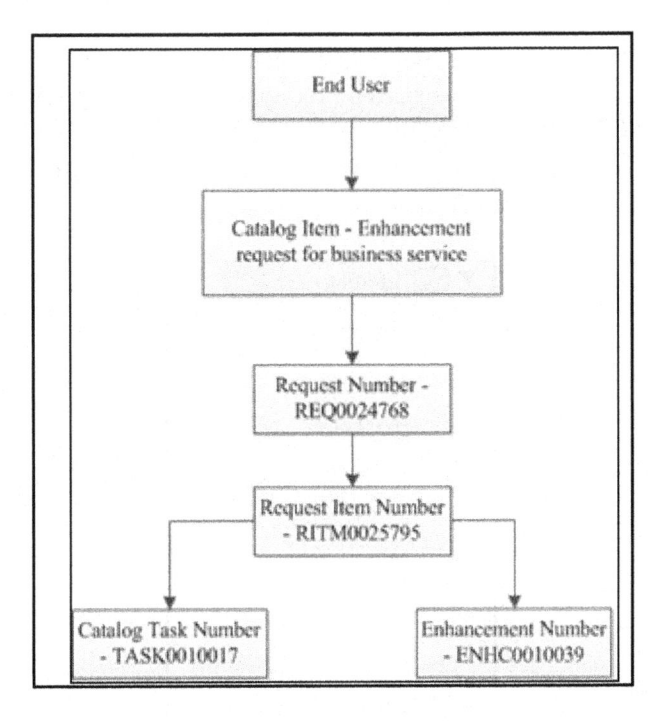

Enhancement task by catalog item workflow

Working with workflow utilities

Utilities are useful workflows activates which are essential for the day to day workflow development, so let's understand this with an example. For instance, if you want to set any value or you want to run any script or join two activities and so on, then you can choose the respective utilities for development purpose from the workflow core section.

Getting ready

To step through this recipe, you should have an active Service-Now instance, valid credentials, and an admin role.

How to do it...

1. Open any standard web browser and type the instance address.

2. Log in to the Service-Now instance using the credentials.
3. On the left-hand side in the search box, type `workflow`, click on **Workflow Editor** Module under workflow application.
4. Now click on workflow core section where you find **Utilities** activates so let's understand some basics first:

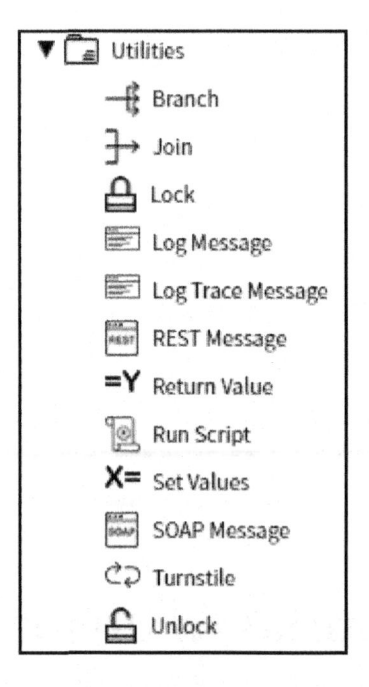

Workflow utilities

- **Branch**: This activity is very useful when you want to split any work in more than one part based on condition, so for better understanding, let's take an example of a task. If any condition is true then a more than one task should be created at same time and in such cases, the branch activity can be applied.

5. To add a branch activity in your workflow, you need to drag and drop it on your canvas.
6. You will now see the following screen where you need to give only the name and stage:

- **Name**: `Split the tasks.`
- **Stage**: Leave blank:

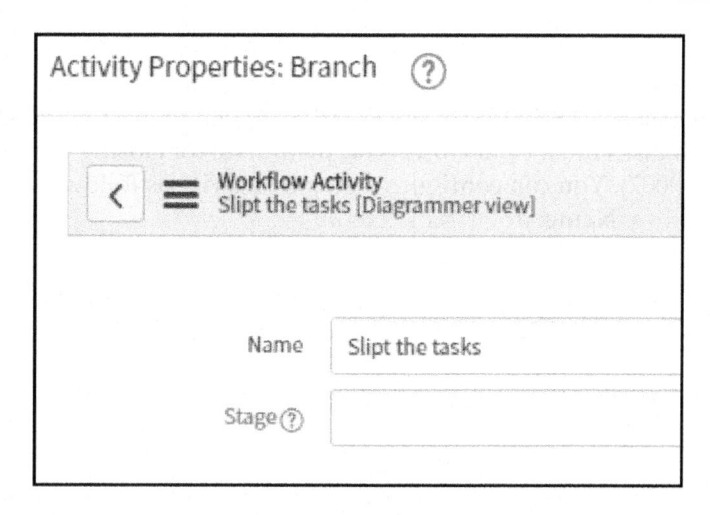

Branch activity configuration

7. Now click on **Submit** button.

In the following workflow for splitting the tasks, the branch activity is being used:

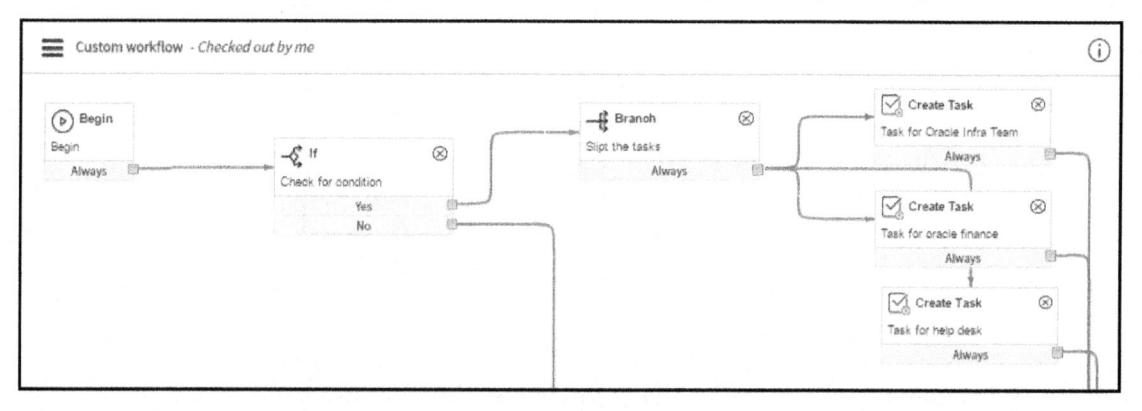

Workflow with branch activity

- **Join**: This activity is less used as compared to other activities when there are multiple current transitions. So let's understand it with an example if there are multiple tasks (TASK0010025, TASK0010016) of a request item (RITM0010008) then both tasks must be at closed complete state for closing the request (REQ0010007). You can configure then join activity as follows :
    - **Name**: `Join all tasks`
    - **Stage**: Leave blank

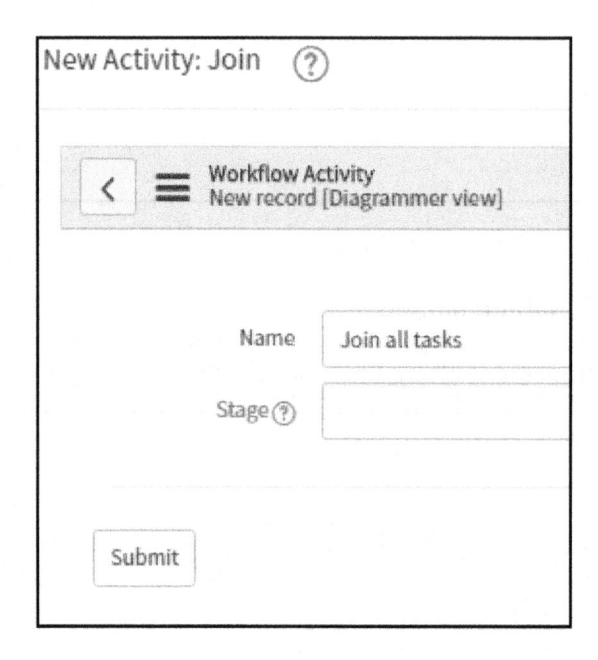

Join activity configuration

8. Now click on **Submit** button.

- For joining multiple tasks, the following workflow is used and as a result if complete is marked, and then all predecessor activities finish executing and transition to the Join activity. If the result is marked incomplete, then All predecessor activities finish executing, but one or more bypass the Join activity:

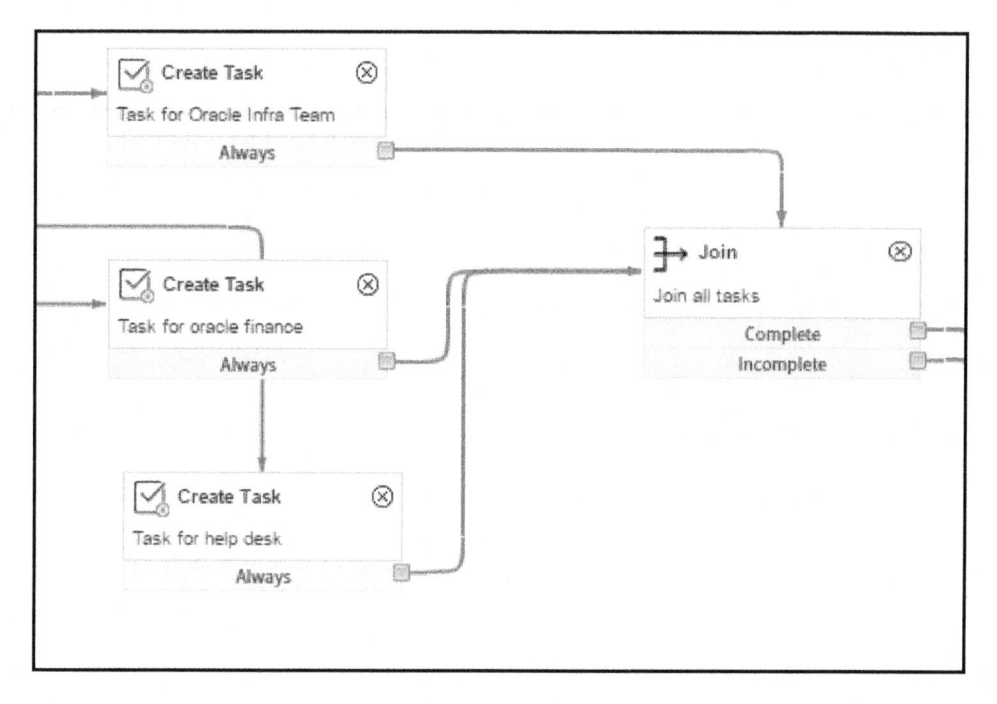

Join activity workflow

- **Run Script**: This activity is very useful in running a script in a workflow, so let's understand it with an example. For instance, if on any catalog item in additional comments field, users enters as `Install Avaya softphone in my system` and you want to make same description as catalog task short description then in such a case, the run script activity.
    - **Name:** `set task short description`.
    - **Stage:** Leave blank:

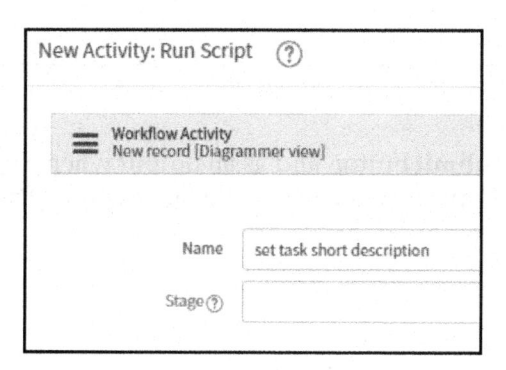

Run script configuration

- In the Script box, you can add your script as shown in following screenshot:

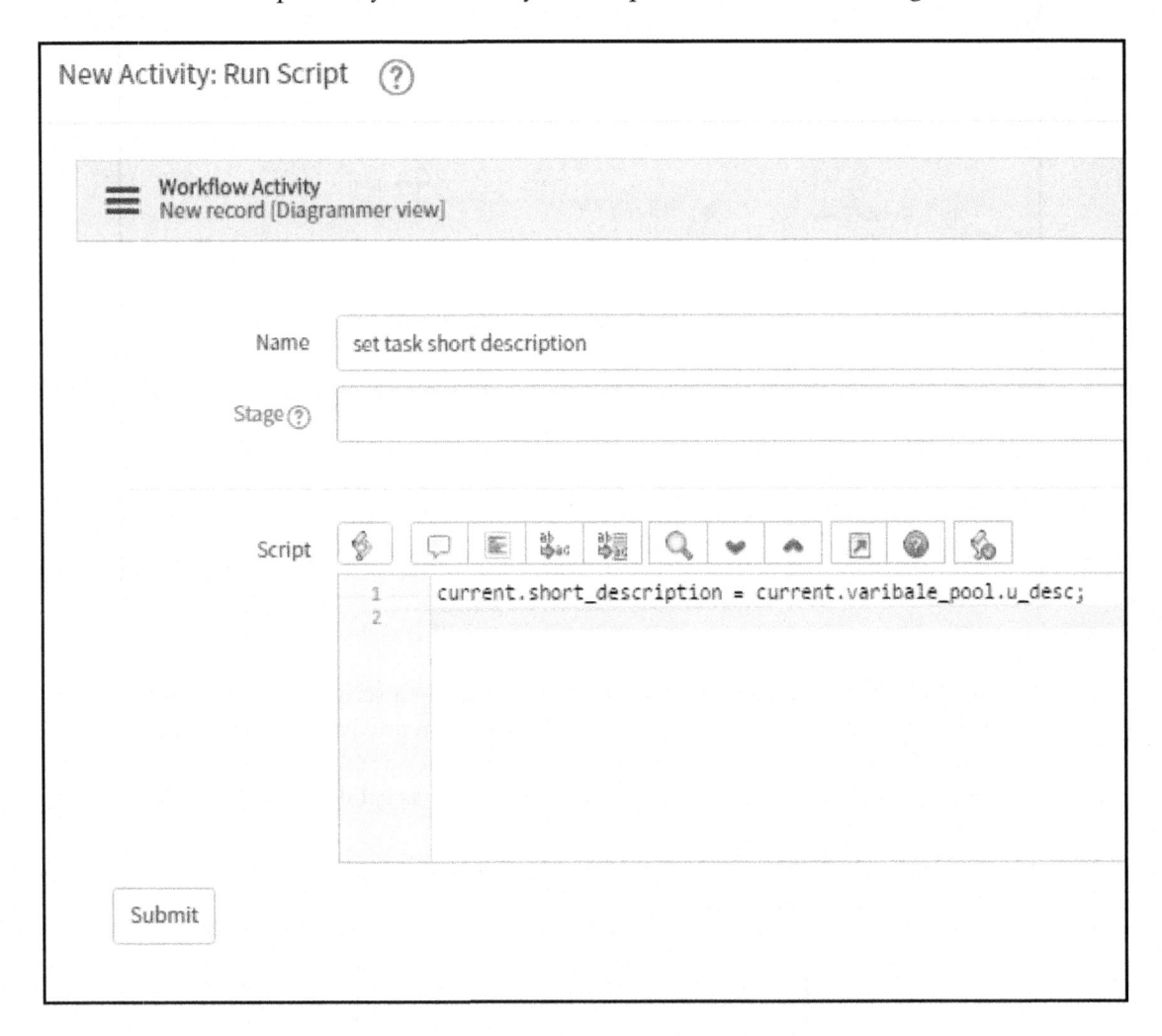

New Activity: Run Script

Workflow Activity
New record [Diagrammer view]

Name: set task short description

Stage:

Script:
```
1  current.short_description = current.varibale_pool.u_desc;
2
```

Submit

Run script – script

- Now Click on **Submit** button and as an output when request is created, catalog task's short description will be set as **Install Avaya softphone in my system**.

- **Set Value**: This activity is very common and widely used for setting the value through a workflow. The set value activity gives the leverage to a developer to set values in any field in the table scope:
    - **Name:** `Set assignment group`
    - **Stage**: Leave blank
    - **Set these values:** `Assignment group = IT finance CAB`

Set value activity

9. Click on **Submit** button as an output whenever request is created, catalog task assignment group will be set as IT finance CAB. Workflow with Set Values is as follows:

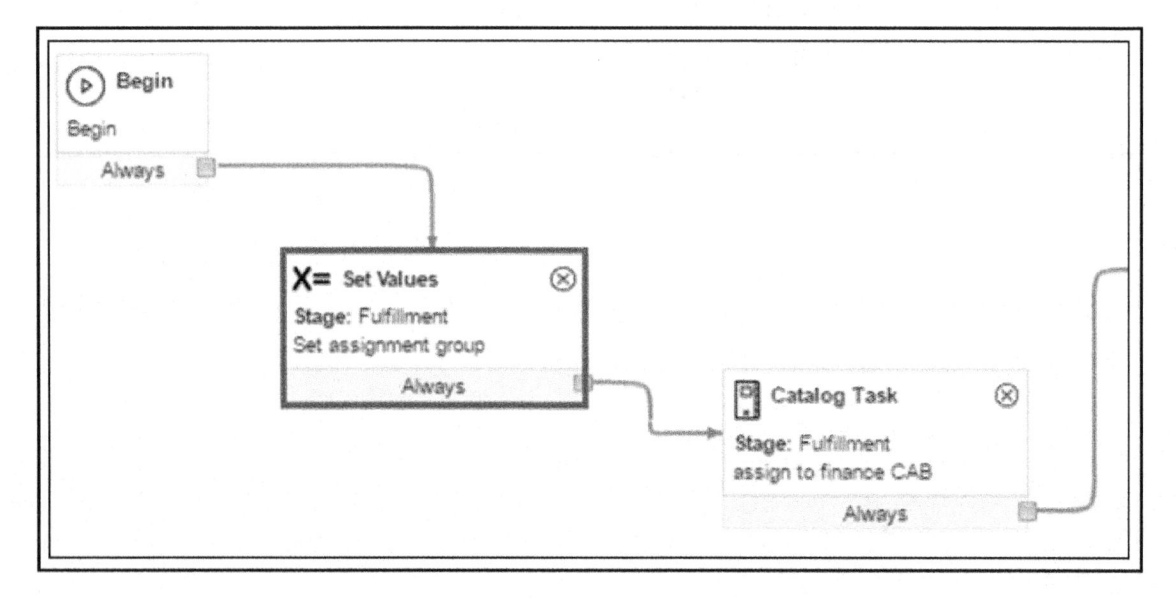

Workflow with set values

- **Rollback to and Turnstile**: These are two different activities but in my experience both are used together in most cases. The rollback to activity is dedicated for restarting any activity without resubmitting the form or in better work I shall say that processing the workflow in backward to a specific activity, but there is some limit to any activity that's why the turnstile activity should be used. In this recipe we are going to see if any request is cancelled for some special catalog item them approval get 3 chances to approve the request.
    - In the rollback to activity, you need to enter the name as `Request Cancelled` and stage as `Request Cancelled`
    - Click on **Submit** button:

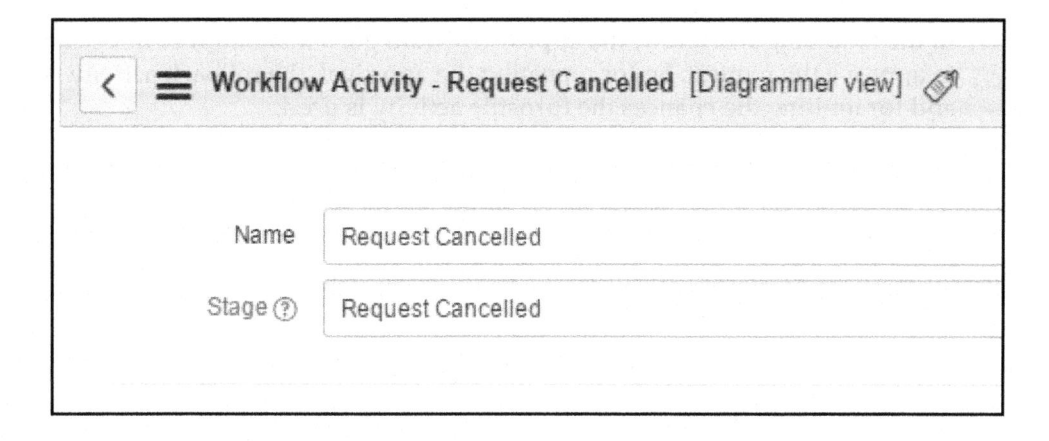

- Rollback to activity configuration
- In the turnstile activity, you need to enter name as `resend for approval for 3 times` and stage as `Request Cancelled`. Here, in the **Allowed Iterations** field, you need to give your count of cycle:

- Turnstile activity configuration

10. Now click on **Submit** button.

11. In the following workflow, the approver would get a maximum of three chances to approve the request. So for repeating the approval, the rollback activity is used and for limiting the chances the turnstile activity is used:

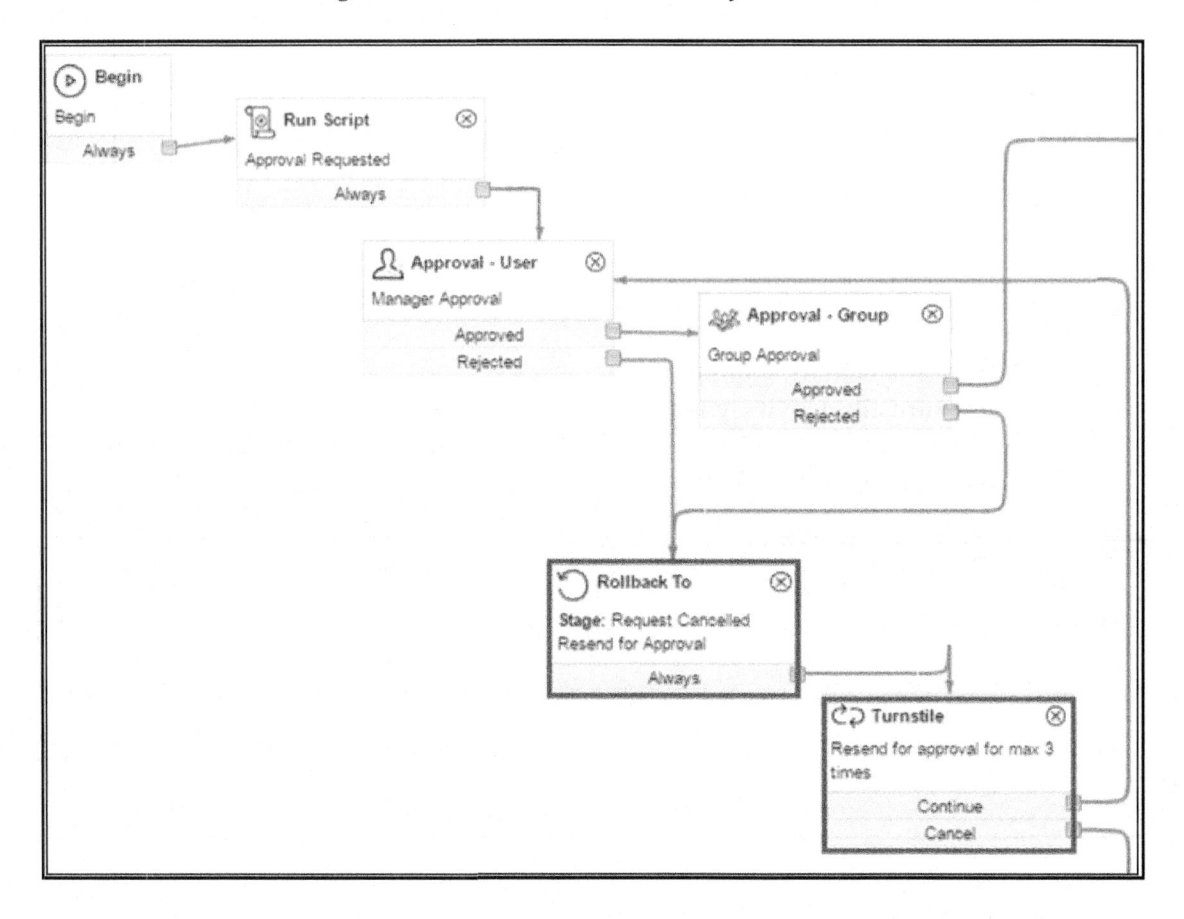

- Workflow with rollback to and turnstile activities

Setting up e-mail notifications from workflows

By Chapter 4, *Configure Alerts* and *Notification*, you can understand the significance of email notifications for end users. Apart of **System Notification** application, service-now allows you to configure notification from workflows as well.

Getting ready

To step through this recipe, you should have an active service-now instance, valid credentials, and an admin role.

How to do it…

1. Open any standard web browser and type the instance address.
2. Log in to the Service-Now instance using the credentials.
3. Now, on left hand side in the search box type `maintain item` and click on **Maintain items** module under the **Service Catalog application** to check the workflow which is attached with it catalog item. Let's suppose, you have opened **Apple iPad3** catalog item as shown in following screenshot:

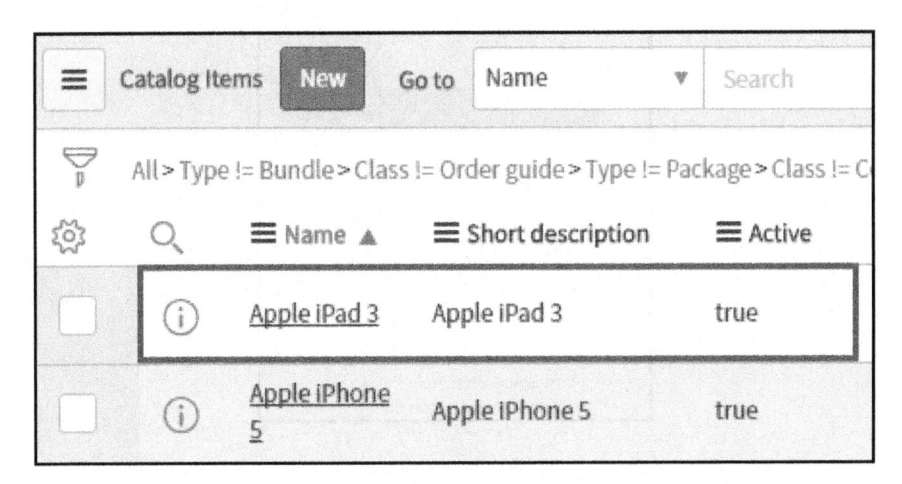

Apple IPad 3 workflow

Creating and Configuring Workflow Activities

4. After clicking on `Apple iPad3` catalog item, you will see attached workflow name `Procurement Process Flow - Mobile` in **Workflow** field of catalog item. You need to click on s**how workflow** button as highlighted as shown in following screenshot:

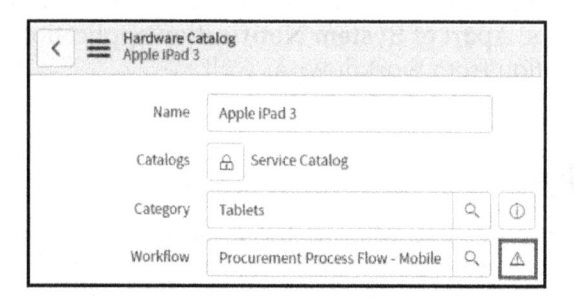

- Show workflow button

5. After clicking on the **show workflow** button, you will able to see the published workflow and you need to Check out the workflow, as shown in the following screenshot, to add the notification activity:

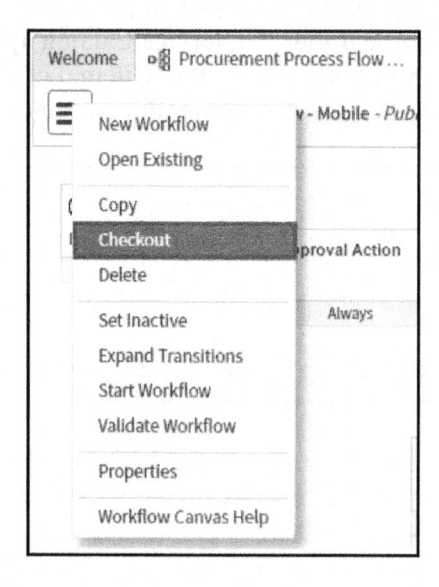

Checkout published workflow

[318]

6. After clicking on the **Checkout** button, the workflow will be unpublished. Now you can add the **Notifications** activity in the workflow:

Workflow notification activity

7. Now you need to drag and drop the **Notifications** activity on the workflow canvas for configuration, as shown in the preceding screenshot:

- **Name:** `Send notification to end user.`
- **Stage:** `Fulfillment.`
- **Subject:** Notification of task processing.

Creating and Configuring Workflow Activities

- **To**: Configuration of the **To** field is very important as if the To field is blank, then no e-mail will be sent out from Service-Now. In To and To (groups) field, you are allowed to give name of users and groups but to include fields in To field you can click on button as shown in following screenshot to add reference fields:

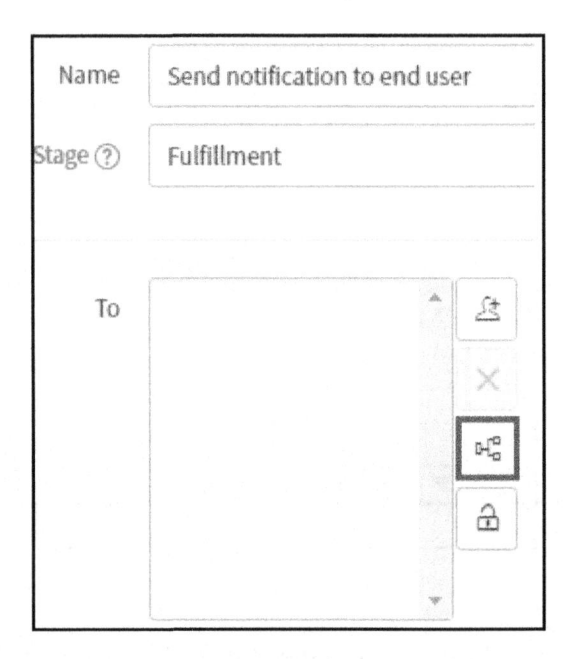

Configure the To Field

8. After clicking on button, you will able to see popup as displayed followng where you can select any fields:

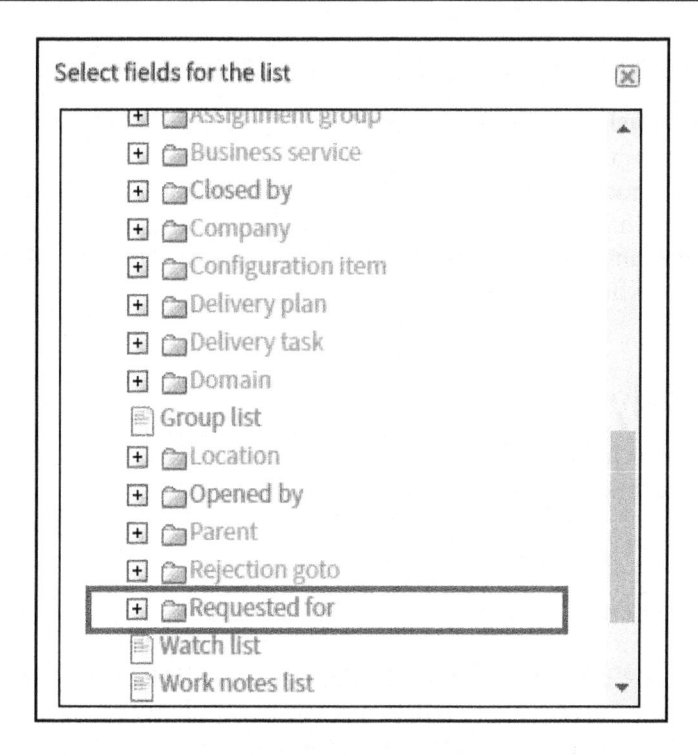

```
Select fields for the list                    [X]
    [+] [📁] Assignment group                    ▲
    [+] [📁] Business service
    [+] [📁] Closed by
    [+] [📁] Company
    [+] [📁] Configuration item
    [+] [📁] Delivery plan
    [+] [📁] Delivery task
    [+] [📁] Domain
    [📄] Group list
    [+] [📁] Location
    [+] [📁] Opened by
    [+] [📁] Parent
    [+] [📁] Rejection goto
   ┌─────────────────────────────────────┐
   │[+] [📁] Requested for                │
   └─────────────────────────────────────┘
    [📄] Watch list
    [📄] Work notes list                         ▼
```

Selecting the field name

9. After selecting the field, **Requested For**, from the options, Service-Now will auto-generate the field path, as shown in following screenshot:

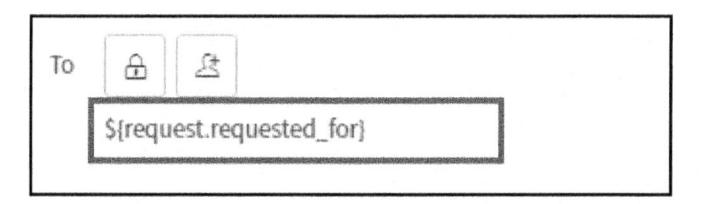

```
To    [🔒]  [👤]
      ┌──────────────────────────────┐
      │ ${request.requested_for}     │
      └──────────────────────────────┘
```

Configured To field

10. Click on **Submit** button and publish the workflow. Now whenever the catalog item, **Apple iPad3**, is submitted, and passed through this activity, it will trigger a notification to the end user.

How to configure a timer in workflows

On many occasions, business requirements are based on time so let's understand this by an example: Send a reminder e-mail for the approver for a request approval or hold the e-mail if you want to send a notification periodically based on the requirements. The important thing to note down is that in such scenarios, you need to configure the time in the workflow. For facilitating a time-related feature, Service-Now provides the **Timer** activity, which pauses the workflow for a specified period of time.

Getting ready

To step through this recipe, you should have an active Service-Now instance, valid credentials, and an admin role.

How to do it...

1. Open any standard web browser and type the instance address.
2. Log in to the Service-Now instance using the credentials.
3. Follow the same process as the last recipe and open **Apple Ipad3** | **Workflow** | `Procurement Process Flow - Mobile` as shown in the following screenshot.
4. Now drag and drop the **Timer** activity in to the workflow's canvas and configure it as shown in following screenshot:

- **Name**: `wait for 24 hours to rollback`
- **Time based on**: `A user specified duration`

Chapter 6

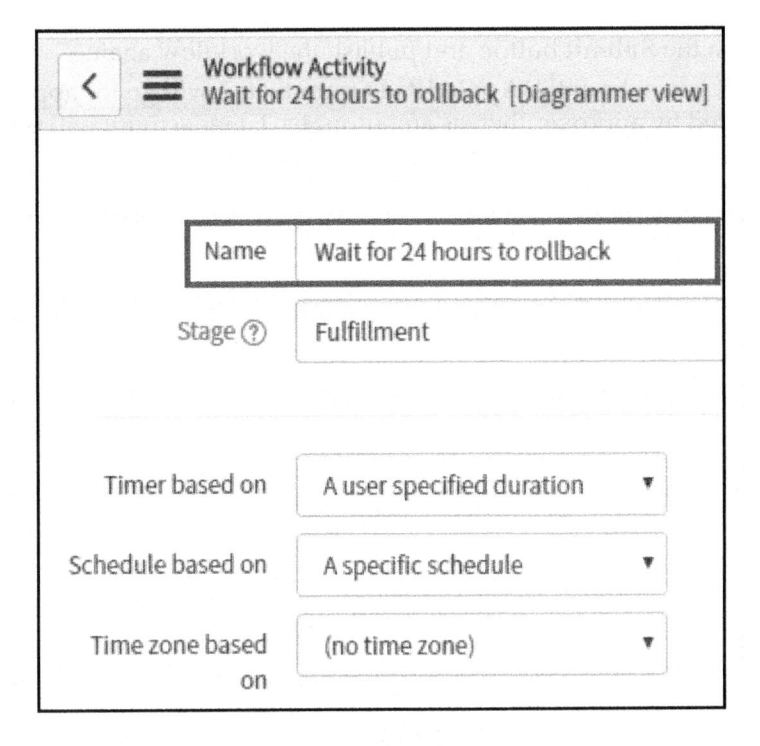

Configure time activity

- **Duration**: 23 Hours 59 Minutes and 59 seconds

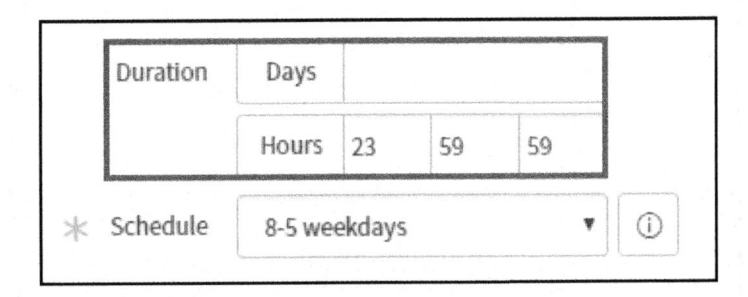

Set duration for timer activity

5. Click on the **Submit** button and publish the workflow again.
6. Now, If you submit the **Apple IPad3** form then it will go for approval .If request is rejected by approver then as an output by Timer activity will pause the workflow for 24 hours to reinsert approval as shown in following screenshot:

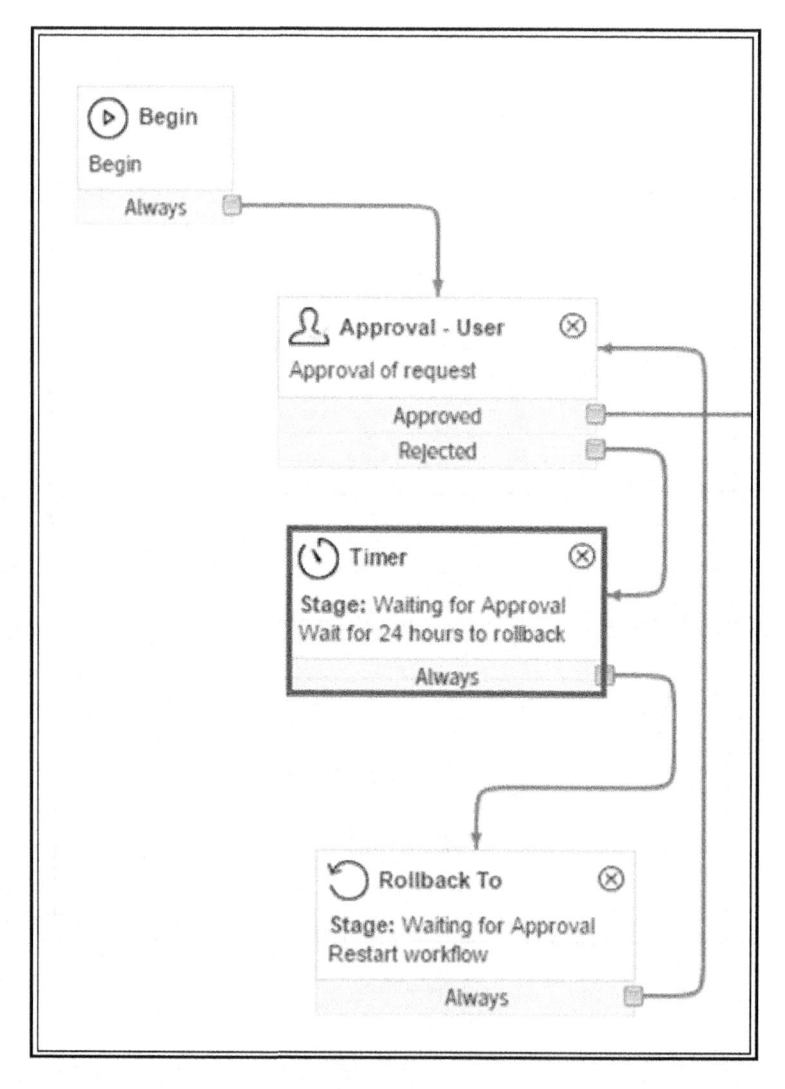

Configured workflow with timer activity

Understanding the approval engine

The approval engine is responsible for maintaining the approval in Service-Now. The approval engine gives you leverage to modify the properties of the approval as well. On many occasions, the approval activity is read only in the workflow, but you want to use the approval activity in the workflow. In such situations, you can modify the approval engine:

▼ Approvals
- Approval - Group
- Approval - User
- Approval Action
- Approval Coordinator
- Generate
- Manual Approvals
- Rollback To

Approval activity read only

Getting ready

To step through this recipe, you should have an active Service-Now instance, valid credentials, and an admin role.

How to do it...

1. Open any standard web browser and type the instance address.
2. Log in to the Service-Now instance using the credentials.
3. On the left-hand side, type `approval`.

Creating and Configuring Workflow Activities

4. Select **Approval Engines** under **System Properties**:

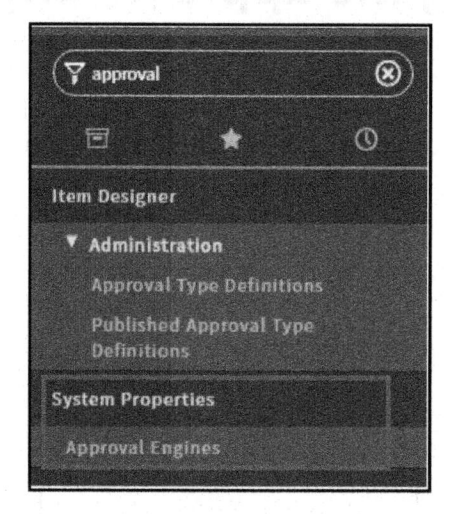

Approval engine

5. The **Approval Engine** has the following options and you can choose the appropriate one for your requirement:

- **Approval Rules**: Use **Approval Rules** to create approvals
- **Process Guides**: Use **Process Guides** to create approvals
- **Turn engines off**: Turn the approval engines off for this table (use this when the workflow is used to manage the approval)

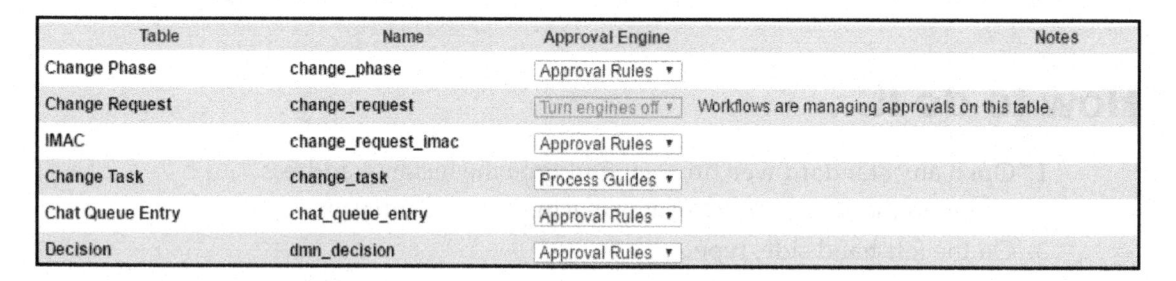

Table	Name	Approval Engine	Notes
Change Phase	change_phase	Approval Rules	
Change Request	change_request	Turn engines off	Workflows are managing approvals on this table.
IMAC	change_request_imac	Approval Rules	
Change Task	change_task	Process Guides	
Chat Queue Entry	chat_queue_entry	Approval Rules	
Decision	dmn_decision	Approval Rules	

Approval engine records

6. Now click on **Save** button and as an output on workflow core section, approvals activities will be available to use.

[326]

7
Auditing and Diagnosing Service-Now

In the Service-Now operational environment, on many occasion you may come across situations where you need to know when any record (incident, change, and so on) was *Created* or *Updated* or *who updated* or *values in the record*, to investigate. Service-now provides many options for debugging and auditing.

In this chapter, we will cover the following recipes:

- Understanding auditing in Service-Now
- Working with auditing tables
- Understanding Service-Now upgrades
- Working with system logs
- System diagnostics
- Working with background scripts
- Working with Field Watcher
- Working with JavaScript logs

Understanding auditing in Service-Now

Auditing is critical while performing troubleshooting. Service-Now has a dedicated audit table(`sys_audit`) table, which stores inserts and changes of records. It is important to note that Service-Now skips business rules or workflow tracking due to performance issues.

Auditing and Diagnosing Service-Now

Getting ready

To step through this recipe, you should have an active Service-Now instance, valid credentials, and an admin or ITIL role.

How to do it...

1. Open any standard web browser.
2. Log in to the Service-Now instance with the credentials.
3. On the left-hand side, type `Incident` in the search box and open any existing record.
4. Now right-click on the header and hover on the mouse over **History** option and select **Calendar**:

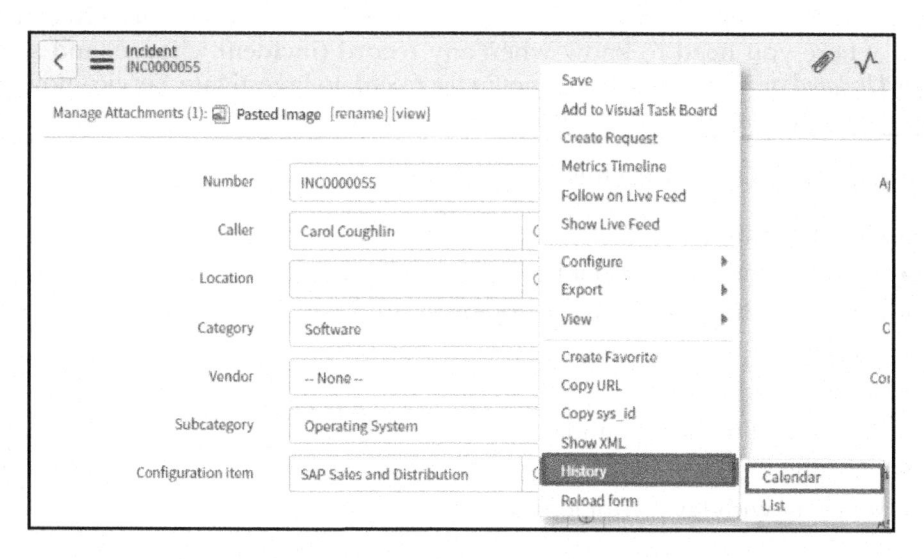

Checking the history of an incident

5. Now you will able to see the following page, where you can see all the activities that were performed on the incident records with user name:

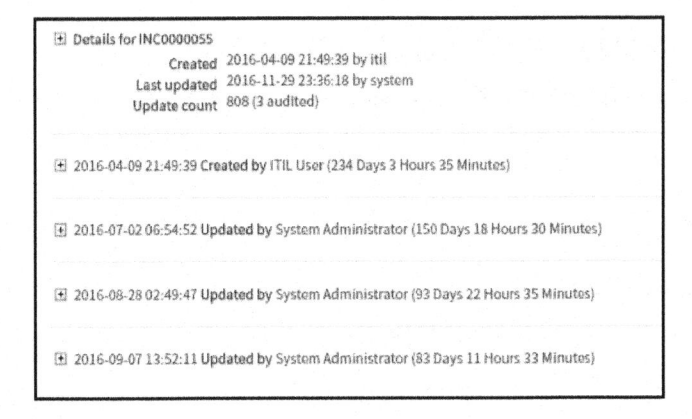

History of the incident

6. If you want to know more details then you need to maximize the record by clicking on the + button so that you can see the **before** and **after** columns for the comparison fields. **Before** column stores last values and **after** column store new values:

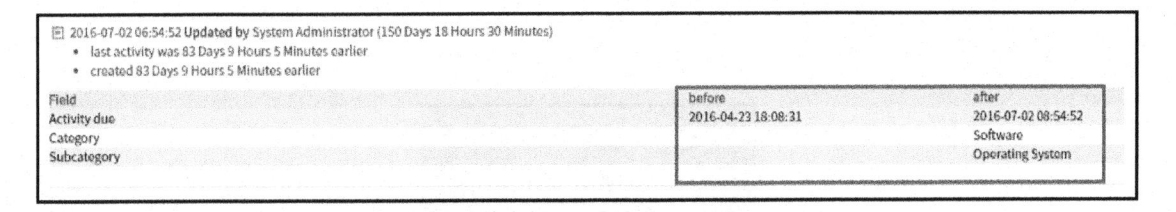

Auditing

If you take a closer look, you can view the time and get the answer to the following issues; moreover, by checking the history of the records, you will be in a better position to troubleshoot issues:

- When the record was updated: **2016-07-02 08:54:52**
- When the category was changed: from **Empty** to **Software**
- When the subcategory was changed: from **Empty** to **Operating System**

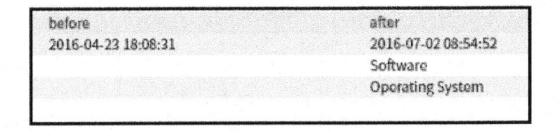

Comparison of before and after state

Working with auditing tables

Out of the box, some tables are already marked auditable in which you can track the respective records, but if a table is not auditable then you will not be able to track changes. In this recipe, you will see *how you can mark any table as auditable*.

Getting ready

To step through this recipe, you should have an active Service-Now instance, valid credentials, and an admin role.

How to do it...

1. Open any standard web browser and type the instance address.
2. Log in to the Service-Now instance with the credentials.
3. On the left-hand side, type `dictionary` in the search box and Service-Now will search the **Dictionary** module for you. Now click on **Dictionary** module under **System Definition**:

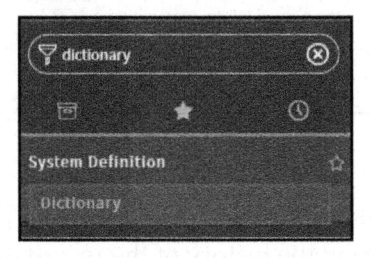

Dictionary

4. On clicking **Dictionary**, you will see the following screen. If the **Audit** column is marked **false**, it means auditing is not activated for that table:

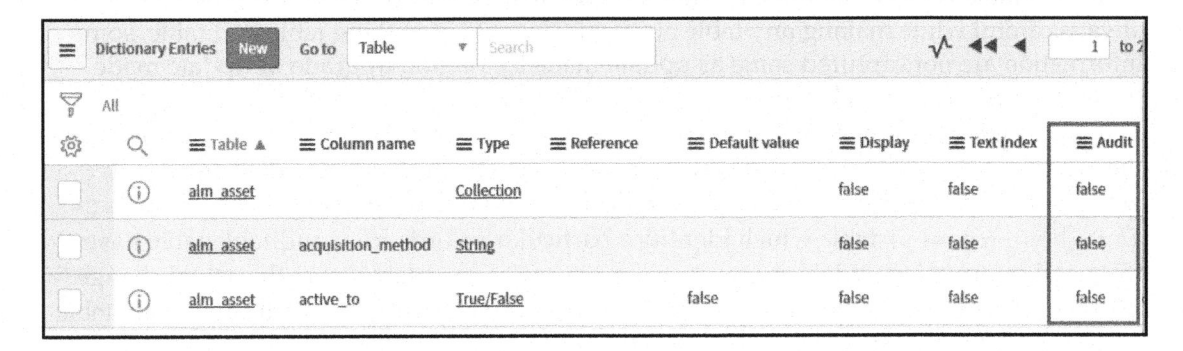

		Table ▲	Column name	Type	Reference	Default value	Display	Text index	Audit
		alm_asset		Collection			false	false	false
		alm_asset	acquisition_method	String			false	false	false
		alm_asset	active_to	True/False		false	false	false	false

Check for auditing

5. Now if you want to enable auditing in any table let suppose **Asset(alm_asset)** for now then, you can open `Asset` table and check the **Audit** field, as shown in the following screenshot:

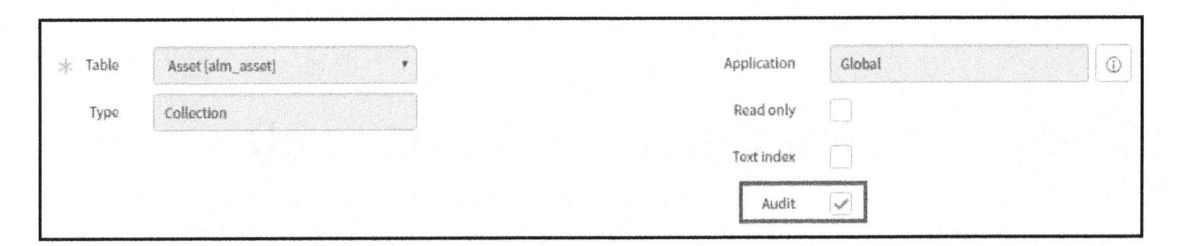

Table	Asset [alm_asset]	Application	Global
Type	Collection	Read only	
		Text index	
		Audit	✓

Enabling audit

6. Now click on the **Update** button.

There's more...

If audited table is receiving huge amount of data then you may face performance issues so always careful while making any table auditable. In spite of making table auditable, some information are not captured same as update made by version upgrade or update made through import set, a field through `no_audit` dictionary attribute and so on. In addition, The `Audit` table is for historical information purpose and intended to keep forever but over the time period size of `Audit` table increases which create performance issue for direct query of records so here service-now for tackling such issue service-now has `History Set (sys_history_set)` table which identifies particular records from auditable table have historical information and `History (sys_history_line)` table store the actual change to the field. Out of the box, Service-Now has *Table cleaner* schedule job which run certain table to prevent data growing exponentially.

See also

To read more about this, please follow https://wiki.servicenow.com/index.php?title=Introduction_to_Managing_Data#Table_Cleaner&gsc.tab=0 link.

Understanding Service-Now upgrades

Service-Now has a yearly conference, **Knowledge**, in which the company releases a new version of Service-Now with new features, new applications, enhancements and so on. So it's very important to keep the Service-Now instance updated for taking the leverage of the Service-Now product.

Getting ready

To step through this recipe, you should have special access. Service-Now has a customer relationship portal (http://hi.service-now.com) where customers can raise product-related issues and the Service-Now customer support team works on these issues. You should have access to this portal (https://hi.service-now.com) to step through this recipe.

How to do it…

1. Open any standard web browser and type the instance address.
2. Log in to `https://hi.service-now.com` with the credentials, as shown here:

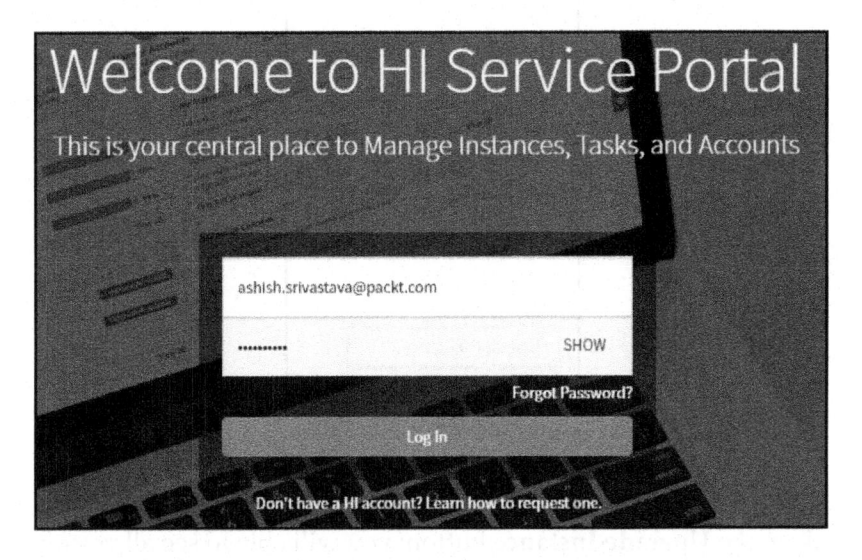

Access Hi- Account

3. After logging in, click on **Manage Instances**:

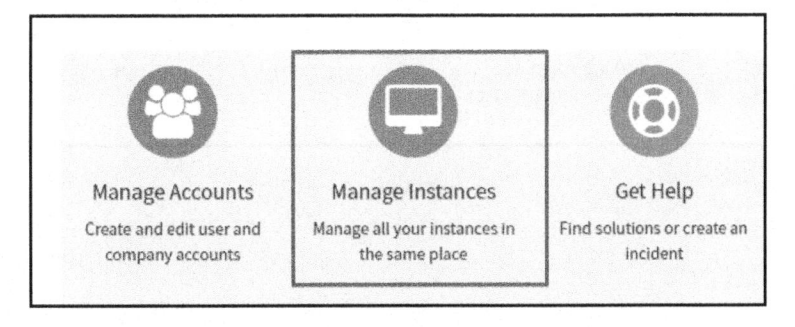

Manage Instances

4. Now you will be able to see all the instances and their status. Now hover on the desired instance; let's suppose it's **Production** in case:

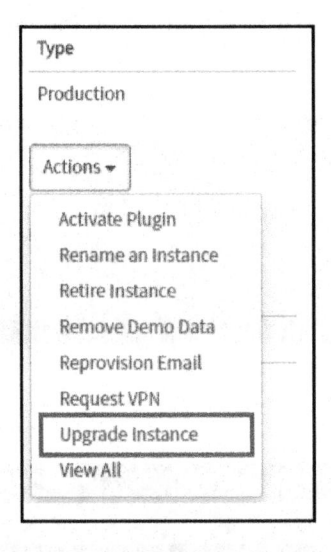

Upgrade instance

5. Click on the **Upgrade Instance** button; you will able to see all your instances, where you can select the desired version upgrade and schedule it:

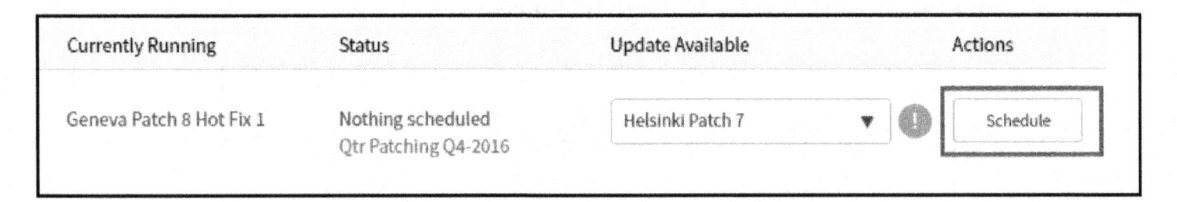

Currently Running	Status	Update Available	Actions
Geneva Patch 8 Hot Fix 1	Nothing scheduled Qtr Patching Q4-2016	Helsinki Patch 7	Schedule

Upgrade schedule

6. It is recommended that you schedule the version upgrade in non-business hours and keep enough buffer time to avoid any issues.
7. Once the upgrade is started, you can see the status of the upgrade in the **Upgrade Monitor** module, as shown here:

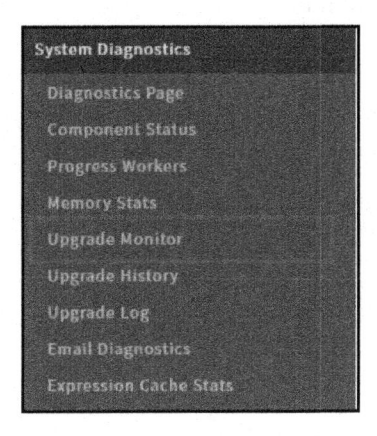

System Diagnostics
Diagnostics Page
Component Status
Progress Workers
Memory Stats
Upgrade Monitor
Upgrade History
Upgrade Log
Email Diagnostics
Expression Cache Stats

Upgrade monitor

8. New upgrades or previously completed upgrades are captured in the **Upgrade History** module, as shown here:

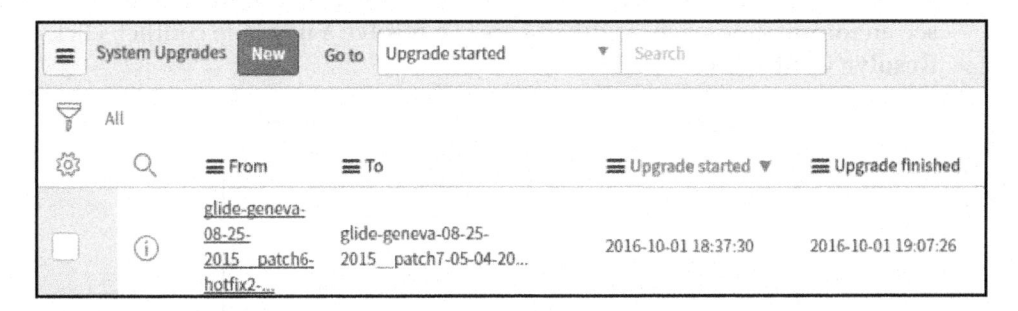

From	To	Upgrade started ▼	Upgrade finished
glide-geneva-08-25-2015_patch6-hotfix2-...	glide-geneva-08-25-2015_patch7-05-04-20...	2016-10-01 18:37:30	2016-10-01 19:07:26

Upgrade history

Auditing and Diagnosing Service-Now

9. Service-Now creates a record for each and every file during upgrade and to see what has changed during the upgrade, you need to click on the records. A `disposition` field plays an important role as it captures the result of the upgrade file as **Skipped**, **Unchanged**, **Unchanged and customized**, and **Skipped error**, as shown here:

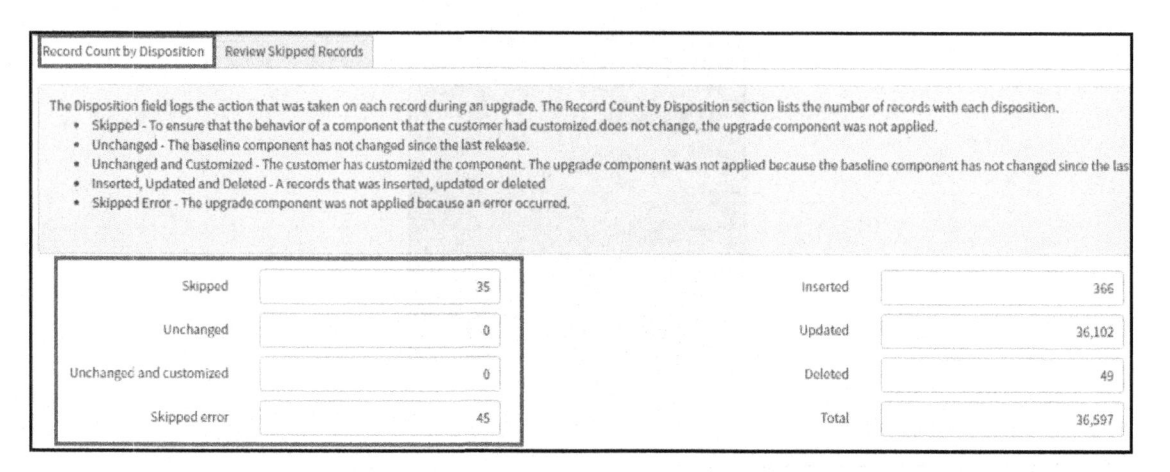

Record Count by Disposition	Review Skipped Records

The Disposition field logs the action that was taken on each record during an upgrade. The Record Count by Disposition section lists the number of records with each disposition.
- Skipped - To ensure that the behavior of a component that the customer had customized does not change, the upgrade component was not applied.
- Unchanged - The baseline component has not changed since the last release.
- Unchanged and Customized - The customer has customized the component. The upgrade component was not applied because the baseline component has not changed since the las
- Inserted, Updated and Deleted - A records that was inserted, updated or deleted
- Skipped Error - The upgrade component was not applied because an error occurred.

Skipped	35	Inserted	366
Unchanged	0	Updated	36,102
Unchanged and customized	0	Deleted	49
Skipped error	45	Total	36,597

Upgrade history by disposition

10. To view the details of a record, you need to click on it, following where you will see an information page, as given here. To resolve a upgrade conflict, click on the **Resolve Conflicts** button:

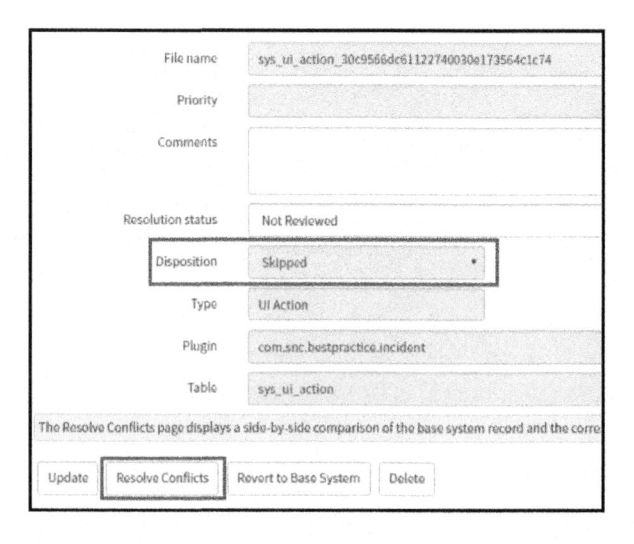

File name	sys_ui_action_30c9566dc61122740030e173564c1c74
Priority	
Comments	
Resolution status	Not Reviewed
Disposition	Skipped
Type	UI Action
Plugin	com.snc.bestpractice.incident
Table	sys_ui_action

The Resolve Conflicts page displays a side-by-side comparison of the base system record and the corre

[Update] [Resolve Conflicts] [Revert to Base System] [Delete]

Skipped record

11. Now, you will now be able to see the **Resolve Conflicts** page. Here you can do a comparison between the base system and the customized system (your customization). If you think reverting to the base system is the best option, then click on **Revert to Base System** and re-apply your customization:

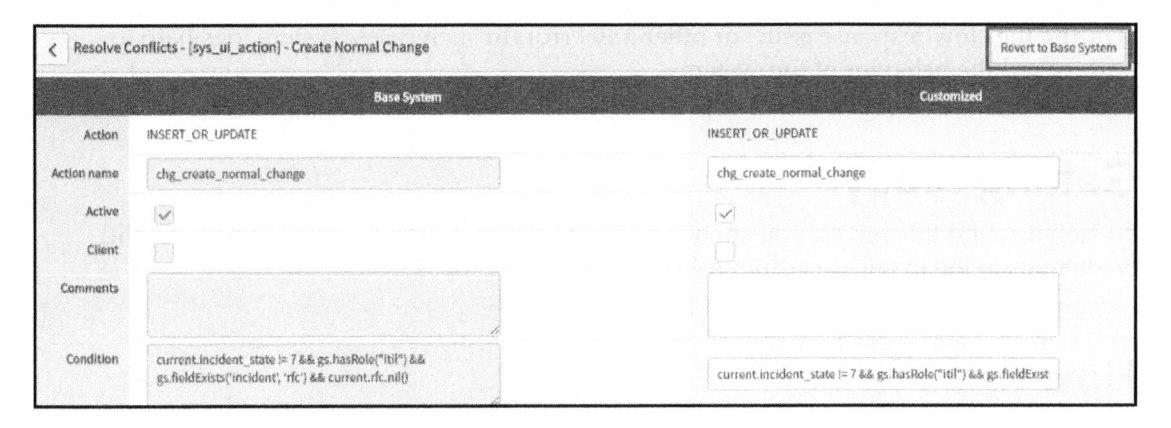

Comparison between base system and customized system

12. As an output, you will able to see the disposition status as `Reverted`:

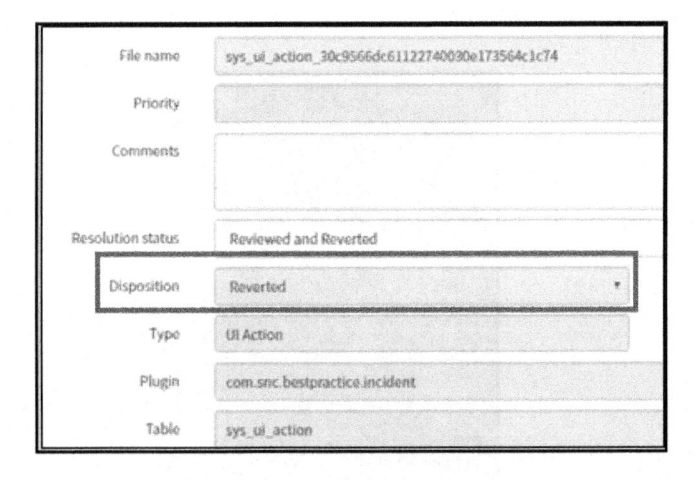

13. Now click on **Update** button and you will see an output message:

    ```
    Your update version entry has been successfully reverted to
    the
    selected version.
    ```

Working with system logs

Out of the box, Service-Now provides the system logs module; system logs are for understanding the system activity. On many occasions, you may come across a situation where you need to check the system logs such as if page loading is slow, a particular region is facing the slow response issue, or other any error. In such cases, system logs help to understand the behavior of the system.

Getting ready

To step through this recipe, you should have an active Service-Now instance and valid credentials to log in and an admin role.

How to do it...

1. Open any standard web browser and type the instance address.
2. Log in to your Service-Now instance with the credentials.
3. On the left-hand side, type `system logs` in the search box and Service-Now will search **System Logs** application for you, as shown here:

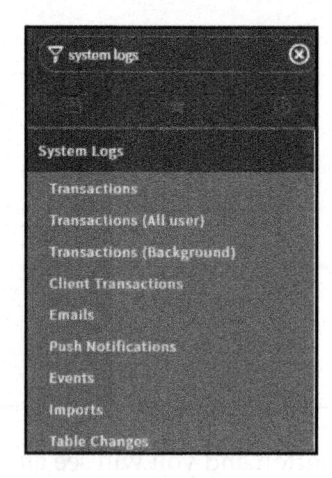

Systems log module

4. It is important to note that only the following activity can be logged in **System Logs** application (reference Service-Now):

    - Workflows
    - Configuration
    - Chat sessions
    - **Transactions** for each view of each page in the system, including load times for networks, servers, and browsers
    - Inbound and outbound e-mail
    - **Events** triggered in the system
    - **Imports** and integrations
    - System warnings, errors, and script logs
    - Upgrade information for any plugin activations, update sets, or system upgrades

5. Often, users report that Service-Now is slow or development or testing instance of Service-Now is slow in a particular region. In such cases, before concluding any result, you should take a look at the transaction logs. As Service-Now is a cloud-based application, the performance of the product is critical. So, to measure the user's transaction details, you should click on the **Client Transactions** module as shown following under **System Logs** application:

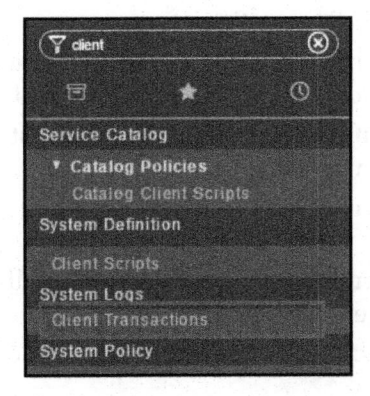

Check users' transactions

6. As an output, you will able to see the following screen, where you will see the **Response time**, **Business rule time**, **SQL time**, **Client response time**, and so on:

	Created ▼	Type	Created by	Response time	Business rule time	SQL time	Client response time
ⓘ	2016-12-01 04:08:49	List	admin	162	0	13	2,594
ⓘ	2016-12-01 04:04:00	Form	admin	334	0	126	1,679
ⓘ	2016-12-01 03:56:19	List	admin	484	0	45	4,742
ⓘ	2016-12-01 03:54:17	List	admin	363	0	58	3,385
ⓘ	2016-12-01 03:51:11	List	admin	169	0	13	965

Client transaction

7. Each and very column of the `syslog_transaction` table, which is the backbone of transactions, represents a different entity. To read more about the transaction log visit:.
   http://wiki.servicenow.com/index.php?title=Client_Transaction_Timings#gsc.tab=0 link.

   - **Response time**: The number of milliseconds spent by the server in fulfilling the transaction
   - **Network time**: the latency time of the network response after the browser request is made, in milliseconds
   - **Output length**: The size of the output string sent by the instance to the browser, in bytes
   - **Business rule count**: The number of business rules executed for this activity
   - **Business rule time**: The number of milliseconds spent by business rules triggered by the transaction
   - **SQL count**: The number of SQL server commands executed for this activity
   - **SQL time**: The number of milliseconds spent by the SQL database
   - **Client response time**: (`load_completion_time`) – (`start_time`), inclusive of server time
   - **Client network time**: The number of milliseconds spent by the network the client is connecting through

- **Browser time**: The number of milliseconds spent by the browser during the transaction
- **Client script time**: The number of milliseconds spent executing client scripts
- **IP address**: The IP address of the client making the request

Whenever a form is loaded in Service-Now, a response time indicator is present at the bottom right of the form and list, which indicates the processing time. **Response time** (ms): 4099, server: 1749, network: 5, browser: 2345, which means the following:

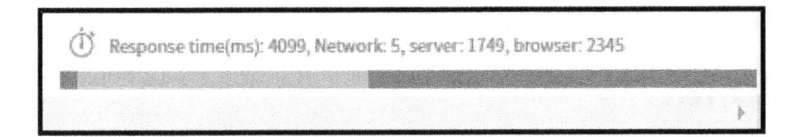

Response time(ms): 4099, Network: 5, server: 1749, browser: 2345

Service-Now form response time

- 499 milliseconds is the total time
- 155 milliseconds on the server
- 172 milliseconds moving data across the network
- 172 milliseconds in the browser, rendering the HTML, and parsing and executing JavaScript

There's more...

Ideally, the response time should be 100 milliseconds in the United States and under 150 milliseconds in Europe or Asia. Please note anything less than 250 milliseconds is not a major issue.

See also

For read more about transaction log
visit http://wiki.servicenow.com/index.php?title=Client_Transaction_Timings#gsc.tab=0 link.

System diagnostics

Out of the box, Service-Now provides the system diagnostics module for troubleshooting, where you can debug business rules, SQL, security UI policy, data policy, and so on.

Getting ready

To step through this recipe, you should have an active Service-Now instance, valid credentials, and an admin role.

How to do it...

1. Open any standard web browser and type the instance address.
2. On the left-hand side, type `Debug` in the search box and Service-Now will search the **System Diagnostics** application for you, as shown here:

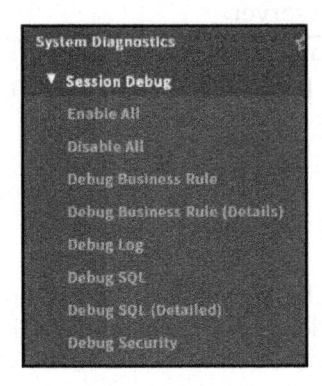

System diagnostics module

3. To understand the debug better, you can open an incident from, as given here, by going to the **Incident** application:

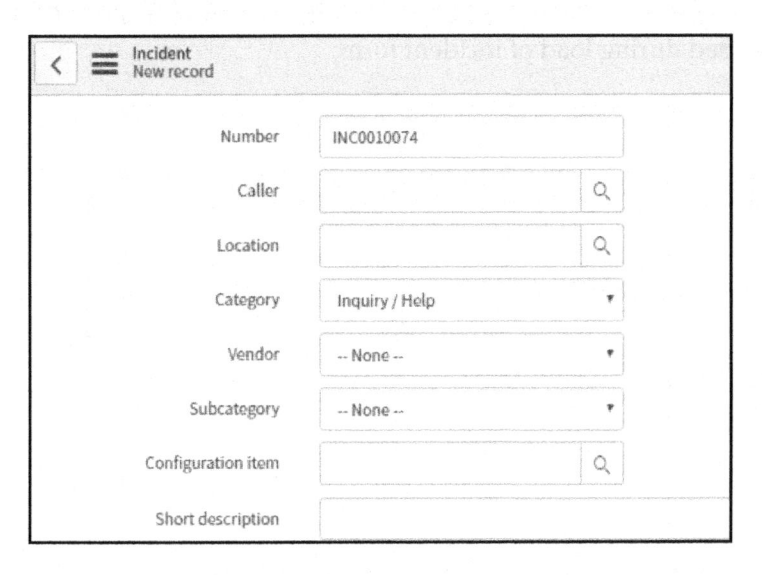

New incident for troubleshooting

4. Now go to **Session Debug** under **System Diagnostics** application and click on **Enable All**, as shown here:

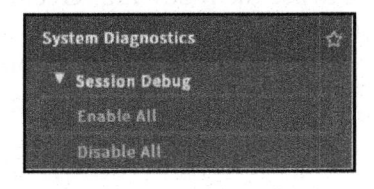

Debugging

5. You will now be able to see text, as given here, where you can see that Service-Now ran a script by clicking on **Enable All**:

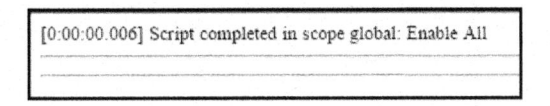

[0:00:00.006] Script completed in scope global: Enable All

Enable All output

6. Now you need to open the incident form again and you will be able to see a new debugging icon on every field, as shown in the following screenshot. If you click on the **icon**, then you will able to see all the **access controls** (**ACLs**) which were processed during load of incident form:

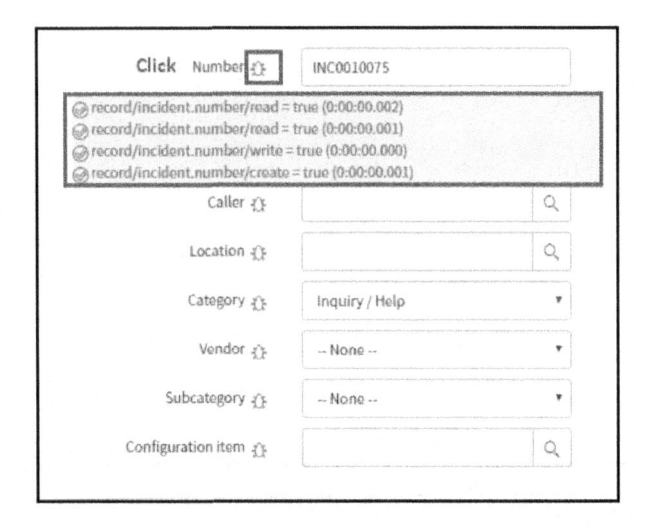

Debugging Form field

7. After clicking on the **Enable All** module, open the incident form and scrolling down, you will be able to see the following screen, where you can view the **Debug Output** of incident form, which gives you the following options and you can filter out these by unchecking the respective box.:

- SQL
- Log
- Business Rules
- Engines
- Security Rules
- Others

Debug output

8. In the majority of cases, you don't need to debug SQL as Service-Now doesn't provide database access to system administrator. Instead of SQL or database layer access, Service-Now provides scripting layer access only.
9. Business Rules runs on the server side and the **Business Rules** option of debug output provides information regarding business rules. Service-Now uses the following indicators in Business Rules: started (==>), finished (<==), and skipped (===):

Business Rules debug

[345]

10. As you will know by now, Service-Now is a role-based system. That's why on many occasions you may face a security role issue. Let's understand this by an example. For instance, if you have made a new role (`ipad_request`) and the access level is not properly set or role is got given to the user, then Service-Now will not allow the user to perform action such as view, write and so on the form. Debug output of **Security Rules** will store such information and if user fails the ACL, it will be marked red automatically, as given here. Let's understand this by a suitable example an end users (user without any role) are not allowed to change the state on the incident form by **record/incident/write** ACL rule as follows:

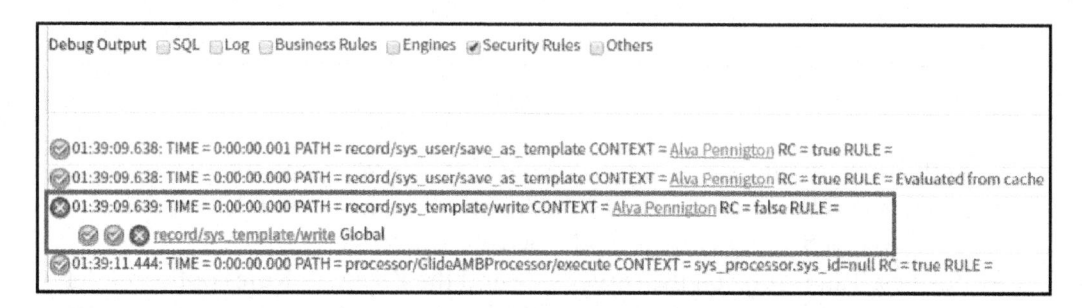

Security Rules debugging

11. If you click on ACL **record/incident /write** then Service-Now will redirect you to the ACL page which is preventing user to access field /table and so on as given as follows:

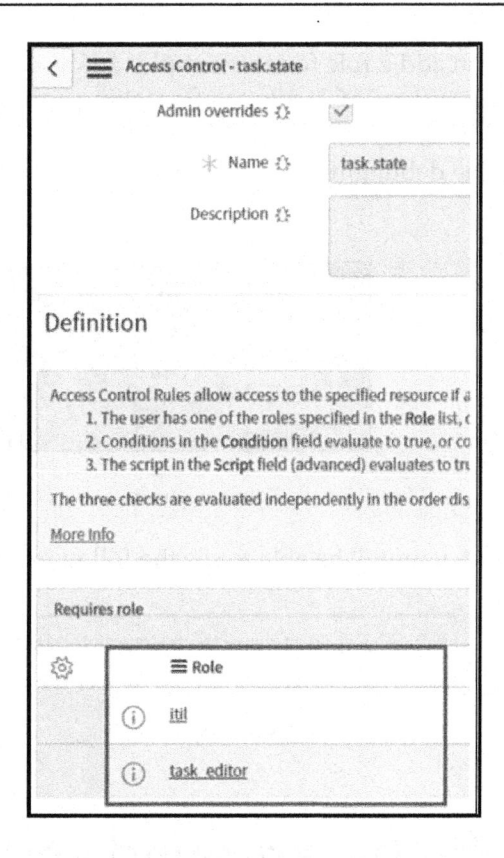

ACL (record/incident /write)

12. As a system administrator by elevating the privilege (`security_admin`), you are allowed to modify the **Access Control** (**ACL**) module records which hold all system and custom roles and available under **System Security** application. It is important to note that without `security_admin` role you are not allowed to modify the ACL rule but you can view ACL rule.

13. Now, you can add a role for an example `ipad_request` in the ACL rule and even edit the system ACL rule so after taking appropriate action, you can update the ACL rule.
14. To disable the debugging, you can click on the **Disable All** module shown as follows:

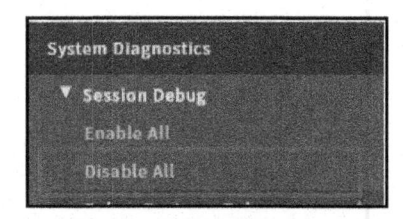

Disabling debugging

15. As an output, you will be able to see the following message:

```
[0:00:00.009] Script completed in scope global: Disable All
```

Disable Debugging message

Working with background scripts

A background script is a place where you can test your server-side scripts, which is same as free text box. To access the background script, you should have a `security_admin` role with elevated privileges.

Getting ready

To step through this recipe, you should have an active Service-Now instance, valid credentials, and a security admin role.

How to do it…

1. Open any standard web browser and type the instance address.
2. On the left-hand side, type `background` in the search box and Service-Now will search the module for you.
3. Click on the **Scripts–Background** module under **System Definition** application, as shown here:

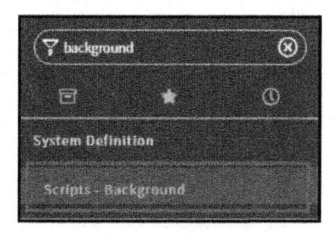

Background script module

4. Now you will be able to see the following screen, where you can place your code and click on the **Run script** button:

Run script

5. Service-Now has an inbuilt `gs.print()` function, which is used to view the output of the script and it also write an entry in a log file, but the `gs.log()` functions in write an entry in the system log and log file as well.
6. It is important to note that the `gs.log()` function can take two arguments, but the `gs.print()` function can take only one argument. You can place your server-side script as shown here:

```
Run script (JavaScript executed on server)
var u_count= 0;
gs.print("server call count"+" "+ u_count);
```

Background script test

7. As an output, you will able to see the following screen with an output:

```
[0:00:00.002] Script completed in scope global: script
*** Script: server call count 0
```

Script output

Working with Field Watcher

Field Watcher is a very efficient way to drill down troubleshooting to the form field level. With Field Watcher, you can view all the actions (UI policy, client script, business rules, and so on) which are being performed on the form.

Getting ready

To step through this recipe, you should have an active Service-Now instance and valid credentials with an admin role.

How to do it...

1. Open any standard web browser and type the instance address.
2. Log in to the instance using the credentials.

3. Click on the **settings** icon, as shown here:

Settings icon

4. Now you will be able to see the following pop-up screen, where you need to go to the **Developer** tab and turn on **JavaScript Log and Field Watcher**, as shown here:

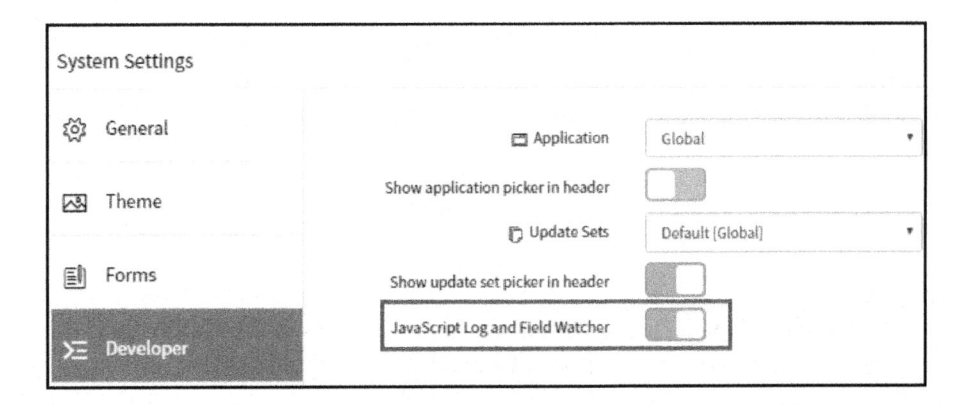

5. Once the **JavaScript Log** and **Field Watcher** field is turned on, you will able to see the **JavaScript Log** and **Field Watcher** sections at the bottom of the page, as given here:

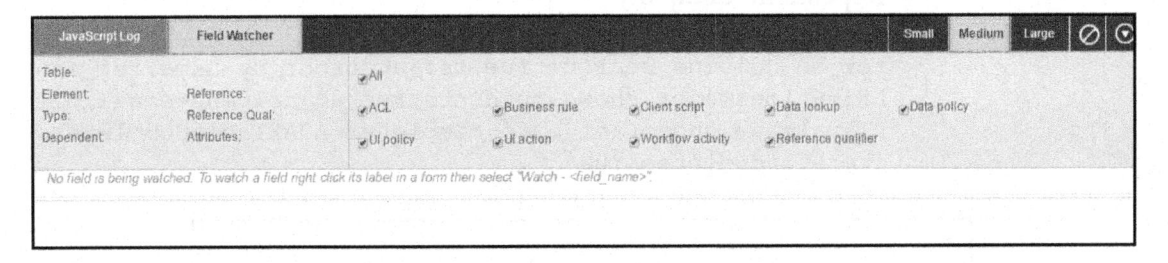

Debug window

Auditing and Diagnosing Service-Now

6. **Field Watcher** provides the functionality to view what component is exactly working on form fields as **ACL**, **Business rule**, **Client script**, **Data lookup**, **Data policy**, **UI policy**, **UI action**, **Work flow activity**, and **Reference qualifier**. To use this functionality, you need to right-click on the form's field and select **Watch-'caller_id'**, as shown here:

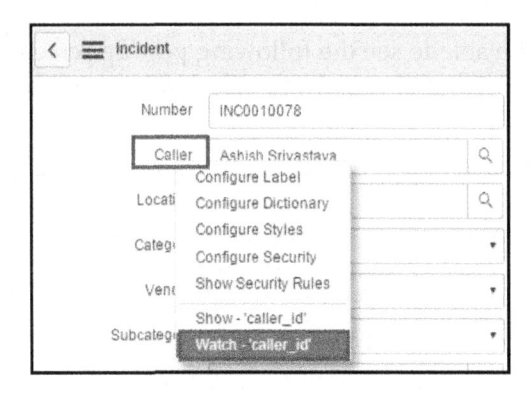

The Watch field

7. After marking the field as **Watch**, you will able to see the **Caller** field details as shown here, which can help you to troubleshoot the issue:

   - **Table**: Incident
   - **Element**: Caller
   - **Reference**: User
   - **Dependent**: Company
   - **Attributes**:
     `ref_ac_columns_search=true,ref_ac_order_by=name,ref_con tributions=user_show_incidents,ref_ac_columns=email,dis play_image=photo,ref_auto_completer=AJAXTableCompleter, iterativeDelete=true`

Field Watcher part 1

8. Now you can mark any component as `true`, as shown here, to view the results:

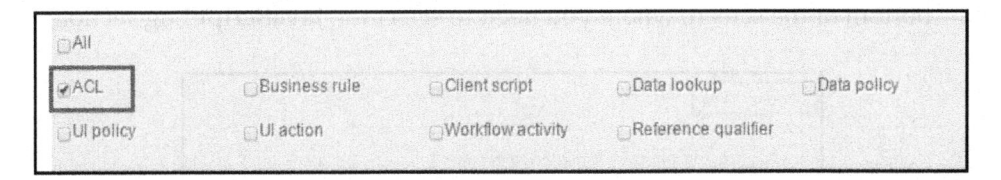

Field Watcher part 2

9. As an output, you will be able to see all those ACL rules which actions are being taken on the form field, as shown here:

Caller field ACL output

Working with JavaScript logs

JavaScript, can run on the client side or on a browser, can use the Service-Now JavaScript log functionality.

Getting ready

To step through this recipe, you should have an active Service-Now instance and valid credentials with an admin role.

How to do it...

1. Open any standard web browser and type the instance address.
2. Log in to the instance using the credentials.

Auditing and Diagnosing Service-Now

3. Now click on the settings icon, select the **Developer** option, and turn on the **JavaScript Log** and **Field Watcher** options. A new pane will be opened at the bottom of the screen, where you need to select the **JavaScript Log** section:

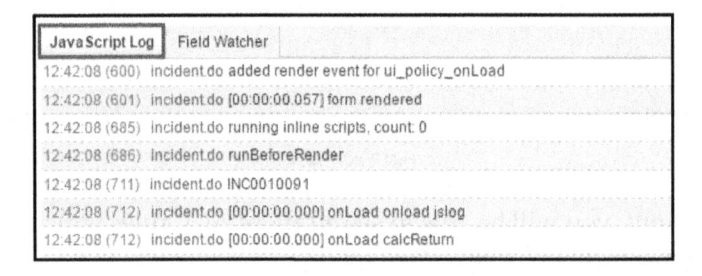

JavaScript Log	Field Watcher
12:42:08 (600)	incident.do added render event for ui_policy_onLoad
12:42:08 (601)	incident.do [00:00:00.057] form rendered
12:42:08 (685)	incident.do running inline scripts, count: 0
12:42:08 (686)	incident.do runBeforeRender
12:42:08 (711)	incident.do INC0010091
12:42:08 (712)	incident.do [00:00:00.000] onLoad onload jslog
12:42:08 (712)	incident.do [00:00:00.000] onLoad calcReturn

JavaScript log screen

4. If you want to log information to the JavaScript log, then Service-Now provides a global `jslog()` function, which passes information to the JavaScript log sections.
5. If you want to capture the JavaScript log to the client-side script, then you can follow this process:
6. Now right click on the header of any incident form and hover the mouse over the **Configure** option, and select **Client Scripts** as follows:

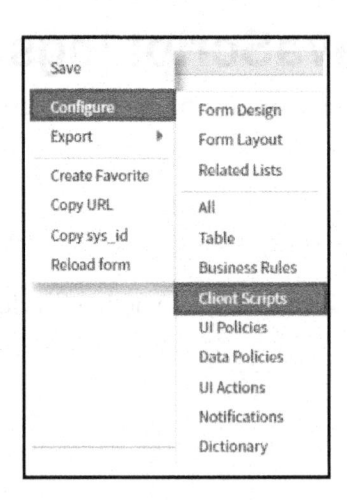

Create Client Scripts

[354]

7. After selecting **Client Scripts** you will be able to see all the client side scripts on screen, where you need to click on the **New** button.
8. Now you need to type **Name** as `onload jslog` and select the **Type** as `onLoad`, as shown here:

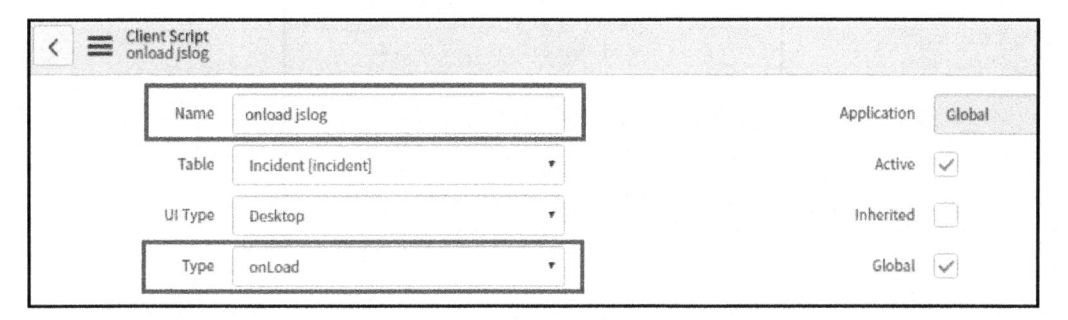

OnLoad client script part 1

9. Here we want to capture the JavaScript log of the incident form's `state` field so that we can check the value of the field when the form is being loaded:

```
function onLoad()
{
  var log = g_form.getValue('state');
  jslog("Log Information:"+ " " +log);
}
```

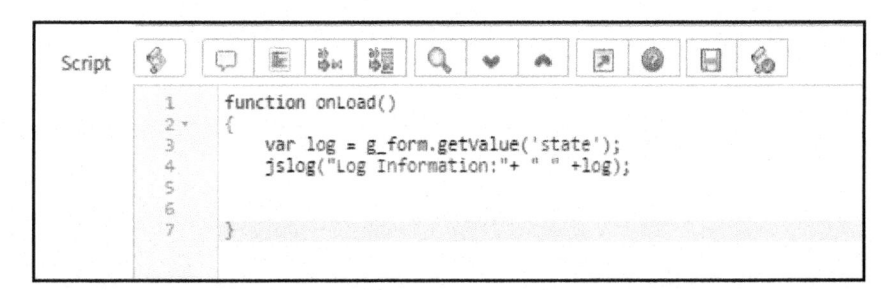

OnLoad client script part 2

[355]

10. Now you can view the **Log Information: 1** which means incident state is new during the incident form load.:

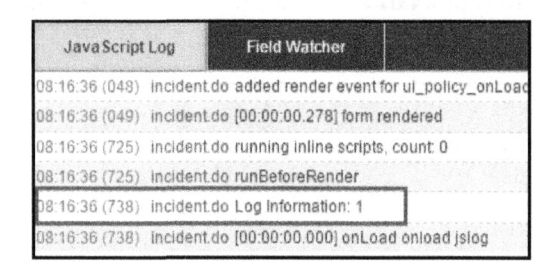

Java Script Log	Field Watcher
08:16:36 (048)	incident.do added render event for ui_policy_onLoad
08:16:36 (049)	incident.do [00:00:00.278] form rendered
08:16:36 (725)	incident.do running inline scripts, count: 0
08:16:36 (725)	incident.do runBeforeRender
08:16:36 (738)	incident.do Log Information: 1
08:16:36 (738)	incident.do [00:00:00.000] onLoad onload jslog

JavaScript log

Index

A

Access Control (ACL) 124, 344, 347
application
  starting 127
approval activity
  setting up 289, 294
approval engine 325, 326
approver 13
auditing tables
  working with 330

B

background script
  working with 348, 350

C

change management application
  URL 51
  using 49, 51
change manager 51
change/problem task
  creating, from incident task 51, 53
change_request table 51
client script
  obtaining 143, 145, 146, 148
condition activities
  working 294, 296, 298, 300
configuration management database (CMDB)
  obtaining 103, 104, 105, 106
  reference link 107
Content Management Application (CMA) 23
Content Management System (CMS) 20
customer relationship portal
  URL 332

D

dashboard
  creating 243, 244, 246
Data Archive 76
data driven application
  about 133
  module, obtaining 134, 135, 136, 137, 138, 140, 142, 143
Data Manipulation Language (DML) 148
database view
  creating 263, 265, 266
deployment 95, 98, 100, 102

E

e-mail notification
  by event registry 211, 213, 215, 216, 218
  creating 179, 180, 181, 182, 184, 185
  script, creating 190, 192
  setting up, from Service-Now workflow 317, 318, 319, 321
  troubleshooting 219, 220, 221
e-mail template
  creating 186, 188, 189, 190
external authentication
  reference link 15, 17

F

Field Watcher
  working with 350, 352
fulfiller 13

G

group administration modules 71, 72, 75, 76

I

inbound e-mail action
  forward prefix, creating 203, 204
  new prefix, creating 197, 198
  reply prefix, creating 207, 208
  setting up 193, 194, 195, 196
incident management (IM)
  application, using 38, 40
  references 20
  URL 41
incident task
  change/problem task, creating 51, 53
Information Technology Infrastructure Library (ITIL)
  framework 8
  about 9, 10
  references 11

J

JavaScript logs
  working with 353, 355
JavaScript
  reference link 143

K

Knowledge 332

L

LDAP server 61, 63, 64, 65, 66, 67
Lightweight Dictionary Access Protocol (LDAP) 18
Login Rules module 23

M

Maintain Item module 26
Measurement Instrumentation Discovery (MID) 64
Microsoft Active Directory
  authentication 17, 19
multiple reports
  sending, in e-mail 234, 235, 236

O

OLA
  setting up 107, 108, 111

P

problem management application
  using 47, 48
problem manager 48
problem table 48

R

related applications
  using 41, 44, 46
report range
  working 260, 261, 262
report sources
  working 256, 257, 258, 259
report's e-mail notification
  date, including 248, 249
reports
  creating 227, 229
  executing 224, 226
  footer template, working 250, 251, 253, 254, 255
  header template, working 250, 251, 253, 254, 255
  scheduling 230, 231, 232, 233
  viewing 224, 226
requester 13

S

self-service application
  about 32, 33, 34
  URL 34
server-side script
  obtaining 148, 150, 158
Service Catalog Application 26
service catalog
  workflow, attaching 280, 281
service desk application 34, 35, 36
Service Level Agreements (SLAs)
  about 36
  reference link 111
  setting up 107, 108, 111
service requests
  creating 23, 26
Service-Now
  about 9, 10

application portal, logging in 20, 22
application, accessing 14, 16, 17
auditing in 327, 329
basic configuration, setting up 56, 58, 61
form, configuring 80, 82, 83, 85, 86, 87
IT view 27, 28, 30, 32
licensing 12
plugins, used 76, 77, 78, 79
prerequisites 9
procurement 12
roles 12
setting up 14
system mailbox 172, 173, 174, 175, 176, 177, 178
tables schema 117, 118, 119, 120
upgrades 332, 335, 337
workflow 270, 272, 274, 277
workflow, attaching with service catalog 280, 281
workflow, e-mail notification setting up 318, 319, 321
workflow, timer configuring 317, 322, 324
workflow, troubleshooting 286, 287
workflow, utilities working 307, 308, 315
workflows, attaching with current module 282, 285
workflows, attaching with new module 282, 285
sys_id
  about 37
  URL 38
system diagnostics 345
  enabling 342, 344, 345, 348
system dictionary 114, 115, 117
system logs
  working with 338, 339, 341
System Policy Application 40
system rule
  setting up 111, 114
System Security 347
system security
  obtaining 120, 121, 122, 123, 124

T

table specific report module
  creating 238, 239, 240, 242
task activities
  working 301, 302, 304, 306
task table 48
team development plugin 158, 160, 161
timer
  configuring, in Service-Now workflow 322, 324
transaction log
  reference link 340, 341

U

UI action
  configuring, on Service-Now form 91, 93, 94, 95
UI policy
  configuring, on Service-Now form 87, 89, 90
underpinning contract
  setting up 107, 111
unique record identifier 37
update set
  about 95, 97, 100, 101, 102
  reference link 95
user administration modules 67, 68, 69, 70

V

view management
  reference link 87

Lightning Source UK Ltd.
Milton Keynes UK
UKOW07f0015100917
308817UK00004B/432/P

9 781785 880520